The Prince, the Princess and the Perfect Murder

Andrew Rose

W F HOWES LTD

This large print edition published in 2013 by
W F Howes Ltd
Unit 4, Rearsby Business Park, Gaddesby Lane,
Rearsby, Leicester LE7 4YH

1 3 5 7 9 10 8 6 4 2

First published in the United Kingdom in 2013
by Coronet

A CIP catalogue record for this book is available
from the British Library

ISBN 978 1 47124 434 6

Typeset by Palimpsest Book Production Limited,
Falkirk, Stirlingshire
Printed and bound by
www.printondemand-worldwide.com of Peterborough, England

This book is made entirely of chain-of-custody materials

For Raoul Laurent

A courtesan is a monarchist at heart
Honoré de Balzac, *Splendeurs et Misères des Courtisanes*

Women are necessarily capable of almost anything in their struggle for survival and can scarcely be convicted of such man-made crimes as 'cruelty'
F. Scott Fitzgerald, *Tender is the Night*

CONTENTS

		INTRODUCTION	1
CHAPTER	1	THE FRENCH CONNECTION	7
CHAPTER	2	'OH FOR THE END OF THIS FUCKING WAR!!'	24
CHAPTER	3	SHE-DEVIL	53
CHAPTER	4	ROYAL FLUSH	78
CHAPTER	5	ENTR'ACTE	113
CHAPTER	6	HONEY AND ROSES	128
CHAPTER	7	MUNIRA	148
CHAPTER	8	STORMY WEATHER	170
CHAPTER	9	ENGLAND 1923	179
CHAPTER	10	STOMPIN' AT THE SAVOY	189
CHAPTER	11	FEMME FATALE	214
CHAPTER	12	WHAT THE 'YELLOW PRESS' SAID	235
CHAPTER	13	'HORRIBLE ACCUSATIONS'	239
CHAPTER	14	NOBLE ROT	251
CHAPTER	15	CONSPIRACY	257
CHAPTER	16	THE GO-BETWEEN	265
CHAPTER	17	THE REAL DEAL	276

CHAPTER 18   THE PRINCE OVER
                 THE WATER   289
CHAPTER 19   THE 'GREAT
                 DEFENDER'   309
CHAPTER 20   CURTAIN UP   321
CHAPTER 21   CENTRE STAGE   353
CHAPTER 22   A FRAIL HAND   375
CHAPTER 23   VERDICT   403
CHAPTER 24   SHOW TRIAL WITH
                 A DIFFERENCE   438
CHAPTER 25   *'MON BÉBÉ!'*   457
CHAPTER 26   ENDPAPERS   482

INTRODUCTION

Years before the tragedy of Charles, Diana and Dodi, an earlier Prince of Wales was embroiled – along with a 'Princess' and an Egyptian multi-millionaire – in a scandal which has been superbly airbrushed from history . . .

This book describes the first significant physical and emotional obsession of the Prince, his liaison with the strikingly attractive Marguerite Alibert, better known in Paris as 'Maggie Meller'. Their affair was, 'a crazy physical attraction'.

I have long been fascinated by the inter-war years, that 'long weekend' from 1918 to 1939, delighting in the more bizarre manifestations of the social, cultural and political history of this febrile period. One of the most extraordinary episodes was the 1923 murder trial of Marguerite Alibert, then known as the 'Princess Fahmy *bey*'.

Her trial was true *Grand-Guignol*. East meets West. Marguerite, a white woman 'with a past' on trial for her life. 'Prince' Ali Fahmy, bestial and sexually perverted Eastern husband. Enormous riches. Couture by Chanel, jewellery by Cartier, accessories by Van Cleef & Arpels and Louis

1

Vuitton. The terrifying *dénouement* of a tempestuous marriage. Shots fired amid a violent thunderstorm. Sudden death in a luxurious London hotel. Triumphant acquittal against the weight of the evidence.

My short account of the trial, *Scandal at the Savoy*, is long out of print. Soon after publication, a mysterious-looking letter arrived, postmarked 'Paris', containing a well-merited rebuke from M Raoul Laurent, Marguerite's grandson. Raoul told me, in no uncertain terms, that I needed to *soulever la voile* [lift the veil] on the case.

Intrigued and suitably contrite, I met Raoul in Paris. He indeed helped lift the veil on the story, telling me what he knew about the affair between Marguerite Alibert and the Prince of Wales during the Great War, about the Prince's love letters to Marguerite. Raoul also gave me a copy of Marguerite's 1934 memoir, which details her relationship with the Prince, an essential source previously overlooked by royal biographers.

I later made contact with Ali Fahmy's great-niece, Dr Faïka B Croisier, then living in Geneva, who revealed how the Fahmy family (still hurt about the way Ali was demonised during the trial) had always suspected official interference in Marguerite's favour.

I discovered that the Prince had torn out most of the passages in his wartime diary referring to 'Maggy'. The prince's spelling, not for the only time, was defective. Marguerite, *demi-mondaine* and top flight courtesan, was best known in Paris as 'Maggie Meller'. My enquiries revealed that British official sources had clearly been 'weeded' at some stage. Important documents (such as a Metropolitan Police Special Branch report on Marguerite, hinting at 'horrible accusations') seemed to have been destroyed or simply removed from the archives.

Incontrovertible contemporary evidence of this conspiracy of silence is to be found in the private papers of Marquess Curzon, that 'most superior person', Foreign Secretary at the time of the trial and a man at the heart of government. I have also tracked down informative, previously unpublished, letters written by the Prince to his second mistress, Mrs Dudley Ward (known to him as 'Fredie'). Unpublished correspondence with fellow Grenadier Guards officers during the Great War also turned out to be highly revealing. Often scabrous, these letters reveal much about the Prince's lifestyle and his attitudes towards women, as well as providing important narrative background. I have also been allowed to see a collection of the Prince's letters held privately in France, showing how the Prince expressed himself in French (the language in which he wrote to Marguerite) and just how indiscreet he could be about military secrets during the Great War.

The Prince, the Princess and the Perfect Murder does not claim to be a new biography of the Prince of Wales, later King Edward VIII and Duke of

Windsor. It is, perhaps, better considered as a biographical study, whose principal characters are the Prince and Marguerite. The narrative tells of their respective backgrounds, their affair, and what happened afterwards in the context of that ill-starred wartime relationship.

For more detailed accounts of the Prince's life and times, *Edward VIII* by Frances Donaldson, the informative unofficial biography first published in 1974, is an invaluable primary source. Philip Ziegler's excellent official life, *King Edward VIII* (containing brief references to 'Maggy') remains the *locus classicus* on the subject.

The Prince's relationship with Wallis Simpson, Duchess of Windsor, has been almost exhaustively documented. Among more interesting recent titles are *Behind Closed Doors: The Tragic Untold Story of the Duchess of Windsor* by Hugo Vickers and Anne Sebba's *That Woman*. In contrast, this book concentrates on the woman before Wallis, telling the previously unknown story of Marguerite and her Prince.

The quest to find the truth about this royal affair has been a deeply personal – at times painful – journey. Years of research have been punctuated by false trails, dead ends and jealously-guarded source material. Some doors have (almost literally) been slammed in my face. I hope that further evidence about this extraordinary episode may come to light as a result of the publication of this book.

Since writing my first account of the trial, the volume of new evidence has changed my mind about two important elements of the story. Marguerite, as will be seen in the book, had a truly protean character. She could inspire loyalty and provoke intense dislike. She could be tender, but she could be very tough indeed.

I now believe that Marguerite ruthlessly exploited Ali Fahmy's possibly ambiguous sexuality to her advantage, deliberately exaggerating and distorting rumours about this aspect of his character. I have accordingly altered my treatment of this issue.

The second re-appraisal is even more important. In my 1991 study of the trial, I had described the shooting as a *crime passionnel*. It was nothing of the kind. This was murder for gain. An execution. A perfect murder.

CHAPTER 1

THE FRENCH CONNECTION

On April Fools' Day 1912, a cross-Channel ferry put to sea in spite of a fierce north-westerly gale and squally snow showers. The dumpy, two-funnelled vessel (a far cry from the elegant lines of the Royal Yacht *Victoria and Albert*) headed unsteadily out of Dover harbour towards the coast of France.

This workaday craft conveyed someone very much out of the ordinary run of travellers: His Royal Highness Edward Albert Christian George Andrew Patrick David of Saxe-Coburg-Gotha, Prince of Wales, Earl of Chester, Duke of Cornwall, Duke of Rothesay, Earl of Carrick, Baron of Renfrew, Prince and Great Steward of Scotland, and Lord of the Isles, 17-year-old heir apparent to the British Imperial Crown.

The Prince was making his first visit to France, a country in which he would live for more than half his adult life.

As the crowded boat yawed about, many of the passengers became seasick. The young Prince, an experienced sailor, had no intention of remaining below decks with the groaning throng, particularly as about ten or so press photographers had smuggled themselves on board, shadowing his every move. Demanding oilskins, the Prince 'rattled up the swinging ladders as nimbly as a cat', joining the ship's captain on the bridge, where he stayed for the remainder of the voyage, seeming reluctant to come down when the ship docked at Calais, more than half an hour late.

The Prince and his two companions, greeted by the British Consul-General, took a late lunch in a private room at the Hotel Terminus, before boarding a reserved First Class carriage, attached to the head of a train drawn by a steam engine massive by English standards and the pride of the Compagnie du Nord. A few years earlier, the Calais-Paris section has been described as 'the least pleasant line in the country' with engines 'burning common coal which fills the . . . eyes with black dust', but no such criticism is recorded of this journey. The driver made up time and the train pulled into the Paris Gare du Nord punctually at 6.45 p.m.

On the platform, in frock coat and silk hat, stood Henri Charles Joseph Tonnelier de Breteuil, 8th Marquis de Breteuil, now 64 and a close friend of the Prince's grandfather, King Edward VII, who had died two years previously in May 1910. Alongside the Marquis stood the remarkable Louis Lépine, Paris Chief of Police since 1900, 'the little man with the big stick', a trenchant reformer who had introduced the study of forensic science and criminology to his metropolitan force way ahead of his London counterparts.

Lépine had also pioneered an attempt to control female prostitution in the city by regulating the enormous number of brothels, introducing a licensing system which created a distinction between *maisons closes* at the lower end of the market and the grander *maisons de rendezvous*, some of which were luxuriously appointed, catering for the richest and most demanding of clients, including industrialists, bankers, aristocrats – and princes of the blood.

The rest of the welcoming party at the Gare du Nord was rather less distinguished, consisting of an official of the railway company, a functionary from Normandy, and two representatives of the British Chamber of Trade.

In accordance with protocol, the first to step down from the special carriage was the tall, grey-moustached figure of Henry Hansell, an amiable non-entity, bachelor and former prep school master, generally regarded as an unimaginative and inadequate tutor to his royal charge. After a short pause (just long enough to heighten public expectation), a shy, slight, but noticeably elegant figure emerged, sporting a high-buttoned grey overcoat, grey suede gloves, black bowler hat and cane. The Prince's comparatively quiet outfit emphasised what was supposed to be an *incognito* visit to France, modestly billed as 'Earl of Chester'. Further back along the platform, the third member of the princely party, the Prince's faithful valet, Frederick Finch, was busy superintending luggage and porters.

At a height of over 6 feet, Hansell towered over the Prince, who stood just 5' 7" tall. Lépine might have mused on whether the Prince qualified for work in the Paris police force. It was Lépine's idiosyncratic rule that no policeman under 5'9" (1.75m) could serve in uniform and no one over the then average height of 5'7" (1.70m) could become a plain clothes officer (in-betweeners had problems). The former had to be built to impress, the latter to be as unobtrusive as possible, and Lépine resolutely excluded anyone of singular appearance from undertaking detective work. On that basis, the Prince's eyecatching good looks, slim figure and blond hair would perhaps have excluded him, although in due course he would demonstrate considerable observational skills, a sharp eye, and a good memory for detail.

When the Prince emerged, a cheer went up from the crowded station concourse, 'press photographers and reporters surged about him . . . in a disconcerting glare of magnesium flashlight', while the Marquis escorted the Prince and his tutor briskly through the Customs Hall to a side exit. Here stood a large and expensive motor-car, with enclosed rear compartment, equipped with a speaking tube for communication with the uniformed chauffeur, a footman sitting alongside him. Finch and baggage following by taxi, the Prince, his tutor and his host were driven through a snowbound Paris to the elegant Breteuil town house at 2 rue Rude, in the fashionable 16th *arrondissement*, a few steps from the Arc de Triomphe.

The stuffiness, the fussiness and the broad gamut of constraints imposed on the young Prince by his parents, King George and Queen Mary, are well known. 'Buckingham Palace . . . unchanged. The same routine. A life made up of nothings . . . The King obstinate, the Queen unimaginative.' King George had seen the Prince off at Victoria, a separation that may have been something of a relief for the young man. At a dreary farewell tea the previous day at Marlborough House, the Prince had to cope with Queen Alexandra (his extremely deaf grandmother) and her querulous unmarried daughter, Princess Victoria, a woman the Prince would later castigate as 'foul' and an 'old bitch'.

Although the London *Times* claimed that 'the Prince . . . has not yet appeared in society', the Prince had made his formal debut the previous year at the Coronation, followed by the Garter ceremony at Windsor Castle, and – most notorious of all – his investiture as Prince of Wales, absurdly robed in an embarrassingly cod medieval extravaganza choreographed by the exceedingly ambitious Chancellor of the Exchequer, David Lloyd George. Official photographs, carefully doctored in an impression of soft focus, transformed the Prince from mere mortal into the company of

11

those young, fair-haired, blue-eyed and very fey saints (so lovingly depicted in Ninian Comper's stained glass windows, fashionable adornments of many contemporary Anglican churches).

Privately tutored, thrust into the uncongenial atmosphere of Osborne and Dartmouth Naval Colleges, it is little wonder that the Prince could seem withdrawn and ill at ease in company. 'A kindly, simple-natured and modest boy, very anxious to do right, never putting himself forward or presuming on his rank,' commented *The Times*. Yet there were signs, even in these early years, of a mulish obstinacy, even wilfulness of character. On his departure from Dartmouth in 1911, fellow cadets had gathered to give 'the Sardine' what was termed 'a good send-off' in 'a natural and well-meaning demonstration'. The Prince slipped away, allegedly 'in a fit of shyness' – or perhaps because he could not be bothered to attend the jamboree, confident in the knowledge that he would not be returning to an institution where he had been numbered with 'an idle, lazy bunch of warts', and constantly risked humiliating punishments. The 'gong-rope' was particularly dreaded. At night, before going to the wash-house, cadets had to undress, but the time allowed was inadequate. The last cadet through the door risked getting a resounding, painful thwack on the back from the 'gong-rope', a thick rope weighted with a solid glass globe.

In joining the Breteuil household, the Prince discovered a very different world from the philistine atmosphere of George V's court. The Marquis moved in intellectual circles and was a friend of Proust, to the delight of that notorious snob and name-dropper. In *Le Côté de Guermantes*, Proust would write sympathetically of the 'Marquis Hannibal de Breaute', a man of erudition and wit, who interested himself in the livelier world beyond the French aristocracy. Bearing the same initials (HB) as Proust's creation, Henri de Breteuil, although cultured, was just as at home in the Paris Jockey Club, fishing in Scotland, or shooting on his estates near the Pyrenees.

A young cavalry officer in the Franco-Prussian War of 1870–1, he had been decorated for bravery, but – disgusted by the slaughter he had witnessed – embraced pacifism and resigned his commission. Serving as parliamentary deputy between 1873 and 1892, Henri believed that a constitutional monarchy on the British model, rather than the flawed constitution of the Third Republic, would bring stability to France. His friendship with the Prince's grandfather began in the 1870s, with a shared passion for Paris, Maxim's Restaurant, and the beauteous *poules de luxe*, such as Liane de Pougy and Agustina Otero Iglesias ('*La Belle Otero*'), probably the most notorious courtesan of her time. Her studbook bristled with the intimate details of European royalty.

The Breteuil family had been closely connected with the French state for three centuries, with a pedigree including generals, government ministers, royal counsellors and the remarkable Marquise du Châtelet (1706–49), *la sublime Émilie,* a scientist whose dissertations on Newtonian theory had drawn the admiration of Voltaire. Henri de Breteuil's maternal grandfather, the banker Achille Fould, had brought the family enormous wealth, enhanced by Henri's advantageous marriage in 1892. 'The American girl is to the fore again,' noted the *New York Times,* when reporting Henri's engagement to Marcellite ('Lita'), daughter of William Garner, a leading manufacturer of cotton goods, who had died some years before in a yachting accident and whose fortune was estimated at some $20,000,000. In 1912, however, *The Times* with brutal English snobbery dismissed the beautiful Lita de Breteuil simply as 'a Miss Garner of New York'.

The Breteuils' Paris residence was a recent confection in classical style, its *ravissant* first floor salon, decorated with the finest eighteenth-century carved boiseries, furniture and paintings, brought in from some of the many other magnificent properties belonging to the family. The Prince and his tutor were shown to their apartment on the ground floor of the building, which the Prince came to love deeply, considering it far superior to his accommodation in England.

At first, the young prince seemed *gauche* to his sophisticated hosts, surprised when asked to take Lita's arm when going in to dinner, and he spoke French awkwardly, though declaring firmly that

English must not be spoken during his stay. The Marquis's sons, François and Jacques de Breteuil, did their best to make the Prince feel at ease in this unfamiliar atmosphere. François, known as the 'Comte de Breteuil', was two years older than the Prince, and an aspiring composer, a leaning that his father strongly disapproved of, regarding it as an unsuitable occupation for a young aristocrat. The Prince, whose interest in the arts would always be limited, magnanimously overlooked so glaring a fault: 'Even the eldest who likes music is very nice,' he wrote in his diary. Just five years later, François de Breteuil was to play a very significant role in the Prince's love life by introducing him to Marguerite Alibert, who would become his mistress, but in 1912 the Prince was probably closer to Jacques, the younger brother, who was the same age, fun to be with, and who liked to ride and play tennis and golf.

Despite a rough-house naval education, including considerable periods at sea that should have been character-forming experiences, the Prince was physically and emotionally a late developer. Today he would be thought of as something of a 'nerd'. Although he was taken to the theatre, to the opera, and to variety shows in Paris, he took only a lukewarm interest and liked to be in bed by 10.30 p.m., rising distressingly early the following morning. The Prince was capable of exhibiting a shy charm in company, but his social skills were still comparatively weak. To the Breteuil family, he must have seemed an idiosyncratic, even prudish, young man. He took little interest in food, almost a capital offence in his host country, and failed to sparkle at the family's weekly lunch parties in Paris, attended by 'statesmen, artists, writers and financiers'. Although the Prince was evidently keen on sports and the racecourse, with a developing taste for adventure, he was unenthusiastic about more formal social life, took little interest in the opposite sex, and – all in all – seems to have resembled a young Mr Pooter in Paris.

In the countryside some 30 miles south-west of Paris stood the mighty Château de Breteuil, dating from the early 1600s. Here, the Prince was accommodated in a pretty, freestanding pavilion, whimsically named 'Chester Cottage' in his honour. The Marquis improved access to the first floor bedroom by installing a fine spiral staircase in mahogany and his guest could reach the main body of the house, in wet weather or simply to avoid observation, by a tunnel, lined with white glazed tiles, appropriately dubbed the 'Metro'.

The Prince's visit was described as having 'no political implication', but both England and France, fearful of the growing power of Imperial Germany, were eager to underline the 1904 *entente cordiale*. The 1912 visit, private though it was supposed to be, served to emphasise the newly forged relationship between the two countries. *Le Figaro* heartily welcomed the young Prince, who 'had recently established himself in Paris at the wish of his august father, King George V'. As *The Times* reported casually, it seemed 'only natural if he were to call on the President'. A supposedly impromptu visit to Monsieur and Madame Fallières at the Élysée Palace took place within a day of the Prince's arrival, the young visitor carefully shepherded by the British Ambassador, Sir Francis Bertie (pronounced 'Bar-Tee').

Although the Prince's general education had been patchy, the King was very keen that his eldest son should learn to speak fluently both French and German. Early attempts to interest the Prince in French had not been successful. His French governess insisted on the language being spoken at mealtimes, but the boy had decided that French was 'effeminate' and would deliberately mispronounce items when presented with a menu. According to his official biographer, the Prince's dislike of the language and reluctance to speak it 'persisted even after he had lived in France for many years'. He showed a greater aptitude for learning German, the language of large numbers of close relatives in the *Kaiserreich*.

But now in France, his new French tutor was well qualified for the task in hand. Maurice Escoffier (no relation of the famous chef), a tall, heavily built man with a full beard, widely regarded as having a brilliant mind, was librarian and lecturer at the École des Sciences Politiques in Paris. Escoffier took his young charge on an extensive sightseeing tour of France.

The diminutive Prince, resembling Gulliver in Brobdingnag in the company of his two far bigger and taller companions, clambered around castles and explored churches all over *la France profonde*. Despite the 'unofficial' label of the visit, the Prince spent an enjoyable few days with the French fleet, cruising in the Mediterranean. In contrast to his almost old-maidish attitude to late nights, romance, strong drink and rich food, a latent sense of adventure took him on a descent in a French submarine, a risky venture at a time of primitive undersea technology. Two French submarines had been lost, with all hands, earlier that year.

The Prince returned to London briefly to celebrate his 18th birthday on 23 June 1912. Although 21 was the age of majority for many purposes in England, reaching the age of 18 meant that there was now no need for a regency in the event of his father's death or incapacity. Another milestone would have less positive consequences. The King, a smoker himself, had refused his eldest son permission to smoke until he became 18, marking the event by the gift of a platinum cigarette case. (The Prince wrote to thank the Marquis de Breteuil for a complementary present, *'la charmante boïte à allumettes'* (the charming box of matches), surely a much more costly item than a simple matchbox.) In due course, the King's gift would be mislaid in very embarrassing circumstances in Paris and, later again, the Prince's persistent smoking habit would cost him his life.

Probably encouraged by the Breteuil boys, the Prince learned to drive, taking an early delight in speeding along newly macadamed roads 'to the terror of Escoffier, who, beard flying, clung by his eyelids to the back seat'. The Prince was well liked by the staff at the Château and his departure at the end of August was to be quite an emotional occasion. 'He seemed as sorry to be leaving us as we were to see him go,' wrote the kindly Marquis, recalling sadness in the Prince's face at a solemn family lunch, which lacked the usual cheerful buzz of conversation. In Paris, the Breteuil car stopped briefly at 2 rue Rude, allowing the Prince to take a last look at his much-loved apartment. After farewells at the Gare du Nord from the Marquis and his younger son, Jacques, the Prince and his tutor journeyed to Amiens, where the Prince was keen to explore the great cathedral.

In October 1912, the Prince went up to Magdalen College, Oxford, a stay that lasted for nearly two years. His lack of education and modest intelligence spared him the trial of 'Smalls', as the college entrance examination was then picturesquely known. Never much interested in books, the Prince reluctantly received instruction in such heavyweight subjects as political economy, history and constitutional law, as well as further instruction in German and French. Emerging from his chrysalis, he continued to nurture a dandified manner already apparent during his visit to France and soon adopted modern fashions, such as flannel trousers (with turn-ups, the latest idea, detested by his father), sports jackets, and soft-collared shirts.

The following month, he showed his power to charm in a letter to the Marquis de Breteuil, who was planning to visit Oxford with his wife, Lita. *'Ce serait un grand plaisir pour moi de vous montrer le collège'* ('It would be a great pleasure for me to show you the college'), wrote the Prince, hoping that they would take lunch in his rooms, *'si vous ne craignez pas un déjeuner étudiant!'* ('if you're not afraid of a student lunch!').

Unlike many undergraduates, the Prince did not have companions from schooldays to help accustom him to university life. Although often seeming ill-at-ease in company (a nervous habit of fingering his tie remained with him throughout his life), he became quietly popular, 'clean-looking and jolly, with no side at all' in the recollection of one contemporary student. Initially, he fought shy of some of the grander personalities, the sons of peers and knights of the shires, fresh from the forcing-houses of Eton, Harrow or Winchester. His choice of friends was modest. One Scottish graduate, rather older than the run of Oxford students, thought the Prince 'not a bad chap'. Another contemporary also found him likeable, 'smaller and more Teutonic in appearance than he had expected, a straw-blond very slight figure in a navy-blue serge suit'.

Although accommodated in college, the Prince had – unusually for those days – a bathroom, albeit primitively equipped. To his irritation, he was still being supervised and escorted around Oxford by the 'melancholy and inefficient' Henry Hansell, a pairing that provoked no little amusement. The oddly-matched couple soon earned the nicknames 'Hansel and Gretel'.

Happily for the Prince, he soon had a decidedly non-intellectual equerry, Major William Cadogan, much more his man. Together they rode, hunted and played polo. Other recreational activities included football and golf, beagling twice a week, and cross-country runs, alongside the usual student experiences of making a good deal of noise, getting drunk (often on 'black-strap' port, supposedly containing rum and molasses) and falling over. He recalled how Gunstone, the college steward, entertained him and other undergraduates with conjuring tricks and off-colour stories after dinner in the hall on Sunday nights. The Prince drove his first car, a grey Daimler, and learned to play the bagpipes, also joining the OTC (Officers' Training Corps), where he target shot, took part in night manoeuvres and went up in an airship.

Among all these diversions, however, there is no record of any romantic affair. The Prince firmly remained a he-virgin, with no obvious interest in female company. 'If only he would bolt with a ballet-girl, say for twenty-four hours!' Lord Crawford wrote despairingly in his diary.

In the spring vacation of 1913, the Prince (accompanied by Major Cadogan and valet Finch) visited Germany for the first time, staying with 'Onkel Willie' and 'Tante Charlotte', the King and Queen of Württemberg, in the royal palace at Stuttgart. On 5 April, he wrote to the Marquis de Breteuil, showing the depth of his affection for his French hosts in an unusual request, made at quite short notice. '. . . *j'ai une petitite demande à vous faire*' ('I have a little request to make of you'), wrote the Prince, explaining that he had a mind to spend a short time in Paris on his way home after leaving Stuttgart '. . . *et j'ose vous demander si je pourrais passer un ou deux nuits chez vous à Rue Rude si cela ne vous incommode pas trop*' ('and I dare ask you whether I might be able to spend one or two nights with you at Rue Rude if that would not inconvenience you too much'). He would be delighted to see the family again and could get to Paris on 15 April, but '*naturellement ma visite sera absolument inofficiel*' ('naturally my visit would be absolutely unofficial') and *incognito*. Only Major Cadogan, whom the Breteuils had met at Oxford the previous November, would be with him (plus, of course, the ubiquitous Finch and the Major's own valet).

In the event, King George recalled his eldest son to London a day earlier than planned and the Prince regretted that he could spend only one night at the Breteuil town house. Nevertheless, the simple act of cadging a bed from friends illustrates the Prince's growing taste for informality, as well as a need for support and affection, elements that

22

were in short supply from his parents. He told the Marquis how, in awful weather, he had had to get up at 3 a.m. to hunt the 'capercailzie' (*Auerhahn* in German). The method of getting close to the birds was *assez bizarre* (quite bizarre), as they could only be detected by their croaking just before dawn.

During his four-month stay, the heir to the throne of the most powerful country in the world had come to feel at ease in France; this youth with 'a dreamy *weltschmerz* look' enjoyed the relaxed company of an amiable aristocratic French family – so different in manner from the stiff and starchy folks back home in Windsor . . .

CHAPTER 2

'OH FOR THE END OF THIS FUCKING WAR!!'

During a visit to Germany in 1913, the Prince met Godfrey Thomas, then aged 24 and attached to the British Embassy in Berlin. Thomas, later to become the Prince's Private Secretary, introduced the 19-year-old Prince to nightclubs and to the city's Palais de Danse, 'frequented by very doubtful women', as recorded by the Prince, who 'danced a good deal' in an atmosphere happily 'devoid of all coarseness and vulgarity'.

In late January 1914, the Prince vividly expressed his distaste for university life at Oxford in a letter to a friend from Dartmouth days. 'I have just returned to this hole for the Easter term,' he complained, 'which does'nt [sic] promise to be less dull than the previous ones I have spent here!!' Aware of the prospect of a European war, the Prince mooted opportunities for military service. Noting the recent 'A7' submarine disaster, the Prince wrote, 'I dont [sic] suppose that decreases the competition for submarines . . . I dont [sic] know whether I should care for the job; I think I would rather join the flying corps.'

With the advent of war in August 1914, other considerations came into play and, after consulting the King, the Prince was gazetted Second Lieutenant in the Grenadier Guards. Even though he stood nearly half a foot shorter than the regulation height of 6 feet, he was proud to have been an officer of the senior British regiment of the line. 'Once a Grenadier,' he would later write, 'always a Grenadier!!' Like thousands of other young men, the Prince was keen to 'do his bit' and it was not his fault that he would spend the war behind the lines in France, not seeing active service because of his position as heir to the throne. For the British authorities, the risk was not that he might be killed, but that he might be captured and used as a negotiating pawn by the enemy. Whatever may have been his moral shortcomings, the Prince cannot be accused of physical cowardice. To friends and family, he constantly complained about being kept out of action on the Western Front.

At the outbreak of war, one of the King's closest advisers was Reginald Brett, Lord Esher. Born in 1852, Esher had served as courtier successively to Queen Victoria, Edward VII and George V, and it was natural that he should seek to advise the young Prince of Wales. Descended from a 'county' family, whose fortunes had been boosted by a distinguished Victorian judge, Reginald ('Regy') Brett was educated at Eton – where he adored the hothouse atmosphere – and Trinity College, Cambridge. With considerable intellectual ability, he was a shrewd judge of character, 'intelligent, able and arrogant . . . with a gift for friendship'.

Although married, with two sons and two daughters, Esher also had a weakness for the company of attractive young men. Although his attentions seem to have been platonic, he expressed his affections in highly charged language, as when he described the Prince as 'the sweetest thing in uniform in all the armies'. Esher's diaries and letters suggest a slightly prurient interest in the Prince's private life, too. Never wholly at ease with Esher, the Prince had written, as early as 1912, 'That man has a finger in every pie and one cannot trust him.' The ambivalent relationship between Prince and courtier endured until the latter's death in 1930. The Prince wrote consolingly to Esher's daughter, 'We have lost a very good & kind friend which Lord Esher has been to me for many years now . . .' – but his private view of Esher was dismissive, regarding him as 'a queer old bird'.

The Prince wrote to Esher in late November 1914 (shortly after his equerry, Major Cadogan, had been killed in action), 'I long to be serving with my reg[imen]t & going thro the campaign in a proper way. I hate leading this comfortable & luxurious life when all my friends are getting hell in the trenches.' It was a huge disappointment that his posting to France should be as a staff officer, initially serving under Sir John French, the first Commander-in-Chief of the British Expeditionary Force (or 'B.E.F.').

The Prince was acutely embarrassed at being accommodated in a series of luxurious chateaux, with excellent provisions, including fine wine, champagne and cigars. In a reply to one of Esher's gossipy letters, he expressed his feelings trenchantly, 'I wish I was serving with 1 of the 2 batt[alions]s of Grenadiers out here instead of sitting here so far from everything . . .' Less reliably, however, the Prince claimed to be a keeper of confidences: 'I realise that all this information is secret & should you be kind enough to send me any papers at any time, they will of course be quite safe.' Despite this assurance, the Prince's frustration with being kept behind the lines may have been the spur to serious indiscretion.

Jacques de Breteuil, fluent in English, had been appointed a military interpreter attached to the British forces in France. The wartime interpreter's life was vividly described by André Maurois in *The Silence of Colonel Bramble*, an elegant dissection of the differences between two cultures. In the book, a British army major claims that the French overestimate intelligence, declaring that 'sport has . . . saved us from intellectual culture . . . We don't go to school to learn, but to be soaked in the prejudices of our class, without which we should be useless and unhappy'.

In the early part of the war, the Prince wrote several letters to Jacques, initially from Sir John French's GHQ (General Headquarters) at St Omer. One early letter, dating from October 1914, bears the legend *Passed by Censor*, but correspondence after this date, sent 'OHMS' and bearing the Prince's seal on the back of each envelope, is not so endorsed. In May 1915, the Prince was transferred to the HQ of 1st Army Corps near Béthune, about 7 miles behind the front line. Subsequent correspondence seems to have been sent privately, using a King's Messenger (usually retired army officers, employed to convey sensitive official documentation). This practice became a favourite device and, later in the war, the Prince would use King's Messengers to carry intimate letters to both his French and English mistresses.

By whatever means the letter reached Jacques de Breteuil, it contained a strikingly careless reference to the effects of the notorious 'shell shortage' of 1915, currently affecting the British front line near Béthune: *'Tout est très tranquil sur notre front à cause de la famine de munitions qui vont aux Dardanelles au lieu de venir ici!! Mais nous espérons en reçevoir plus tard!!!!'* ('Everything is quiet on our front because of the shortage of munitions which are going to the Dardanelles instead of coming here!! But we are hoping to receive more very soon!!!!') German agents were active in northern France and might have ascertained the Prince's location at 1st Army Corps HQ. Although Jacques was an absolutely secure recipient, wartime conditions heightened the risk that the letter might fall into the wrong hands before it could be delivered. These thoughtless words were potentially of value to the enemy, with grave consequences for British armed forces. In other circumstances, such foolish comments could have resulted in court-martial.

Unhappily, this would not be the only example of indiscreet correspondence by the Prince during the Great War. In one instance, the Prince's loose words about the state of the conflict in October 1915 seem culpably defeatist from a serving officer: 'I am a pessimist at the best of times!! I always look facts in the face & now see the Germans beating the Russians & Serbians & absolutely holding up ourselves & the French!!' As will be seen, he later wrote a series of dangerously indiscreet letters to his Paris mistress, by no means a safe recipient – a folly that would have dramatic consequences for both the Prince and the Royal Household.

The exquisite boredom of life behind the line among the 'Red Tabs' (staff officers) was trenchantly expressed to his French friend. Wistfully recalling pre-war game shoots on the Breteuil estate and on Scottish grouse moors, the Prince complained bitterly: '*Je suis "absolutely fed up"* . . . *La vie ici est bien ennuieuse et monotone . . .*' ('I'm "absolutely fed up" . . . life here is really tedious and dull . . .'). He wrote later of being 'too bored for words . . . with a lot of old generals who liked to pretend they were "boxed" [drunk] . . .'

Very early in the war, using his knowledge of German, the Prince was briefly allowed to take part in the interrogation of prisoners, a rare practical exercise, and occasionally visited the front line, experiencing shelling and gaining some impression of death and destruction. He had a narrow escape in September 1915, after his transfer to XIVth Army Corps HQ, under Lord Cavan (or 'Fatty', as the Prince called him, with apparent affection). While the Prince was close to an active sector of the front near Loos, his stationary car was strafed with German gunfire and the driver killed by shrapnel. The Prince, only yards away, was deeply upset by the death of 'an exceptionally nice man'. After this, the bulk of his time was taken up with banal administrative tasks, such as organising the collection of firewood, supplies of ammunition, and carrying out observations behind the lines. Lord Lee, professional soldier and politician, recalled seeing a mud-spattered Prince of Wales tramping the Flanders roads alongside columns of marching men and slow-moving lorries. Arthur Lee found the Prince 'incorrigibly self-effacing . . . his main desire appeared to be to get either killed or wounded'.

Formal parade duties and a few days' leave (usually spent in London) to a degree enlivened the tedium. Visiting hospitals became an important part of the Prince's wartime calendar. There is no doubt that he was acutely aware of the privations endured by ordinary soldiers and of the terrible consequences of war. On one occasion, the Prince toured a unit dedicated to the treatment of facial disfigurement, where – understandably – patients were extremely sensitive 'to any suspicion of curiosity or recoil on the part of a visitor'. One case was thought to be of such a 'frightful . . . repulsive character' that the man's bed was screened off as 'it was not thought well to include him' with the other patients. The Prince took a different view, went straight up to the patient and kissed him, a gesture of humanity that, even to the most sceptical of observers, is deeply moving.

As to his private life, he remained the Sleeping Prince, lacking adult sexual experience until well into the war. By the summer of 1914, he started going to dances, held during the London Season at the great town houses of the aristocracy. The Buckingham Palace ball, of course, was a stuffy affair. Dancing the 'royal quadrilles' (a hopelessly out-of-date hangover from Victorian days), the Prince – 'a very shy young boy' – was obliged to partner his stately mother, who 'firmly piloted' her unenthusiastic son around the dance floor.

Once away from the Palace, however, there was fun to be had. The Prince 'danced without stopping all evening' at the Devonshire House ball. In July, just before the outbreak of war, he told the Prime Minister, H. H. Asquith, that he 'had not been in bed more than 4 hours in any night this week'. In sharp contrast with the plain, high-minded regimen adopted when staying with the Breteuil family in Paris, he was on the way to developing that notorious taste for entertainment, drink and late hours which would characterise his post-war life.

On 23 June 1915, however, the Prince gloomily described his 21st birthday as 'a sad & depressing occasion . . . it didn't interest me at all & did my best to forget it!! Emotionally immature, he was ill-prepared to face the normal challenges of adult life, let alone the awesome responsibility of a King-To-Be. His childhood and adolescence have been described in painful detail by biographers and by the Prince himself, in books and magazine articles.

Although the Prince claimed to have endured 'a wretched childhood', his early upbringing in the unlovely York Cottage at Sandringham, little more than an overgrown suburban villa, was in many ways conventional for an upper-class child. He had a Nasty Nanny, who would pinch the little boy till he cried, but the Prince was not alone in such Victorian sufferings. A generation earlier, George Curzon (destined to provide vital evidence for this book) was the victim of a sadistic governess, who delighted in beating and humiliating her small charges.

Customarily in those days, such parents saw little of their offspring and it was not at all unusual to be packed off to boarding school or junior naval college, as was the Prince, at the age of 7. His father, successively Duke of York, Prince of Wales, and King George V, was an upright man of limited intelligence, who felt it was his duty to play the role of a stern parent towards his firstborn son. George was not a completely cold, unfeeling father, but he was a remote figure, a martinet, and certainly not the Prince's 'best friend' as he claimed to be.

His mother, the future Queen Mary, was kind and affectionate in a rather remote way, but was an unreliable ally, always deferring to her husband. Although the Prince undoubtedly found happiness with his younger siblings, poignantly evidenced in family photographs of the period, he lacked a full measure of love from his parents, remote figures in his landscape. Spoiled to an extent by his indulgent grandfather, Edward VII, who died in 1910 when the Prince was 15, he found for a time a grandfather substitute in the Marquis de Breteuil, whose kindly manner and relaxed family life were clearly much appreciated by the adolescent Prince. By 1915, however, the Marquis was a sick man. The European War had been a terrible blow, adversely affecting the health of a man who had worked so hard to promote harmony between nations, and by the following year he was dead.

At first the Prince seems to have obediently accepted his royal destiny, but the war brought enormous changes in his life. The ribaldry of the officers' mess, perhaps even 'the rough male kiss of blankets' (army issue, of course), prompted a growing coarseness, exemplified in correspondence with brother officers, accompanying a measure of selfishness in his private life. As will be seen later, long-serving courtiers, such as Regy Esher, were increasingly sidelined. Unfortunately, the Prince's self-effacing nature rendered him susceptible to unwholesome influence exerted by rackety men older than himself, though junior to the Esher generation of High Victorians. The Duke of Westminster, a hardened *roué*, became a close wartime friend. Later on, in the 1920s, Brigadier Gerald, 'G', Trotter (born 1871) and Major Edward 'Fruity' Metcalfe (born 1886) would become ill-chosen accomplices in sexual adventure.

Back in 1915, the Prince was still very much an innocent abroad and that year saw a series of seemingly platonic involvements with women, celebrated in wildly romantic letters. Unmarried girls of his class and age group were constantly chaperoned and, although dances, tennis-parties and the hunting field were useful social occasions, more intimate physical contact was rarely possible before marriage. Married women, paradoxically, had greater freedom to indulge in sexual adventures. There were rigid conventions, the breach of which could result in social excommunication. On the other hand, within this framework – provided that secrecy was maintained – a married woman could take a lover of her own social class.

Even King Edward had a slow start to his private life. In 1861, aged 20 and then Prince of Wales, he had not yet slept with a woman. Brother officers smuggled Nellie Clifden, an 'actress', into his bed at an army camp at The Curragh in Ireland and Edward's world suddenly became a much brighter place.

In 1915, the first target of the Prince's affections

was Viscountess Coke, known as 'Marion', a married woman twelve years his senior who became for a time his closest confidante. As with many other women in his life, the Prince turned nasty when relations cooled. By early 1920, he was repeatedly referring to her in correspondence as 'that little bitch'.

Much the same treatment was meted out to 'P', Lady Sybil ('Portia') Cadogan, a rather lumpy girl who throughout most of 1916 seems to have shared his attentions simultaneously with Marion Coke. When Portia's engagement to his old friend Lord Edward Stanley was announced the following year, to the surprise of many in Society, the Prince commented 'alas it's not me that's engaged to Portia, but <u>old Edward</u>'. Since the Prince already knew that the couple had been 'spieling [romancing] . . . for some months now', the effect of the supposed disappointment was rather diminished. As with Marion Coke, he turned against Portia (including her sister, Lady Hillingdon, in his rogues' gallery), writing darkly of 'that gang' and of having once been 'in their clutches'.

The Prince found some relief from his boredom by frequenting The Globe in the Grande Place at Béthune, a café reserved for British officers and French civilians. Sometimes billetted in the Hotel de France nearby, the Prince made use of the nearby public swimming baths, where the writer Robert Graves, then a junior officer in the Royal Welch Regiment, once shared a 'bloody cold' shower with him. 'We were very pink and white,' Graves remembered, 'and did exercises on the horizontal bar afterwards.'

The Prince did not make use of other forms of horizontal exercise available in Béthune. The Red Lamp, a British Army brothel, could be found just off the main street. Graves once saw a queue of 150 men outside, patiently waiting for a few minutes with one of three resident prostitutes, each of whom had served nearly a battalion of men every week 'as long as she lasted'. Three weeks seems to have been the limit, after which the woman 'retired on her earnings, pale but proud'.

Mingling with other ranks was contrary to the Army Act amounting to 'conduct unbecoming the character of an officer', so separate arrangements were made for the pleasure of the officer class. Robert Graves, like the Prince at this time, was reluctant to lose his virginity, partly on moral grounds, partly from fastidiousness (some of the women were 'pols' (prostitutes) or otherwise distinctly shopsoiled, having passed through many hands), and partly from fear of a 'dose'. Sexually transmitted diseases were, of course, widespread. Antibiotics were decades away. Syphilis was an omnipresent risk, treatable only with the recently discoversed neosalvarsan, an arsenical compound with uncertain side effects, including liver damage. Less serious, but equally common, was gonorrhoea. Silver nitrate-based preparations, with such alarming labels as 'Protargol', 'Collagol', 'Albargin' or 'Collosol Argentum', were applied to the affected member in the hope of a cure.

Despite the temptations offered in nearby towns, the Prince continued to lead – perhaps even slightly to enjoy – a quiet, undemanding existence. *La vie à Calais quoique monotone est toujours confortable* ('Life in Calais though dull is comfortable'), he wrote to François de Breteuil in November 1915, adding breezily *Au revoir mon cher François et "Best of Luck".*

Comfortable conditions at XIVth Division HQ were in sharp contrast to the damp and muddy accommodation of the trenches. On one evening in late November, Raymond Asquith – the Prime Minister's son, a Lieutenant in the 3rd Battalion, Grenadier Guards – was the guest of 'Fatty' Cavan. (Asquith, one of the most brilliant minds of his generation, was killed on the Somme later that year.) The Prince's presence in the mess went largely unremarked by Asquith, who quietly damned with faint praise the shy, intellectually undemanding, young man. The Prince gave Asquith a good cigar – 'his only contribution to the evening's sport, but a sufficient one.'

In February 1916, Jacques de Breteuil joined the Prince, Lord Claud Hamilton (the Prince's new equerry), Lord Edward Stanley and other friends for dinner in the Hotel Continental at Calais. 'The Lord Claud', as he was known, was the youngest son of the Duke of Abercorn and a tall, spare man with a round face embellished with a handlebar moustache. Hamilton, five years older than the Prince, had been a career soldier and had a robust personality, not afraid to give the Prince unpalatable advice when necessary.

Escaping from the tedium of his administrative duties in France, the Prince visited Egypt, braving a Mediterranean infested by German U-boats. Unknown to him at the time, the young Frenchwoman who would become his first mistress had made a similar journey the previous year, spending several weeks in Cairo as 'guest' of Cherif *pasha*, a redoubtable public figure, before her return to Paris.

The expedition, said to have been the Prince's own idea, seemed 'a glorious picnic after Flanders', although he felt 'such a swine having a soft comfortable time out here while the Guards Division is up at Ypres'. The official reason for his six-week visit to the Middle East was to report on the defences of the Suez Canal, though his contribution must have been modest, and one historian has condemned the visit as 'unnecessary'.

On the other hand, there is evidence that his appearance raised the morale of ANZAC (Australian and New Zealand forces), who had been evacuated from Gallipoli. The expedition had been a disaster, with heavy loss of life, and the military authorities feared disaffection. True to their reputation, the antipodeans were a rumbustious and at times ill-disciplined crowd. Writing from Ismailia, the

Prince reported that 'various filthy shows' were to be seen in 'a hot quarter of the town' and that he had heard that an Australian had shot dead a donkey during a particularly revolting display. 'Not such a bad effort!!' was the Prince's wry comment.

Much of his time was spent in the vicinity of Cairo. Although the Prince expressed 'every intention of spending an unofficial 24 hours there', official duties inevitably took up most of his time. Ronald Storrs, at that time Second Secretary at the British High Commission, escorted the Prince on a decorous tour of bazaars and of the old quarters of Cairo, including an ascent of the famous minaret of Sultan Hassan. Storrs, a shrewd witness, was greatly impressed by the Prince's 'quick, human directness' and considered that he had not previously acted as *cicerone* to 'any person who entered more swiftly into the spirit of the place', even to the extent of haggling with a Jewish merchant, seemingly unaware of the buyer's royal identity, for a 'Qubba' rug.

Later, Storrs joined the Prince at Atbara, travelling on the royal *dahabeeyah* (private riverboat) from Wadi Halfa to Luxor. At Abu Simbel, the Prince astonished his perspiring British companions by going for a two-hour run, in intense heat, accompanied by 'four tall Sudanese guards'. He left Egypt for Italy on HMS *Weymouth*, escorted by a destroyer and an aeroplane, a measure of insurance against attack by 'Turco-German' aircraft, which had recently bombed Port Said.

Back in France, the Prince settled unwillingly into life at XIVth Corps HQ. Among the English recipients of the Prince's many letters was his counsellor, 'Regy' Esher. For years he had written fairly regularly to Esher, but as war progressed a subtle change crept into the Prince's attitude to his elders. When in England for a short period of leave in March 1916, he avoided meeting the ageing courtier at Buckingham Palace. He had delayed replying to one of Esher's gushy letters, eventually giving the older man a gently worded but firm discouragement by writing 'I am very busy just now & so can't be sure whether I shall be free tomorrow evening between 6 & 8.00PM. I should hate for you to come & find me out!!'

In May 1916, the Prince was posted to Chateau Louie, near Poperinghe. '2 miles N of "POP",' he wrote, '& [we] are most palacial [sic]; I live in a hut in the grounds!!' He was nearly 22 now. The war, the sights he had seen, and his slow progress to maturity were causing profound changes to his personal life and attitude to sex. He had visited a Calais brothel as one of a party of officers, but felt only disgust at the sight of naked prostitutes on display, his 'first insight into these things'. Other items of Calais merchandise prompted a good-humoured ribbing in a letter to a brother Grenadier officer. 'Do you remember when my sister [Princess Mary] caught you looking at those filthy Calais photographs. I've never laughed so much . . . .' The Prince declared to his friend that he was not experiencing 'sexual hunger', adding, a little inconsistently, 'that doesn't prevent me hankering after <u>fair</u> women, not a bit!!'

The Prince was physically a late developer and some royal biographers have commented on his apparent lack of body hair, noting that, during his time at Dartmouth in 1911 or 1912, the Prince suffered from mumps. There have been suggestions of possible sterility and the effects of a lack of testosterone, coupled with loose talk about something 'wrong with his glands' on reaching puberty. Complete sterility and loss of testicular testosterone after mumps is unusual.

A waspish memoir by a former private secretary suggests that the Prince suffered from arrested development, both mentally and morally, illustrated by sleeping for unusually long periods, by repeatedly (and in in an infantile fashion) playing the bagpies or the accordian, and by a 'mulish obstinacy' if asked to change anything which he had made up his mind to do. Although his doctors were said to have found evidence to support this contention, the only example given in the memoir is that the prince rarely needed to shave, which is hardly convincing evidence of a serious glandular disorder.

Given the Prince's emotional limitations, speculation about the physical effects of mumps or of some other, unknown, condition overlooks a few significant factors. First, the Prince was very fair and may not have had much body hair in adult life.

Second, his extreme vanity may have led him into 'manscaping' his body at various times. Third, and most important of all, the evidence revealed later in this book provides no support for the contention that the Prince was sexually inadequate.

Quite the reverse.

Paris was the venue of choice for young army officers with money to spend during their short periods of leave. When the Prince thanked Jacques de Breteuil for his birthday greetings in June 1916, he wrote, '*Quelle joie de passer 2 jours à Paris pour voir vos parents ETC!!*' ('What fun to spend 2 days in Paris seeing your parents <u>ETC</u>!!'). The following month, he congratulated his friend Captain Bailey for having had 'the hell of a time in Paris', hoping that 'you are all the better for it, tho' perhaps a trifle tired!!'. He added wistfully, 'You must have "met" some d-d fine women I bet!!'

One event, however, which was recorded in the pages of the *London Gazette* for 3 June 1916, deeply discomfited the Prince, now promoted to the rank of Captain in the Grenadier Guards. He was ashamed of having received the wholly unmerited award of a Military Cross, writing bitterly to his friend Captain Bailey, 'All I can say about my M.C. is that I wish to hell that it had been given to <u>you</u> and not to me who has no more earned it than a pol [prostitute] in London.'

Among that day's list of recipients was the name of Captain Ernest Herbert Campbell Bald, Reserve of Officers, late of the 15th Hussars, who won his MC for his role in a dashing expedition in western Egypt under the command of his friend, the Duke of Westminster. After the war, the future Major Ernest Bald MC would play a significant role behind the scenes in a drama involving the Prince's first mistress, a scandal that risked serious damage to the reputation of the British monarchy.

That summer, during the terrible Somme offensive, the Prince was posted to chateau after chateau – Louie, Marieux, Bryas, Etineham. Kept away from active service, he endured a form of luxurious captivity, unable to play a serious military role, curiously resembling the fates of medieval Scottish kings, such as David II and James I, both of whom idled away their youth in castles, prisoners of the English, constantly seeking ways to alleviate the challenges of boredom.

Château Louie, near Poperinghe, was only a few miles from the front line in an area subject not only to the noise of bombardment, day and night, but also to the risk of German air-raids. With that backdrop, the Prince dined with officers of the 3rd Grenadier Guards, including Raymond Asquith, on 21 July 1916. Just before returning to the trenches, the officers organised an open-air ball in camp, accompanied by bagpipes. Whether or not the Prince joined in the dancing (probably an all-male affair), he would have enjoyed hearing the pipes, which he had learned to play at Oxford. He might have been less amused to know about

43

a humorous reference to him in Asquith's letter. Diana (the future wife of Duff Cooper), a vivacious and beautiful young woman, had many admirers in Society. Asquith slyly added 'the Prince of Wales' (your 'future'?)' to his description of the impromptu dance at the chateau.

Eventually, in August 1916, the Prince was transferred to a camp near Meaulte, which was near Amiens and in fact not far from the front line. Here he would remain (subject to two further spells of chateau life, including a week spent accompanying the King) until May the following year. 'You know how it sickens me not to be allowed back to regimental duty myself,' he wrote to Captain Bailey in October 1916 in a spirit of self-deprecation, 'not that I should be the least use, for I'm a wretched specimen really . . . , an embusqué [shirker] sitting on one's ass the whole time!!'

The Prince's last letter to the Marquis de Breteuil, the man who had entertained him so generously before the war, was written on his birthday, 23 June 1916. In very affectionate terms, the Prince described his recent visit to Egypt, the heat of which was unfavourably compared with the incessant rain and bitter cold (*'un froid de loup'*) of Flanders. The Marquis died early in November 1916. Perhaps symptomatic of the Prince's changing attitudes to an older generation of advisers, the event passed unremarked in his diary.

At about this time, the Prince was accorded a second equerry. The Hon. Piers Legh, known as

'Joey', was another Grenadier Guards officer of his acquaintance. Tall, of slender build, with a receding chin, Joey Legh resembled the stereotypical silly-ass English aristocrat. He was more intelligent than the Prince, which is not saying a great deal, and has been described as being, if not exactly a half-wit, 'at any rate a three-quarter-wit'. Legh was a man of dry humour, 'a marvellous raconteur' of imperturbable character, whose facial immobility surely helped make him 'redoubtable at poker'.

Legh, already familiar with the Paris *demi-monde* and without doubt a man of the world, became a close confidant during the Prince's military career. Philip Ziegler has elegantly described how the Prince finally discovered the facts of life. 'Towards the end of 1916 . . . Claud Hamilton and Joey Legh decided that his virginity had been unhealthily protracted, took him to Amiens, gave him an excellent dinner with much wine, and entrusted him to . . . a French prostitute called Paulette', said to have been permanently attached to an RFC officer and therefore only 'on loan' to the Prince.

Amiens, if not quite Paris, had become a very popular destination for officers with twenty-four-hour leave passes. In September, Raymond Asquith, Oliver Lyttelton (the future Lord Chandos) and another Guards officer persuaded the Prince to lend them his grey Daimler car for the short journey over to the cathedral city, where they booked themselves into a comfortable hotel for the night. Asquith, during a wholly plantonic encounter, took a fancy to 'a perfect *femme du monde* accompanied by sweet champagne and all manner of lingeries . . .'

The Prince seems to have enjoyed more than one encounter with Paulette in Amiens, but reconstructing a timetable of these early amorous adventures is not easy. Although he kept a wartime diary, written up in some detail, until mid-June 1917, the Prince later ripped out parts of the narrative, some of which seem to have related to sexual escapades. The sequence of missing sections suggests that the 'excellent dinner' at Amiens might have taken place on 18 November 1916. Omissions occur in respect of four dates in mid-December, on one of which the Prince is known to have been with Paulette, with a further deletion at the end of that month, which also seems to refer to a meeting with her.

Other missing passages occur in February 1917, after he had returned to chateau life, now posted to the 3rd Army Artillery School at the Chateau de Hautecloque, near St Pol and 70km from Amiens. As Paulette was another officer's 'keep' and presumably had to be given back, the Prince may have started looking closer to hand for female company, this time in Arras. One of the diary deletions hints at a trip there on the weekend of 10–11 February 1917. In a letter written a day later to Captain Cecil Boyd-Rochfort (later to become the Queen Mother's racehorse trainer), the Prince recorded that 'we always get Sundays free for joy rides'.

Hautecloque was, in the Prince's opinion, 'a luxurious chateau which is easily the best billet I've ever struck in France; a good room & a large fire mean a g[rea]t deal these arctic days!!' Although he never ceased to complain about being kept away from the fighting, the Prince's correspondence with contemporaries from 1916 onwards suggests a coarsening of attitudes, a burgeoning enjoyment of the comfortable lifestyle available behind the lines, and increasing devotion to pleasure. After his first encounter with Paulette, the Prince – to use a homely sporting expression – resembled a dog put to a bitch for the first time. 'He was never out of a woman's legs,' was the trenchant recollection of Lady Diana Cooper. So started the obsessive pursuit of women, of all sorts and conditions, which would become the overriding objective of his private life.

For the moment, however, London outpaced Paris as the object of his off-duty interest. 'London is absolutely the only place to spend one's leave,' he declared to Boyd-Rochfort, adding, 'Oh for the end of this fucking war; I am getting so sick of being exiled in France!!' Nevertheless, he managed to get away for a couple of days to the Hotel Continental at Le Touquet (a future favourite destination), followed by eight days' leave in London, safely cocooned with his parents in Buckingham Palace.

During this period of leave in 'Blighty', on 19 March 1917, the Prince's diary records an evening spent at Prince's Restaurant, 190 Piccadilly, then a fashionable rendezvous for dinner and dancing. ('Isn't there a bishop or somebody who believes we shall meet all the animals we have known on earth in another world?', wrote 'Saki' in one of his *Reginald* stories, 'How frightfully embarrassing to meet a whole shoal of whitebait you had last known at Prince's . . .') Among the company helping to celebrate the 38th birthday of the Duke of Westminster was Lord Edward Stanley, son of Lord Derby, appointed British Ambassador in Paris the following year. (Stanley was soon to marry 'P', Portia Cadogan, one of the Prince's cast-off obsessions.) Another guest was Godfrey Thomas, already a close friend of the Prince. Shortly after the war, Thomas was appointed the Prince's first Private Secretary and would in later years become only too familiar with the indiscretions of the increasingly feckless Prince.

Known to intimates as 'Bendor' (from the name of a famous racehorse) and one of the richest men in Europe, Hugh Richard Arthur Grosvenor, 2nd Duke of Westminster, had been a frequent visitor to France for many years. From early in the Great War, Bendor had been in command of a fleet of Rolls-Royce armoured cars, commissioned by him and generously donated to the war effort. Unsuitable for use on the trench-ridden terrain of the Western Front, this mobile force was ideal for desert-based operations. In March 1916, with his ADC, Captain Ernest Bald, Bendor had led an overnight 120-mile dash across the desert, raiding a camp of the

Senussi, a pro-Ottoman tribe. For several months, the Senussi had been holding hostage, as 'living skeletons', a large number of British sailors, seized after their ships had been torpedoed by German U-boats in the nearby Sollum Bay. It was a daring operation and Bendor was awarded the DSO, narrowly missing a VC.

After a bout of fever in June that year, Bendor was shipped back to France, where he had a shooting lodge (designed by the famous architect Detmar Blow) on a large estate near Mimizan in Les Landes, later to become a popular destination for the Prince. In the course of convalescence, Bendor was to be seen at Nice and Cannes. Joining his friend Captain Bald in Paris during the latter part of 1916, he enjoyed the company of a certain Marguerite Alibert, alias 'Maggie Meller', a *grande cocotte* very much in demand at the time . . .

Fifteen years older than the Prince, the aristocratic libertine Bendor was already a close friend. Though his personal courage was never in doubt, he proved to be a dangerous role model for a young Prince already rebelling against the advice of more conservative elders, such as the King, Lord Stamfordham (the King's Private Secretary) and Regy Esher.

Tall and brutally handsome, with 'blue eyes and a debonair manner', the modern epithet 'male chauvinist' brilliantly describes the actions and attitudes of a supremely arrogant man. Serial womaniser and heavy drinker, he regarded wives (there would be a total of four), mistresses and sundry squeezes with equal contempt, treating them as little more than objects strewn across the path of life.

His first wife, Constance Cornwallis-West (sister-in-law of Lady Randolph Churchill), bore him two daughters and a son, who died as a child in 1909. The failure to possess a living male heir was a bitter blow to Bendor's ego, but even before the boy's death he was enjoying numerous affairs both in England and in France. In Paris, he was fond of using the Hotel Lotti, just off the Place Vendôme, as a base for amorous assignations, but just as happy to patronise high-class brothels, such as the notorious establishment at 12 rue Chabanais, often used by Edward VII when Prince of Wales.

One of Bendor's most bizarre habits was that of locking out unwanted wives. In March 1913, late one night, Constance Westminster was refused admittance to Grosvenor House in Park Lane and had to find shelter, via the milk-train, at the Duke's enormous country seat, Eaton Hall in Cheshire. Here, 'the edict had not gone forth', the words of a shocked Alan Lascelles, who considered that Bendor 'ought to be whipped round London' for his behaviour. Ten years later, the Duke's second wife, Violet Nelson, was locked out of Bourdon House in Davies Street, Mayfair. With the help of a servant, she climbed in through a window, assisted by a friend, one Cyril Augustus Drummond.

Bendor promptly locked the pair in the drawing-room, telling Cyril, 'Take her. She likes fucking.'

Bendor's third wife, Loelia Ponsonby, became very scared of him, and was at times frightened simply to come home. On many occasions as Loelia was attempting to get her key into the lock of the front door of Bourdon House. 'My hand trembled so much that I could not get it in.'

Though Marguerite could take care of herself, Bendor cowed other mistresses, exhibiting a sadistic tendency in his relations with women. Although the Prince could adopt an abject, fawning, seemingly submissive pose when infatuated, the Duke's malign influence can be detected in the younger man's increasingly crude, sometimes abusive treatment of discarded favourites.

At the Duke's raffish birthday party, gossip among the all-male company must have centred on Paris and its sensual attractions, already sampled by a high proportion of the guests. The impressionable Prince, newly initiated and about to return to France, needed little encouragement to move upmarket, away from workaday 'pols' in the dull, damaged northern cities of Amiens and Arras. His aim was now to explore the superior delights offered by *la ville lumière*, the City of Light. On return to service life in France a few days after the Westminster birthday dinner, getting to Paris became the object of the Prince's most fervent desire. He must have a 'pol', a 'keep' there, a woman he could brag about to his male contemporaries.

In April, he determined to take full advantage of three days' leave, making preparations for the long drive from St Pol to Paris. If the Prince was to find *the* woman, arrangements had to be made post haste. That weekend, it seems, he contacted his old friend, François de Breteuil, whose knowledge of Parisian society far outstripped that of Joey Legh, Claud Hamilton, or even Bendor.

The Prince was about to embark on the first great sexual obsession of his life, his affair with Marguerite Alibert, 'Maggie Meller', an expert in the arts of love and – in every sense – a woman of the world.

CHAPTER 3

SHE-DEVIL

The Prince of Wales was born in White Lodge, a handsome Palladian mansion in Richmond Park, west of London. The woman who would become his first mistress saw the light of human day in one of a row of cast-iron beds, crowded into the public ward of a massive and forbidding metropolitan maternity hospital in the south of Paris.

'A Parisian in mind, in taste, to the fingertips', her real name was Marie Marguerite Alibert, but she would become known to the Paris *demi-monde* as 'Maggie Meller' and (in later strivings for respectability) 'Mme Laurent', 'Mme Fahmy', even 'the Princess Fahmy *bey*'. Her date of birth became a movable feast (sometimes 1892 or 1895), but the official record establishes incontrovertibly that she was born just before midday on 9 December 1890. Outside the foetid warmth of the great Paris maternity hospital of Port-Royal, near Montparnasse, bitter easterly winds kept the street temperatures around zero. The baby, known to her family as Marguerite, was the eldest surviving child of Firmin Alibert, *cocher de fiacre*

53

[cab driver], and his wife Marie Aurand, *femme de ménage* [charwoman].

The family lived for a time in the rue d'Armaillé, in the 17th *arrondissement*, not far from the Arc de Triomphe. Marguerite had a much younger sister, Yvonne, born in 1900, with whom she had a stormy relationship, eventually becoming completely estranged. A brother was said to have been killed during the Great War in an attack south of Rheims. One of her two highly coloured attempts at autobiography mentions a second brother, also allegedly a victim of the hostilities.

Family sources confirm, however, that Marguerite had just one brother, who was killed, at the age of 4, by a lorry while playing in the street, an accident blamed on Marguerite's wilfulness in failing to look after him properly. As a result, she claimed, Marguerite was sent to board with the Sisters of Mary, 73 rue des Ternes, not very far from her home, a religious house where the nuns solemnly reminded her each day that her sins had dispatched her brother, the 'little angel', to heaven.

Marguerite may indeed have been entrusted into the care of nuns after this or some other juvenile misdemeanour. She aptly described her character as 'mercurial' and Paris, of course, hosted all sorts of temptations. Understandably perhaps, Marguerite resented her sojourn among the nuns, ironically describing this period as 'a great start in life', gleefully recalling that the institution was later turned into a garage. The experience had a few good points: Marguerite was given the smatterings of an education and taught to sing, developing an attractive mezzo-soprano in which she would warble 'sacred solos'.

In later years, Marguerite posthumously moved her parents up the social ladder. Firmin and Marie were promoted respectively to lawyer's clerk and milliner (after all, Marguerite's *couturier* Gabrielle 'Coco' Chanel had started her working life making hats).

In the 1890s, Maître Elie-Henri-Jules Langlois, a lawyer originally from Nîmes and with a very shady past (including imprisonment for assault), acted for Thérèse Humbert, *La Grande Thérèse*, prime mover in the colossal 'Humbert-Crawford' financial scandal that convulsed France in 1902, a drama of which Marguerite would have been well aware. By the simple ruse of inventing a rich American benefactor, Thérèse and husband Frederic persuaded scores of people, of modest means as well as the super-rich, to 'loan' them money at absurdly attractive rates of interest. Overall, the Humbert scheme netted around 100,000,000 gold francs (perhaps £350,000,000 at present-day values).

Although discovery and retribution were inevitable consequences of so colossal a deception, one valuable lesson was almost certainly not lost on Marguerite. The fraudsters had succeeded in duping the public because they aimed high, brazenly keeping up their act to the very end. The luxuriously appointed mansion at 65 Avenue de la Grande Armèe, the Humberts' Paris home for twenty years, was just a few steps from the cramped and modest apartment shared by Marguerite's family.

In Marguerite's account, she left the spartan convent of her own volition, moved in with the Langlois family, and began enjoying *le haut luxe* (the high life) of Paris. She claimed that Mme Langlois was her godmother. In reality, Marguerite may have entered the household as a domestic servant (perhaps placed there by the nuns), giving her the chance to see the workings of an *haut bourgeois* household and to use her nascent observational skills to the full. The Langlois were cultured, as well as rich, interesting themselves in music and the arts. Marguerite undoubtedly profited from the brief association.

The idyll did not last long. Although Marguerite considered herself to have been 'devout . . . in a mystic way as young sensitive girls sometimes are', she fell from her state of grace rather rapidly. By the early summer of 1906, she was pregnant. On 21 January 1907, her only child, a daughter christened Raymonde, was born in the grim maternity hospital at Port-Royal. Marguerite was just 16 years old.

Many years later, it was suggested in the American press that Raymonde's father had been a penniless art student, but he might just as easily have been a member of the Langlois family or another male servant, perhaps a footman or a coachman. Marguerite, typically, has left two completely different accounts of the father's identity, neither of which is convincing. The first finds her engaged to a man of 28, whom she had known since childhood, but – as she wrote airily – 'unfortunately I had not a sufficient dowry and the beautiful dream collapsed'. The second version involves an Englishman, younger son of a colonial administrator in India and killed in the Great War. His name is given, quite improbably, as 'André Mont-Clarc'. Under the age of 21 at the time of the romance, the young man required his father's agreement to marry, a consent that unsurprisingly never came. Whoever fathered baby Raymonde, this episode put an abrupt end to Marguerite's association with the Langlois family.

In the straitened circumstances of the Alibert household, there were few resources to spare for Marguerite and her child. Raymonde was sent away to be looked after on a farm near Moulins, in central France and remained there for seven years. Marguerite never visited her during this period. Later, after Marguerite's circumstances had dramatically improved, Raymonde returned to live with her mother in Paris, before being sent to school in London after the Great War.

But for now, untrammelled by early motherhood, Marguerite was free to pursue her quest for upward mobility. Her prime asset was her body. Although not a chocolate-box beauty, she was petite, with a shapely figure, expressive greenish-grey eyes, a pretty mole on her left cheek, and a large sensuous mouth. At this time, she wore her striking auburn hair in long tresses, 'falling to my knees'.

What happened in the year or so after the birth of Raymonde is obscure, and Marguerite, understandably, glossed over what may have been a particularly unpleasant period in her life. This was a time when – like Edith Piaf a decade or so later – she may have been forced on to the streets, earning a living by 'polite prostitution', singing in cheap cabarets and restaurants. Unlike Piaf, however, Marguerite already had a veneer of sophistication, the legacy of her brief convent education and time spent with the Langlois family. She also had the advantage of having been brought up in a smart area of Paris, affording her countless opportunities to see how the rich led their lives. Marguerite, a quick learner, soon honed the skills necessary to support herself in the only practicable way open to her. 'She was tough. She had to be.'

Marguerite came (or brought herself) to the attention of a Mme Denart, who ran the kind of high-class brothel known as a *maison de rendezvous* at 3 rue Galilee, in the heart of the fashionable 16th *arrondissement*, not far from Marguerite's modest childhood home on the other side of the Arc de Triomphe. Mme Denart, for reasons which will be seen, later developed a jaundiced view of her young *protégée*. Marguerite came to her 'ill-mannered', with 'no accomplishments', unpleasant disparagements which do not quite fit the facts. Mme Denart, for all her sour recollections, probably did help develop Marguerite's social skills. Elocution lessons were arranged (Marguerite would learn to speak French with slightly old-fashioned formality). The daughter of a cab driver and a charwoman was taught how to dress in style and keep her demanding customers entertained in restaurants or the theatre. With some exaggeration, Mme Denart boasted that her *ingénue* had been made to study the piano for three years 'so that she could go out with my clients'. Mme Denart undoubtedly had an eye for talent and Marguerite evidently had what was needed to become a successful courtesan. In time, Marguerite became 'the mistress of nearly all my best clients, gentleman of wealth and position in France, England, America and other countries . . .' All in all, Mme Denart declared modestly, 'It was me that made . . . a sort of lady of her.'

Even by 1907, Marguerite, a very self-possessed 16-year-old, was the sort of lady known as *'une dame à cinq heures'* ('a 5 o'clock lady') or *'une cinq à sept'* ('a five to seven'), references to the late afternoon, a popular time for sexual assignations in *maisons de rendezvous*. When not accompanying a client to dinner or to the theatre, there were excellent opportunities for such working women to gain custom in the music halls springing up all over Paris as the new century progressed, such as the Palais Persan (Persian Palace) at 'Magic-City', near the Eiffel Tower; the Casino de Paris; and,

59

most famous of all, the Folies Bergère at 32 rue Richer in the raffish Pigalle district.

At the Folies, business was booming and, despite prudish attempts at municipal regulation, stage acts were becoming steadily more *risqué*. The management of the Folies actively encouraged the presence of attractive, well-dressed and elegant young women as expensive bait front of house, greeting the regular incoming procession of rich men eager for sensual diversion.

There were broadly three types of what would now be called 'sex workers' operating in Paris. Commentators noted the difficulty of distinguishing from each other *la courtisane, la fille d'occasion et la prostituée professionelle* (the courtesan, the woman for hire, or the professional prostitute). Marguerite's aim in life was very clear from the start. She had no intention of standing in a darkened doorway in a draughty street in order to drum up trade. She never regarded herself as a common prostitute, some diseased whore from the pages of *Bubu de Montparnasse*, a widely read contemporary novel. In the manner of another fictional courtesan, Marguerite Gautier, doomed heroine of Dumas *fils'* maudlin novel *La Dame aux Camelias* (and others in the long line of Parisian *poules de luxe*), she would succeed in creating a glamorous, almost wholesome, image for herself. In due course, she was able to manage, with considerable professional skill, the simultaneous attentions of a number of wealthy men. Perhaps her closest literary forebears are the courtesans who feature in *La Comédie Humaine* by Balzac. Marguerite's rapacity, ambition and desire for social acceptance mirrors the hypocritical Valérie Marneffe, while her gentler side, love of style and fashion, is reflected in the character of Josépha Mirah, the 'tart with a heart'.

In real life, nineteenth-century Paris had seen a parade of *grandes horizontales*, seeking to exploit the riches of the City of Light. One of the most avaricious was Esther Lachmann, 'La Païva', born in Moscow of Jewish parentage. In around 1838, abandoning husband and child, she moved to Paris, becoming mistress of a concert pianist, who introduced her to the fashionable world. In 1851, now widowed, she married a Portuguese nobleman, obtained his title, then abandoned him for Count von Donnersmarck, a much younger man, 'whose income never fell below three million francs a year'. Esther, always a heavy spender, built the 'Hôtel Païva' on the Champs-Élysées, a temple of luxury, which featured a 'Hollywood style grand staircase' and a salon lined with costly Lyons damask. Her 'great bed was carved from precious woods inset with ivory', next to 'a large safe which kept her jewels'. Esther was grasping, greedy and, it was said, particularly unpleasant to her servants. After her death at 64, her husband allegedly preserved the body of 'La Païva' in embalming fluid.

Some courtesans became acknowledged figures in the field of art, music and literature. Apollonie Sabatier, born in 1822 and known as 'La

Présidente', was famous for her Sunday dinners, attended by literary lions such as Gustave Flaubert, Ernest Feydeau and Théophile Gautier. Mistress of the banker Hippolyte Mosselman, Apollonie was acidly described by Edmond de Goncourt as 'a biggish woman with a coarse, hearty manner . . . [a] rather vulgar creature endowed with classical beauty . . . a camp-follower for fauns'.

Emma Crouch, born in England and educated in Boulogne, reinvented herself as 'Cora Pearl' for the Paris market of the 1860s. Cora, very beautiful with tremendous dress sense and strikingly auburn hair, was quickly taken up by French nobility, including the Duc de Morny and Prince Napoleon, the Emperor's cousin. She sang, wearing the skimpiest of costumes, in operetta by Offenbach. In association with Charles Worth, the English *couturier*, her style of dress, her *maquillage* and her *coiffure* became the talk of Paris. She even out-dressed the Empress Eugénie on one evening at the opera, when all eyes turned to look at Cora, causing Eugénie to leave in a jealous huff. Her château at Beauséjour, near Orléans, was the scene of extravagant parties, during one of which Cora, nude, was carried around on a large silver charger, covered only in parsley. Like Marguerite, Cora became an accomplished horsewoman, riding in the fashionable Bois de Boulogne. Like Marguerite, too, she kept a studbook of her lovers, recording all manner of intimate performance data.

Nearer Marguerite's time, as the turn of the

century approached, the reigning Paris beauties were 'La Belle Otero', Liane de Pougy (a glamorous reinvention of Anne-Marie Chassaigne) and Lina Cavalieri, originally from Belgium. All these women served their time at the Folies Bergère.

Otero, who traded on her image as an exotic Andalusian dancer and was pursued by legions of royal and noble admirers, had a kind heart. She promoted the career of Marguerite Boulc'h, a penniless 14-year-old errand girl (born in 1891), who would become the great *chanteuse*, Fréhel. De Pougy 'was famous for the splendour of her jewellery, her luxurious town house, the "secondary residences" . . . in Brittany and Saint-Germain'. Something of a wit, de Pougy was once asked her opinion of Otero and Calavieri. 'It's like this,' she replied, 'when Calavieri wears real jewels they look false and when Otero wears false jewels they look real.'

It was in 1907 that André Meller first came into Marguerite's life. Meller was a married man of 40 with, as Marguerite ruefully recalled, a roving eye for women. He was tall, good-looking and slim. Meller was also rich, the son of a successful Bordeaux wine *négociant*, who supplied claret to the Vatican. Marguerite may have been introduced to Meller by the friend of a friend. Or she may have encountered him in the street, outside the famous early motor showroom, Neubauer, where he had just bought a Renault. Or she may simply have been picked up by him one night at the Folies.

Meller had a racing stable at Bordeaux, which seems to have been the spur to Marguerite's passion for horseflesh (in contrast to the unsteady seat of her future lover the Prince of Wales, Marguerite became an excellent mount and also adored attending fashionable race meetings). With little Raymonde safely out of the way, Marguerite cultivated her affair with Meller, who set her up, as a 'kept woman', in an apartment in the rue Pergolese (the 16th *arrondissement*, of course). Unlike strait-laced London, there was no shame in a man appearing in public with his mistress in Paris and Marguerite made an attractive companion for Meller in and around town. Over the course of a seven-year affair, Meller took her duck-shooting (staying at his villa in Arcachon on the coast, west of Bordeaux), and on trips abroad, including to Morocco and Venice. Although there was talk of annulment, Meller does not seem seriously to have contemplated marrying Marguerite, who none the less styled herself 'Mme Meller', although *tout Paris* was getting to know her simply as 'Maggie Meller'.

Meller's business interests in Bordeaux, coupled with his status as a married man, allowed Marguerite – like many other 'kept' women at the time – to carry on the rewarding business of Paris courtesan. She continued to feature as a major attraction at the *maison de rendezvous* and, aiming unswervingly for the top, would now be seen in the most luxurious hotels and expensive restaurants. People were beginning to notice Maggie Meller.

And Marguerite took notice of the world around her. She lived through the sensational trial of Mme Steinheil in 1908. Jeanne-Marguerite Japy had been the mistress of President Felix Faure and, as legend has it, was engaged in an act of *fellatio* at the Élysée Palace, when the President suddenly died. Jeanne-Marguerite's fair hair was held tightly in the dead man's grip and had to be cut away. In her haste to escape from this most embarrassing situation she abandoned her corsets before slipping out of the palace by the tradesmen's entrance.

A few years later, now married to Adolphe Steinheil, a rich and well-connected artist, Jeanne-Marguerite was charged with strangling her husband (and murdering her mother-in-law) in obscure circumstances, apparently for gain. Her testimony was wildly inconsistent and there was evidence that she had tried to implicate innocent people. Nevertheless, after a spirited performance in court, Jeanne-Marguerite was acquitted. The verdict showed the world, including Marguerite, that a beautiful woman could murder her husband, tell a preposterous story, walk free from court and collect an inheritance.

One summer afternoon in 1912 (during the Prince of Wales's first visit to France and the year when the first completely nude woman appeared on the stage of the Folies Bergère), Marguerite was introduced by a mutual admirer to

Pierre-Plessis. The young journalist, poet and author was a friend of Jean Cocteau, the current *enfant terrible* of Paris. At *l'heure du thé* ('tea-time' is a wholly inadequate translation), amid the opulent surroundings of the Ritz Hotel in the Place Vendôme, a string orchestra essayed sentimental melodies amid a forest of palms. The young romantic was captivated by Marguerite's large, deep, seemingly melancholy eyes (*'les grand yeux doux et tristes'*). She was wearing a conspicuously large diamond ring, displaying the first fruits of what would soon become a formidable collection of jewellery. Pierre-Plessis was struck by her apparent air of simplicity, even of artlessness. Marguerite spoke demurely of going that evening to the Theatre-Français, and of how much she admired the writings of Pierre Loti, Charles Farrère and Alfred de Musset.

Pierre-Plessis's sympathetically written account of meeting Marguerite at the Ritz shows how well she could marshal her attractive qualities, but she did not always show her gentle side to the world. Her dry Parisian wit could be corrosive and was combined with a fiery temperament. At times, Marguerite could exhibit a violent temper, as the Prince of Wales would discover to his cost. However rich and well-connected her lovers might be, she was not afraid to show her contempt when circumstances required. Mme Denart remembered a celebrated occasion when Marguerite vigorously slapped a wealthy admirer about the face as they sat in an expensive restaurant, in the full view of other customers.

André Meller, despite having provided his lover with a smart apartment, jewellery and access to Parisian *haute couture*, was not exempt from Marguerite's whiplash. Pre-war Morocco seemed old-fashioned and, despite her own well-practised profession, she expressed distaste for holiday accommodation set among camels, prostitutes and slave-dealers. As to Venice, at the Danieli there was a violent scene in a bedroom (once occupied by the novelist George Sand), when Meller – increasingly jealous of the attention Marguerite was attracting from other men – lost his temper, slapped her, and had his face deeply scratched in return.

The quarrel was soon patched up and, the following year, Marguerite joined Meller Deauville at the Villa Paradou, a neo-gothic extravaganza which still stands behind the famous Casino. Marguerite was beginning to cut a figure among the swarm of ambitious and attractive women, wasps around the honey-pot in this most fashionable of resorts.

One writer with a sharp eye for beauty and the ways of high society was Georges Dreyfus, better known as Michel Georges-Michel, author of *Les Montparnos*, a novel based on the life of his friend Modigliani (later adapted into a film, *Les Amants de Montparnasse*, starring Gérard Philipe and Anouk Aimée). Artistic adviser to Diaghilev, helping produce the Ballet Russes between 1913 and 1929, organiser of the first Picasso exhibition in Rome, Georges-Michel wrote extensively, and amusingly, about the society that preened itself in fashionable resorts such as Deauville. Many of his books were illustrated by leading contemporary artists, such as Van Dongen and Raoul Dufy.

Georges-Michel's first encounter with Marguerite was at Deauville, during the summer season of 1913, and, although they would not meet again for nearly twenty years, her style and beauty made an unforgettable impression on the 30-year-old author.

Meller was by now almost pathologically jealous of his young mistress. Marguerite, with remarkable candour, described herself as being *une fichue diablesse* ('a terrible she-devil'), and, after yet another row, she had the gates of the villa locked, the doors barred, and Meller's horses set free to roam the property. Police were called, Deauville was scandalised and, in the end, Meller decided to break off the relationship. Marguerite secured a settlement of 200,000 francs, which she brazenly described as a pittance little more than a bag of beans, blaming her comparative youth and naivete for not having secured more.

Leaving rue Pergolèse, she moved to an even grander apartment at 6 square Thiers, off the avenue Victor Hugo in the 16th. Here she employed two indoor servants and kept a stable of horses. Marguerite, with the security of Meller's cash behind her and using her remarkable power to charm and fascinate, was now in a position to make further attempts to conquer the *beau monde* of Paris. Some doors would never open to her, but Marguerite's determination was harvesting some very useful contacts.

Once more, the Folies Bergère would play a dramatic role in Marguerite's life. Nicole de Montjoie, who had a financial stake in the great Paris music-hall, was the owner of the Chateau de Montjoie in Touraine, south of Paris. Whether Nicole encountered Marguerite through her presence at the Folies or, as Marguerite claimed, at one of the elaborate balls held at Magic-City, they became firm friends. Like others of her class anxious to break away from stuffy convention, Nicole was flattered to make the acquaintance of a true *femme du monde* (woman of the world), an excellent companion around Paris, and was delighted to show off her new discovery to influential friends. Marguerite, who was now becoming rather a name-dropper, not to say snob, relished Nicole's introductions to high society figures, young men such as the Marquis de Pracomtal and André de Fels, grandson of Max Lebaudy, the fabulously rich 'sugar king' of France. Such men might avail themselves of Marguerite's sexual services, but this was not always the case. Some friendships would remain platonic. Experienced courtesan that she had become, Marguerite deftly compartmentalised the differing aspects of her life.

A typical day just before the outbreak of war would see Marguerite and Nicole riding together in the Bois de Boulogne, having lunch at the Café de Paris, going to the races in the afternoon, and – leaving Marguerite free for professional diversions during the *cinq à sept* – dining with aristocratic friends at the newly opened Ciro's Restaurant at 6 rue Daunou.

For much later entertainment and opportunities to encounter the eligible rich, one of Marguerite's favoured Paris nightclubs at this time was in the bohemian *quartier* of Montmartre. The Abbaye Thélème was wickedly named after Rabelais's fictional monastery in Gargantua, notorious for its motto '*Fais ce que vouldras*' ('Do what you want').

Until wartime restrictions forced an early curfew, a fashionable clientele crowded into the tiny confines of the Abbaye after midnight, enjoying a late supper before taking to the tiny dance floor. Although the Abbaye may have affected an off-piste air, its visitors were not slumming. This was by no means a low dive. The high standard of service, accompanied by an excellent *cuisine* approached 'that pitch of perfection which almost amounts to scandal'. Pre-war, the partying could continue until three or four in the morning.

Since the beginning of the decade, two dance crazes had swept across the Atlantic. The first came from North America. The second – with even greater *éclat* – originated in the south, from Argentina. Raucous New York favourites, such as the 'Ramshackle Rag', 'Rum Tum Tiddle' and 'Hitchy Koo', imported on single-sided gramophone records, soon featured in the night clubs of Europe. By 1912, however, the Tango, a less frenetic, definitely more sensuous style of dancing than the bouncy 'two-step', took centre stage.

In Paris, noted an observer, the Tango '*a envahi les salons, les theâtres, les bars, les cabarets de nuit, les grand hôtels et les guingettes* [has invaded the drawing-rooms, theatres, bars, nightclubs, great houses and dancehalls]'. There were Tango teas, Tango exhibitions, Tango lectures. '*La moitié de Paris frotte l'autre* [Half Paris cuddles up against the other half]'

During that last summer of peace, Marguerite began the pattern of travel that she would re-establish after the war, beginning the season at the Villa d'Este on Lake Como and renting a seaside property at Dinard in Brittany.

On 16 March 1914, Gustave Calmette, polemical editor of *Le Figaro*, the leading right-wing newspaper, was shot dead in his Paris office by Henriette Caillaux, wielding a 6.35mm Browning automatic pistol. Mme Caillaux, a beautiful, intelligent woman who cut an impressive figure in court, considered that her victim had slandered her husband, a Socialist minister. Represented by the great Maître Labori (defender of Émile Zola) and despite the strength of the case against her, Mme Caillaux was acquitted of murder. In the course of evidence, she declared that she did not intend to kill M Calmette, only to frighten him. She did not know whether the safety catch was on or off. 'My finger was on the trigger. I pressed it.'

The verdict was also prompted by a curious precedent. In the late nineteenth century, two other French wives had been acquitted of murder after shooting dead men who had allegedly insulted their honour. The Steinheil case, five years earlier, had been a revealing exercise, but had not involved the use of firearms. Mme Caillaux had shot an unarmed man dead at point blank range, but nevertheless secured an acquittal. Marguerite would take note of this well-publicised case.

On 31 July 1914, three days after Mme Caillaux's triumph and on the eve of war, Jean Jaurès, prominent Socialist and anti-war campaigner, was shot dead by a right-wing activist. On the day now considered a landmark in French history, news of the assassination reached Marguerite, now a beautifully coutured adornment of the best restaurants, sitting at a table in Maxim's as guest of her rich admirer, André de Fels, enjoying the last days of the *belle époque*.

The crisis brought new opportunities to Marguerite, now the owner of a smart new '20-30' Renault. She was delighted to be able to offer her services as a driver to the Baroness Lejeune (née Murat, a family closely connected to Napoleon Bonaparte) who seems to have directed Red Cross work in Touraine, south of Paris. The Baroness, also christened Marguerite, had a vast gothic palace, the Château Mothe-Chandeniers, in Vienne, south of the Loire.

Personal comforts, of course, could not be overlooked and Marguerite, travelling as 'Mme Meller', was cosseted by her personal chef and Vietnamese maid, driving doctors and nursing nuns to and from hospitals whose wards were rapidly filling with soldiers and airmen, the first of many casualties arriving from the Western Front.

Marguerite's altruistic commitment to social services in the international emergency did not last long. At the end of the year, she became ill with an unspecified ailment, for the alleviation of which her helpful doctors recommended a warm climate. Marguerite's indisposition conveniently coincided with midwinter, the most agreeable and fashionable season for Westerners in Egypt. Risks of her ship being torpedoed by German U-boats were weighed alongside opportunities available in Alexandria, Cairo and Luxor. Marguerite, a risk-taker by nature, made a shrewd decision, took ship from Marseilles and, a few days later, had installed herself in Cairo. Here she received the unwanted attention of a rich and powerful Egyptian *pasha*. Skilfully evading the advances of this *pasha*, Marguerite secured the protection of another, Mehmet Cherif, described modestly as 'a friend' she had made in Paris.

Cherif cut a striking figure with his enormous bushy (and very Turkish) moustache. He was famous for his love of Paris (his *'parisianisme'*), as well as a flamboyant lifestyle and 'stable' of Rolls-Royce cars. He was the brother-in-law of the Grand Vizier of Turkey and was married to a member of the Egyptian royal family. A former Turkish Ambassador to Sweden and reformer, he had at first supported the 'Young Turks', the nationalist group which overthrew the Sultan in 1908, but disliked their extremism and soon left their ranks to found the Turkish Liberal party.

Cherif survived four assassination attempts, the most serious being in January 1914, when a Turk (armed with a pistol, dagger, Koran and 200 francs) burst into Cherif's Paris apartment, shooting dead a valet before being killed himself by Cherif's son-in-law. In Cairo, a disgruntled ex-employee had tried to shoot Cherif while he and Marguerite were strolling through the *souk*. Instinctively (Marguerite claimed) she threw herself in front of the intended target, later finding Cherif's signed photograph in her hotel room, When Marguerite returned to France, avoiding the heat of an Egyptian summer, Cherif prudently moved to Geneva, where, in October 1915, he bravely drew attention to the persecution of Armenians, fruitlessly trying to arouse world opinion in their favour. Cherif *pasha*, one of Marguerite's top-flight international clients, maintained relations with his favourite *parisienne* for many years afterwards.

With Marguerite safely back in Paris, it may have been about this time that she broke with Mme Denart, who had originally guided her career as a courtesan. The rupture explains the latter's barbed references to her quondam *protégée*, recollections later given to an English private detective. There is certainly evidence that, by the second half of the war, Marguerite was on the books of one of the grandest Paris *maison de rendezvous*, that of Mme Sonia de Théval at 20 rue Bizet (in the 16th, of course).

Marguerite's new workplace was in no danger of raids or summary closure. The male clientele was necessarily rich and often powerful. Discretion was the keynote. Customers would be received by a maid, formally dressed as the sort of servant found in any upper-class Paris household. Such a *maison* might sport an impressive marble staircase, bordered by elaborate wrought-iron handrails. The maid would indicate a waiting-room, elegantly furnished in Empire style, in which the client would find, artfully displayed among newspapers and society magazines, some albums of photographs. These would show courtesans in a variety of poses, catering for all tastes and including married women (long predating *Belle du Jour*), *trottins* (errand girls) and attractive actresses seeking to augment their income from theatre work. Prominently displayed would be photographs of the *grandes vedettes*, the 'big stars', the most sought after and expensive on the list, women – like Marguerite – who had special skills, equally happy to play the dominatrix, wielding the horsewhip, to take part in lesbian activity staged to the customer's requirements, and even to indulge a client's taste for sodomy.

The atmosphere of the *maison* was calm, quiet and unhurried. Mme de Thèval (or her *sous-maîtresse* Ginette Folway, a former revue actress) would note the client's selection and requirements, then agree a price. The woman of choice would be contacted (often by telephone), and, after an interval, the customer would be shown to a suitable *salon* in the building, two of which were on the same floor as the waiting-room. Most liaisons were of the *cinq-à-sept* formula in the late afternoon, but the *maison* was allowed to open at noon and earlier assignments were possible.

Number 20 rue Bizet, with a handful of other establishments (such as the old-established brothel at 12 rue Chabanais in the Marais, which had so often sheltered the Prince's grandfather), attracted members of the English aristocracy, for whose entertainment Mme de Thèval demanded astro-nomical sums. During periods of wartime leave in Paris, members of the Prince's close circle – such as Joey Legh, 'the Lord Claud' and Captain Bailey – may well have made their way to this quiet corner of the 16th *arrondissement*.

During 1916, Marguerite was taken up by Achille Fould, *richissime* son of the financier who had bankrolled Louis Napoleon's *coup d'état* of 1852 and a close relation of the old Marquis de Breteuil, who had been the Prince's host during his first visit to France. That year also brought the Duke of Westminster to Paris and Deauville. Recovering from illness contracted during his Egyptian service and already estranged from his first wife, Bendor was ripe for diversion. Marguerite, already a favourite of Captain Ernest Bald (Bendor's ADC and close friend), entertained Westminster before his return to England in the latter part of 1916. It was Marguerite's association with the fabulously rich 'Bendor', and his exclusive social circle, that would secure for her the greatest prize of all, the patronage of the Prince of Wales.

By the following year, Marguerite had secured for herself a significant niche in wartime Paris society. In her elegant apartment, seeking to emulate the true *grands salons*, Marguerite held court at her own *soirées*, at which minor aristocrats, artists, writers, singers, actors and actresses could be seen, respectable people content to enjoy the hospitality of a woman who was willing, on more *louche* occasions, to offer herself for reward to the highest bidder.

Definitely not the Anglo-Saxon model.

CHAPTER 4

ROYAL FLUSH

The Prince was determined to enjoy his three days' leave, an escape from dreary routine made possible by his commanding officer, the amiable General 'Fatty' Cavan. As 'Earl of Chester', driving his new Rolls-Royce *coupé* to Paris on the morning of St George's Day, Monday 23 April 1917, he installed himself (with his valet, Finch, now in uniform) in the Hotel Meurice, a comfortable establishment in the Rue de Rivoli, which was to remain his favourite Paris hotel for many years.

The Hotel de Crillon, a magnificent exercise in French classicism, was created in 1758 at the whim of Louis XV and designed by the architect Jacques-Ange Gabriel. Originally intended as a government department, this most imposing building was soon sold to a noble family and, apart from a temporary state confiscation under the Revolution, remained a private residence until the early twentieth century. In 1909, the Crillon was transformed into a luxurious hotel, patronised by the rich and famous, then as now, and conveniently just a few steps away from the Élysée Palace, from the Chamber of Deputies at the Palais Bourbon, and from the British and American Embassies.

Although the object of the Prince's attention was a notorious *demi-mondaine*, Parisian etiquette demanded formal introduction. This first encounter with Marguerite, formally presented to the Prince by François de Breteuil, whose family had entertained the Prince in 1912, took place at lunch in the hotel's restaurant, the magnificent former ballroom of the Crillon family, now known as Les Ambassadeurs. The restaurant looked directly on to the Place de la Concorde, where the Prince's distant kinsman, Louis XVI and his queen, Marie Antoinette, were guillotined during the French Revolution.

Lunch, though leisurely, would have been a light affair. Marguerite's slim figure was one of her prime assets, while the Prince, image-conscious from early youth, was never much of a trencherman. A light eater, he developed a taste for seafood and was often content to toy with a plate of oysters or a lobster.' The couple drank only water and conversation would have been conducted entirely in French, which – thanks in part to his connection with the Breteuil family – the Prince could now speak with reasonable fluency. Marguerite, who had no English, was immediately entranced by this shy, eager young man. He spoke French, she recollected, remarkably well, with only a slight accent, which was very appealing to her.

For his part, the Prince was bowled over by this

petite, strikingly attractive young Frenchwoman, dressed by the leading couturier Paquin, her auburn hair (then worn long) and her hazel eyes beautifully complemented by a gleaming ensemble of emeralds and pearls. At table, Marguerite would soon be aware of an early transatlantic affectation on the part of her new companion, perhaps picked up from his contacts with Canadian army personnel. The Prince, having cut up his food, ate only with his right hand, waving his left hand around while talking.

From all the available sources, it is clear that Marguerite – when she was in the right mood – could be excellent company, delightful and charming. Highly skilled in the arts of her profession, she no doubt hinted discreetly over coffee at the delights which awaited the Prince later that day. After lunch ended, perhaps beyond three o'clock, there might be a drive around Paris. Edith Wharton, writing just before the war, described 'the afternoon motor rush to some leafy suburb . . . the whirl home through the Bois to dress for dinner and start again on the round of evening diversions . . .'

Marguerite's apartment at 67 avenue Henri-Martin was conveniently close to the Bois de Boulogne, where, in the next two days, the Prince and his delightful new companion could enjoy a morning ride on the best horses of her stable. A Paris police report confirms that Marguerite's practice, in keeping with many other *demi-mondaines*, was to leave afternoons free for liaisons. After that memorable first meeting, the Prince noted Marguerite's address in his pocketbook, then asked her a highly significant question, *On se tutoie?*, which derived from the verb *tutoyer*, an untranslatable French expression signifying the intimacy of lovers.

That evening, the Prince may well have taken Marguerite 'back to the Bois, with supper in one of its lamp-hung restaurants', such as Au Pré Catalan or the Château de Madrid. On the other two nights of his all too brief leave, they might go to the cinema or to 'the little play at the Capucines or the Variétés', or even to a Montmartre nightclub, such as the Abbaye Thélème, though wartime restrictions now meant that licensed premises had to close early. As a result, clandestine establishments were set up in *la banlieue*, on the edge of the city. Chauffeur-driven limousines decanted their expensively dressed occupants, who found late-night entertainment sometimes in lonely houses, set behind crumbling walls in unfashionable quarters, where (from bribery or indifference) the police were unlikely to cause trouble.

Duff Cooper, then a First Lieutenant in the Grenadier Guards, recorded such a late-night visit in a diary entry made the following year. His account illustrates how Marguerite and her Prince might have spent an evening together in that latter part of the Great War. Duff had taken a fancy to a woman seen at Maxim's. 'When she left the restaurant I . . . boldly followed her – drove her to her flat and then back to the Folies Bergère where we had taken two boxes for the performance of *Zig-Zag*. Afterwards I went off with my new friend to an establishment where one could dance and drink – a pleasant place more like a private house. We drank a little and danced a little and then went to her flat . . .'

It was, of course, the lady's performance in bed which was the most desirable and significant feature of the Prince's stay in Paris, but, for the time being, the young man was giving nothing away. When Regy Esher had a 'delightful talk' with the Prince over lunch at the Crillon on Thursday 27 April, the last day of his Paris leave, the infatuated Prince made no mention of love sessions with Marguerite, the beauty who had sat so demurely opposite him in the same restaurant just three days before. 'A real affectionate little talk,' Esher crooned and, unaware of the facts, described his young companion as 'looking splendid . . . one of those fine lads that one loves and admires more day by day'.

The Prince's own record of these pleasurable rites of passage has been largely torn out of his wartime diary, but fragments remain, hinting at the depth of passion felt for his new love. A few days after his return from Paris to the humdrum life at XIVth Division HQ, the Prince wrote '. . . how perfectly bloody this endless war is!! Of course those 3 days bliss in Paris have made it all the more bloody . . .

Dinner was rather an ordeal after Paris & I've develloped [sic] that "feeling of revulsion" for the whole corps staff except Fatty, Claudie, Joey and Bucknall who shoved off for Paris this morning.' This brief, but intense, episode of sensuality had upset the Prince. 'I simply could'nt [sic] write & turned in about 12.00!!'

Trench filling and army paperwork were no substitute for Marguerite. The Prince, determined to keep fit, went on long solitary runs. 'Heavens how I sweated which only shows how fat one gets in Winter,' he recorded in his diary, adding confidently, 'I'm getting rid of the flesh all right now.' The even tenor of life in camp near Meaulte had become hopelessly disturbed by thoughts of Marguerite. 'I still cant [sic] settle down to any writing,' he noted two weeks after meeting her, 'its [sic] fearful what a change in my habits "48 hours of the married life in Paris" has wrought.'

On 11 May 1917, he crossed the Channel for two weeks' leave in London, somehow managing to escape the constraints of family life with the King and Queen. 'I had a wonderful time,' he wrote to Captain Cecil Boyd-Rochfort, 'went to 3 or 4 dances & 1 pols dance . . .' The 'pols dance', probably attended by 'fast' women rather than by working prostitutes, enabled the Prince to try his luck with chorus girls and actresses, such as Madge Saunders, the same age as the Prince and originally from Johannesburg. Madge, 'a dark-haired voluptuous woman with a full bosom and an even broader sense of humour', turned out not to be the expected pushover. Using a motoring metaphor, the Prince recalled ruefully how 'I tuned up Madge, tho' there was absolutely <u>nothing doing</u>!!' – later writing wistfully to his friend, 'You think Madge is a cock teaser; I think so!! What can be done?'

Despite the fun and the London shows (the Prince enjoyed *The Bing Girls*, *Zig-Zag* and *Under Cover*, hugely successful reviews), he yearned for the City of Light. 'It's so bloody being so far from Paris . . . Oh!! bugger this war!!!! . . . I shall have a shot for Paris leave later on.' Both Paris and Marguerite had a certain something noticeably absent from the London scene: 'A little of the English tart goes a long way & they aren't a patch on the French ones, are they?'

On his return to France, the Prince spent a couple of weeks at Flêtre, on the Cassell-Bailleul road, followed by a spell in June in the rather odd surroundings of a 'Trappist Convent' at Saint Sixte. Although after the first fine careless rapture with Marguerite the Prince had found it hard to get down to writing letters, the gnawing absence from Paris could be assuaged, in part, by the act of correspondence. Late at night, the Prince would lie in bed, using pencil to avoid spilling ink on the sheets, writing innumerable letters to family, friends, acquaintances, and to his new inamorata. During 1917 and 1918, the Prince wrote some twenty letters to Marguerite, greeting her as '*Mon*

Bébé', signing himself 'E'. He enclosed photos of himself, uniformed or in shirtsleeves, in camp or at table, sometimes adding souvenirs from the front, such as Prussian tunic buttons or even a German helmet. As with Jacques de Breteuil, correspondence was sent by King's Messenger to avoid interception, a practice that the Prince foolishly seems to have thought would ensure complete security.

Letters to a later mistress, sent the following year, contain elaborate romantic flourishes in French, a style surely honed during his extensive correspondence with Marguerite. A typical example is, '*Bonne nuit et à bientôt petite amour chérie à moi; ce n'est que TOI seule qui occupe toutes les penseés de ton petit E qui t'adore chaque jour plus follement et qui t'appartient entièrement entièrement!! Tous, tous mes baisers les plus tendres . . . Ton E*' ('Good night and see you soon little love dear to me; it's YOU alone who occupies every thought of your little E who adores you every day more crazily and who belongs to you completely, completely!! All, all my most tender kisses . . . Your E').

The letters to Marguerite, no doubt written in this slightly formal French, were indiscreet. Just as he had done in correspondence with Jacques de Breteuil, the Prince made comments about the conduct of the war which could have damaged the Allied cause had they fallen into enemy hands. He also mocked his father, the King (a few years later, he would refer scathingly to 'my charming father, the one & only royal beaver'). Such passages were not likely to do much harm if confined to trusted recipients, male family members, Regy Esher or other courtiers, brother officers in the Grenadier Guards, or to French aristocrats such as the old Marquis de Breteuil and his sons. Nevertheless, the Prince, with remarkable naivety, even stupidity, given three years' experience of life in an army HQ, chose to send this dangerous material to a Paris *poule de luxe* . . .

The Prince, thrilled by Marguerite's replies, recorded eagerly that she 'writes me the most wonderful letters!!' In addition to sharing these stimulating literary talents, Marguerite sent her lover small presents ('I got a box of chocolates from Paris this morning!!'), as well as mildly erotic literature, such *Les Aventures du Roi Pausole*, a witty fantasy by Pierre Louys, featuring gender confusion, cross-dressing and lesbian themes, later adapted as an opera by Honegger. The Prince appreciated the gift and was much taken by its contents. Marguerite later recalled that she had never seen the Prince so amused by any other book.

A more heavyweight title, galumphingly British in its approach to matters of sex, came into the Prince's hands in the summer of 1917. Captain Wilfred Bailey, the young Grenadier Guards officer whose 'hell of a time' in Paris had won the Prince's admiration a year before, sent his friend a copy of 'Walter'. The full title of this notorious work is *My Secret Life* by 'Walter' and the identity of its author has never been definitely established. First published in Amsterdam in 1880, the book ran to no less than a thousand pages in eleven volumes.

The text suggests that the author of *My Secret Life* was British, though the narrative takes the reader to the naughty Continent from time to time. Every possible permutation of heterosexual activity is chronicled in inordinate detail, with lesbianism and some male homosexuality added to a text liberally sprinkled with f- and c-words. The female characters, often domestic servants, dairy maids or shop assistants, are treated as lower-class sex objects, fit only for a wealthy man's pleasure. In a relatively mild example, one episode refers to a workman's wife, who – of course – has eagerly accepted Walter's advances: 'I was in a bursting state of randiness and she must have been the same; for I had no sooner entered her than her breath shortened, she clasped me tight, shivered and wriggled and we both spent . . .' *My Secret Life* also includes sequences set in the brothels of Paris, one of which intriguingly refers to 'the red-haired French woman'. Marguerite, rightly proud of her auburn tresses, was unlikely to have been impressed by the reference.

My Secret Life, banned in the United Kingdom until the 1960s, was extensively pirated abroad. The Prince's copy may have been an edited version, but its content seems to have pleased him greatly. A week after receiving the book, he wrote that the '<u>album</u> poem' (perhaps a saucy squib) sent to him by Captain Bailey, 'isnt [sic] a patch on "Walter"'.

The Prince's hopes for a further short spell of leave in Paris and the chance to see Marguerite again were cruelly dashed by knowledge that he would be required to attend King George and Queen Mary on a morale-boosting visit to France in July 1917. Amid a blanket of Allied press secrecy, the Prince greeted his parents at Calais on 3 July. They had crossed over in HMS *Pembroke*, accompanied by two destroyers, with seaplanes flying overhead for the duration of the voyage. Lunch at Boulogne station was grim. Food was already rationed in France and it was a 'meatless day', the dull fare accompanied by what turned out to be 'aperient mineral water'. Although the King had foresworn alcohol for the duration of the war, this attempt at healthy refreshment by the French authorities was not appreciated by the royal party. The King, especially, deeply affected by the process of war, 'looked old and tired & was occasionally very cross . . .'

Within two days of his parents' arrival, the Prince was standing with his father and other senior British army personnel on the battlegrounds of Messines and Vimy Ridge. Great care was taken not to draw enemy attention to the sightseeing party. The Germans had posted observers in balloons behind the German lines, who could have noticed a procession of official-looking cars, signalling the fact to their long-range gunners. As it was, some shelling occurred in the vicinity but later the Prince was seen to be poking at the ground, looking for relics, some of which may have found their way to Marguerite in Paris, enclosed with those unwisely written love letters. Whatever his private opinions of his father, the Prince played the role of dutiful son, even to the extent of clambering with the King into a tank (then a very new military development), which was then driven off, bumping over the disturbed ground for some ten minutes, King-Emperor and Prince crouching uncomfortably in its smelly and cramped interior.

The German intelligence network was not to be underestimated. The owner of a nearby château was not surprised to discover that the Germans were aware of the royal visit, but unluckly the enemy's intelligence network had not accurately ascertained the dates.' The night after King and Prince had left Messines, the town suffered a severe air-raid, so bad that HQ General Staff were transferred to the chateau at Flêtre.

The Prince stayed at the King's side until the end of the week, when – with some relief – he joined his mother at the Château de Beaurepaire, near Montreuil, on Saturday 7 July. Many young officers relished 'joy rides', short excursions which offered the hope of sexual adventure, but the presence in France of his royal parents threatened to put a brake on the Prince's amorous adventures.

The Queen (accompanied by the redoubtable

Mabel, Lady Airlie, as her lady-in-waiting) had created her own special itinerary for this short visit to France. Their first Sunday together was spent at Albert, where they lunched with 'Bungo', better known as Lord Byng of Vimy, one of the few competent British generals on the Western Front. Mother and son then 'motored' to a chateau near Rouen, so that the Queen could see Rouen Cathedral and the almost equally magnificent church of St Ouen, plus take a look at Amien Cathedral, her unflagging energy taking in hospitals, aerodromes, nursing hostels and casualty clearing stations. The Queen did not flinch at touring the killing grounds, 'the devil's charnel house' in Lady Airlie's words: The Queen's face was ashen and her lips were tightly compressed. I felt that, like me, she was afraid of breaking down.'

The Prince accompanied his mother on some of her visits, including a trip to the site of the Battle of Crécy. He longed to get to Paris or Deauville, 'the latter place would do me best . . . and you can guess why!!' The Prince's interest in Deauville, a fashionable resort on the Channel coast some 60 miles from Rouen, arose from the presence there of Marguerite, who had installed herself at the Hotel Normandy for the summer season.

The temptation of seeing Marguerite again was too much. 'It is a sin to waste another Summer on war!!' he wrote. Perhaps the breathless accounts of sexual exploits described by 'Walter' motivated the Prince – once so reluctant to pursue the opposite sex – to take a radical course, effectively under the nose of his royal mother. 'Four days running,' recorded Regy Esher in words of manifest astonishment, 'the boy started off for Deauville in his open motor, driving himself, and was back in Rouen by 7 next morning. I doubt whether King Edward [VII] ever showed more spirit . . .'

On the first day of these flying visits, the Prince drove Marguerite in his open Rolls-Royce some 12 miles for lunch at the Auberge de Guillaume le Conquérant, a world-famous restaurant, subsequently patronised by the likes of Winston Churchill, Max Beaverbrook and Duff Cooper. Afterwards, they drove to Caen, then a city of great beauty, with its half-timbered medieval houses, stone guildhalls and great Norman churches, almost entirely razed to the ground in 1944. On another day, they toured the unspoilt fringes of the Seine estuary, visiting Touques, from where William Rufus embarked to claim the English throne after the Conqueror's death, and on to the fishing port of Honfleur.

Although it was wartime, the Deauville season found ways to carry on as if nothing had happened. At the outbreak of hostilities, the Prefect had roped off the 'Potinière', the promenade beloved of fashionable visitors, closed the Casino bar, forbidden the playing of baccarat, and banned the tango as a symbol of decadence. As a result, clandestine nightspots and gambling joints mushroomed in cellars around the town. Eventually the authorities had to relent and, by 1917, entertainment was more or less at pre-war levels, the smart set unfazed by exorbitant prices. That summer, despite the terrible fighting on the Western Front and food shortages, the Casino's grill-room was packed with celebrities from the world of finance, the arts, the law and the armed forces sharing grilled chicken at sixty francs a wing.

Prominent among the visitors, as the Prince would surely have noticed, were large numbers of American and British officers, often drunk on the gamut of wartime cocktails available from Charlie, the 'king of cocktails', whose American mahogany bar offered such delights as the 'Whizz-Bang', the 'Bulldog', the 'B.E.F' and the 'Canadian Corps Special'.

At the Casino, supper was served in the early hours. Free from wartime restrictions in Paris, Marguerite and her Prince could dance until dawn, far from the theatre of mud, misery and death a hundred miles away. They would not have been alone in trying to forget the horrors of the Western Front. One summer morning that year, at 3 a.m., a naked woman was seen running along a bedroom corridor of the Hotel Normandy, in hot pursuit of a dinner-jacketed man, whipping him mercilessly with her rope of pearls . . .

Regy Esher, always the eager recipient of confidences, concluded that the Prince's 'first amourette' was going rather well. Marguerite (described archly as 'the little French lady') had shown 'the assurance and persistency to overcome his extraordinary shyness'. Esher's source for this intimate intelligence may have been Joey Legh or even the Prince himself, now confident enough to declare his new infatuation. In any event, it appears that Esher was given no hint of Marguerite's more adventurous tutelage in the arts of love.

After the departure of the King and Queen, safely back in England, the Prince resumed his dull round of duties at XIVth Army HQ, escaping for short periods of leave in Paris, where he could visit Marguerite again. By now, the Prince was becoming more of a party animal and seemed to enjoy the gatherings held at Marguerite's apartment.

Marguerite was keen to impress her latest catch with her artistic and cultural connections, perhaps not realising how little such matters meant to the Prince. Among her guests, the Prince would have encountered the classical music singer, Hélène Baudry, *protégée* of François de Breteuil (whose family thought that Hélène's collatura voice enchanted him more than her physical beauty). At one party, the Prince had a gramophone delivered to Marguerite's apartment, wound it up himself, and amused the company by dancing with the glamorous Suzanne Dantès, then a young actress in her mid-twenties, later to become a French film star, playing alongside the likes of Arletty, Sacha Guitry and Jean Gabin. Marguerite, with her very special skills, had no reason to fear introducing the Prince to attractive women from the *beau monde*. In any event, according to Marguerite, the Prince always remained *très reservé, très prince* (very reserved, very much the prince).

For variety and perhaps more advanced diversions, the Prince could be taken to perhaps Mme Théval's *maison de rendezvous* at 20 rue Bizet, a few steps from Marguerite's apartment. The Prince, evidently intrigued by the lesbianism explored in *Le Roi Pausole*, may have witnessed performances involving Marguerite and the *demi-maîtresse* Ginette Folway. In this context, a few years later, an English private detective wrote – evidently with the most extreme embarrassment – of news gleaned in Paris that Marguerite had been 'addicted . . . to committing certain offences with other women and . . . there is nothing that goes on in such surroundings as she has been moving in in Paris that she would not be quite well acquainted with . . .'

Among her *specialités*, Marguerite enjoyed a reputation as dominatrix. Her skill at riding and stable of ten horses provided the inspiration for a photograph of herself, probably part of an album available to clients at the *maison de rendezvous*, showing her dressed mannishly in riding gear, horsewhip prominently displayed. As is now well known, the Prince was drawn to women with strong, dominating personalities, an attraction suggestive of elements of masochism in his character. 'Please come up to London,' he wrote to a later mistress, 'to give me that hiding.'

Poules de luxe do not, as a rule, give their services

free. The Prince was an exceptional catch. 'The Prince of Wales never pays' was the motto although favours, in the form of jewellery or expensive scent, were expected and received. The Prince could be delightfully responsive to the wishes of his women friends. 'I was able to slip out early to get your Chypre from Coty which I'm sending by the same K[ing's] M[essenger] as this letter . . .' he wrote to a later mistress, 'tho. I must apologise for the "flacon" looking like a soda water darling tho. its [sic] the only one they had'.

Despite this broadening of sexual experience, the Prince remained pathetically immature for someone of his age, army service and social background. 'He is almost a child in appearance and character,' commented Esher at this time, 'and utterly without guidance.' To be fair to the Prince, his advisers sometimes gave out mixed messages. Joey Legh had robustly enjoyed the attractions of wartime Paris. In May of that year, the Prince recorded that 'Joey got 5 days leave there . . . & they were some days from all his accounts . . .!!' Legh, who had accompanied the Prince and Marguerite on outings to the theatre or to the cinema, seems initially to have made no objection to the liaison (indeed, it would have been difficult to have done so, since he had been jointly responsible for introducing the Prince to 'Paulette' in Amiens the previous November). Towards the end of the year, however, Legh became concerned about the possible risks of the affair and advised the Prince to break off the relationship.

An ideal opportunity to bring the affair to an end arose in November 1917, when XIVth Army HQ was dispatched to Italy, but the Prince, still in thrall to Marguerite, was in no mood to listen to advice, again showing the mulishness which would become characteristic of his later life. He was irritated by having to leave France, particularly as he had been due some three weeks' leave. The Prince managed to spend only three days in London, but even this short break was marred by 'a stupid old uncle of mine' who 'must needs die the day before I got back', plunging the royal family into mourning. Luckily, he was able to get twenty-four hours in Paris, where he spent one 'undisturbed night' with Marguerite, which 'made up for a little of the leave I missed . . .'

The sudden deployment of the XIVth Army corps to Italy arose from the need for Allied reinforcements after the collapse of the Italian army at Caporetto. The Prince had a low opinion of the Italian armed forces, frequently making disparaging references in correspondence ('It is by no means certain that these bloody "Ice Creamers" are going to fight'). Italian women fared even worse, losing heavily in comparison to his Paris love: 'These Italian women are the uggliest [sic] collection of bitches I've ever seen,' he wrote frankly to Boyd-Rochfort, adding 'I've hardly seen a fuckable one yet.' Bemoaning his 'ghastly exist- ence' in Mantua, 'tied to the generals & isolated from the ladies', the Prince consoled himself by remembering that, 'Paris is always on the direct route home . . .'

In January 1918, still chafing at his unwanted Italian assignment, the Prince put in for forty-eight hours' local leave, hoping to get to Bologna, but his thoughts soon turned to France: '. . . thank goodness PARIS is the direct route to England . . .'.

The Prince was allowed a relatively long period of leave in England between mid-February and the latter part of March 1918 and so could enjoy a brief rendezvous with Marguerite on the way home. There, risking the disapproval of his father, the Prince had 'taken to going to all the dances', causing 'wild excitement' among Society girls. 'So far,' noted Lady Cynthia Asquith in her diary, 'he dances mostly with Rosemary [Leveson-Gower] and . . . motors with her in the daytime.' Lady Rosemary, daughter of the Duke of Sutherland, held a temporary attraction for the Prince, who thought her 'such a darling', even briefly considering her to be the only girl he could ever marry.

The Prince's involvement with Rosemary Leveson-Gower ended, for once, without rancour. In any event, whatever the shortcomings of her blood line, Rosemary was a single girl. From Marguerite onwards, the Prince showed a decided tendency to pursue married women and, in late February 1918, an air-raid introduced him to the Englishwoman who would become his London mistress and long-term confidante.

The Prince had gone to a party, hosted by Mrs

Kerr-Smiley, at 31 Belgrave Square. At that stage in the war, London was suffering a series of night-time air-raids by German Zeppelin-Staaken aircraft, sometimes called 'giant bombers'. Air-raid warnings were not, as in the Second World War, given by sirens. In a more primitive system, maroons were fired and cyclists would roam the streets ringing handbells, each with a large placard tied in front bearing the words 'TAKE COVER'.

On the night of 16–17 February, the Royal Hospital Chelsea, not far from Belgrave Square, had been hit, causing a number of fatalities. A few nights later, presumably dressed for an evening out, Mrs Dudley Ward, the estranged wife of a Liberal MP, and her companion, one 'Buster' Dominguez (said to be 'some kind of Latin American diplomat'), were walking in Belgrave Square when the alarm was sounded. Seeing an open door, they sought temporary refuge in the hallway of Mrs Kerr-Smiley's town house and, when discovered there, were invited to take shelter in the cellar. After the air-raid wardens had been heard shouting 'ALL CLEAR' in the street outside, festivities resumed. The Prince, immediately attracted to the new arrival, danced with Mrs Ward until the end of the party in the small hours. Nobody seems to know what happened to 'Buster'.

Before the year was out, a new and growing obsession with Winifred (or, gratingly, to modern ears, 'Freda') Dudley Ward would cause the Prince to abandon his Paris *bébé*, Marguerite, with alarming and wholly unforeseen consequences for the supremely self-centred heir to the throne . . .

'Fredie', as he would call her, was almost exactly the same age as the Prince. She not born 'in the purple' and came from a middle-class background. Her father, Sir Charles Birkin, was 'in trade', a manufacturer of Nottingham lace, and, as often happened in the late nineteenth and early twentieth centuries, the dowry available from a manufacturer's daughter had overcome the snobbery of an increasingly impoverished landed class. In 1913, Fredie married William Dudley Ward, a cousin of the Earl of Dudley and an MP who was nineteen years her senior.

Like Marguerite, Fredie was 'petite, elegant and pretty' and enjoyed the attentions of a number of men – her 'barrage' as she called them. Lady Cynthia Mosley, Marquess Curzon's daughter, later waspishly claimed that when Fredie Dudley Ward went to her first coming-out party, 'nobody knew her. She was terribly dressed.' Ali Mackintosh, one of the barrage then 'in charge of something at Barkers', took Fredie in hand and was responsible for teaching her the art of *couture*.

Duff Cooper, a good judge of character, thought Fredie 'very nice', also 'charming and [with] such a good sense of humour'. Outside her narrow social circle, many of whose members were little more than vacuous pleasure-seekers, she would have been thought immoral, rather 'loose', a 'woman of easy virtue'. Despite having two young children to care for, she took a succession of lovers, including the Prince, Michael Herbert (a cousin of the Earl of Pembroke), Major Reginald Seymour, and, in the later 1920s, the American socialite Rodman Wanamaker II. Michael Herbert, about the same age as the Prince, was a longstanding rival for Fredie's affections. She seems to have relished playing the Prince off against Michael Herbert, a process that lasted well into the 1920s.

Fredie had a strong personality (another trait shared with her Paris rival and with Wallis Simpson), although she 'contrived to appear feminine and frail'. She was discreet and, true to the rules of contemporary upper-class (and upper-middle-class) etiquette, was the safe recipient of myriad confidences imparted by the neurotic Prince. Although Fredie kept several hundred of his letters, written between 1918 and 1930, she never made use of the material for her own advantage and, to the end of her long life, was reluctant to discuss the relationship. The Prince, on the other hand, seems to have destroyed her letters to him.

An English listener described Marguerite's voice as 'rather shrill'. Fredie, according to Duff Cooper, spoke in a 'rather high childish voice', also thought to be 'oddly attractive'. Perhaps the Prince had a taste for women with unusual voices. The BBC television interview of the Duke and Duchess of Windsor, recorded in 1970, suggests that Wallis also spoke in a distinctive manner, slightly harsh and rasping, consistent with her own forceful character.

On his way back to Italy at the end of March 1918 and staying, as usual, at the Hotel Meurice, he was able to spend three nights in Paris, where 'the Lord Claud & I will probably have lots of adventures . . . !!!!' Having Marguerite as his royal 'keep' in Paris would always be an edgy enterprise for the wayward Prince. On one occasion, he left a platinum cigarette case, given to him by his father for his 18th birthday, in the back of a Paris taxi. Despite an extensive search and the offer of a reward, the cherished item was never recovered.

A far more serious and unwanted adventure took place at the end of March 1918, when the city, now within artillery range, was subjected to indiscriminate shelling by a huge German gun, positioned some 125km north of Paris. During Good Friday liturgy, over eighty people (mostly women and children) were killed when a shell exploded on the roof of the Church of St Gervase et Protais, near the Hotel de Ville. The Prince, all too familiar with the noise of shellfire, heard the strike, noting that 'there was no mistaking the sound!!!!'

The final attempt by Germany to break through the allied lines was at St Quentin in April 1918. With 'our backs against the wall', the words of Field Marshal Haig, the tide of war gradually turned against the Central Powers. The loss of Russia as an ally after the Bolshevik *coup d'état* of October 1917 had been offset by the arrival of increasing numbers of American troops and the near-starvation imposed on Germany by an efficient seaborne blockade.

The Prince was not able to return to Paris from his Italian posting until August 1918. He wrote frequently to Fredie and from early April began to use romantic phraseology in French which almost certainly derived from the style used in his letters to Marguerite (*'Milles et milles baisers, Bébée'*). A letter to Fredie, written on 10 June 1918, however, suggests that the Prince was still corresponding with the other woman in his life. He told Fredie that he was 'rather frightened' about Paris in the light of a recent German advance. 'I hear that the morale of the Parisians is good!!' he noted, with the significant addition, 'Anyhow of "les Parisiennes"!!!!' Although there are hints of sexual adventures in his letters to Fredie, the evidence suggests that the Prince took care not to let Fredie know about his mistress (his 'keep') in Paris.

In any event, it seems that the Prince was not completely faithful to either his English love or his French love. One awkward incident, undoubtedly arising from some sexual adventure(s) by the Prince and involving women of the Voluntary Aid Detachment (known by the unhappily worded initials 'VAD'), occurred during a short stay in Rome during May 1918. 'The Lord Claud' Hamilton, angered by the Prince's behaviour, threatened to resign. 'I have had a straight talk and said it must stop or I shall go,' he wrote crisply to Marion Coke, the 'little bitch' now no longer the object of the Prince's callow romantic affections.

The Prince's long summer exile in Italy, punctuated by tedious official functions (or 'stunts', his own word), eventually came to an end. Saturday 17 August 1918 saw an open Rolls-Royce 'tourer' stationed outside the Hotel Meurice, awaiting the arrival of its princely owner. That morning, the Prince called on Lord Derby, the British Ambassador, but declined his invitation to lunch, evidently having other plans for the afternoon. The pattern of earlier meetings suggests a daytime liaison with Marguerite, his *dame à cinq heures*.

Later on, accompanied by 'The Lord Claud', the Prince attended a 'small dinner' in his honour at the Embassy. The guest list was suitably grand, including the Duchess de Tremouille, the Duke and Duchess de Gramont and their daughter ('23 and quite lovely'), and Madame de Polignac. Arthur 'Boy' Capel (Coco Chanel's lover) was there with his wife, the former Diana Wyndham, together with Portia Stanley, not yet the object of the Prince's vilification.

The Prince, with a low boredom threshold, often found these occasions tedious, but – perhaps mindful of an enjoyable afternoon – was in excellent form that evening. Derby recorded that he had never seen anyone enjoy himself more. The Prince, in cheerful mood seems to have joined in when some of the Ambassador's younger guests later danced to a gramophone.

The Prince spent one more night in Paris before returning to London, accompanied by 'The Lord Claud' and Joey Legh. Derby accurately foresaw the gloom awaiting the Prince at Windsor Castle. There was a national food shortage and the Ambassador considered that the young, pleasure-loving Prince 'at all appreciates the rationing and teetotal diet . . .' in the home of his parents.

The Prince returned to Paris two weeks later, but it is clear that circumstances had changed in the meantime. During his days in England, the relationship with Fredie had deepened considerably.

Marguerite claimed that the coming of Peace had brought an end to the relationship with the Prince and her chronology was only a week or so out. Around August 1918, she had an operation, supposedly an appendicectomy, though evidence was later produced to show that it had been a procedure to remove her ovaries. Whether because the Prince, smitten by Fredie Dudley Ward, was now tiring of her company (and that of her intellectual circle) or because Marguerite was temporarily out of circulation, or because the war was coming to an end, the relationship was cooling. The Prince's earlier zest and enthusiasm for Parisian life was clearly beginning to wane. 'Paris falls very flat just now & I'm not enjoying it at all,' he declared to Fredie, writing from the Hotel Meurice on 4 September. It was perhaps at this time that he stopped seeing Marguerite, who would likely have known, from her many contacts, if the Prince had passed through town without seeing her.

After a further spell of duty in Italy, the Prince spent a short leave in England, where he saw Fredie and admitted having lied about the episode involving the VADs in Rome during May, hinting about other affairs. More worldly-wise than the Prince, Fredie claimed not to be bothered about his 'medicine' when he was away from her, as, in her words, *'les petits amusements ne comptes pas'* ('little diversions don't count').

Spending the latter part of October at the HQ of the Canadian Corps in northern France, the Prince continued to bombard Fredie with gossipy letters, none of which refers to his entanglements in Paris. It seems that, by late October 1918, the Prince had finally decided to break off his relationship with his 'Paris woman'. The Prince should have been aware that Marguerite was a woman of fiery spirit and no respecter of persons. Not for the only time in his life, he chose the path of denial, hoping that Marguerite would quietly accept being dropped after an affair that had lasted the better part of eighteen months. Her ability to look after herself was not to be underestimated. She would make a great deal of trouble for the King-Emperor's eldest son.

Around 1.30 a.m. on 1 November 1918, he began a long letter to Fredie, who was in low spirits recovering from a bout of 'Spanish flu'. The Prince, just back from a party at the Canadian 1st Division HQ, was feeling bullish, having '<u>so so</u> enjoyed & loved reading your 2 divine long letters. Gud!! what a happy man I am to-night (or rather this morning).' The Rome incident now ancient history, the Prince confidently reported that '6 Canadian VADs were brought up by car from Boulogne & 3 of them were "divine women" . . . tho' of course it was a case of "single girls are much too tame" not that your E tried (or wanted to) find out if this was so!!' The party was also enriched by '½ dozen nursing sisters from a Can[adian] C.C.s . . . as ugly as sin . . . I longed to have my own little girl there to dance with . . .' At this point, feeling sleepy and having to go forward in a few hours to see the Canadian attack on the German lines at Valenciennes, the Prince broke off his letter.

Unscathed by shellfire, he returned to HQ the next evening and, to his horror, found a bombshell awaiting him. A letter, 'a regular stinker', from Marguerite reminded the inconstant Prince that she still had his love letters, with all those foolish, indiscreet comments about the conduct of the war, insulting abuse about his father, letters very probably scabrous into the bargain. Although this letter seems to have been lost, there is evidence that it contained some very damaging personal allegations. And Marguerite, in bitter mood, had money in mind.

'Oh! Those bloody letters, and what a fool I was not to take your advice over a year ago!!', he wrote despairingly to Joey Legh. 'How I curse myself now, tho' if only I can square this case it will be the last one, as she's the only pol I've really written to . . . I'm afraid she's the £100,000 or nothing type, tho' I must say I'm disappointed and didn't think she'd turn nasty: of course the whole trouble is my letters and she's not burnt one!!'

Eager to catch that night's King's Messenger, the Prince hastily finished his letter to Fredie. The last two scrawled pages reveal an unpleasant side to the Prince's character, moral cowardice in continuing a grubby little deceit upon a woman he claimed to love deeply. For nine months he had kept Fredie completely in the dark about his lengthy affair with Marguerite, despite all the breastbeating about the Rome affair and his promises to be truthful in future. Now, at last, Fredie might have to be told about the French mistress, but although he had just written a letter of alarming candour to Joey Legh, he was not ready to tell Fredie about his predicament, certainly not in a letter, however frank he had promised to be about his sexual foraging.

'How I long to get home to England & my own little angel for I've got so much to talk to you about & to tell you about beloved one that I just cant [sic] write,' he wrote coyly, adding an exquisitely tortuous passage, 'tho its [sic] nothing serious; if only I could write it but I just cant [sic] as I'm so hopeless at expressing myself!! But it can wait sweetheart so dont [sic] worry; if it worried me I would <u>try</u> to write it but as it doesn't (& I think I know when its [sic] a case of worrying!!) I wont [sic] try!!!!'

The Prince had funked telling Fredie the truth. Revelations about Marguerite would be deferred until he was back in England. Although he wrote several more letters before returning to London, he made no further mention of the problems with his Paris 'pol'.

The Prince, of course, was not without advice and support. In his immediate household, Joey Legh and 'the Lord Claud' were eminently men of the world and could call in reinforcements. The royal solicitors could liaise with French lawyers in the event of a demand for money. Similarly, Special Branch of the Metropolitan Police could ask the Paris *securité* for information about Marguerite's character and background, facts duly noted in the *renseignements generaux*, secret files kept on those French citizens (whether convicted of criminal offences or not) who were deemed to be of interest. Marguerite, with her *eblouissante notoriété* (dazzling fame) and her circle of the rich and famous, was an obvious candidate for official attention.

There was, in truth, a great deal for the Prince to worry about. He might have avoided scandal over the affair with the VADs earlier that year, but Marguerite's furious reaction to his neglect of her posed a much greater threat. She was rich, she was determined, and she had influential friends in

Paris, with access to the best lawyers. Marguerite could afford to wait.

Shortly after the Armistice, the Prince returned to royal duties in London until the end of November and it appears that he took this opportunity to tell Fredie (something at least) about the long affair with his Paris 'keep'. He affected a measure of denial about his difficulties with Marguerite and, for a while, his correspondence with Fredie made no mention of 'those bloody letters' and the looming threat to his reputation and credibility.

A month after receiving Marguerite's 'regular stinker', he allowed himself some cautious optimism. 'I have'nt [sic] heard another word from "IT" in Paris sweetheart so that I'm hoping its [sic] all blown over & that I shant here [sic] any more; but si ça continue I have expert assistance to hand so I'm less worried than I was tho. Gud! what a fool your E has made of himself darling & he deserves any thing except that he was very young at the time & I dont [sic] think he's exactly the first to be had like this!! Gud!! this is a sordid life belovèd one . . .'

If Marguerite had suddenly turned nasty, the Prince was responding in kind. As with Marion Coke ('bitch'), Portia Stanley ('clutches'), and other discarded favourites, he employed a crude disparagement. 'Marguerite, mon bébé', the young woman who had brought him so much 'bliss' in Paris and Deauville, who had written him 'the most wonderful letters' in response to his own foolish correspondence, was now reduced to no more than 'IT'.

As to the 'expert assistance' to hand, this may have included advice from the royal solicitors, but with the national interest at stake, Special Branch was the obvious source for more robust protection. Founded in 1883 as part of a drive to combat the activities of the Irish 'Fenians', Special Branch became an early intelligence network for the British government, though by 1918 some of its remit had passed to MI5 and MI6.

During the interwar period, as will be seen, Special Branch provided a team of protection officers, who had the not always agreeable task of looking after the heir to the throne and keeping him out of trouble. Reports (sometimes with updates) were regularly filed on individuals considered to pose any sort of threat to the Prince and his reputation. The subjects included several women 'stalkers' and, during the tense days of 1935, a year before the Abdication, a supposed lover of Wallis Simpson.

For now, the very considerable risk posed by Marguerite to the good name of the Prince amply justified the attention of Special Branch and a report was duly compiled about her, probably in late 1918. Sir Basil Thomson, then head of Special Branch, spent time in Paris in December 1918 and during the following month, officially superintending preliminary arrangements for next year's peace conference. (Thomson prided himself on his friendship with the Prince and dined privately with him later in 1919, clearly thrilled that the Prince, 'a charming host' who 'knew exactly the moment for leaving the table', had personally 'followed me to the main door [of York House] to see me off'.)

So, in those first days of peace, a month after the 'regular stinker', no mail for the Prince arrived addressed in Marguerite's handwriting, postmarked from the 16th *arrondissement*. For the moment, all was quiet on the Western Front. A week after his reference to 'IT', the Prince was telling Fredie, 'Touching wood I think the Paris trouble is over, though I must get all those letters back somehow.' But Marguerite was biding her time. By the middle of December, six weeks after Marguerite's 'stinker' and evidently still a worried man, the Prince wrote to Joey Legh: 'Not another word from Maggy, thank God, so here's to hoping.' If the Prince had persuaded himself that all danger was past, he was wrong. While convalescing in the Paris nursing home during August, she discovered that another patient was Charles Laurent, a young air force officer. Laurent had just returned from Russia, where he had been serving with the White Russian forces under General Wrangel, fighting the Bolsheviks.

A blunt and impulsive character, Laurent quickly fell under Marguerite's spell. For her, the handsome officer had very particular attractions. His father, Henri Laurent, was a director of both the Grand Magasins du Louvre, a large department store, and of the company that owned the Hotel Crillon, where Marguerite had first met the Prince of Wales some eighteen months before. While there was no chance of Marguerite ever marrying the Prince, Charles Laurent was unmarried and very rich. He could provide her illegitimate daughter, Raymonde, with an excellent Parisian surname and, best of all, could give Marguerite financial security, plus a measure of respectability and access to at least some of the Paris salons.

Charles Laurent was too good a catch to miss and for the time being there was little point in pursuing a crude scheme of blackmail which could result in legal proceedings and, quite possibly, muffing her chances with Laurent.

She had the letters.

CHAPTER 5

ENTR'ACTE

After the end of the Great War, the Prince continued his affair with Fredie Dudley Ward, sending this complaisant, perhaps slightly dull woman a regular supply of abjectly worded love letters, prominently sealed on the back of the envelope with the likeness of a spider (or 'thpider' in royal baby talk). The Prince's letters could be carried by King's Messenger, but sometimes his correspondence, conspicuous black wax seal and all, was dispatched by ordinary mail, another example of risk-taking (or sheer carelessness, perhaps even arrogance) on the Prince's part.

After spending time with British and Empire forces in northern France and Belgium, the Prince returned briefly to Paris in February 1919. This was an official visit and much of his time was taken up with duties connected with the forthcoming Versailles Peace Conference (although there was an opportunity to buy some 'filthy French [sex] toys' in a Paris shop). The Prince would not return to Paris until January 1924.

The long absence is partly explained by the extensive series of Empire tours (Canada, New

Zealand, Australia, India) which reduced the time available for private excursions abroad. The first Empire tour took him to Canada between August and November 1919; to Australia and New Zealand between March and October 1920; to India, taking in Ceylon, Malaya, Japan and Egypt, between October 1921 and June 1922.

Nevertheless, bearing in mind his frequently expressed fondness for life in the city, the length of time that elapsed between these Paris visits seems curious. During 1920 and 1921, his affair with Fredie Dudley Ward was at its zenith, an entanglement that took up much of his free time in England, and during his New Zealand tour in 1920, the Prince had written to Fredie, 'As regards Paris . . . it's unique . . . & I used to love Paris too when I was "jeune homme". I've never been there as a "married man" . . .' He enjoyed the Season, went hunting and steeplechasing, played tennis and golf, and performed his quota of official 'stunts', but for some reason did not make the short journey across the Channel and visit the French capital.

The Prince knew that Marguerite had kept his letters. Early in 1920, the Prince gave a warning talk to his three younger brothers (Albert, Henry and George), arising from 'some of my experiences in Paris etc. which you've heard so often!'

The Prime Minister, David Lloyd George, had made a discreet mistress of his secretary, the quietly perceptive Frances Stevenson. Like so many of her contemporaries, Frances was at first entranced by the Prince, 'a dear thing, with beautiful eyes, but such a boy'. Two months later, however, she was writing that she disliked his hard sounding voice, a less favourable observation, perhaps prompted by a tactless inquiry as they sat together, dinner guests of Sir Philip Sassoon. The Prince had asked her with a 'meaning look' why Mrs Lloyd George did not spend much time in London.'

In the summer of 1919, the Prince finally succeeded in persuading his father that he needed a home of his own, away from the confines of Buckingham Palace. He set himself up in York House, part of the sprawling complex of St James's Palace. The mostly north-facing accommodation was unpretentious. The Prince's bedroom had just a 'narrow, single bed with a table beside it on which there was often a glass of milk and an apple.'

At the same time, the Prince took the opportunity to reorganise his personal staff. Godfrey Thomas was 'poached' by the Prince, leaving the Foreign Office to become Private Secretary, with Joey Legh and 'the Lord Claud' remaining as equerries, until the latter was replaced by the Hon. Bruce Ogilvy in 1921.

Poor eyesight had kept Thomas away from military service and he had served in the Foreign Office for the duration of the Great War. At the Foreign Office, Thomas had been head of the 'cipher department' and was succeeded by Archibald Hay-Drummond (known as Archibald Hay), brother-in-law of Captain Ernest Bald, friend of the Duke of Westminster and Marguerite's onetime lover in Deauville and Paris.

Sir Godfrey John Vignoles Thomas was the only son of a Welsh baronet and Brigadier-General, and succeeded to the title after his father died on active service in 1919. The title, dating from 1694, had a respectable antiquity and the family fortunes were boosted by his father's marriage to Mary Frances Isabelle Oppenheim, daughter of Charles Augustus Oppenheim (a name worthy of inclusion in one of Hilaire Belloc's *Cautionary Tales*). Oppenheim, a successful London businessman, left a family very comfortably provided for with an estate valued at some £160,000 (£9,000,000 today) at his death in 1878. Charles had married Isabelle Frith, daughter of the celebrated Victorian painter William Powell Frith, a union that may have brought Godfrey Thomas a measure of cultural sensibility.

Thomas became a close associate of the Prince after their first meeting in Berlin the following year. 'Whenever the Prince was on leave, he received permission from the Foreign Office to join him,' so Godfrey Thomas would have been well aware from the start of the Prince's romantic entanglements, including the eighteen-month affair with Marguerite.

The Prince's new Private Secretary, then aged 31, has been described as 'dark and good-looking – a bit like . . . Cary Grant'. Thomas 'usually wore a troubled air, as if he had just been slightly done

116

down'. Though 'much liked and respected', he was thought 'a shade dull'. The Prince, for his part, considered Thomas 'really my greatest man friend & the only one to be trusted absolutely'.

Stamfordham crisply defined the qualifications for such a post: 'Someone with brains, a facile pen – a nice fellow.' Thomas, who eminently fitted the bill, was quintessentially a figure of discretion, keeping a low public profile, his working persona steeped in Foreign Office culture. 'For all his . . . self-effacing manner,' wrote an anonymous obituarist in 1968, 'he had much ability, a most resourceful tact, and an unfailing memory'. Described also as 'a quiet man', whose tastes were said to be of 'an intellectual kind', Thomas comes across as a shrewd, if rather indolent, observer of the Prince's failings. From time to time, he would exert himself to give sound advice, but Thomas seems to have deliberately avoided confrontation. 'A stronger personality . . . might possibly have curbed some of the Prince's excesses, but more probably the two men would have quarrelled and greater mischief been done than good.'

Thomas, however, had learnt the value of secrecy in his official work and would serve his master well during the crisis of 1923. His political views, in so far as they can be ascertained, seem to have been deeply conservative. Thomas, for example, 'always felt that the Prince should not marry a commoner . . . .'.

Alan 'Tommy' Lascelles joined the Prince's staff

at York House as Assistant Private Secretary in November 1920. At first, like so many others, he was overwhelmed by the Prince's charm. 'He won me over completely. He is the most attractive man I have ever met.' Lascelles, born in 1887, was a grandson of the 4th Earl of Harewood. He was a first cousin by marriage of Princess Mary, sister of the Prince of Wales. A highly intelligent man, tall, spare, handsome (though with a slightly receding chin), some people considered Lascelles to be a snob. 'It was when he reached public school that he first became aware of his own aristocratic nature', but alas the public school was not Eton, Harrow or Winchester (all ancient foundations and top of the range), but Marlborough, a redbrick boarding school less than a century old. Hopelessly middle class, Marlborough contained 'not a soul brought up to the same social traditions as myself . . . they knew none of the people I knew, or knew of . . .' Lascelles hated his school.

Class was a sensitive issue in those days (it still is) and Lascelles was not alone in his sufferings. He would have empathised with a slightly younger victim, George Harcourt Vanden-Bempde-Johnstone, Baron Derwant (pronounced 'Darwent'), who bemoaned days spent at his 'ordinary' public-school, Charterhouse. Like Lascelles, Vanden-Bempde-Johnstone felt keenly that his true place was at Eton, Harrow or Winchester. Instead he was obliged to rub shoulders (and other bodily parts) with 'sons of chemists and Indian Civil Servants, Trinidad sugar-merchants and country doctors . . .'

When in England, the Prince continued his usual diversions, both sporting and social. In June 1922, Harold Nicolson glimpsed him over lunch at the Marlborough Club, then at 52 Pall Mall (a club whose membership included Lord Stamfordham and Godfrey Thomas, perhaps some small guarantee against princely mischief). 'P of Wales there,' he wrote, 'talking polo: very red: his little red hands flicking all the time about his neck-tie.'

The Prince also sought amusement in the company of men who had been (or were still) part of Fredie's 'barrage' of admirers. A good example is Captain Alistair Mackintosh, charitably described by one of the Prince's set as 'witty, kind and generous to a fault'. Ali Mackintosh was, like Fredie, a product of the prosperous middle class and met the Prince in Italy during the summer of 1918. Friendly with Bendor, the Duchess of Sutherland, 'Fatty' Cavan, Loelia Ponsonby and scores of Society figures, Ali took his idle charms to Hollywood, where he married the silent film star Constance Talmadge in 1926.

By the latter part of 1922, the Prince's relationship with Fredie Dudley Ward was under severe strain. She was now contemplating divorce from William Dudley Ward ('Duddie') and seems to have been playing the Prince off against Michael Herbert, who had been a member of Fredie's 'barrage' for several years. 'In the spring of 1923 . . . . Freda must have stated bluntly that their relationship could never be what it had been and that he would have to content himself with friendship.'

He was now Prince Charming, an international media celebrity, arbiter of fashion, surrounded by crowds of adoring admirers and pursued relentlessly by legions of press reporters and newsreel cameramen. Yet the smiling, relaxed image that Thomas and Lascelles worked so hard to maintain was always vulnerable to disclosures, particularly in the American press, about the Prince's private life, not always consistent with the clean-limbed, elegantly dressed sportsman of the public arena.

In 1920, there had been a sharp reminder of this exposed flank. By this time, Lord Louis Mountbatten had succeeded in becoming close to the Prince, although young 'Dickie' was cordially detested by some members of the Prince's entourage for his perceived arrogance and duplicity. Mountbatten had kept a diary during the antipodean tour, full of what he thought was amusing anecdote, and some twenty copies were privately printed aboard ship, HMS *Renown*. Although not scurrilous, the diary was 'extremely frank' about aspects of the journey and could have damaged the Prince's burgeoning reputation as poster boy for the British Empire. Unfortunately, the ship's doctor made off with a copy and, once back in England, tried to sell it. 'The culprit was eventually tracked down to Kettner's restaurant [in London's Soho], where he was bargaining with an

American journalist, the diary on the table . . . The asking price was £5000.'

The content of letters written to Marguerite by the Prince was potentially far more damaging than this artless account of high jinks on the ocean wave. Worries that the 'little French lady' might decide to market her treasures across the Atlantic must have been omnipresent in the minds of those few courtiers in the know, especially Godfrey Thomas and Tommy Lascelles. There were wider implications than simply royal scandal. In January 1922, the Chancellor of the Exchequer, Stanley Baldwin, had voyaged to America in a humiliating exercise, an attempt to reduce the crippling level of interest payable on Britain's war debts. Settlement was eventually reached, but deep concern remained about the financial implications of unfavourable American attitudes towards Britain. A positive image for the Prince could be an enormous boost, but the situation was delicate. According to Lascelles, newspapers in the USA (including 'the Sunday rags . . . notoriously filthy and scandalous . . .') often gave 'exaggerated publicity to his amusements, expensive tastes, uselessness etc', but the Prince had the power to 'change . . . American opinion towards us, & the debt & 100 other things'. Given the unpredictable behaviour of the heir to the throne, that change of opinion could go either way.

The Prince, in his voluminous correspondence with Fredie, wallowed in self-pity and neurotic reflection. Marguerite, his cast-off mistress, had no such concerns, forging ahead in the years that followed the break-up. Early in 1919, Charles Laurent, her latest rich suitor, proposed marriage. He was well aware of Marguerite's chequered past, but unaware of her true motive in encouraging his affections. In early 1919, Marguerite told Mme Denart, her former *maîtresse*, that she was only marrying Laurent for the sake of her daughter and would 'kick him out' after six months. On the other hand, she claimed to find Laurent's solemn, thoughtful manner a refreshing change from the flippancy of other friends and she could hardly complain of his lack of generosity. With Laurent's help, she moved from square Thiers (itself no slum) to a magnificent apartment at 67 avenue Henri Martin, in the heart of the 16th. Laurent made her an annual allowance of 36,000 francs (£450) and paid the yearly rental of the flat, a substantial 18,000 francs (£225).

The Laurent family opposed the match and, though banns were published for the requisite period at the *marie* (town hall), there was to be no Paris wedding. Instead, as the social column of *Le Figaro* reported on 2 May 1919, '*Lundi a été celebré à Venise, par le consul français, le mariage de Capitaine Charles Laurent avec Mme Marguerite Meller*' ('In Venice last Monday Captain Charles Laurent and Mme Marguerite Meller were married by the French consul'). *Le Figaro* was (and is) a newspaper of record for the aristocracy and *haute bourgeoisie* of France. Marguerite had made another significant step in her quest for social acceptance and financial security.

For the honeymoon, Laurent had taken a lease of the fifteenth-century Palazzo Tiepoletto, overlooking the Grand Canal and not far from the Rialto Bridge. Unlike her stormy visit to Venice with André Meller in 1913, there were to be no lively parties at the Danieli or at the Hotel Excelsior on the Lido. Charles Laurent was a young man of sober tastes, loved the history of Venice and its glorious architecture, and had no time for conventional partying. Disagreements began almost at once. Marguerite was eager to visit the *chic* Venice bars, showing herself at the costume balls and at the many private parties to which they were invited, invitations that Charles would usually refuse. After their return to Paris, Charles expected his new wife to accompany him to concerts, recitals and the opera, while Marguerite pined for the glamour of Ciro's, the racecourse, and riding in the Bois.

Matters came to a head when Charles was offered a diplomatic post in Japan. He told Marguerite that she could not go on living her pre-war life. Marguerite would have to choose between life in Japan and life in Paris. She chose Paris. And divorce.

On 30 March 1920 (plaint no 267 at the Paris Tribunal of the Seine), the marriage was dissolved. Marguerite's cool stratagem had paid off handsomely. She secured considerably more by way of settlement than the 'little bag of beans' reluctantly handed over by Andre Meller in 1913. With the money from Laurent, Marguerite became a rich woman. She could easily afford the apartment at 67 avenue Henri-Martin, with several indoor servants, a stable (now accommodating ten horses), a full-time groom, and two limousines, driven by her loyal chauffeur, Eugéne Barbay. Eugéne, a handsome man originally from Alsace, which was under German occupation between 1870 and the end of the Great War, had escaped to France and been severely wounded at Verdun in 1917. Provided staff members could put up with Marguerite's unpredictable temper, she seems to have been a generous employer, perhaps conscious of her own youthful privations.

Her next major conquest was to be Juan de Astoreca, whose family fortune was created in the nitrate mines of northern Chile. The coming of war saw enormous growth in their profitability, since nitrates were used in the manufacture of high explosive shells. After 1917, however, the development of new processes saw the virtual collapse of the Chilean nitrate industry.

Around 1920, the time he and Marguerite became acquainted, Jean d'Astoreca (as he now gallicised himself) was permanently resident in France, and his riches, though diminished, remained substantial. Jean (or 'Pépé' as she called him, mocking his heavily accented French) offered Marguerite the life she loved. That wealth and a mutual love of horseflesh (Astoreca adored the races) brought them together and, although the physical side of the liaison was to end dramatically, the couple kept up a more or less amicable relationship for several years.

Raymonde, abandoned for so long, had now returned to Marguerite's care. Raymonde closely resembled her mother and in later years this provoked Marguerite's jealousy, a major cause of their ultimate estrangement. Raymonde's father may, after all, have been an Englishman, for Marguerite decided to give her daughter an expensive private education in England. To that end, she enrolled Raymonde in The Grange, a girls' boarding school in Totteridge, then a leafy suburb of north London.

Astoreca was the man of the moment, but this did not prevent Marguerite seducing the aristocratic husband of a near neighbour in the Avenue Henri-Martin, a young *vicomte* who had, in just a month, spent 800,000 francs in a vain attempt to make Marguerite his mistress, sweet revenge for a perceived social snub on the part of his wife.

Like many of her other suitors, Astoreca did not escape the full force of Marguerite's temper. An absurd argument about the price of trout at the Moulin de la Planche, near Versailles, led to a furious row between the pair in front of an exclusive clientele at the Dauphine. Astoreca, a mild man, eventually told Marguerite to be quiet, whereupon she grabbed her horsewhip and struck him across the face, breaking his glasses. Astoreca stormed off and, sitting in the back of his car, angrily refused to take Marguerite home. Unfazed, she ordered his chauffeur to get out and proceeded to drive herself and her astonished lover back to her apartment. The next day, the couple went out riding in the Bois as if nothing had happened.

Further scenes and threats of suicide by Astoreca prompted Marguerite to make a second journey to Egypt later that year, as temperatures cooled and the Season began.

Taking Raymonde and an English schoolfriend with her, Marguerite arrived in Cairo in December. Harvesting contacts made during her previous visit to Egypt in 1915, she set herself up as mistress of Mosseri, rich banker and prominent member of a Sephardic Jewish family of Italian origin.

Around the turn of that year, a young playboy experienced an event of the most profound significance. Amid the grandeur of the Semiramis Hotel in Cairo, Ali Kamel Famy *bey* had his first glimpse of 'Mme Laurent' (as Marguerite now styled herself). Just as the Prince of Wales had been enraptured on meeting Marguerite for the first time at the Hotel Crillon, Ali was immediately drawn to this vision of style and fashion, born and bred in Paris, a city he loved.

Marguerite, though attracted by gossip that Ali was a millionaire umpteen times over, kept her guard. Ali was prone to wild acts of generosity, but could – it was said – behave callously to his

126

mistresses. Ali is supposed to have whispered to a mutual friend, 'Tell her I will give her a *fête Venitienne* in her honour,' ordering his *dahabeeyah* to be decorated with the letters 'MM', displayed in flowers and also illuminated on the stern of the yacht. Marguerite, mindful that a rich businessman in the hand was worth a young millionaire in the bush, politely refused to go aboard, and played hard to get, leaving Egypt without saying goodbye to her latest conquest. With her usual acumen, Marguerite had made a mental note of this very interested party for future reference in Paris.

CHAPTER 6

HONEY AND ROSES

Even to a sceptic's eye, the brief life of Ali Fahmy cannot be robbed entirely of exoticism and romance. Some hard facts exist, like rocky outcrops piercing a miasma of sensationalism. Ali was born, probably in the Ismailiya district of Cairo, on 10 August 1900, the only son of Ali Fahmy El-Mouhandez *pasha*, a civil engineer and member of the Egyptian upper middle class. When Fahmy *père* died in 1907, he became a rich man. His young son was left two-fifths of his father's estate, then worth perhaps £800,000, the balance being divided between four older sisters, three of whom (Aziza, Fatima and Aicha) were alive in 1923.

As the benjamin and only boy, brought up by mother and sisters, Ali had a very spoiled childhood in a society that generally cosseted the young male. He attended the reputable Nasrieh School in Cairo, but was said to have been too delicate to be sent to university. When his mother died, he came into his inheritance at the early age of 16, two years before the legal majority. Feebleness vanished at once as Ali took enthusiastic possession of his fortune.

And it was some fortune. Ali's father had dabbled in cotton, but the Great War had done wonders for the Egyptian cotton industry. The price rocketed, increasing nearly seven times as the war progressed. As prices rose, Ali's estate bought land in Upper Egypt, amounting to some 4,500 *feddans* (acres) of prime cotton-producing land. His agents also established links with banks and trading companies in France and England. The banker Émile Miriel, long-serving director of Crédit Foncier, a major French banking house in Egypt, became a personal friend. By the end of the war, Ali's inheritance was producing over £100,000 annually and, even though the post-war slump caused a sharp decline in cotton prices, his annual income never fell below £40,000 (around £2,000,000 today).

Ali tried to buy friendship and entertained generously. Cairo society smiled indulgently on his growing extravagance, but also because he had charm and cut an elegant figure. He loved to dance and was often to be seen at Shepheard's, the Semiramis, the Continental-Savoy and other smart hotels of Cairo and Alexandria.

It is not surprising that so enormous an income should have turned the head of a youth whose earlier life had been so sheltered and indulgent. Possibly in an attempt to provide some stability in his new life, Ali was provided with a private secretary. The first to be appointed was Mahmoud Abul Fath, later to become editor of *Al Ahram*, a prominent Cairo newspaper and a man who came to know a great deal about Marguerite.

Said Enani was six years older than his employer and had previously worked at the Ministry of the Interior in Cairo. A well-educated man who spoke fluent French and English, he served as a sort of guardian, as well as confidant, to a young man who was, in truth, rather unsure of himself.

Ali was 5' 9" tall and comparatively light-skinned. He was later described by Said as being 'nervous', with a weak personality. His behaviour had its neurotic side and Ali appears initially to have had difficulty making friendships with his peers. Ultimately, he came to enjoy the company of a young, intellectual set that included Mahmoud Abul Fath and Mukhtar *bey*, a distinguished Egyptian sculptor. Ali is said to have loved opera and was a keen amateur photographer. His small circle of friends had nationalistic leanings, keenly aware of the humiliation caused by the British occupation of their country during and after the Great War. Some were attracted by the heady rhetoric of the veteran Saad Zaghloul, founder of the nationalist Wafd Party.

Though his behaviour could be profligate, Ali's short life reveals a sense of social responsibility far ahead of his time. During the war, in his extreme youth, he had donated substantial sums to the British Red Cross and later set up a fund, administered by the Ministry of Education, to enable poor Egyptian students to visit and study in Europe. He planned to set up a new ophthalmic hospital at Maghagha, on the west bank of the Nile, some 90 miles south of Cairo: the foundation stone was laid by the portly King Fuad II. Ali was honoured with the title *bey*, a Turkish word formerly signifying the rank of provincial governor. It has been argued, however, that Ali was entitled to the more senior title of *pasha*, inherited on the death of his father. Although Ali undoubtedly lived on a princely scale, his status as *bey* did not make him a 'prince', arising from mistranslation in the foreign press, a bogus attribution he seems to have done little to discourage.

Although Ali had no need to work and never gained any professional qualifications, his excellent French gained him the honorary post of Press Attaché to the French Legation in Cairo. France had taken a close interest in the Middle East and been involved in Egyptian affairs at least since the time of Napoleon Bonaparte. Many of the Egyptian upper class were both francophone and Francophile and particularly so since Britain had established an unwanted hegemony over Egyptian affairs.

In 1914, the crumbling Ottoman administration was replaced by a British 'protectorate' and only in 1922 would Egypt be granted a measure of internal self-government, Britain continuing to control foreign policy and all matters connected with defence and the security of the Suez Canal, regarded as an Imperial lifeline. There was considerable friction between Britain and France throughout the 1920s: at one time, Saad Zaghlul had found sanctuary in Paris, much to the chagrin of Whitehall.

France was also popular as a playground for the Egyptian rich. As many as 3,000 Egyptian families were said to visit every year. 'Egyptian visitors at watering-places, the Egyptian customers of smart restaurants, fashion houses and gaming tables were prodigal of the wealth they had made from cotton.' Ali eagerly joined the throng of his high-rolling fellow-countrymen, making extended tours of Europe each year, taking in Paris, Deauville, Biarritz and Monte Carlo.

In this heady milieu, Ali developed a taste for speed, importing the latest fast cars from France, Germany and England. By 1923, his garage was said to contain a 90hp Mercedes, a Renault coupé and a Buick, together with two Rolls-Royces (one open, with whitewall tyres, the other a more sober saloon), a Berliet, a baby Peugeot, two 'runabouts' and several powerful motor-cycles. He would drive at great speed through the narrow, crowded streets of Cairo, indifferent to the confusion and upset caused. When Ali visited Europe, a selection of his vehicles would be shipped out with him.

Ali's playboy image was also displayed on the waters of the Nile. Thorneycrofts of England supplied a 450hp racing motor-boat, which, with its aeroplane engine, was reputedly the fastest on the river and capable of crossing the English Channel. Ali would race along the Nile, the wash of his craft disturbing, even capsizing, all manner of lesser craft. Another speedboat was commissioned from Neuilly of Paris at a cost of 440,000 francs (£5,500). It was purchased on the recommendation of a member of the French colony in Cairo, one Count Jacques de Lavison, who illustrated the mercenary character of some of Ali's 'friends' by claiming 55,000 francs (£687) commission on the sale after Ali's death.

With one of his powerful speedboats, Ali won first prize at a Monte Carlo regatta, but the pride of his little fleet was probably the steam-powered *dahabeeyah*, luxuriously fitted out, in which he could transport his secretary, associates and assorted hangers-on up the Nile to Luxor, fashionable in the cooler months between November and May.

Early in 1922, Ali began to refurbish a small palace in Cairo, on the El Gezira side of the Bulaq Bridge at Zamalek, the most *chic* quarter of the city. King Peter of Yugoslavia had lived there until his death in 1921. No expense was spared in fitting out the palace: a firm of Parisian interior designers was engaged and an 'Italian garden' planned at an overall cost of £120,000 (the equivalent of over £5,000,000 today). Ali owned a villa, slightly more modestly appointed, in Alexandria and a suite of offices in central Cairo.

Life in the fast lane inevitably had a sexual dimension. Ali was handsome as well as extremely rich and from the day he came into his inheritance he would have been the target of those with matrimony in mind. He seems to have had a number of short affairs with women in Egypt and France. For a while, a Mlle Bosini was his mistress, but behind the façade of conventional high life lay a rogue factor, which set Cairo buzzing in 1922 and which would later be appropriated by Marguerite for some very murky purposes indeed. Said Enani, as befitted the private secretary of a multi-millionaire with so many business and social interests, now had a secretary of his own. The three men began to look like an inseparable trio, both in public and in private.

The satirical Cairo weekly *Al Kashkoul* (favourite reading at the British High Commission as a barometer of 'native' opinion) published a cartoon, rendered in French as *l'ame damne de Fahmy* (the captive soul of Fahmy). The accompanying Arabic text referred cryptically to the three men depicted as 'The Light, the Shadow of the Light, and the Shadow of the Shadow of the Light'. The punch line may simply have been a comment on the self-serving influence that the two secretaries had on Ali, still only 21, but, as will be seen, Westerners chose to interpret the cartoon as somehow referring to homosexual entanglements.

Homosexual behaviour, though barely spoken of in Egypt, could be looked on as a passing phase in a young man's development or as an adjunct to a basically heterosexual life. Many of the male prostitutes in Cairo would have had wives and families of their own. Although Said knew his master by the familiar, distinctly unoriginal, nickname of 'Baba' (after Ali Baba of Forty Thieves fame), there is no evidence of any physical involvement between the two men. In fact, allegations were made that Said sometimes procured women for Ali. As to Said himself, an English private detective's report of 1923 suggests that Ali's secretary was resolutely heterosexual, reported as regularly entertaining women in his room at the Hotel Majestic in Paris.

By 1921, whatever may have been Ali's innermost thoughts, he was having to contemplate marriage. There must have been strong family pressure on him, as the sole male heir, to carry on the Fahmy line. He may also have been anxious to scotch rumours, however unfounded, about his private life.

Ali had his first sight of Marguerite at the Semiramis Hotel in Cairo. In the spring of 1922, he travelled restlessly about Europe, taking in a stay at the Savoy in London. By the middle of May, he was back in Paris, where he saw Marguerite again, prominent among the crowd of like-minded women and their admirers, brilliantly on display in fashionable restaurants and nightclubs. Although the weather was generally poor that year, the few fine days of May would see society heading for one or other of the two (partly) open-air restaurants in the Bois de Boulogne. Au Pré Catelan was in the park itself, while the Château de Madrid stood near the Porte de Madrid, then one of the gates of the Bois. This building was a pastiche of a chateau built by Francois 1er in 1528 and it was here that 'the élite of Parisian society resort to dine . . . and dance on summer evenings'. A dance floor was set up under the trees, with space for a large number of tables. Marshal Pétain, the hero of Verdun (and in 1940 the controversial architect of armistice with the invading German armies), was a frequent visitor, and at 66 still possessed a lively interest in women.

Marguerite was aware that Ali Fahmy, whose wealth was by now well known in Paris, was attracted to her: she noticed how he would look intently at her on the many occasions their paths crossed, but somehow the necessary introduction eluded him. Marguerite, the mistress of Jean d'Astoreca, was playing hard to get, treading cautiously in a city notorious for gossip. In early July, she spent a few days in Deauville, where she met Madeleine Martinet, 'an exceedingly charming woman . . . I felt very sympathetically attracted to her and to her young sister, a remarkably pretty girl, and took them back in my car to Paris'.

Later that month, Marguerite's warm feelings for her new friend paid dividends. One day she was telephoned excitedly by Madeleine, who said that she knew someone who absolutely had to meet her. 'He said it was his sole ambition while he was in Paris,' added Madeleine by way of encouragement and so, supposedly mystified,

Marguerite duly arrived at the Hotel Majestic at noon on 30 July 1922.

This *hôtel de luxe*, which stood in the avenue Kléber a few metres from the Arc de Triomphe, vied in 'its splendours, comforts and cuisine' with the Ritz. The headquarters of the British delegation at the Versailles Peace Conference, the hotel was soon 'restored to its usual guests to whom display, luxury and wonderful ladies have never seemed scandalous'. There, on 18 May 1922 and in a private *salon*, Proust, Joyce, Picasso, Stravinsky and Diaghilev gathered for supper, the only time that these emblematic figures of the Modernist movement were together in one room.

Madeleine duly effected the required formal presentation, beginning an ill-fated acquaintance with the handsome young man whose dark, intense eyes Marguerite had seen so often around town. 'I felt,' she later wrote, 'a curious *tresaillement* [thrill]', but if thrill it was, the sensation was as likely caused by the thought of Ali's bank balance, and what it might mean for Marguerite and her daughter, than by any truly romantic yearnings of the heart.

Quickly abandoning her new girlfriend, Marguerite accepted Ali's offer of lunch at the Château de Madrid. As they left the Hotel Majestic, Ali indicated two cars waiting outside. One was his Rolls-Royce coupé, with attendant burly Sudanese chauffeur, while the other was a gaudy sports model shaped like a torpedo. Marguerite, well aware of Ali's reputation for crazy driving in Cairo, wisely chose the Rolls.

The acquaintance soon ripened. Two or three days after the rendezvous at the Hotel Majestic, Marguerite met Said Enani for the first time, and wondered exactly how deep the friendship was between her new friend and his older secretary. She was also introduced to the secretary's secretary, and to Ali's own lawyer, the peripatetic Mahmoud Fahmy. Marguerite later wrote of a whirlwind courtship in which she was pursued by Ali, abrim with *des avances furieuses* (madcap advances) for over a month in Deauville, in Paris, and back in Deauville again. The truth was more prosaic. Not long after their informal introduction, Marguerite moved into Ali's suite at the Majestic (which cost him 10,000 francs (£125) a week), living with him there for a few days before he left for Deauville.

Ali had taken a suite at the Hotel Normandy, one of the best hotels in the little town, an unlikely-seeming resort for the smart set, situated as it was on the chilly north-western coast of France, opposite Le Havre and the great mouth of the Seine. July and August saw its small resident population swamped by a horde of migrating rich, who travelled there by luxury train, expensive chauffeur-driven motor-car, or by yacht. That season, the Cornelius Vanderbilts were aboard the *Sheelah* (chartered from Admiral Lord Beatty), Earl Fitzwilliam had brought the *Sheemara*, while

Lord Dunraven thrilled onlookers with his speedboat *Sona*, a recent sensation at Cowes.

In that *Année des Rois* (Year of the Kings), the King of Sweden, the Dowager Queen Olga of Greece and ex-King Manuel of Portugal were in town. King Alfonso XIII of Spain could be spied playing a chukka of polo, under the transparent sobriquet 'The Duke of Toledo', before returning to his private villa at nearby Hennequeville. Another monarch who patronised the Deauville Season of 1922 was Ahmad Shah of Persia, the occupant of a very wobbly Peacock Throne. A few weeks later, Olga was forced into exile. Both Alfonso and Ahmad would be ousted within a decade.

In the early evenings, people strolled along the promenade des Planches, maybe pausing at La Potinière, with its pretty green tables, for an aperitif. Vermouth cassis was popular and, in place of the battery of wartime cocktails, unchauvinistic French nationals might sip a 'Dempsey' (one part gin, two parts Calvados, two dashes of anise and a teaspoonful of grenadine), in honour of the American bruiser who had demolished gentlemanly Georges Carpentier the previous year. And not a few of Deauville's more antique summer visitors might have been tempted by the promise of a 'Monkey Gland Cocktail', another favourite of a year when post-war Deauville really got into its stride.

After dinner, society migrated to the Casino.

During the second week of August 1922, Winston Churchill regularly tried his luck at the tables, in the company of press baron Max Aitken (later Lord Beaverbrook) and his gossip-columnist friend Lord Castlerosse, an Irish peer of enormous girth and zest for life. André Citroën, the car manufacturer, won 750,000 francs (£9,375) on Friday 10 August and lost most of his gains the following Monday night. On the dancefloor, 'there is no tangoing . . . no foxtrotting, always the "Shimmy" with its dry and monotonous rhythm and lack of grace, to which the dancers lugubriously revolve'.

The Hungarian-American Dolly Sisters were a great attraction of the Casino's cabaret, appearing in fantastic costumes. Tall white ostrich plume head-dresses crowned the effect, creation of the internationally renowned English couturier, Colonel Edward Molyneux, another of Deauville's seasonal residents.

The inimitable Mistinguett, Queen of Paris vaudeville, was also in town, wearing what *The Tatler* described as 'a very short frock' (at a time when the hem-line still hovered just above the ankle), showing a glimpse of those famous and highly insured legs, encased in shiny silk stockings. That autumn, she would play at the Casino for 20,000 francs (£250) a performance, plus a hard-nosed 15 per cent of the box-office.

Marguerite, despite her dalliance with Ali, still considered herself the mistress of Jean d'Astoreca. According to her rather florid account, she and

Astoreca set themselves up at the Hotel Royal. That night at the Casino, Marguerite saw Ali, who greeted her warmly, before she joined Astoreca at the tables of the *salle de jeu*, only to find her protector with cards in one hand, the other caressing the thighs of a woman sitting next to him.

Ordering her maid to pack her bags, Marguerite marched over to the Hotel Normandy, moving in with Ali, who later gave her a diamond-encrusted powder compact worth 35,000 francs, bought from Van Cleef & Arpels and the first of many bejewelled gifts from her Egyptian suitor. Marguerite also savoured the heartier pleasures of the resort, mixed bathing now allowed, also playing tennis and golf while Ali made a short excursion to Verona, from which he returned on 21 August. He was now calling her 'Bella', while Marguerite – taking her cue from Said Enani – designated her new Egyptian lover as 'Baba'.

As autumn approached, the fashionable world drifted down to Biarritz on the Atlantic coast, not far from the Spanish border. Ali Fahmy and Marguerite were now living as man and wife, but Ali never travelled without his entourage, the 'shadows of the light', and Said Enani was always at hand to give advice, even if it was not always heeded. More experienced in the ways of the world than his new master, Said viewed Marguerite's patently strategic manoeuvres with suspicion, though a strange intimacy was growing between them. They had, after all, some coincidence of interests arising from their mutual interest in the fortune of a very rich young man.

From Biarritz, excursions were made to St Jean-de-Luz and over the Spanish border to San Sebastián. On these trips, Ali would often insist on taking the wheel, fully earning Marguerite's description 'velocimaniac', as he sped recklessly along the narrow, twisting roads in the foothills of the Pyrenees. In 1922, the modern syncromesh gear system had not yet been developed. To change gear, it was normally necessary to slip into neutral before re-engaging, a process that could cause considerable loss of speed. Ali was a proud exponent of the 'racing change', a risky technique calling for deft use of the accelerator and a cavalier disregard for the welfare of the gearbox.

Marguerite particularly liked the Biarritz set and, in the first major disagreement of their relationship, declared herself reluctant to break her stay in order to go to Milan, as Ali wished. Angrily, he set off alone in mid-September, hoping Marguerite would follow, but with her own strong will (and a well-developed sense of strategy) she would not be persuaded to leave. Marguerite nevertheless agreed that she should go to Cairo in the latter part of the year, though – for form's sake – she put up token resistance, claiming that she had already planned a winter trip to Cannes.

Ali, completely smitten, returned to Biarritz, where Marguerite was photographed in the fashion of 1865, appropriate dress for the Second Empire Ball, which took place that evening. This was one of the great social events in France, rivalling the Bal du Grand Prix at the Paris Opera, held in June.

Immediately after the ball, Ali returned to Egypt for family reasons, taking ship from Marseilles. He arrived at Alexandria lovesick and in poor spirits. Although he had sent Marguerite romantic letters from Milan, she was perhaps not prepared for the long, emotional letter written to her from Cairo on 26 September. Described coldly by an English writer as 'written in abject and sickening terms of flattery', the (admittedly inadequate) English translation reads as a statement of courtly love. Extracts convey something of Ali's passionate lovelorn style, addressed naïvely to an older woman brought up in a tough school:

My Dear Little Bella,
. . . I landed on Monday and my first . . . thoughts are for you who, by your bewitching charm, your exquisite delicacy, the beauty of your heart . . . have brought out all that is good and generous in human nature . . . that indefinable radiance, proceeding from you, invades and envelops me. Your image everywhere incessantly pursues me . . . Torch of my life, your image appears . . . to me surrounded by a halo and your head, so dear, so proud, so majestic, is brightly encircled by a crown which I reserve for you in the beautiful country of my ancestors . . .

Both unsure of himself and uncertain whether Marguerite would keep her promise to revisit Cairo, Ali seems to have been trying, in this revealing passage, to dispel rumours about other affairs, his sexual orientation, and his very close relationship with Said Enani:

> . . . If, by chance, your journey should be thwarted and if – giving credence to stories, something I would never believe of you – you abandon your planned journey, you will unwittingly have made my life aimless. Envy, jealousy and distraction are common at all times and in all countries. They should never have sway over noble natures like yours . . .

The letter ends with a hint of emotional blackmail:

> . . . Let me insist . . . that you embark so as to arrive here at the beginning of November . . . Come quickly and see the beautiful sun of Egypt . . . Ill, saved from death in bed, my only consolation is you. My recovery . . . I owe largely to your sweet and beneficent vision.
> Believe me, I love you very much
> From your faithful little Baba . . .

Enclosed were tickets for the journey, but Marguerite was not ready to make the trip. She had other strings to her bow and, once back in Paris, resumed her liaison with Jean d'Astoreca, whose sharp-eyed secretary, Miguel-Surgères, had discovered that Marguerite would always sleep with a loaded pistol under her pillow, morbidly fearful that someone would try to steal her jewellery.

Ali was not to be fobbed off by Marguerite's excuses. His melancholia may have brought on some kind of psychosomatic illness, though hardly serious enough to warrant the absurd series of telegrams despatched on his behalf by Said Enani:

CAIRO: 4 OCTOBER 1922: NO NEWS FROM YOU. BABA SERIOUSLY ILL SINCE HIS ARRIVAL. HAVE NOT BEEN ABLE TO WRITE TO YOU BEING BUSY WITH HIM BUT HOPE FOR PROMPT RECOVERY . . . SAID

CAIRO: 7 OCTOBER 1922: DESPERATE STILL. GRAVE DANGER TODAY. TOMORROW TELEGRAPH HIM HOW YOU ARE – SAID

CAIRO: 9 OCTOBER 1922: BABA BETTER TODAY. FIRST WORD YOUR NAME. TELEGRAPH DAY OF DEPARTURE – SAID

Marguerite does not seem to have taken this nonsense seriously, but was considering her

145

options. 'This is the time o' year,' commented the Paris correspondent of *The Tatler*, 'when *affaires du coeur* frame up their winter programmes!' Perhaps Marguerite had been hoping that Astoreca would make an honest woman of her or maybe she had quarrelled once more with a man almost as neurotic as Ali. At all events, accompanied by her younger sister, 21-year-old Yvonne, Marguerite boarded the Simplon-Orient Express on 16 November 1922, arriving in Trieste the following day. Waiting for them there was SS *Helouan* (10,000 tons), of the Italian Sitmar line, bound for Alexandria. 'Mrs Laurent' and 'Miss Alibert', as listed in the 'Arrivals' column of the English-language *Egyptian Gazette*, were to have distinguished company on the voyage. Also aboard ship was Emir Abdullah of Transjordan, 'a strikingly handsome man of about 40 . . . of fair complexion and with slender delicately-formed hands'.

The voyage afforded Marguerite and Yvonne a glimpse of this real Arab prince, uncompromisingly dressed in the raiment of his ancestors. The Emir wore 'an Arab *kufiya* and *argai*, with a deep plum-coloured *zabun* and a gold mesh belt, the clasp of which was formed by the highly worked gold and silver scabbard of a large dagger'.

On Monday 22 November, in brilliant winter sunshine, the SS *Helouan* put in to Alexandria. Marguerite recalled how the white mass of buildings on the shoreline was gradually transformed into low houses, overhanging buildings and minarets.

As the vessel docked, scores of porters noisily vied with each other to claim passengers' luggage. The Emir, formally greeted by the British Consul, was whisked off to Cairo in a special saloon attached to the boat train. The two Frenchwomen, on a very different errand, were met on board by Ali, miraculously restored to ebullient health. A limousine was waiting on the quayside, engine running, to take the party to Ali's private villa, overlooking the Mediterranean, a few miles out of town.

CHAPTER 7

MUNIRA

Ali's seaside villa could not compete for splendour with his mansion at Zamalek, so the day after disembarkation they took the train to Cairo, a journey of three and a quarter hours. The party was chauffeured across the city in a procession of three cars (the last of which carried a mass of luggage and assorted servants), over the Nile to the building that Ali unblushingly called his 'palace'. On the steps leading up to the entrance, twelve liveried Nubian footmen, glittering in gold braid, greeted Ali and his two guests, ushered into salons furnished and decorated in what was supposed to be the style of Fontainebleau. Marble columns, Gobelin tapestries, Aubusson carpets, venerable Persian rugs and eighteenth-century French furniture, carefully selected (on commission of course) by Fahmy's agents, filled the ground floor rooms, in some of which Ali had attempted to reproduce the parquet flooring of the Hall of Mirrors at Versailles.

The Fahmy monogram, a fantastic reproduction of his name in Arabic, designed by Ali himself, was to be seen everywhere, often spelt out in precious stones, on lamps, chairbacks and picture frames, as well as on a surfeit of gold cigarette-boxes strewn throughout the building. As a tribute to his principal guest, Ali had commissioned a special dressing-table set: four hairbrushes, six perfume dispensers, hand mirrors, a manicure set and scissors, each one wrought in gold and tortoise-shell and adorned with the letter 'M' in small diamonds.

Marguerite's bedroom had been fitted out with items once belonging to King Peter of Serbia, who had died in 1921. The décor was very much in the style of the French Empire, possibly reflecting an admiration by the late King for Napoleon Bonaparte. Peter was invited to assume the Serbian throne in 1903 after the previous incumbent and his wife had been brutally murdered in a military *coup d'état*.

In those first days as resident mistress, Marguerite would go horse-riding with Ali, early in the Cairo mornings. It was always a delight when 'there was nothing to be seen but masses of white mist . . . In a minute or two, as the sun strikes over the hills . . . and the mist turns a delicate pink, in the far distance the bright blue hills of the western desert begin to show, and the horizon line is cut by the pyramids, starting out of the sea of blushing cloud. Incredibly quickly, change follows change. The cloud now turns to a liquid translucent gold and through it dimly appear the feathery palms and the graceful sails of passing boats. In a moment

more the rising breeze has swept away the cloud
. . . and the morning pageant is over.'

Marguerite had come to Egypt, just as she had
done in 1915 and 1921, to become the mistress
of a rich man. Ali Fahmy differed from his prede-
cessors, not merely because he was very young,
handsome and super-rich, but because – shortly
after Marguerite's installation at Zamalek – he
asked her to marry him. The real reasons behind
his proposal will probably never be known, but
the very intensity with which he expressed his
feelings suggests some inner conflict which could
not be resolved by marriage alone, especially
marriage to a woman who, despite her air of
charm and sophistication, had made her name as
a high-class Paris whore.

Marguerite, for her part, had the simplest of
motives for becoming Ali's wife. Though she was
already a rich woman, she had an expensive lifestyle
and a daughter to maintain. Marguerite, who had
been the mistress of a future king, had high social
ambitions and Ali's wealth might open doors of
Paris salons currently closed to her. So she accepted
Ali's offer of marriage, but prudently engaged the
services of Maître Michel Assouad, a Cairo attorney
of considerable guile.

Ali's family strongly opposed this marriage to a
non-Muslim foreigner of dubious antecedence, an
older woman, whom they suspected (with good
reason) of being little more than a gold-digging
hustler. But Ali would not be deterred, even

150

though the faithful Said Enani did his best to fight a corner for the family. The civil ceremony was fixed for 26 December 1922, with a religious marriage planned early the following year.

The Cairo winter season had begun, almost the very day Marguerite arrived with her younger sister. The active social scene at first masked deep and irreconcilable differences in temperament between Marguerite and her fiancé. One common bond was a love of the bright lights and in the last weeks of 1922 they could be seen dining and dancing in Cairo's best hotels and restaurants.

There was an added excitement for partygoers that year, an attraction that was drawing more than the usual complement of well-to-do tourists. On 5 November 1922, an archaeological expedition headed by Howard Carter and the Earl of Carnarvon had discovered the entrance of a large and apparently undisturbed ancient royal tomb in the famous Valley of the Kings. An outer section of the tomb was officially opened at the end of the month and there was intense speculation as to what might be revealed in the inner chamber, an exploration scheduled to take place early in the New Year. Westerners were already beginning to call this the 'Tut-Ankh-Amun Season'.

A dancing craze had taken hold in Egypt, just as it had in Europe. 'Cairo is not particularly up-to-date; it generally takes Dame Fashion a little while to travel across the Mediterranean,' observed one English-language newspaper, but the writer

151

conceded that the ballroom of the Semiramis Hotel, where Ali had his first sight of Marguerite the previous December, gave a creditable impression of Paris or the West End of London. The dances were attended by people of all nationalities, but the British, a conservative bunch, disliked the sexually charged exhibitions of dancing at teatime, tending to restrict their appearances on the dance floor to after dinner.

Shepheard's was a hotel particularly favoured by Ali, whose fluent English enabled him to stay well informed about British attitudes, a useful conduit of intelligence during his time as press attaché to the French Legation. Built in the 1840s (and destroyed in the riots that followed the Suez crisis of 1956), Shepheard's was very popular with the British, serving as a sort of annexe to the High Commission.

The popular RAF Jazz Band played for the foxtrotting young in the hotel ballroom. If this suggested a peaceful social life, the impression was misleading. The British community in Egypt was decidedly nervous about the rise of militant nationalism in Egypt: a number of British officials and soldiers had been murdered in recent years and street demonstrations, strikes and riots were frequent occurrences in Cairo and Alexandria.

Ali and Marguerite were less vulnerable than British expatriates to the prevailing tensions. In December, Ali persuaded two Italian opera stars, Nino Piccaluga, the romantic tenor, and his wife,

Augusta Concato, to join an expedition by river boat to the pyramid of Saqqara. Here an elaborate banquet was served, complete with orchestra and dancers, in a restaurant once the home of the great French archaeologist Mariette. Later the party descended into the tombs, where by candelight Piccaluga and Concato sang *mourir si jeune et belle*, the final aria from *Aida*, which Radames and Aida sing before their entombment. Within a few months, Ali – a young and handsome man – would die violently before his time.

It was almost as if Ali and 'Mme Laurent' were having their honeymoon before the marriage, but living together was already beginning to expose strains in the relationship, problems that would grow rather than diminish as the months went by. Ali was turning out to be intensively possessive of his new love, as if to play down the rackety image of his past, while Marguerite was hedging her bets. Despite that notorious row at the Deauville Casino, she had not lost contact with her old flame, Jean d'Astoreca, and an unfortunate incident happened during mid-December. While out shopping in Cairo, she dropped a telegram and left the premises unaware of her loss. The finder noticed that it was signed 'Jean' and that the message was expressed in very affectionate terms. When it was restored to Marguerite, on a later visit to the shop, she was visibly embarrassed.

Whether or not Ali found out about this indiscretion, the couple certainly had a major argument three days before the civil wedding, a dispute sufficiently serious for Marguerite to book a return passage on the SS *Helouan* for herself and her maid. The row may have blown up, as a French woman friend recalled, because Marguerite was 'addicted to flirting' and expected Ali to put up with her well-practised ways.

The quarrel was patched up in time for a large pre-wedding reception and dinner at Shepheard's on Christmas Day 1922. Ali unwisely confessed to his fiancée that his friends had been betting on whether he would be able to keep her, but, once the capable Maître Assouad was satisfied that the civil contract was in order, there was to be no hesitation on Marguerite's part. Although the Prince of Wales had been her finest trophy, marriage to the heir of the British Crown was impossible, and Ali made a very desirable second-best.

Marguerite brought the Prince's letters to Egypt and most of the correspondence seems to have been handed to Maître Assouad for safe-keeping. As will be shown later, Marguerite was on very close terms with Assouad. With her customary caution, she would have been wary of depositing such valuable items in any of Ali's properties. Two or three letters, however, were kept separately, perhaps left in Paris in the hands of a trusted friend, such as the singer Hélène Baudry, or Madeleine Martelet, who had introduced her to Ali. This was a prudent course to take. Marguerite would not put all her eggs in one basket.

Marguerite undertook to produce evidence of her divorce from Charles Laurent (this was resolved by the roundabout declaration of the French consul that she was 'free from any bond of marriage'), while Ali agreed to pay her a dowry of £8,000, with £2,000 to be paid on signing the contract, the balance on his death or if he should divorce Marguerite. Ali's lawyer insisted on a clause by which Marguerite stood to lose the £6,000 and her right to alimony if she divorced him. Ali would not be 'kicked out' quite as easily as Charles Laurent had been, but the prize of his fortune made up for this slight restriction on her freedom of action.

Another major provision of the contract was that Marguerite should convert to Islam, ostensibly because of a term in the will of Ali's mother excluding Ali from her inheritance if he married a *kufar*, but it also served to strengthen Marguerite's position if Ali, with his reckless taste for speed or from some other cause, should happen to predecease her. Marguerite, a lover of Parisian *haute couture*, was not obliged by contract to wear Islamic dress. She retained her French nationality. All in all, she had been well advised and, far from being a defenceless Frenchwoman in a foreign land (as she would later claim), she had not only the services of an experienced Cairo lawyer, but the support of a former lover (possibly General Cherif *pasha*), who acted as witness at the civil ceremony, a favour for which Ali may not have been too grateful.

Five nights after the civil marriage, Shepheard's was packed with 1,200 diners celebrating a rowdy New Year's Eve. Some young British bucks doused diners unfortunate enough to be sitting near the fountain in the Moorish Restaurant, while bread rolls and cotton-wool pellets were hurled from table to table in the ballroom, used as an overflow dining area. After supper, a 'jazz band' belted out the latest favourites, 'I'm Just Wild About Harry', 'My Sweet Hortense', and 'Ain't We Got Fun'.

There was barely ankle room for dancing under the great chandelier, decorated in 'magnificent cascades of bougainvillaea [with] a profusion of flowers everywhere'. At midnight, the lights were dimmed and two dozen white doves released from a balcony, an effect rather spoiled by the wags who lowered a squealing piglet (not the most tactful of gestures in a Muslim country) on a rope from an upper fanlight. Bags of red and white confetti were emptied on the heads of the crowd, 'everybody whistled and screeched, cushions were thrown about and a rugger scrum indulged in by the . . . men'. In the early hours, a full moon lit the departing *gharris*, as guests forsook the hotel for Ciro's nightclub or, more romantically, journeyed out of town to gaze upon the pyramids by moonlight.

After the civil wedding, the process of conversion to Islam of the woman who had once considered herself 'devout . . . in a mystic sort of way' proceeded according to the regulations. Marguerite was obliged first to consult a priest of her own religion, who would be given the opportunity of trying to persuade the intending convert to remain Christian. At the house of the civil governor of Cairo, Father Maréchal of St Joseph's Church vainly attempted to keep Marguerite within the folds of the Mother Church, but to no avail. Assuring the priest that she would not betray the faith of her childhood, raised as she had been by the Sisters of Mary, Marguerite confessed that this was all about money. Since Ali risked losing his inheritance if he married a Christian, Marguerite felt she had to take his interests into account. Nevertheless she gave the church a handsome donation. In return, the priest, undaunted, presented a breviary to Marguerite, now formally sundered from the body of the Holy Catholic Church.

On 11 January, after proclaiming in Arabic 'There is one God and Mahomet is His Prophet', Marguerite added another to her string of *noms de plume*. She had become 'Munira', after her husband's mother, and to mark the occasion had herself photographed demurely wearing the *choudri*.

Within a week of Marguerite's conversion to Islam, Ali was writing a revealing letter to Yvonne Alibert, in terms that suggest a reason for the younger sister's rapid departure from Cairo. Ali's emotional immaturity and his wife's unwillingness to change her 'bad habits' were rapidly propelling the marriage towards disaster:

. . . You may rest assured, my little Yvonne, that I have no reproach with regard to you. I would much like you to have spent the winter season with us, but the question of my marriage with Munira – ha, ha, ha – caused a delicate situation which, being considered, perhaps it was in your best interest to return to France. Just now I am engaged in training her. Yesterday, to begin with, I did not come in to lunch or to dinner and I also left her at the theatre. With women one must act with energy and be severe – no bad habits. We still lead the same life of which you are aware – the opera, theatre, disputes, high words and perverseness. We leave for Luxor next week.

Accept, my dear child, my affectionate sentiments . . .

Ali was probably writing jokingly to Yvonne, but any attempts to 'train' his new wife were doomed to failure. Five days after he had written to Yvonne, a terrific quarrel erupted, in the course of which each spouse threatened to kill the other. As with so many of their arguments, jealousy was at the root. Marguerite rushed up to her room and, mindful at this early stage of the need to keep a record of events with a view to divorce proceedings, wrote an emotional denunciation of her husband:

Yesterday, 21 January 1923, at three o'clock in the afternoon, he took his Bible, or Koran, I do not know which, kissed it, put his hand on it and swore to avenge himself on me . . .

Unconvincingly, she declared that 'this oath was taken without any reason, neither jealousy, bad conduct, nor a scene on my part', adding a post-script which showed where her priorities lay:

PS Today he wanted to take my jewellery from me. I refused, hence a fresh scene.

Calm had been briefly restored when, at daybreak on 25 January, the steam-powered *dahabeeyah* cast off, on a major voyage up the Nile to Luxor. Ali took command, clad in tarboosh, pyjamas and a pair of red heelless slippers, or babouches and, with evident pleasure, successfully negotiated two of Cairo's awkward bridges before going below for breakfast. The pride of Ali's little fleet, the boat was crewed by some twenty-five Nubian sailors, whose complement included a chef, six cooks and two stewards, one of whom was styled Maître d'hôtel, both in uniforms bearing Ali's self-designed monogram. Fahmy had his valet aboard, Marguerite was accompanied by her maid Aimée, and, unsurprisingly, Said Enani completed the party.

After ten days of tortuous progress, the craft

drew near to its destination and, eager to exchange the comparative loneliness of the *dahabeeyah* for the cosmopolitan society of Luxor, Ali helped Munira into his speedboat, which had been towed up from Cairo. Together they went ahead of the yacht, making for the jetty in front of the Winter Palace Hotel. Here two of Ali's sisters, Madame Said and Madame Roznangi, were waiting with warm greetings for their brother but conspicuously less affection for his bride.

Moored opposite the hotel, among the other luxury craft, the *dahabeeyah* boasted an impressive list of guests. Lord Carnarvon accepted an invitation to lunch, and the lavish shipboard parties given by the Fahmys during their two visits to Luxor that February were attended by some of the best-known personalities of the 'Tut-Ankh-Amun Season', including Howard Carter, the popular and gregarious Maharajah of Kapurthala (a great Francophile who, to Marguerite's delight, spoke excellent French), a Greek archaeologist, a distinguished Egyptian poet, various financiers and an assortment of local dignitaries. In a diary entry for 6 February, General Sir John Maxwell recorded that '[Howard] Carter came over . . . had tea with Ali Kamel Fahmy and Mahmoud Abul Fath on their [sic] richly decorated steam *dahabeah*'.

The reason for this visit is unclear. Maxwell, a career soldier, had served in Egypt for many years, becoming C-in-C British forces there in 1908 and again at the beginning of the Great War. Appointed

C-in-C and Military Governor of Ireland immediately after the 1916 Easter Rising, he took
responsibility for the execution of fifteen of the
leading rebels, earning the nickname 'Bloody
Maxwell'. By 1923, at the age of 63, he had retired
from active duty, but had close links with Allenby,
the High Commissioner, and British officials.
Maxwell may have used the visit to sound out
educated Egyptian opinion on matters of importance to British Imperial interests. The fact that he
was accompanied by Howard Carter, already
famous as the discoverer of Tut-Ankh-Amun's
tomb, testifies to the importance of the meeting.

In between hosting these entertainments, the
Fahmys, evidently gripped by the prevailing
Tut-Ankh-Amun fever, hired a pair of donkeys,
on which they travelled to Karnak and the Valley
of the Kings. En route, they were spotted by an
English journalist, H. V. Morton, later to become
well known as a travel writer and a shrewd observer
of humanity, with a gift for the syrupy phrase,
already very much part of his style in 1923. Morton
described 'one of those crystal-clear mornings
which come only in Egypt, bringing with them a
sense of indescribable dancing happiness. There
was not a ripple on the blue waters of the Nile,
the miles of sugar-cane stood motionless and not
a breath stirred the tall, feathered palms on the
road to Gurnah . . .'

After an hour's ride between the baking-hot rock
walls that lead into the famous valley, he saw a

little way ahead of him a man and a woman mounted on donkeys. 'At first,' recalled Morton, with a hint of racism, 'I thought he was a European. He was wearing a grey sun helmet, a well-cut shooting jacket and a pair of Jodhpur riding breeches.' He heard them speaking French and asked an English friend if he knew who they were. 'The Fahmys,' came the reply, delivered patronisingly with 'the peculiar smile with which a white man in the East refers to a mixed marriage'.

Morton asked his friend if they were part of the Egyptian royal family. 'No,' he said. 'Just a *bey*. Pots of money . . . I'll introduce you.' The prevailing contempt felt by the British for most things Egyptian can be discerned in Morton's thumbnail sketch of Ali:

> [He] impressed me as a very polished upper-class Egyptian, not very dark, clean-shaven and possessing in a marked degree that dangerous magnetism of the eye which attracts more white women than most untravelled people imagine. He was too well dressed to look exactly right. Like most Oriental men, he reeked of scent . . .

Ali discussed London and Paris, speaking of the journey back to Cairo for the Islamic wedding, now near at hand. No, they were not staying at the Winter Palace, declared Ali with evident pride, as he swished the ever-present flies away with an ivory-handled whisk of white horsehair. 'I have a yacht.' Morton was very suspicious of this glib, disgustingly rich foreigner. 'All the time he talked, he smiled,' and, subtle Easterner that he was, 'had a trick of looking at your mouth when you were speaking to him . . .'

Marguerite was very quiet, possibly because the journey had tired her, but she was a practised rider and may just have been out of sorts, in no mood for polite chatter. Morton spoke to her in English, but in French she replied that she did not understand and, after a few commonplace remarks, settled down to watch the porters removing artefacts from the great royal tomb.

After four or five days of this crowded social programme, a telegram arrived on 9 February stating that preparations for the religious wedding were complete. The couple, leaving their luggage on the *dahabeeyah*, boarded the *train de luxe* for the thirteen-hour journey back to Cairo, arriving at nine o'clock on the evening before the ceremony.

Clothed entirely in black, with only her large, intriguing eyes visible, Munira was driven early the following afternoon to Ali's large suite of offices, in the business quarter of Cairo. The white-bearded *cadi* formally asked her if she had received her dowry. Her answer, duly recorded in a register by the *cadi*'s clerk, was in the affirmative, although she would later claim that she had only been paid the equivalent of £450, instead of the promised

£2,000. She also alleged that Ali, without warning, had suddenly insisted that she should forgo her right of divorce. There was said to have been a long argument about this, after which, browbeaten, she was cajoled into accepting the provision.

An Islamic marriage contract does not automatically give a wife the right to divorce her husband (who is always permitted to divorce his wife): it is for the woman to claim the insertion of such a clause, which many brides have been reluctant to do. Although it appears that the religious settlement did not give Marguerite the right of divorce, her own account of the episode seems improbable, not only in the light of her assertive nature, but because her lawyer, Maître Assouad, was present throughout the proceedings. Whatever the position might have been in Islamic law, the civil contract, drawn up according to the Egyptian legal code, clearly protected Marguerite's right to divorce her husband.

In the presence of Ali's brother-in-law, Dr Assim Said *bey* (a Cairo gynaecologist), lawyers for both parties and the bridegroom's closest friend, Said Enani, marriage documents were signed in front of the *cadi*. Ali and Munira became man and wife, according to Islamic rite. Marguerite was now to be known as 'Munira Hanem El-Faransawiah', recorded as 'non-virgin, daughter of Farman [sic] . . . French subject'. The party made its way to Shepheard's Hotel for the wedding feast, a junket which lasted well into the small hours and at which, in defiance of religious proscription, the 'costliest wines' were served.

Next day, they took the train to Assiout, between Cairo and Luxor, where the *dahabeeyah* was waiting for them. Using the motor-boat intermittently for excursions, the honeymoon party reached Luxor with decidedly frayed tempers. This time Ali and Marguerite came to blows. Ali had tried to lock his wife in her cabin during the journey, provoking violent resistance. The arguments continued at Luxor, when he pompously forbade her to leave the ship, posting members of the crew at each end of the gangplank.

With so many Europeans around, including some very distinguished acquaintances, it seems highly improbable that Marguerite was ever a true prisoner. Even by her own account, she was never physically abused by the servants and, as appears from the divorce-minded letter that she wrote to her lawyer, her main fear appears to have been a public scandal, news of which might trickle back to the gossips of Paris:

Dear Maître [Assouad]
I have to bring to your notice very grave incidents. For the last three days, I have been a prisoner on board. I am absolutely unable to get out. Threats were made and to avoid a scandal, I had to go inside. This evening I have to go to bed at 7 o'clock. I have on my arms the marks of my husband's

gentleness. I ask you to send here one or two persons, who will have this condition established, so as to make use of it . . .

On 16 February 1923, the inner chamber of the great royal tomb was formally opened. Although the greatest artefacts would not be revealed for some months, it was clear that this had been a major archaeological find, though some Egyptian newspapers were tartly critical of Lord Carnarvon's style and motives. *Al Ahram* complained that, by giving the London *Times* a monopoly of access to the team's discoveries (in return for a handsome consideration), Carnarvon had forced them to take the news regarding their national treasures from non-Egyptian sources: 'He [Carnarvon] has come to regard the tomb as his own creation', was one caustic comment.

British newspaper moguls fell over themselves to get in on the act. First Lord Beaverbrook, then Lord Rothermere, trumpeted his imminent arrival in the land of the pharaohs. 'Lord Beaverbrook is expected to arrive in Cairo next week . . .', said the *Egyptian Gazette* on 22 February, later announcing that 'a wireless message has just been received by Shepheard's Hotel that Lord Rothermere is arriving at Port Said . . . in two days' time . . .'

The Fahmys' second visit to Luxor was noticeably less successful than the first had been. Marguerite's maid returned to France for a holiday on 10 March, leaving her mistress feeling isolated and without a confidante. There were some lighter moments, as when the pair made a second trip out to the newly opened tomb of Tut-Ankh-Amun: as if to mark the occasion, Marguerite had climbed into a nearby open sarcophagus and lay down inside it. Clad in riding habit and with her arms folded in front of her, she became the subject of a zany snapshot. But the bickering soon began again. Ali wrote to Yvonne Alibert on 16 March, describing the trip, together with a little macho blustering, an evident nostalgia for Paris and a romantic flourish:

> . . . but I quarrelled all the time. I showed her I could act with energy and this is what is needed with women. I hope you will make a journey with us next year. Give me details about the pretty women in fashion [in Paris]. If you see [. . .], tell her my heart, my soul, my sentiments are at her feet and I am still in love with her. I hope she has not forgotten me . . .

The Luxor season wound down after mid-April, as the heat became steadily less tolerable. The *dahabeeyah* returned to Cairo, a bad-tempered voyage in which the vessel was frequently marooned on sandbanks. Ali, in sulky mood, behaved badly to his wife, his crew, and to any hapless native boatmen or fisherfolk who chanced to get in his way.

Once back in Cairo, claimed Marguerite, Ali renewed his acquaintance with the seedier type of dancehall and café, in which prostitutes, both female and male, and hashish were freely available. Hashish could be either smoked or chewed and some low dives offered *manzoul*, normally an inoffensive sweet paste, transformed into a kind of 'space-cake' of opium, hashish, even strychnine, taken 'for its aphrodisiac properties'. The user of hashish, reported the *Egyptian Gazette*, 'sees visions, voluptuous or merely grandiose . . . To promote the hallucinations, the walls of hashish-smoking dens are often covered with pictures of elephants, dancing girls and other imagined accessories of regal pomp . . .' And there were new opportunities for the well-to-do. 'Since the War, the [Egyptian] upper and middle classes . . . have succumbed to the lure of morphine and cocaine . . . [a habit] imported with the French prostitutes who flocked to Cairo in the winter of 1919–20 . . .'

Marguerite, although not fully confined within the traditional boundaries of the Egyptian wife, was getting dangerously bored. Occasional outings to the theatre with one of her sisters-in-law, who had slightly unfrozen from the early days of their acquaintance, were no substitute for the gay life in Paris. By late April, fashionable society had already left Cairo for more temperate climes.

One night, escorted by Ali's diminutive Nubian valet, Marguerite went to the cinema. Ali's close friend, the sculptor Mukhta *bey*, unwisely took her back to Zamalek in a taxi. Ali, who had returned home earlier than expected, was waiting for his wife in the grounds of the mansion. A violent argument took place during which Ali punched his wife on the face, an ugly incident, even if Marguerite's allegation that she had sustained a dislocated jaw seems to have been a later embellishment.

At last, the day came to set off for summer in Europe. On the morning of their departure, Marguerite's heart missed a beat when Ali capriciously announced that he had decided not to go after all, but at 7.30 a.m. on 18 May 1923, the boat-train pulled out of Cairo on its way to Alexandria, with the Fahmy entourage on board. Just after 1 p.m., their ship was making its way out into the Mediterranean, bound for Brindisi, Venice and Trieste, with its onward rail connection to Paris. The vessel was the SS *Helouan*, on which Marguerite and her sister had travelled to Egypt six months before. On this voyage, Ali and Marguerite fought so much that they became the talk of the ship and the captain had to be called in to act as umpire.

CHAPTER 8

STORMY WEATHER

The Fahmys argied and bargied, clawed and scratched, bit and kicked their way from the heat of Egypt to a chilly, wet Paris, where they took a suite at the Hôtel Majestic, the scene of Ali's first formal introduction to Marguerite the previous July. Marguerite, delighted to be back in her home town, exchanged scandal with her women friends, discreetly renewed some valued male acquaintances, bought another horse for 12,000 francs (£150), ordered several new dresses and, while the going was still good, expanded her collection of jewellery. Her personal wealth was now estimated to be in the region of 3,000,000 francs (£37,500), a very comfortable sum in 1923.

Despite the ever-present risk of friction, the couple made regular appearances at the smart nightspots, dancing into the small hours most mornings in the swing of the Paris June Season. They would go to Claridge's, the Carlton, the Club Daunon, Le Perroquet and Ciro's, from which they emerged early one morning arguing furiously. As they were motored home by Marguerite's loyal chauffeur, Eugéne Barbay, Ali was heard to shout angrily, 'I've had enough of you,' before getting out of the car, slamming the door shut, and walking off into the night.

One of Marguerite's friends later recalled those troubled days in Paris. '[She] was playing with fire and making the Prince crazy with jealousy . . . Her marriage to this wild youth of 23 [sic] was a mistake and worse – a crime. Heedless of everything, she went on in her married life like an emancipated Parisienne. She received all her admirers with smiles . . .' Ali felt himself to be humiliated. 'I was a witness to many scenes,' continued the friend, 'and, though I assured the Prince that his wife was flirting and nothing more . . . his ideas were so narrow that they had no relation to the society life he was leading. One day he insisted that his wife, who was wearing a gown very slightly décolleté, should put a shawl over her shoulders . . .' Marguerite did not easily accept these attempts to restrict her freedom in Egypt, still less so in her native Paris. 'I can't go on living like this,' she confided to her friend at the end of the month, 'We must get a divorce.'

Ali, a strange mixture of martinet and libertine, was himself the butt of his wife's criticism. He had always been generous to the principal members of his all-male entourage, rewarding them with cash and other presents at his whim. Said Enani was the principal beneficiary, but the others, including the boy valet, were not left out. Marguerite grew increasingly resentful of the intimacy between Ali

171

and his staff, which now included a 'minder', one of whose nicknames, 'Le Costaud', reflected his strapping build.

Ali's fondness for wearing jewellery was a trait common enough in rich Egyptian men, but Marguerite felt that it ought not to be extended to subordinates. Harsh words ensued and Marguerite's will prevailed. 'He had a habit, which I succeeded in breaking,' she said imperiously, 'of letting his suite adorn themselves with some of the contents of his jewel cases.'

Marguerite was particularly suspicious of Said Enani. His friendship with Ali, for the association between the two men went well beyond that of master and servant, predated his acquaintance with Marguerite by several years and, what was more, Said was very close to the surviving members of Ali's family, a rich and powerful lobby not greatly enamoured of the new Madame Fahmy. She resented the way they talked together in Arabic, which she could not understand, as well as Ali's frequent late-night practice of slipping up to Said's room for an hour or so before returning to his wife.

Ali's relationship with his secretary seems to have been platonic, but Marguerite complained that he was spending time with 'men of bad character'. She had flatly refused his suggestion, made after a visit to the Folies Bergère (one of Marguerite's beats in her professional days), that they should go on to 'a certain disreputable resort in Paris to which as a rule only men were admitted'.

By mid-June 1923, Marguerite wanted rid of Ali. She kept in touch with Maître Assouad in Cairo and engaged a French private detective, a M. Gasser, whose instructions seem to have been to follow Ali and report on his sexual encounters. If it came to a divorce, Marguerite's own past and her present fairly louche behaviour would undoubtedly be a handicap: if, on the other hand, she could show that Ali had been unfaithful, perhaps even associating with homosexual men, her chances of a substantial pay-off would considerably increase. To avoid scandal, Ali and his family might be willing to settle on terms a good deal more generous than those provided for by the strict wording of the civil marriage contract.

On 17 June, Ali left Paris for a few days in Stuttgart, glad to be away from the domestic maelstrom and able to indulge another of his passions, high-performance cars. He was uneasy at the prospect of what Marguerite might get up to, alone and unchaperoned in Paris, and Said Enani was charged with the unenviable task of trying to secure Marguerite's chastity during her husband's absence.

Ali's obsessive jealousy gnawed at him while they were apart. He wrote her a bitter letter, warning that if she kept on seeing other men, he would publicly call her a very rude name – this was perhaps 'une salope' (a slag). It was a timely threat: one of the glittering social events so loved by Marguerite was to take place on Saturday 23 June and she would have been anxious not to give the scandalmongers yet more ammunition.

Le Bal du Grand Prix, held amid the splendour of the Paris Opera, was the last great event of the Paris Season, taking place on the eve of the Grand Prix of the Longchamps race meeting, an event at which *tout Paris* could see and be seen. For the occasion, Jean-Gabriel Doumergue (who, with the artist Georges Scott, had staged the Second Empire Ball at Biarritz in September 1922) employed the exotic theme of the Far East in the Eighteenth Century, enabling the great ladies of France to appear in a series of tableaux that uneasily linked Imperial China to the Court of Versailles. A staircase and walls draped in black velvet symbolised the eastern night, and a procession of rajahs and nautch girls gave way to the France of Louis XV, whose mistress, the notorious Madame de Pompadour, was represented by 'none other than Mlle Cecile Sorel [the noted French actress], borne in a palanquin by negroes . . .', amid a painted, powdered and bewigged retinue gorgeously costumed in the fashion of the 1750s.

There were elaborate representations of the treasures brought back from India by Joseph Dupleix, the French adventurer defeated by Clive, and of the court and theatre of China. In one of the latter, the Comte Étienne de Beaumont presented the Prince of Wales's American friend, Nina Crosby, now Marquise de Polignac, and other society beauties in extravagant oriental costume. The final tableau, and the most spectacular, depicted the flowers and birds of the Orient. 'Then appeared floral cascades of lotus, of chrysanthemums, of orchids, [with] pagodas, porcelain bridges, parasols, roses, fountains . . .' Women, gilded eyelids and vermilion-coloured nails aglint, were dressed as subtropical flowers and fantastically coloured birds. Then, at 2 a.m., it was time for the company to foxtrot into the dawn on any one of a number of dance floors, each with its own orchestra.

Convulsions at the ball seem to have been avoided, but two nights later, during a heated argument in their suite at about 2 a.m., the Fahmys came to blows. Marguerite pulled her pistol out from under its usual hiding place, the pillow of her bed, pointed it at Ali and threatened to shoot him. Things were getting out of hand. Ali would appear in public with scratches on his face, while Marguerite on occasion sought to disguise bruises with cream and powder. There was a disturbing tendency to wave guns around: Ali also had a pistol, probably a .25 automatic, whose butt was elegantly decorated with mother-of-pearl and gold-leaf chasing.

A violent scene took place in the lobby of the Hôtel Majestic, in front of Ali's sister, Aicha, and his brother-in-law, Dr Said, who were also staying there. People were startled to see a well-dressed couple loudly insulting each other, heedless of passers-by. Ali, carrying out his earlier threat, shouted that she was nothing more than a tart, while she called him 'un maquereau' (a pimp) and, very likely, '*un pédé*' (a pederast), '*un salaud*' (a bastard) or '*un salopard*' (a sodomite). Ali, now furious, grabbed at her left wrist, wrenching off an expensive bracelet – his recent gift to Marguerite – and threw it contemptuously back at her. Dr Said and Said Enani had to separate the pair as they tried to smack each other's faces.

Dr Said took the view, supported by the rest of Ali's family, that a separation was desirable. 'The cause seemed to me,' he wrote, 'that being a Christian woman and having taken the Mohammedan vows, she would not fall in with her husband's wishes, as it is generally understood that a wife must strictly obey her husband. He did not like her to go out alone, particularly as he knew of her former conduct and this, I believe, is the cause of the whole trouble. She resented this surveillance upon her and wished to follow her usual bent . . .'

Marguerite's friends and acquaintances in Paris were also getting worried. One woman, signing herself 'Nouile', wrote on 30 June from 9 rue Duphot, a smart address close to the Élysée Palace: '*Tu sais que mon amie Fahmy est au plus mal avec son mari ça ne marche pas de tout ce ménage. J'ai grand peur pour son peau. C'est à ce point que ça barde! . . .*' ('You know that my friend [Marguerite] Fahmy is on the worst terms with her husband . . . the two don't get on together at all. I fear greatly for her skin. It's got to the point of an armed contest! . . .')

It was about this time that the second series of SEM's album *Le Nouveau Monde* appeared, its coloured lithographs eagerly scanned by the fashionable world, scandal-mongers and journalists. Since the *belle époque* of the 1900s, the mordant brush of Georges Goursat had satirised the foibles of the rich and famous, as seen in the great hotels, fashionable restaurants and theatres of Paris and at resorts such as Deauville, Cannes and Biarritz.

SEM, 'a funny little monkey of a man', could be savage and his art sometimes provoked victims, or lovers of victims, to fury. He observed people unaware that they were being watched. He would wait for weeks, even months, and then 'suddenly I think, that woman, she was like a horse, or that fellow, he resemble [sic] a camel. Then I draw.' Duff Cooper noted a 'hectic evening' there in August 1922, 'a free fight' between a banker called 'Bamberger and an American a propos of a caricature that SEM has done of Idina'. The American had mistaken the banker for the artist. Lady Idina Gordon had been represented as a heron, and, in consequence, declared an unrepentant SEM, 'everybody would remember Idina as a heron for the rest of her life.

In addition to Marguerite's marital disharmony, another high-profile union was on the rocks, this time between the super-rich Maharajah of Kapurthala and his wayward wife. The former Anita Delgado, in her youth a beautiful Spanish dancer, was a woman with a lively private life, about the same age as Marguerite. SEM, who knew both women well, used the caption *une desenchantée* (a disillusioned woman) as an echo of *Les Desenchantées*, title of a popular romantic novel by Pierre Loti. Marguerite and Anita were both women cast off (or in danger of being cast off) by their wealthy protectors. The link was not by chance, for SEM chose his victims with the greatest care. Marguerite, depicted shrewishly, featured as part of a double bill in typically cruel caricature, with the well-padded form of Anita, looking rather like an overfed turkey.

The last few days of June had seen a considerable improvement in the Parisian weather. *'C'est samedi et il fait beau'* ('It's Saturday and the weather's fine'), wrote the Parisian lady of 3 rue Duphot on the day Marguerite, Ali and their retinue were seen off at the Gare St Lazare by Dr Said and his wife, Ali's sister. They did not foresee the drama that would take place across the Channel. 'There seemed to be the usual misunderstanding, but nothing unusual,' remembered the doctor.

CHAPTER 9

ENGLAND 1923

Marguerite, in her first-class cabin aboard the cross-Channel steamer plying between Le Havre and Southampton, knew that she had some potentially powerful allies in England. She had kept in touch with Major Ernest Bald, close to Bendor, a close friend of the Prince of Wales. In June 1923, Major Bald had taken up residence in his London club for the Season. The social column of *The Times* noted his presence at a dance held at Claridges Hotel, joining a preferred list which included the Duchess of Norfolk, Viscount Churchill, Lord Clifton, Lady Lilian Grenfell, Lady Clodagh Anson, The Hon. Lady Lloyd-Mostyn, Lady Malcolm and Mrs Stanley Baldwin, wife of the Prime Minister.

A few weeks earlier the *Daily Mail* had trumpeted 'The 1923 Season has begun', in the middle of a dismally wet April, brightened only by the wedding of Lady Elizabeth Bowes-Lyon to the Prince's younger brother 'Bertie', now Duke of York, assisted by his bachelor brothers, the Prince of Wales and Prince Henry. To celebrate the occasion, the principal chef of the Savoy Hotel, M. François

Latry, successor to the incomparable Escoffier, prepared such unlikely delights as *poussin de printemps Glamis Castle* and *fraises glacées Elizabeth*.

For the new Season, wet or dry, more dances and receptions were planned since the golden year of 1914. If the April newspapers were correct, 130,000 American tourists were expected to arrive in London at any minute.

The war, of course, had been the great divide. Britain's various Expeditionary Forces had been literally decimated: one in ten had been killed – some 800,000 young men – and the overall casualty figure was one-third of the enlisted total. Though France, Germany and Russia had suffered proportionately worse losses, the psychological impact of the war on British society was immense. If the crass lyrics of 'It's a Long Way to Tipperary' had epitomised the thoughtless mood of 1914, its glum post-war successor was 'I'm Forever Blowing Bubbles', an artless elegy for lost youth and vanished hope. A brief boom temporarily shielded demobbed soldiers from the unemployment that would become so persistent a feature of the interwar years. Already in 1923 over a million people were out of work. In August, an unemployed ex-Colour Sergeant of Marines leapt to his death from a road bridge in Kent. A pawn ticket for eight wartime medals was found on his body.

In the early 1920s, there was a fierce determination, if not to forget the war, at any rate to get back to 'normal', inducing a pervasive nostalgia for the world before the Great War, perhaps prompted by the thought that it was something that the boys who had died in France, Flanders, Palestine and Mesopotamia would have wanted. Newspapers and magazines habitually drew comparisons between life pre- and post-war, usually to the detriment of the present, depicted as shallow and decadent. 'And what did you do in the Great War, Daddy?' was the damning question posed in the famous *Punch* cartoon, in which a small boy unwittingly skewers his father, a well-dressed 'shirker' comfortably seated in a peacetime armchair, whisky-and-soda in hand. Fortunately for the Royal Household, British readers were not to know what the Prince of Wales had been doing during the Great War, enjoying the favours of a Paris mistress, exploring a variety of sexual adventures in a smart apartment and an expensive brothel, all safely behind the lines.

In this bitterly retrospective atmosphere, many found inspiration in what Signor Musssolini was doing for Italy. The podgy dictator had no more fervent admirer than Lord Rothermere, proprietor of the mass-circulation *Daily Mail*. 'This young, vigorous ardent Italian,' wrote the noble lord in 1923, 'did more than save Italy . . . he saved the whole Western world . . . The idea that he is a blustering, flag-waving agitator is foolishly wrong.' Lord Rothermere was particularly impressed by the Duce's 'caution . . . skill and . . . gentleness' and he was not the only fan. Lord Curzon, the

Foreign Secretary, saluted Italy's 'strong man' and Winston Churchill was, for a time, 'favourably impressed' by the blackshirt leader.

In contrast to Mussolini's machismo, British youth was seen as decidedly effete. Worries arising from this perception could sometimes be oddly worded. A clergyman, preaching at Windsor in September 1923, was worried that many young men were being 'lured by the attraction of the opposite sex to the tennis court and the foxtrot, when they ought to be playing cricket'. At Oxford, another reverend gentleman roundly condemned contemporary morals, complaining bitterly that 'girls go about as if to attract men'.

There was a widespread feeling that moral standards were in hopeless decline. In July 1923, the Bishop of Durham warned that the nation's sexual morality was 'on the brink of complete disintegration'. That month, the self-appointed inspectorate of the London Council for the Protection of Public Morality was duly scandalised (though presumably not surprised) by the goings-on in London's parks and open spaces. Such *bien-pensant* groupings often had powerful supporters. The Director of Public Prosecutions, Sir Archibald Bodkin (such a fine name), a perfervid moralist, was a keen supporter of another high-minded caucus, the National Vigilance Association, or 'NVA', whose unexceptionable work among young prostitutes was marred by religious bigotry.

The equivalents of today's tabloid press played

the old game of prudery and prurience: in 1923, transvestism seems to have been Grub Street's favourite sin, with lurid reports of cross-dressing in Surrey and Wiltshire. Sensational news of a bank robber in drag filtered across the Atlantic from Chicago. The President of the Methodist Conference warned that 'the nation's girlhood is exposed to terrible risks of alcoholism, indulgence, midnight follies . . . and licentiousness'. 'The Midnight Follies' was in fact a cabaret, of more or less complete propriety, which entertained late night diners at the luxurious Hotel Metropole (now the Corinthia Hotel) in Northumberland Avenue. Patrons paid 30 shillings (£1.50) each to dine, dance and watch two high-quality 'turns', entertainment ending at 12.30 a.m. on the dot.

The war had brought in all manner of restrictions on social life, not least in regard to the liquor trade, supposedly a result of the 1915 'shell shortage', which the Prince had so rashly reported in a letter to his friend Jacques de Breteuil. Emergency licensing restrictions were crystallised in the 1921 Licensing Act, the product of an unholy alliance in Parliament between total abstainers (such as Lady Astor) and the 'beerage', the brewing lobby well represented in the House of Lords. Weekday closing time in London was set at 11 p.m., but, as so often in England, a class distinction crept into the draft legislation and a 'theatre-supper' clause was inserted, providing for a 'Supper Hour Certificate', whereby the well-to-do were granted an extra hour's drinking time by paying for a meal that was a legally required accompaniment to the liquor.

By mid-1923, the major London hotels provided dinner-dance facilities, competing for business with nightclubs proper, such as the Embassy in Bond Street, already a favourite haunt of the Prince of Wales. Though the Prince thought the Embassy the 'Buckingham Palace of night clubs', the venue was little more than a luxuriously appointed basement. On a balcony, above the hubbub of diners, was the bandstand. The male clientele wore evening dress, dinner jackets for some, though the 'full soup and fish' of white tie and tails was socially more acceptable. Women now wore their hair short, in styles of which the boyish 'Eton Crop' became the most extreme form.

Other London nightclubs favoured by the Prince included Ciro's in Orange Street, the Grafton Galleries, the Queen's Hall Roof and, perhaps the most exclusive of all (including the Embassy), the Riviera Club, which overlooked the Thames from its elegant rooms in Grosvenor Road.

During the war, clubs of all sorts – authorised or unlawful – had mushroomed in the East End, catering for the hordes of restless young servicemen on leave in Town. Many were simply unlicensed drinking dens or, like 'Ma' Meyrick's notorious '43' in Gerard Street, simply flouted the rules. Some were illegal casinos, some were what would later be called 'clip-joints', and a few catered discreetly for homosexual men, a feared and despised minority which, according to the puritanical weekly *John Bull*, 'should be hunted out of clean and decorous society'. Some clubs tolerated drug use: cocaine was available on the streets, with cannabis (or 'hashish') not yet on the list of prohibited substances. The popular press regularly ran sensational features alleging a drug menace, usually associated with black and Chinese immigrants.

By 1923, London already had a sizeable community of African or Afro-Caribbean origin. The term 'black' at that time was used indiscriminately to embrace virtually anyone with a skin darker than pink. Thus Egyptians, such as Ali Fahmy, were 'coloured' or 'black', as were all Asians in the Indian Empire. The term 'coloured' also embraced Chinese and Japanese. Indeed, almost the entire population south of the Mediterranean and East of Suez was liable to be described in these terms.

Contemporary references to 'black' people in the British press make dismal reading. 'BLACK DEVILS AND WHITE GIRLS' headlined *John Bull* that autumn, alleging that 'coloured men are still lurking in our cities. Living depraved lives on the immoral earnings of the white girls they have lured to their betrayal.' In London, these 'degenerate negroes' lived in the streets around Tottenham Court Road and the eastern end of Shaftesbury Avenue, areas 'honeycombed with black men's . . . nightclubs . . . and thieving lodging houses . . . They run gambling houses, they trade in dope,

185

they spread disease.' This crude racism was not confined to *John Bull*. Other newspaper reports spoke of 'negro haunts of crime . . . hotbeds of evil', adding, for good measure, that an accused black man was 'a member of a jazz band'.

An unmistakably sour note of sexual jealousy can be detected amid the racial stereotyping and reports of 'flashily-dressed, bejewelled negroes', men who – as a shocked *Daily Mail* revealed in September 1923 – were found to be dancing with white women at the ironically named 'British Colonial Club' in Whitfield Street, Soho.

The principal feature of London life in 1923 which distinguished it from the pre-war world was the extraordinary popularity of dancing. 'Bulldog Drummond', the loutish creation of the pulp novelist 'Sapper', could boast that he and a girlfriend had 'jazzed together', but English dance music was performed in homespun ways, betraying the influence of brass and military bands, often far removed from the vitality of the Afro-American rhythms, the true roots of ragtime and jazz.

Tunes were often catchy and robust, but there was a brittleness about popular music at the time. Jerky, staccato foxtrots and one-steps were the most popular dances, though the sentimental waltz (often spelt 'valse') and the sinuous tango provided some relief. The craze of the 'shimmy-shake', which had taken New York by storm in 1919, was now being challenged by the 'blues' or 'blues trot', which first made its appearance in London ballrooms during July 1923, a foxtrot played 'a quarter slower . . . and jazzed up to quaint effect'. The blues proved to be a temporary diversion before the arrival from America of the super-athletic, shin-busting Charleston eighteen months later.

Dancing, in this early post-war period, had become an almost manic phenomenon, resembling medieval displays of mass hysteria, perhaps due to the widespread sense of release after the war's end. Early in July 1923, the *Daily Mail* noted disapprovingly that 'everyone dances on almost every possible occasion. Dancing teas, dancing dinners and dancing suppers . . . succeed each other in a giddy whirl.' *The Observer* reported that 'almost every West End hotel runs a dinner dance and in many cases a tea dance as well'. A 'Harley Street woman specialist' was of the opinion that 'a great deal of evil . . . goes on in the modern dance hall' and a 'psychoanalyst' informed readers of *Lloyd's Sunday News* that consulting rooms 'were filled with dancehall wrecks'. Despite the alleged risks to mental and physical health, the young loved to dance.

One spur to the dancing craze was the coming of radio. The London station of the BBC began regular broadcasts in November 1922 ('2LO calling') from studios in the Strand and the first dance music was transmitted shortly before Christmas. Two months later, the BBC moved to Savoy Hill, a narrow street opposite the Savoy Hotel. The

187

BBC and the hotel shared the same electrical generator and, from April 1923, ordinary 'listeners-in' were able to get a taste of the high life when the Savoy Havana Band began broadcasts that became hugely popular.

A simple overhead microphone was fitted to the ceiling of the hotel ballroom and a BBC announcer (suitably attired in white tie) waited backstage to announce the numbers that had been played, poised to operate a cut-out switch if any of the dancers misbehaved by bawling something undesirable at the microphone. According to one early announcer, it was not shouted obscenities that were feared, but a much graver possibility, stigmatised – in a very British way – as 'the chance of a possible advertisement'.

CHAPTER 10

STOMPIN' AT THE SAVOY

O n the morning of 1 July 1923, the Fahmys took up residence at the Savoy Hotel. With them was Said Enani and also an entourage including the chauffeur and Marguerite's current personal maid, Mlle Aimée Pain (allotted a room on the hotel's eighth floor, sharing accommodation with other guests' servants). Their suite (which cost 9 guineas a day) was on the fourth floor of Savoy Court, luxuriously furnished apartments attached to the hotel, decorated in the pastiche Adam style then popular. As Marguerite and Ali emerged from a lift, they were directed to the door to their suite, number 41, on the opposite side of the corridor, slightly to their right. The hotel understood that 'Prince' Fahmy and his wife intended to remain until the end of July, when the Goodwood Races brought the London Season to a close and Society emigrated to the grouse moors or to Continental resorts such as Deauville and Le Touquet.

Ali had brought his personal valet, the unnamed illiterate Sudanese youth, part of the Egyptian household, who would spend much of his time crouched in the hallway outside his master's door, patiently waiting to be commanded. Marguerite's Paris chauffeur, the handsome Eugéne Barbay, was available to drive the party about London and also responsible for exercising Marguerite's beloved lapdog.

The entrance to the suite was formed by a double set of doors, one of which opened outwards into the main corridor. Inside, a marbled bathroom could be found immediately opposite the entrance, to the left of which lay a short passage leading to the principal bedroom, its doubled bed covered by silk sheets, on which guests sometimes lay 'private embroidered pillows'. This was very much Marguerite's room, as her young husband chose (or was allotted) a second, slightly smaller, bedroom next to the bathroom.

From the suite, looking down on to Savoy Place, there was a fine view of the River Thames, flowing lazily beyond the broad sweep of the Victoria Embankment, busy with cars, taxi cabs, lorries, horses and carts and trams. Eastwards, the elegant but now crumbling Georgian structure of Waterloo Bridge spanned the river, on the other side of which could be seen Waterloo Station, newly rebuilt, and – like a lighthouse that had lost its way and wandered inland – the Shot Tower, a stumpy London landmark of the time.

The Savoy has accommodated the royal, the rich and the famous for well over a century, but – despite the best efforts of its management – has fallen prey to scandal from time to time. Oscar Wilde stayed there in the early 1890s, originally in room number 361, where he entertained a depressing collection of rentboys, hospitality that formed a basis for the prosecution's case against him in 1895. Mata Hari, the exotic dancer and supposed German spy, had visited the Savoy in 1915 and 1916. A more recent embarrassment was the discovery of a woman's body in her apartment in Savoy Court, the block where Marguerite and Ali would later stay. Billie Carleton, aged 22, already a well-known *soubrette* of the theatre, had overdosed on cocaine after a night out at the Victory Ball of November 1918, held at the Albert Hall.

By 1923, the Savoy's autocratic and highly efficient manager, George Reeves-Smith, must have hoped that damaging scandals were in the past. He was to be disappointed by what happened outside suite 41, Savoy Court, in the early hours of 10 July that year.

In addition to the delights of room service, the newly arrived Fahmys – briefly on their best behaviour in a foreign land – had the choice of two world-renowned restaurants within the hotel complex. The lively Savoy Grill (sharp left at the Strand entrance foyer) was crowded with business types at lunchtime, personalities from media and theatre adorning the evening supper tables. The Grill offered its lively clientele no music, but in the Savoy Restaurant, with its panoramic view of the river, a sedate orchestra played 'Hungarian melodies . . . [of] melancholy sweetness for a clientele unkindly described as "a few truly smart people and a crowd of well-dressed . . . nonentities".'

Sparkling or dull as the diners might be, the menu – set out entirely in French, of course – included a four-course *Diner du Jour* on offer at 15/6 (77.5p) (*Vin Blanc par Carafe* 3/6), with the alternative *à la carte*, on which the most expensive item was chicken, suitably dignified as *Poularde de France Dorothy*, which came in at a hefty 30/- (£1.50).

The smart set, after the latest dance music, would make their way along the broad corridor from the restaurant, downstairs to the magnificent ballroom, decorated in a style that cheerfully commingled Louis Quatorze with his great-grandson, Louis Quinze, displaying a wealth of Corinthian capitals and gilded moulding. Here the Savoy Havana Band held sway. BBC broadcasts secured excellent publicity for the hotel and a lucrative recording contract with Columbia, the most prestigious record company of the day.

On their first evening at the Savoy, Ali and Marguerite chose to take dinner in the hotel restaurant, the summer light still affording diners the breadth of views over the river. Later that evening, as on all the nights of her brief stay at the Savoy, Marguerite gently placed under her pillow a .32 semi-automatic Browning pistol, loaded with six bullets.

In London, after a dreary June, 'July made its debut yesterday in half-hearted fashion. For an hour or two in the afternoon, the sun managed to burst through a pall of clouds, but the temperature was below normal, the Kew maximum being 65° . . .' The Fahmys, not expecting too much of an English summer, sought entertainment in theatres and nightclubs. As if in desperation, they went out, accompanied by Said, on every night of their short stay together.

Likely attractions at the theatre included the revue *Brighter London* at the Hippodrome, where Paul Whiteman's Orchestra, led by an amiable 280-lb giant from Denver, Colorado, had been playing to packed houses since April, and George Gershwin's *Stop Flirting?* at the Shaftesbury Theatre, in which London theatregoers could see the young Fred Astaire dance with his sister Adele.

The Fahmys did the rounds of the nightclubs. London Ciro's, in Orange Street, off Leicester Square, was enjoying a record season that year and was a possible venue early in the week. The Fahmys may also have gone to hear Jack Hylton's Band, recording stars since 1922, play at the Queen's Hall Roof, a very popular rendezvous at the side of the famous concert hall where Sir Henry Wood conducted the Proms each summer. There the cabaret included The Trix Sisters and Divina and Charles, who, later that year, earned the peerless accolade 'Banned in Bournemouth', when the local watch committee responded apoplectically to their apache dance, 'Rough Stuff', performed with the help of cracking whips.

On Tuesday 3 July, a letter postmarked Paris arrived for Marguerite at the Savoy. It was written in French and unsigned:

> Please permit a friend who has travelled widely among Orientals and who knows the craftiness of their acts to give you some advice. Don't agree to return to Egypt for any object or even Japan. Rather abandon fortune than risk your life. Money can always be recovered by a good lawyer, but think of your life. A journey means a possible accident, a poison in the flower, a subtle weapon that is neither seen nor heard. Remain in Paris with those who love you and will protect you.

Marguerite excitedly showed it to her husband, who cynically replied that she had probably written it herself. The letter has a distinctly bogus air about it and, if not Marguerite's handiwork, may have derived from one of her circle of friends at home in Paris, perhaps a former lover who knew about the marital breakdown. There may have been a more sinister purpose, with the letter pre-prepared as part of the 'programme' Marguerite had hinted at to a Cairo manicurist and in conversations with Ali's friend, Mahmoud Abul Fath.

Towards the end of the first week in London,

the Fahmys, still together for the moment, went to the exclusive Riviera Club at 129 Grosvenor Road SW, formerly the home of a brother of Lord Derby. The elegant single-storey house, on the site of some old wharves, faced on to the Thames. The former drawing-room, which became the club's ballroom, enjoyed an excellent view of the river, if not quite 'Venetian in its beauty', as the *Referee* would have its readers believe. The Prince of Wales was among those who sometimes made the pilgrimage to Pimlico, an open secret to the press ('a very eminent person indeed is to be seen there very often . . .'). It seems that HRH was not present when the club's patrons were treated to the spectacle of a Fahmy row, in the course of which, as the couple stood in the hall overlooking the Thames, Ali shouted, 'I'm tired of you – I've a good mind to throw you in the river.'

Marguerite did not pay much attention to the threat: two or three nights later, she travelled to an out of town nightspot on the banks of the self-same Thames, The Casino at Molesey. The party included Ali, Said Enani and another Egyptian, Gallini Pasha. On the way, they stopped the car to look at Hampton Court Palace. Here another dispute began, blows were exchanged, and Gallini tried to separate the warring couple.

The Fahmys and their party experienced the novelty of being ferried across to the island on one of the hotel's private punts and this open-air excursion may have been prompted by a change in the weather, the start of a ten-day heatwave. Harold Nicolson, congratulating himself on having written in one day 10,000 words of *Byron*, noted the rapidly increasing heat, soon to become 'boiling hot'.

The Fahmys had made plans to visit the Embassy Club at 6 Old Bond Street, the Prince's favourite nightspot, during the second week of their stay. M. Gelardi of the Savoy had recommended them, as potential members, to the famous 'Luigi', who endeared himself to London's high society by his agreeable manner and strong sense of discretion. Events conspired to prevent what might have been an interesting confrontation between the Prince, his former mistress, and her new – and very jealous – husband.

On Thursday, further upstream at Henley '. . . the morning was overcast, but late in the day the sun came out gloriously, the Americans arrived and the world of fashion seemed assembled on the lawns and in the boats by the riverside . . .' The transatlantic oarsmen were described as 'serious, wide-shouldered young men in low-crowned felt hats and horn spectacles . . . whose accent was a quaint combination of Harvard, Yale, and Oxford or Cambridge'. Those young men either not in training or careless of it might well have slipped up to town that Thursday or Friday, joining the likes of the Fahmys for dancing at the Grafton Galleries or for cabaret at the Metropole Hotel's 'Midnight Follies'.

Friday saw the temperature reach 84°F at Kew and, as usual, London found itself unprepared. '[The] traffic chaos seemed worse than ever, the fumes of the endless motor traffic mingling with the tropic heat . . .' With no air-conditioning to dispel the sweltering atmosphere, London life grew more than usually sticky. Marguerite, already suffering from a very personal complaint, found that her discomfort had acutely increased.

Dr Edward Francis Strathearn Gordon was a physician and surgeon with consulting rooms at 26 Southampton Street, on the north side of the Strand, opposite the Savoy Hotel entrance. In 1923, he had the good fortune to be the hotel's doctor, a post that he held for many years afterwards. He was well liked and a practised exponent of the bedside manner demanded by the Savoy's rich and often temperamental clientele.

Marguerite Fahmy summoned Dr Gordon to see her on Wednesday 4 July. It was an afternoon consultation and Ali kept well out of the way elsewhere in the suite. As might be expected, the doctor spoke excellent French, murmuring sympathetically when Marguerite showed him the bruises on her arms, inflicted during some of the more recent matrimonial barneys. She also gave chapter and verse about Ali's generally disgraceful behaviour. It was unlikely to have been the first time that Dr Gordon had come across this kind of injury, accompanied by complaints about the violent conduct of a husband or lover.

But Marguerite's allegations also included a distinctly uncommon element, intimately connected with a painful condition.

Marguerite had developed external haemorrhoids, which were in an inflamed state, as Dr Gordon could plainly see. He examined her again on each of the next two days, telling Marguerite that if no improvement had occurred by the following Monday, 9 July, the advice of a specialist surgeon should be sought. Haemorrhoids, hardly the most fashionable of complaints, are extremely common, come and go rather unpredictably, and often affect women who have given birth. Earlier that summer, in Paris, Marguerite had undergone ultraviolet ray treatment (a medical fad of the day, administered by a special quartz applicator), but it does not appear to have had the desired effect.

At the Savoy, she alleged to Dr Gordon that her husband had 'torn her by unnatural intercourse'. Marguerite said that Ali was 'always pestering her' for this kind of sex, implying that he was not interested in vaginal penetration. She repeatedly asked Dr Gordon to provide 'a certificate as to her physical condition to negative the suggestion of her husband that she had made up a story'. The document, useful in divorce proceedings, might have also served for the purposes of her more sinister 'programme' against Ali.

Soothing ointments brought a little relief to Marguerite during that very warm weekend. Friday's heat was such that a train was derailed near Lewes because the rails had buckled in the heat, tar melted in the streets and four ladies playing tennis doubles in Burton-on-Trent were suddenly engulfed in hay, the remains of a haystack which had taken off in a summer whirlwind. At Wimbledon, women spectators fainted, but, braving the soaring temperatures, the mighty Suzanne Lenglen careered around the court in a calf-length skirt, walloping Kitty McKane in straight sets, 6–2, 6–2, to win the championship.

On Saturday, Kew recorded a temperature of 89°F. Women brought out the parasols, prettily decorated with Japanese paper, which had stood undisturbed in umbrella stands since the blistering summer of 1921. Combining the dictates of fashion with propriety and comfort was not easy, but much could be achieved with lightweight material. 'Diaphanous dresses' made a rapid appearance and the *Daily Mirror*'s Wimbledon reporter could describe 'the pretty girl in gold gossamer, so to say, whose waist was over the hips and skirt touching the ground'. For men, straw hats and panamas came into their own and one exhibitionist was observed strolling along the Strand in full colonial outfit of 'white duck' suit, canvas shoes and sola topi. At Henley, a fairly conservative occasion, 'a few bolder spirits donned tennis shirts open at the neck'.

Sleep did not come easily on these humid nights. In the roof gardens of Kensington, merrymakers in evening dress stayed up till all hours, regularly sending out for new supplies of ice to cool their drinks. One Clapham resident gave up the attempt to sleep and sat, wearing his pyjamas, in a garden chair until daybreak, drinking iced lemonade. For daytime relief, the British Museum was voted a first for coolness, closely followed by the Victoria and Albert Museum.

Sunday's temperatures were a little lower, at 80°, but blue skies had given way to angry masses of cloud: thunderstorms broke out, two people were killed by lightning in the Midlands, and a fireball exploded in the clock tower of Dunsford Church, near Exeter. There was a brief electrical storm over London in the early hours of Monday, a day that brought no respite, for the temperature rose again to 84°. Not everybody was behaving decorously; fifteen lads, aged between 16 and 19, appeared in court charged with 'wilfully trespassing upon the towpath of Regent's Park canal for the purpose of bathing'. They were an unlucky sample of about a hundred youths who had been seen 'bathing with nothing on and using obscene language . . .' The defendants were each fined 2 shillings and advised to use the public baths.

Milk was often already sour by the time it was delivered: 'it goes bad when you look at it . . .' reported the *Daily Graphic*. That Monday the Oxford v. Cambridge cricket match, a great social occasion, opened at Lord's. 'Summer frocks made a conspicuously cool contrast to the regulation morning dress worn by most men . . .' Dame Clara

Butt (whose Junoesque form towered above her slightly built husband), Mrs Stanley Baldwin, Field-Marshal Lord Plumer and the Duke of Rutland were snapped by the press photographers, as was the Jam of Nawanagar, better known as Ranjitsinhji, legendary cricketer of the 1890s.

The Fahmys took a cooling drive that morning, returning to the Savoy at 1 p.m., in time for lunch in the restaurant with Said Enani. Marguerite's discomfort as she sat at the table did nothing for her temper and the customary quarrel broke out. Probably as a diversionary tactic after promptings by the restaurant's head waiter, the orchestra leader came over to the Fahmys' table, bowed low, and asked politely in French whether Madame would care to select a tune for the band to play.

In an act of pure melodrama, Marguerite looked up demurely and said, 'Thank you very much. My husband is going to kill me in twenty-four hours and I am not very anxious for music.' The conductor replied, 'I hope you will be here tomorrow, Madame,' a model of hotel diplomacy. Marguerite told Ali, 'I'm going to leave you and you'll pay dearly for it.' Her husband, for once, responded half-heartedly and went up to his room for a nap after lunch.

At 3.30, Dr Gordon arrived at suite 41, accompanied by Mr Ivor Back, a consultant surgeon: after a brief examination, Mr Back recommended an operation. Marguerite agreed and Dr Gordon telephoned a London nursing home there and then, arranging for Marguerite to be admitted the next day, to have the necessary minor surgery on the Wednesday. Marguerite asked Mr Back if he would provide her with a certificate as to her physical condition, but it seems that the surgeon politely demurred, just as Dr Gordon had done.

After the consultation was over, Marguerite, with a sudden perversity, decided to use the operation as a pretext to return to Paris. After ordering train tickets for herself and her maid, she took Said Enani with her on a shopping trip to Selfridges, where she bought some new clothes for the trip. They returned for tea at about 5 p.m., after which Marguerite calmly kept an appointment with the hotel's hairdresser.

Shortly before 8 p.m. that evening, the trio met up in the Fahmys' suite, the men in full evening dress (tailcoat, white tie, starched white shirtfront and waistcoat), Marguerite wearing a white satin evening dress, embroidered with small pearls, designed for her by 'Coco' Chanel, now the star of Paris *haute couture*, at a cost of 8,000 francs. On an oddly still, humid evening, they were chauffeured to Daly's Theatre, which then stood in Coventry Street, just off the north-east corner of Leicester Square. At 8.15, the curtain rose on a musical comedy which turned out, with hindsight, to have been a grimly humorous choice. It was *The Merry Widow*.

This was a popular revival of Lehár's operetta, starring pert Evelyn Laye (a day short of her twenty-third birthday) and handsome Carl Brisson. Even on a Monday night, the house would have been well attended as the three took their seats in the box reserved for them by the ever-efficient Said. The first duet, titled 'A Dutiful Wife', was soon followed by 'Maxim's', a celebration of Parisian nightlife, which must have been a pointed reminder to the couple of the city in which their relationship, now so bitter, had begun only a year before.

In the warm, sticky atmosphere of the crowded theatre, Marguerite would very likely have shuffled uncomfortably on the plush upholstery of her gilt chair. The first act lasted about three-quarters of an hour and her irritability surfaced in the first interval. Ali told her how much he wanted her to remain in London, but Marguerite angrily insisted that her mind was made up and that she was going back the next day. She probably asked Said to send a telegram at once to Paris, notifying friends of her impending arrival. The telegram was dispatched 'at nine p.m. on the evening of July 9th'.

Not to be outdone and with the tit-for-tat attitude characteristic of the Fahmy marriage, Ali immediately ordered three telegrams of his own to be sent to Paris. It seems that the faithful Said either telephoned his employers' instructions to the Savoy or hurried down to the West Strand telegraph office, which was open twenty-four hours a day. Ali's cables were each timed at 9.10 p.m.

and contained an identical message, which reveals that relations between the couple were now near to breaking point.

The wording was English and read: 'NOTHING TO BE DELIVERED TO MY WIFE ON MY ACCOUNT DURING MY ABSENCE. FAHMY.' The addresses were Cartier of the rue de la Paix, Van Cleef & Arpels of 22 place Vendôme, and Louis Vuitton of 70 avenue des Champs Élysées. The first two firms held substantial quantities of jewellery on Ali's behalf, worth in all around £5,000. Vuitton was holding a gold-fitted handbag, valued at 162,000 francs (£2,025), and the company had recently been commissioned to prepare a similar bag, bearing Marguerite's monogram, at an estimated cost of 157,000 francs (£1,962). It appears that this latter item had been ordered just before Ali's trip to Stuttgart in June. While he was away, Marguerite had called at Vuitton, saying that she wanted it there and then. On being told that it would take another fortnight to complete, Marguerite appeared very annoyed and left the shop.

The last two acts of *The Merry Widow* are set in Paris, a fact that did nothing to calm the growing tension between husband and wife. As they left Daly's, towards 11 p.m., the distant growling of thunder could be heard above the noise of homeward-bound theatregoers. Over in Mayfair, one of the Season's great dances was well under way at the home of the Hon. Rupert and Mrs

Beckett at 34 Grosvenor Street, a fine Georgian town house sadly marred by heavy Edwardian embellishments. The considerable Beckett fortune derived from 'trade', interests in the Westminster Bank and ownership of the *Yorkshire Post*, but Mrs Beckett was closely related to the Marquess of Anglesey and socially ambitious. The Becketts' youngest daughter, Pamela, had been noted in the past by gossip columnists as dancing with the Prince, but she seems to have had emotional problems. In October 1921, then aged 18, Pamela (who had just 'come out' as a debutante) abruptly disappeared from her Mayfair home and was 'lost' for two days before being discovered by police wandering aimlessly in the distinctly unfashionable north London suburb of Cuffley, near Potters Bar.

The glittering styles and titles of Muriel's dinner guests duly reflected her social aims. The Prince, of course, was Guest of Honour, joined by the Duke of Sutherland, the Duke of Portland, Lord 'Fatty' Cavan, Prince Obolensky, Lord Crewe, Ettie, Lady Desborough, Lord Revelstoke, Lord Alington, Lord Romilly, and Sir Robert Horne, former Chancellor of the Exchequer. Fredie Dudley Ward was there (her name discreetly tucked away in the middle of the guest list) and the presence of Michael Herbert no doubt disturbed the jealous Prince, despite a supporting team of Godfrey Thomas and Joey Legh. Pamela Beckett, happily restored to the bosom of her family, joined the thirty or so diners, whose ranks were supplemented after dinner by a gaggle of other luminaries, including Marquess and Marchioness Curzon, Prince Paul of Serbia, the Earl of Lonsdale, and an assortment of de Traffords, Granards, and Lytelltons. Also present, but not yet worthy of mention in the printed record, was the American *arriviste*, witty diarist and mega-snob, Henry 'Chips' Channon. Years later, using curious phraseology, 'Chips' recalled that stormy night in 1923 when 'I, the Prince of Wales, and Prince Paul were dancing at Muriel Beckett's ball'.

Once back at the Savoy, Ali's patience snapped during a late supper and a loud argument broke out, worse even than the contretemps at lunch, causing heads to turn at this strictly unofficial cabaret, now a twice-daily performance. Ali roundly told Marguerite that as his legal wife she should not go to Paris on her own. He wanted her to have her operation in London so that they could spend the remainder of the Season in England. Marguerite maintained that she was going to Paris the next day, whereupon the argument degenerated, as so often before, into mutual vituperation. Eventually, Marguerite picked up a wine bottle from the table, shouting in French, 'You shut up or I'll smash this over your head.' 'If you do,' replied Ali, 'I'll do the same to you.'

No doubt to the relief of the restaurant's staff, the Fahmys and the ubiquitous Said then went down to the ballroom, where the Savoy Havana Band was entertaining hotel residents and guests.

Without doubt, the band would have played (probably several times) 'Yes! We Have No Bananas', the smash hit of the moment. This utterly banal tune, whose lyric crudely mocked fumbling attempts at English by an immigrant Greek greengrocer in New York, was an enormous success. Why this should have been so remains a mystery, but by mid-July 1923 sheet-music sales were running at the rate of 37,000 a day. The song was recorded by five British bands between July and September and was a regular feature of dance-music broadcasts until well into the following year. Queen Mary took the trouble to learn the words and, duetting with Lady Airlie, cheerfully sang 'Yes! We Have No Bananas' at the top of their voices for the 'joy of shocking' a stuffy member of the Royal Household.

More discriminating dancers might prefer Gershwin's 'I'll Build a Stairway to Paradise', the bouncy 'Toot-Toot-Tootsie, Goodbye', or, in more reflective vein, 'Three o'clock in the Morning', a slow waltz of enduring popularity. Unfamiliar today, but featured in the summer of 1923, were 'Dancing Honeymoon', 'I Ain't Nobody's Baby', 'Oh Star of Eve' and, perhaps most forgettable of all, 'Oogie oogie Wah Wah'.

A tense and gloomy threesome sat on their white and gold lyre-backed chairs at one of the numerous tables in the ballroom. Ali tried to defuse the situation by asking Marguerite to dance, expressing the vain hope that they could make things up, but she curtly refused. Although she had refused to dance with Ali, she later took the floor with Said. He tried to persuade her to be reasonable and stay on in London. 'Nothing doing!' came the determined response.

Shortly before 1 a.m., Marguerite announced that she was going to bed. Said escorted her to the lift and returned to Ali for a brief heart-to-heart. Ali seemed very depressed, concerned that, with Marguerite going back to Paris alone, the marriage was finished. The two men went back to the foyer, from where it was evident that a tremendous thunderstorm was raging outside. When it rains, taxis become a rarity in London and almost an extinct species during a thunderstorm, but the Savoy is a powerful magnet and, even on this wild night, there were one or two cabs hopefully waiting under the entrance canopy. Said Enani went to bed immediately after his chat with Ali, but his younger master had other ideas. He was seen by hotel staff, still wearing formal evening dress, standing for a short time in the entrance lobby at 1 a.m., before the Savoy's doorman ushered him into a cab, whose driver was instructed to take Ali in the direction of Piccadilly.

While Ali was away, Marguerite was putting pen to paper. She was writing to Dr Gordon, as yet unaware that his patient had decided not to go into the London nursing home after all. As the translation reveals, Marguerite was now being a little less than frank about the substance of the disagreement with her husband:

Gerard 4343 *lundi soir*
Savoy Hotel, London WC2

Docteur

Les événements ce sont precipités et mon mari refuse de prendre la responsibilité de mon opération. Je dois donc regagner ma famille, c'est à dire demain je pars pour Paris. Veuillez m'excuser au pres du Docteur qui avait bien voulu me donner ses soins et croyez Docteur

à mes sentiments reconnaissants.

M. Fahmy

P.S. Veuillez Docteur avoir l'aimabilité de donner au Docteur pour son derangement le compte m'est personelle et ancien

Le Docteur Gordon, 26 Southampton Street, Strand WC2

[Doctor

Affairs have come to a crisis. My husband refused to take the responsibility for my operation. I am therefore returning to my family. That is to say, tomorrow I leave for Paris.

Will you excuse me to the doctor who was kind enough to look after me and, believe me, yours gratefully, M. Fahmy.

P.S. Will you please pay the doctor for his trouble? This account is a personal one.]

If she was implying that Ali had refused to pay for the operation in London, Marguerite was not telling the truth. While he may have been reluctant to have his wife treated in Paris, away from him, the evidence suggests that he would have been only too pleased for Marguerite to be operated on in London. Marguerite, of course, had to give some excuse to Dr Gordon for her perverse conduct. She enclosed a cheque for £15. Marguerite also penned a polite note to her friend the Maharajah of Kapurthala, apologising for not being able to accept his invitation to dinner the following night.

Shortly after 2 a.m., with almost continuous thunder and brilliant flashes of lightning all around, Ali returned to the Savoy and went up to their suite. Soon another violent argument broke out between husband and wife, while Ali's black valet crouched in the corridor outside the door, waiting to be discharged from service for the night.

Half an hour later, John Paul Beattie, night porter at the hotel, was taking some luggage to another suite on the fourth floor of Savoy Court, apparently for some late arrivals that stormy morning. As he came out of the lift, almost opposite the Fahmys' suite, the door suddenly opened and Ali, wearing a brightly coloured dressing-gown over a white silk *djellaba*, came rushing out, closely followed by Marguerite, still in the white satin evening dress she had worn to the theatre. Marguerite's little dog ran about yapping noisily.

'Look at my face,' cried Ali excitedly to the astonished Beattie. 'Look what she's done.' Ali pointed to his left cheek, on which could be seen a slight red mark, and also a mark near his right eye. Marguerite interjected in rapid French, which Beattie did not understand, gesturing towards her face, but he could see no sign of any injury.

'Please get back into your room,' asked Beattie, mindful of other guests, despite the storm, 'and don't kick up a disturbance in the corridor.' By now, Marguerite was trying to pull Ali back into the suite, but he was in no mood to return, insisting that Beattie should send for the night manager, Arthur Marini.

There were two adjacent lifts on the fourth floor and, as one was descending, Beattie was able to attract the attention of the lift attendant, who was told to pass the message on while the porter continued with his work, wheeling his luggage round the corner, a sharp left turn, then along another short stretch of corridor (with the door to suite 42 and, beyond it, the emergency stairs), and round to the left again on his way to number 50.

As he rounded the second corner, Beattie heard a low whistle and, looking back, saw Ali Fahmy stooping down outside the door of suite 42, apparently whistling to Marguerite's lapdog, which had been following Beattie along the passageway. The porter continued on his way, but after going only about 3 yards, he heard, above the roar of thunder, the unmistakable sound of three shots, fired in rapid succession.

He ran back in the direction in which he had come and, as he rounded the corner of the short corridor, saw Marguerite throw down a large, black handgun and stumble towards him. On the floor, just by the door to number 42, some 24 feet away from his own suite, and with his head towards the direction of the stairs, lay Ali, on his right side, crumpled against the wall. He was unconscious, breathing stertorously, and bleeding profusely from a head wound from which protruded fragments of brain tissue and splintered bone. Alongside him lay a pool of blood in the corridor, about 5 feet from the door of number 42.

Beattie pushed past Marguerite, who was shouting hysterically in French, picked up the pistol, and put it in one of the two adjacent lifts. Marguerite made as if to follow him, but he caught hold of her arms and led her towards the stairs, where there was a service telephone. Keeping hold of Marguerite with one hand, Beattie told the hotel telephonist to send for a doctor and ambulance. Amid the flood of voluble French, Beattie recognised the English word 'cloak' and took her back to suite 41 so that she could get her wrap.

Arthur Marini was in the night service room when he received a message from the hotel reception that he was urgently wanted at suite 41. Thinking that he was being called in to calm yet another Fahmy altercation, he hurried up the stairs to the fourth floor, where he was horrified to find Ali, terribly injured, lying just to the night manager's left as he emerged from the staircase. Turning the corner of the corridor, he saw Beattie leading Marguerite out from number 41. 'Go and telephone the police at Bow Street,' said Marini crisply, 'and tell the general manager to come here at once.'

Marguerite had some explaining to do.

CHAPTER 11

FEMME FATALE

Crying out in French, over and over again, 'What shall I do? I've shot him', Marguerite clutched desperately at Marini's sleeve as he tried to persuade her to return to the drawing-room of the suite. Gelardi, the general manager, was slow to get to the scene, but his two assistants, Clement Bich and Michael Dreyfus, soon arrived. Dreyfus, in his room at the hotel, unable to sleep because of the heat and the thunder, had himself heard the loud, arguing voices, then three shots. Not able to tell where the sounds had come from, he had taken the lift down to reception: the liftman, warned by Beattie, already knew that there had been trouble outside suite 41. Dreyfus, after giving instructions to the reception staff, ran up to the fourth floor in time to find Marguerite, bending over Ali's body, holding his head and repeating '*Q'est-ce que j'ai fait, mon cher?*' ('What have I done, my dear?')

Beattie was ordered to bathe Ali's face in cold water, upon which it became clear that he was gravely wounded both in the head and in the nape of his neck. Marguerite, grabbing at Clement

Bich's arms, again said, 'What have I done?' Bich replied, 'You know that better than I do,' at which Marguerite raised her hands to her face, saying desperately, '*J'avais perdu ma tête. J'ai lui tire.*' ('I lost my head. I've shot him.') After she had been escorted back into the suite by Marini, Marguerite kept asking to go back into the corridor, but she was prevented from returning to Ali's stricken body. Instead, Marini agreed to telephone Said's room. Said, already in bed, was alarmed to hear a strange man's voice saying an urgent 'hello, hello', seconds before the receiver was seized by Marguerite, who shouted excitedly, '*Venez vite, venez vite. J'ai tire à Ali.*' ('Come quickly. I've shot Ali.')

'We were quarrelling over the divorce,' she unwisely told Marini, before suddenly asking, 'Where is my revolver?' As if in a daze, she hunted through the drawers of the wardrobe and looked under the pillow, saying, 'I kept it there always, as I am so frightened of him.' Her composure was now beginning to return. Marguerite changed out of her evening gown into a jade-green blouse and skirt (bought specially for her return to Paris), put on some lipstick and tidied her hair, and awaited the arrival of the police.

At the Savoy, 'cases of death . . . were . . . hushed up [and] bodies . . . removed surreptitiously'. Ali, his face covered, was being taken away on a stretcher as Said arrived panting outside suite 41, out of breath after running, almost falling, down four flights of stairs. A bystander idiotically told him, 'Everything's all right.' At the same time, Sergeant George Hall, hot foot from Bow Street, was marshalling the gathering in the fourth floor corridor, a small crowd that would have included a number of bemused and horrified guests. Dr Gordon, too, was soon on the scene, where he was surprised to find Fahmy's Nubian valet still waiting, crouched outside the door of the suite. Nobody paid the slightest attention to the silent youth, of whom Ali had once said, 'He is nothing.'

Gordon found Marguerite to be 'excited and dismayed . . .' He recalled that she kept exclaiming, 'Oh, what have I done?', but was evidently not completely out of her wits. She handed her doctor the letter in which earlier that fateful morning she had written of her intention to leave London for Paris. Marguerite was very eager, at this crucial early stage, to get across the story that Ali had refused to allow her to have the operation in London. Marguerite was going to keep her head, whatever happened.

Ali Fahmy had been removed from the Savoy in an LCC ambulance, as discreetly as circumstances permitted. At 2.55 a.m., still clinically alive, the dying man was seen by Dr Maurice Newfield, the house physician in the casualty department of Charing Cross Hospital, which then stood 200 yards from the Savoy, in King William Street. Dr Newfield would have realised at once that there was little to be done for Ali, unconscious and still bleeding profusely, brain tissue bulging from the wound in his left temple. Bandages were applied,

216

and blankets and a hot water bottle put round him, but Ali died at 3.25 that morning.

Fifteen minutes later, Marguerite arrived at Bow Street police station by taxi, escorted by Sergeant Hall and Dr Gordon. At Bow Street, the matron, Mrs Greenwood, had been sheltering in the inspector's office, fearful to remain alone in the matron's room during the storm. If Marguerite had been a male prisoner, she would undoubtedly have been incarcerated in one of the evil-smelling cells, lined with glazed brick and devoid of adequate sanitary facilities, which lay beyond the custody area and its 'No Spitting' notice.

Marguerite was more fortunate. She and the matron huddled in a corner of the inspector's office, while Dr Gordon, later to be a vital witness at Marguerite's trial, played the role of detective and tried to find out what had happened. Marguerite was anxious to show her doctor a fresh scratch on her neck which, she claimed, had been inflicted by Ali. In her bedroom, she said, he had approached her 'in a threatening manner'. Marguerite had snatched up her pistol, fired a shot out of the window, hoping to frighten him, and, thinking that the gun was now unloaded, pointed it at her husband and pulled the trigger 'several times', after which Ali fell to the ground. At first, she thought he was shamming. When she realised she had shot him, she said, 'I then gave the alarm by telephone.'

For someone who had undergone a shocking experience, Marguerite was able to give Dr Gordon a surprisingly coherent account of her side of the story, a version, not yet complete, that would later form the germ of her defence. And she needed a good lawyer. Dr Gordon, well versed in the ways of the rich in trouble, suggested that Marguerite should instruct Freke Palmer as her solicitor as soon as possible. At that time, Palmer probably had the largest and certainly the most fashionable criminal practice in London. Luckily for Marguerite, money was no problem, as Palmer's services did not come cheaply. Palmer was no altruist and the Poor Prisoners' Aid Scheme held little attraction for him. His long experience extended back to the 1880s and he had worked on innumerable murder cases with the leading criminal barristers of his time.

Shortly before 4 a.m., Dr Gordon broke the news to Marguerite that her young husband had died. She wept. The doctor then wrote out a two-page statement (on the approved police form no. 992) in a fastidious but attractive hand, amazingly legible for a medical man. As the thunder began to die down, Marguerite dozed for a while in her corner of the inspector's office, until the change of shift at 6 a.m. brought an inevitable disturbance and the offer of a welcome cup of tea. Dr Gordon, who had left the station after writing his statement, probably telephoned the solicitor at his home, before snatching an hour or two's sleep. Freke Palmer was instructed to begin the arduous process of establishing a defence to the capital charge of murder.

By this time, the exceptionally violent weather, which had convulsed southern England for over twelve hours, was almost over. From late the previous afternoon, there had been a series of isolated electrical storms in Surrey and Sussex. At Croydon Aerodrome, an Instone Air Liner from Cologne and a big twin-engine Rolls-Royce Handley Page just managed to land before a thundery squall struck at 7.15 p.m., but soon the really severe storm began to sweep over the Channel from northern France, reaching the coast at about 9 p.m.

Between midnight and 1 a.m., the 'stupendous thunderstorm' reported the next day by the *Star* was at its first great intensity over central London. There was almost continuous lightning and even the most solid buildings vibrated with the thunder. The storm ebbed slightly for a while, before rising to another climax between 4.30 and 5 p.m. In the six hours from midnight, 2.57 inches of rain – the entire average rainfall for July – was recorded in Hampstead, in north London.

'Last night was awful,' recorded Jean, Lady Hamilton, in her diary, 'it seemed as though the world really was smashing up . . . the thunder never stopped for four or five hours . . . the sheet lightning was continuous . . . and the horrible fascinating forked lightning . . .'

During the downpour, at about 2.30 a.m., a woman was found by police in Parliament Square, screaming hysterically in her nightdress, as MPs attempted, with varying degrees of success, to get back to their homes. Viscount Curzon (a distant cousin of the Marquess, later known as the racing driver, Earl Howe) was reported as having bravely 'jumped into his swift little 2-seater and careered out of the gates as if it were a lovely moonlight morning', while less adventurous MPs bedded down in the corridors of Westminster, and four representatives of the people were later found asleep in their cars.

Some 3,000 telephone lines were put out of action, and wireless reception suffered severely. 'Broadcatching [sic] in the London area was badly interfered with by atmospheric disturbance . . .' This, at any rate, had the merit of preventing listeners from hearing John Henry, an early radio 'comedian', with lugubrious Yorkshire voice, who seems to have been both very clean and consistently unfunny. Although the newspaper pointed out that 'properly made aerials act as lightning conductors providing they are earthed', a wireless set exploded at Thames Ditton and in nearby Walton a worse fate befell Mr Justice Russell, whose country house was completely burnt out.

The Times reported 'one of the most remarkable and spectacular [thunderstorms] seen in London for many years . . . a journey through the streets of London between 1.00 and 5.00 a.m. was a thrilling experience'; to the *Daily Mail*, it was 'the greatest thunderstorm by far in this country that living man can remember'. And at the Star & Garter Home in Richmond, many of the resident ex-servicemen, still traumatised by the horrors of the trenches, were reported to have been severely disturbed by the noise of thunder and the brilliant flashes of lightning, cruel reminders of the Great War.

The charge was not administered until mid-morning. Superintendent Parker of Special Branch (whose responsibilities included royal protection issues) was now in overall charge of the investigation. Acting under his authority, Divisional Detective Inspector (DDI) Alfred Grosse had first gone to the mortuary at Charing Cross Hospital, where he viewed the body of Ali Fahmy at about 5 a.m., before examining the scene of the shooting at the Savoy.

The method of collecting of forensic material in this case was distinctly odd from the outset, which suggests that someone in a position of authority had already told Superintendent Parker and DDI Grosse, to 'go easy' on the process.

In the first place, although a handwritten record was made of the bloodstained area, the management of the Savoy Hotel should not have been allowed to clean up the scene of the shooting by ordering the night porter to wash down the corridor and remove bloodstains from the carpet. That early mistake may have resulted simply from the inexperience of the first police officer on the scene, PS Hall, but the failure to take photographs was the responsibility of senior Yard officers.

Although Ali had to be taken to hospital, there was ample opportunity for photographs to be taken of the corridor and rooms in the suite as they were when first seen by investigating officers. Photography of a crime scene was feasible at that date (examples can be found in official files on other high-profile English murder cases, such as that of David Greenwood in 1918 and Norman Thorne in 1925). Photographs could have been of great value to the prosecution. Furthermore, no photographs were taken by the police of Ali's body, showing the position of injuries, although, for example, Leon Beron's body had been photographed for use in the Stinie Morrison case of 1911.

The police search of the scene was perfunctory from the start. After PS Hall had arrived on the scene, Beattie went to the luggage lift where he had placed the pistol and – presumably without gloves – was allowed to handle the gun for a second time. Beattie also handed over the three empty cartridge cases he had found scattered on the floor outside the Fahmys' suite. He also recovered two spent bullets from the area adjacent to the nearest stairwell, the wooden bannisters of which had been damaged by a shot or shots. This was work that should have been carried out by police.

Extraordinarily, it was not until the next day that a chambermaid found another cartridge case in Marguerite's bedroom. Over a week later, on 18 July, a hotel valet discovered the third of the three bullets that Marguerite had fired at her husband. The missing bullet was lying underneath a grating over a radiator opposite the stairs to the fourth floor and had obviously been missed by the police. Grosse was an experienced officer, who had investigated several important murder cases. His failure to conduct a thorough examination of the scene of the crime is astonishing and quite out of character.

There were ricochet marks on the wall to the left of the door to suite 42, as well as on a set of folding doors immediately to the right of the stairs. Bloodstains could be seen on the carpet in the corridor. After their position had been noted (but not, it seems, photographed), Beattie, by night the hotel's jack-of-all-trades, was ordered to clean them away. His duties were by no means over: he had to wait until 6 a.m. to make his first statement to the police.

In Marguerite's bedroom, Grosse took possession of the white Chanel evening dress, which Marguerite had been wearing when Ali was shot: there was some blood on the hem and beside the bed in Ali's room DDI Grosse found a number of crushed beads (or small pearls) which matched those sewn on the dress.

When Grosse returned to Bow Street and first saw Marguerite at 7 a.m., it was merely to order her removal to the matron's room, above the cells, and to ensure that the prisoner had a cup of coffee. Not until two hours later did the legal formalities begin. Accompanied by Detective Sergeant Stewart Allen, who acted as interpreter, Grosse introduced himself. The bald statement, 'I am a Detective Inspector', was rather beautifully rendered in

French as '*Je suis le chef inspecteur de la Sûreté ici*'. Grosse, a dapper, clean-shaven man, who sported a bow tie under his wing collar, told Marguerite that she would be charged with Ali's murder and cautioned her in customary fashion: 'Anything you say will be taken down in writing and may be used in evidence.'

The Metropolitan Police files record the following statement. Marguerite was quite calm by now:

> *Je dis au Police que je le fais. J'ai dit la vérité. Ce ne va rien. Il m'a battue devant tout le monde depuis nous avions été mariés. Il m'a dit plusiers fois, 'me tué', et il y a des personnes qui l'ont entendu.*

> [I told the police that I did it. I have told the truth. It doesn't matter. He has assaulted me in front of many people since we have been married. He has told me many times, 'kill me', and many people have heard him say so.]

A police telegram was dispatched at 9.40 a.m. formally informing the Metropolitan Police Commissioner and his senior staff of Ali's death by shooting and of his wife's arrest. In contrast to modern practice, in which lengthy interviews are the norm, Marguerite was not interrogated at any stage by police officers. When she was charged, at 11 a.m., Marguerite replied simply, '*Je comprends.*

Je comprends. Je perd la tête.' ('I understand . . . I lost my head.')

Sometime after noon, Marguerite's fingerprints were taken by an officer who thought her 'a perfect little doll'. Her personal details were recorded, including two beauty spots, one on each cheek. Shortly afterwards, Aimée Pain, Marguerite's personal maid, arrived from the Savoy. She probably brought her mistress scent, soap and towels and took instructions concerning the jewellery that madame would wear at her first appearance in court that afternoon. Marguerite also had the opportunity to speak to her maid about other matters. Aimée had already made her statement to the police, but Marguerite was anxious to talk to her about events on the night of the shooting. 'Madame Fahmy' was beginning to marshal her forces.

After lunch, Freke Palmer walked into the matron's room with his managing clerk, Collins. Because of his busy professional schedule and with the clout that comes from regular appearances as an advocate, Freke Palmer had persuaded the police, who controlled the list of cases of Bow Street Court, to put Marguerite's appearance at the end of the afternoon, so as to give time for preliminary instructions to be obtained.

The storm and the Savoy shooting had both occurred too late to be included in the daily press, but the first 'evening' newspapers (which started publishing around midday) were carrying the sensational story in their 'STOP PRESS' columns.

225

Already a small crowd was gathering outside Bow Street Court, which forms part of a building also housing the police station, in the hope of securing a place in the limited accommodation available in Number Two Court, on the first floor of the court-house, up a flight of stone steps and along a narrow corridor.

'Bow Street' always had, despite the best efforts of its cleaning staff, a smell of 'old lag' about it and on that broiling July afternoon the heat in the court, which had a glass roof, must have been intense, creating a particularly unpleasant atmos-phere. The small dock, with its iron railings, stood a few feet from the door to the custody area, through which, at about 3.30, Marguerite made her entrance, looking pale and tired, escorted by Police Sergeant Claydon of the 'Woman Patrols' (who had relieved the matron two hours before). Necks craned forward to see her, and reporters' pencils scribbled away.

Despite the difficult circumstances, Marguerite had taken some care over her appearance. She was now a widow and the green silk blouse she had put on at the Savoy would have seemed a little too jaunty for so grave a charge as murder. Aimée had access to madame's wardrobe at the hotel and so, despite the intense heat, Marguerite entered court wearing a long, satin 'charmeuse' coat, suit-ably black. The softly draped coat, comparatively lightweight, had a smooth, semi-lustrous finish and was trimmed with fur at the neck, sleeves and hem. She wore a small mushroom-shaped black felt hat, around which lay a lightly patterned strip of silk.

Most eyes, however, were riveted on Marguerite's jewellery, which she could not resist displaying, despite the pressing need for a sober look. Large, pearl-drop earrings matched a plain, but elegant, pearl necklace. Above her gold wedding band, she wore 'a big square marquise diamond ring' and on the third finger of her right hand, an even larger emerald, 'set in quaint oriental style'. On her left wrist she wore a magnificent three-tier diamond and sapphire bracelet, set in turquoise, probably one that Ali had torn off and thrown at her in the lobby of the Majestic in Paris a fortnight before.

Though these were hardly widow's weeds, the press responded sympathetically to this wan, petite form, 'typically Gallic, [whose] pallor emphasised dark marks under the large and impressive eyes . . .' Those compelling eyes were seen to fill with tears during the brief hearing and from time to time she would dab them dry with a large, green silk handkerchief.

DDI Grosse told of the arrest and gave a short description of the scene of the incident to the Stipendiary Magistrate, Rollo Graham-Campbell, who agreed to Freke Palmer's request that his client should not be transported to Holloway Prison in a van, like the common run of prisoners, but rather in the comfort of a taxi cab.

More details about the Savoy Hotel were now

appearing in the newspapers and the *Evening Standard*, *Evening News*, *Star*, and *Pall Mall Gazette* were splashing news of the night's events on billboards. Front pages highlighted references to the French nationality and Parisian origins of the woman who had shot her Egyptian 'Prince'.

The storm had not cleared the air. That day, even hotter than its predecessor, was the date of a large evening party thrown by the Prince of Wales at St James's Palace, entertaining 'the most beautiful debutantes of the Season, men of distinction in politics and diplomacy', prominent industrialists, and a bevy of Society matrons, including 'the Duchess of Northumberland, the Countess of Birkenhead and Mrs Baldwin'.

A dinner for 'fifty to sixty' personal friends began at 8.15 p.m., followed by a large reception in the Banqueting Hall. Princess Mary 'in glittering white', acting as hostess for the bachelor Prince, had the unenviable task of shaking her gloved hands with some 800 guests, whose names were sonorously announced by Bruce Ogilvie, the Prince's junior equerry. Coping as best they could with the sweltering night, the company could admire the banks of red and white flowers on display, while the subdued roar of conversation largely drowned music played by the accompanying Band of the Welsh Guards.

The Prince felt ill at ease at such formal gatherings, where tailcoats and decorations were *de rigueur* for the men, but that night, for whatever reason, he was able to disguise his feelings, 'played the part of host with a charm which robbed the party of all stiffness and formality' and 'looked so alert, so genuinely happy in himself'.

On 11 June, the 'yellow press' (a contemporary term for modern-day 'tabloids' and 'redtops') went to town, with front-page headlines in the *Daily Mail, Daily Express, Daily News, Daily Chronicle, Daily Sketch* and *Daily Graphic*. More conservative newspapers, such as *The Times, Daily Telegraph* and *Morning Post*, carried the news in measured reportage, adding various layers of information to the bald facts of the shooting.

By this date in 1923, York House at St James's Palace was staffed by a 'handpicked team', comprising the private secretaries, Godfrey Thomas and Tommy Lascelles, together with equerries Joey Legh and the Hon. Bruce Ogilvy (who had replaced 'The Lord Claud' in 1921), with other personnel of military experience, Rear Admiral Halsey, sometimes called 'The Old Salt', and Brigadier-General Gerald 'G' Trotter', a one-armed veteran of the South African War with a taste for late-night entertainment. The team seem to have worked reasonably well together, although the appointment of an 'outsider' the previous year had introduced a measure of disharmony.

The newcomer was Captain Edward 'Fruity' Metcalfe, 'one of the Indian Army ADC's the Prince [had] retained to look after his horses'. Metcalfe, whose influence on the Prince has been noted earlier in this book, was a professional soldier, son of an official in the Irish prison service, and not quite out of the same stable in terms of social background as the 'handpicked team', who were also dismayed by his easy familiarity with the Prince. Metcalfe was 'very nice and irresponsible', in the opinion of Godfrey Thomas, 'a wild, wild Irishman', according to Admiral Halsey.

The few people 'in the know' about the Prince's liaison with Marguerite had something very important to talk about that evening. Joey Legh had met Marguerite on several occasions in Paris during the war and may have picked up the unwelcome news from early press reports. Thomas and Lascelles, too, must have been well aware of their master's fateful wartime liaison. Special Branch, with a pre-existing file on Marguerite and possibly with knowledge of her movements, might have tipped off York House soon after the Savoy Hotel incident. By whatever means, the Prince, his secretaries, 'Fruity' and all, would have become aware during that Tuesday of the identity of the young woman described as a 'Princess' in a welter of lurid press reports.

All of the Prince's team, including even the *blasé* Metcalfe, are known to have been 'terribly afraid' of what might come out at a murder trial. The priority, beyond doubt, was secrecy – at almost any cost. The fewer who knew about the Prince's *mésalliance* with Marguerite, the better would be the outcome. The wartime letters had to be recovered and Marguerite stopped from revealing the affair. The Prince's people must have been concerned from the outset to know what Marguerite would accept in return for handing over the letters and remaining silent. She had, as they well knew, already threatened blackmail in 1918.

The fear was stark. Backed up by the evidence of the letters, Marguerite could easily make the Prince an object of ridicule, contempt, perhaps even hatred in Britain and abroad, by revealing stories of partying in Paris and Deauville, jollies in his Rolls-Royce, a luxurious existence enjoyed in chateaux and high-class *maisons de rendezvous* safely behind the lines, while men were being blown away in their tens of thousands on the Western Front. There was a real risk too that Marguerite might simply sell the letters abroad (in the USA, for example), causing enormous damage to the credibility of the British monarchy.

Circumstances dictated that Thomas, assisted by Lascelles, should take prime responsibility for dealing with the acute problem presented by Marguerite. The Private Secretary and his Assistant were by far the most intellectually able members of the Prince's personal staff. As will be seen later, their personal correspondence indicates a close involvement in protecting the good name of the Prince throughout the 1920s. Their first response to the challenge seems to have been made with commendable speed.

'It is fortunate that he [the Prince] is off to

Canada,' later wrote the Foreign Secretary, Marquess Curzon. Although *The Times* had reported in early July that the Prince would visit towns in both Wales and England during mid-October, his engagement programme was abruptly altered on 11 July, just one day after the shooting. The good burghers of Aberystwyth and Winchester would now have to wait rather longer to salute their Prince. Given the urgent circumstances, this unexpected announcement cannot be seen as coincidence. The Prince would now be travelling to Canada for some six weeks, leaving in early September, ostensibly to visit his ranch near Calgary in Alberta, his return scheduled for 21 October. With suitably deferential hyperbole, the news was declared to be of 'exceptional interest' by *The Times*, apparently unaware of the real reason behind the sudden change of plan.

Quite apart from official inside information, the earliest press reports showed that Marguerite, whatever her defence might be, would have a case to answer. A trial would have to take place, probably at the Old Bailey. It is not difficult to see why the Royal Household should have wanted to ensure that the Prince was away from England during so sensitive a period. Sir Archibald Bodkin, the Director of Public Prosecutions, was the man to ask about trials, dates and judges. At that time, the DPP's office was in Richmond Terrace, Whitehall, no great distance from St James's Palace, but a confidential meeting might just as easily have taken place over lunch or dinner in a London club.

Tommy Lascelles, for example, was a member of the Travellers' Club (and two other West End clubs, the Beefsteak and Pratt's). He frequently lunched at the Travellers', on occasion sitting near the Prime Minister, Stanley Baldwin. 'The PM is sitting exactly 3 feet from my pen,' Lascelles confided to his wife later that year. Bodkin, exemplifying the close connection between advocacy and the acting profession, belonged to the Garrick Club in Garrick Street, near Covent Garden. These clubs, with a carefully selected upper- and upper-middle-class male membership, were ideal places to meet and converse, often in subdued voices in a quiet corner of one of the club rooms (perhaps in a 'morning room' or a 'smoking room' equipped with comfortable leather armchairs) about confidential matters of the day.

Marguerite's arrest posed some awkward questions for the Prince's people. In the circumstances, it is most likely that one or other of the private secretaries approached the DPP within hours of the shooting, asking for essential information to help keep the Prince's name out of the media. As DPP, Bodkin cut a hard-working, possibly obsessive, figure. 'He took an active part in the direction of enquiries prior to trial and on occasion prior to arrest . . .' Bodkin was also willing to advise 'any government department' (read this to include the Royal Household) on matters arising from the conduct of criminal prosecutions. This being the case, Bodkin was an ideal recipient for sensitive information involving the heir to the throne.

The Prince's secretaries needed to know when any resulting murder trial would be held. Bodkin, aware of the Old Bailey calendar, fixed well in advance, would have had no difficulty in responding that the trial would take place at the next session, starting on 10 September 1923. At this time, trials rarely lasted longer than a week. There was a risk that a jury might disagree on its verdict, with the prospect of a re-trial, but this was unusual and could be accommodated if the Prince were to be away for as long as six weeks. Armed with this information from the DPP, the Royal Household could safely announce that the Prince would visit his ranch in Alberta during September and October.

The High Court judge already assigned to that session was the recently appointed Sir Rigby Swift KC, which was an excellent stroke of luck for the Royal Household, for reasons that will be made clear in due course. The DPP would have been appraised of the background to the case by either Thomas or Lascelles, emphasising the importance of absolute secrecy. At all costs, the Prince's name must not be 'dragged in' to the proceedings. At this very early stage, of course, there was a rogue element. Its name was Marguerite.

CHAPTER 12

WHAT THE 'YELLOW PRESS' SAID

The *Daily Mirror*'s headline of 11 July 1923, 'A PRINCE SHOT IN LONDON', was typical of its contemporaries, accompanied by a report that seized eagerly on the two exotic birds of paradise who had so suddenly found violent notoriety. At first, the references were generally sympathetic to both parties, the affair being seen as a domestic tragedy between two foreigners, a *crime passionnel* worthy of a novel by Zola. For example, the *Sunday Express* referred to 'the painful sensation in those social and Bohemian circles where the "Prince" and his beautiful French wife were very vivid and decorative personalities . . .'

In some early reports, Ali Fahmy was depicted as an ardent young lover, dashingly handsome, regarded by his contemporaries, according to the *Daily Express*, 'with affection, commingled with amusement created by his extravagance . . . His charming manners, happy smile and immaculate appearance placed him in the forefront of Cairo's gaieties, spending lavishly for his own and other people's pleasure . . .' The *Daily Sketch* printed a long article, almost certainly based on an interview with Said Enani ('one who has been the Prince's constant companion for the past five years'), which gave some reasonably correct background material and was headed 'WELL-BELOVED BY ALL HIS PEOPLE'.

Inaccuracies abounded. The *Daily Chronicle* reported that Marguerite was 'a descendant of a noble Turkish family of Alexandria'; according to the *Sunday Illustrated*, she was from 'a good family . . . born just on thirty years ago in the south of France . . . lapped in luxury from earliest hours'. To the *Daily Mirror*, mindful of the year's Tut-Ankh-Amun discoveries, Ali had been a member of 'one of the oldest Egyptian families', a misstatement which paled in comparison with the *People*'s inventive streak, demonstrated on the first Sunday after the shooting. Ali, it declared, had been in London some months ago, helping to revive an ancient Egyptian dance, a visit at which 'a private, but most allegorical [sic], ceremony was performed to celebrate a festival called Amun Toonh (established . . . in 1403 BC . . . to celebrate the goddess of the Sun, Ta Aha) . . . [and] carried on with many mystic movements'.

But there were less favourable references to Ali, a trend to which eventually the entire English press succumbed. The *Daily Mail* was one of the earliest to make use of the 'oily Levantine' approach: 'He was a notorious spendthrift and, being ignorant and vain, had long been the victim of a crowd of

236

sycophants . . . He was very fond of jewellery . . . his glittering diamonds used to attract attention at the [Paris] Opera House . . .' *Lloyd's Sunday News* accused Ali of 'voluptuousness truly Eastern . . . every form of excitement that could appeal to a sensuous nature . . . notorious for the lavish expenditure he incurred in entertaining stage stars of both sexes [in] Paris . . .' This flashy, effeminate foreigner had not so easily impressed the English upper classes as he had their gullible French counterparts: 'From time to time, he was received in good London society, but his vulgarity and extravagant habits caused him to be dropped . . . [He] next drifted into the night clubs and dancing resorts, wearing . . . conspicuous jewellery . . . naturally, he was blackmailed heavily.'

The *Illustrated Sunday Herald* splashed a denunciation of Fahmy across half a page, using information that can only have come from someone close to Marguerite. Headed 'SECRET LIFE OF BOY "PRINCE"', it contrasted 'the beautiful and the bestial . . .' Readers were left in no doubt who was beautiful and who was bestial. Marguerite was the 'radiantly beautiful wife', who, before the ill-fated marriage, had 'flitted from capital to capital . . . carrying off in the gay whirlwind of her life a legion of untiring admirers . . .' Although the article hinted at Marguerite's background ('. . . her smart frocks were discussed; her horses and motor-cars were the envy of the grand cocottes . . .'), the fire was reserved for Ali, 'madly jealous', who, 'when she asked him for fidelity . . . pursued the trend of his own devices . . .' Marguerite's alleged imprisonment in the *dahabeeyah* at Luxor became marvellously garbled: 'On one occasion, when Maggie had again gone out at night in Cairo, the Prince had her abducted by his dusky slaves and carried to his yacht . . .'

One vital aspect of the story was missing from this wealth of reportage: any mention of the involvement between Marguerite and the Prince of Wales.

CHAPTER 13

'HORRIBLE ACCUSATIONS'

By coincidence, 'Ali Fahmy Kamel' happened to be the name of a prominent Egyptian nationalist, not in good odour with the British authorities. Exiled in Paris, Kamel hurriedly telegraphed home to contradict the rumour that he had been the victim of the Savoy Hotel shooting. On the other hand, 'Prince Ali Kamel Fahmy' had worked as Press Attaché at the French Legation in Cairo. The British were as suspicious of French political activity in Egypt as they were fearful of the ever-stronger Egyptian nationalist movement. An example of British official attitudes arose that year, when an Egyptian civil servant in the Cairo Ministry of Education had the temerity to propose that French should be placed on an equal footing with English in Egyptian schools, also recommending a French company's scheme to take Egyptian students round France at low cost. To the British, this was all 'part of the usual policy of intellectual propaganda . . . the real object . . . is intended to encourage young Egyptians to acquire a knowledge of . . . French life and ways of thought'.

Immediately after the shooting, Scotland Yard's Special Branch, with its interest in royal protection, was in the frame. A senior officer's minute in the Metropolitan Police file, dated 13 July 1923, ordered that Grosse's original ten-page police report be sent to 'H[ome] O[ffice] for F[oreign] O[ffice]', adding '[Superintendent] E [Division] to see attached papers from Special Branch. I understand that – as we expected – the wife is making horrible accusations against the husband.' These words give a clue to the content of the Special Branch file, which has since gone missing, and suggest that Marguerite had made 'horrible accusations' on an earlier occasion, this time against the Prince. The 'stinker', sent by Marguerite to the Prince in late October 1918, may have contained some extremely unpleasant allegations.

Postal communications between Marguerite and the outside world were immediately put under official surveillance and the prison governor, aware of the public furore surrounding the case, had acted swiftly. 'She sent out two letters last Saturday [14 July],' he told the head of Special Branch, also emphasising the lack of francophones at Holloway by adding 'as these were in a foreign language they were sent to H[ome] O[ffice]'.

Major-General Sir Borlase Elward Wyndham Childs was Assistant Commissioner of the Metropolitan Police and head of Special Branch. Familiarly known as 'Fido', Childs had spent part of the war in a mysterious role as 'Director of

Personal Services'. On 16 July, a peremptory message was telephoned to the prison governor: 'Sir Wyndham Childs . . . wishes you to supply him with the names and addresses of all persons who have visited Marie Marguerite Fahmy . . . and the names and addresses of all persons to whom she has written and who have written to her . . . He also wishes to see all letters written by her and sent to her from this date.'

'I quite understand,' the governor replied soothingly to a highly unusual request. This was a catch-all demand, open to legal challenge had it become known, as it would have included confidential and legally privileged written communications between Marguerite and her solicitor, Freke Palmer.

Marguerite had no complaints about her reception at Holloway. After arriving by taxi from Bow Street Police Court late on the afternoon of 10 July, she was taken immediately to the hospital wing, well away from the common run of women prisoners.

She undressed for the compulsory 'mental and physical' examination, carried out by the prison doctor, Dr Morton, who had many interviews with her during the period of remand. Marguerite, he reported, was kept under 'continuous mental observation' during her period of remand. Morton had taken care to read the court depositions before making his final report to the DPP, Sir Archibald Bodkin, and his findings were manifestly sympathetic to Marguerite.

She was thought to be 'depressed, dazed and sleepless' on admission to Holloway and would suffer 'recurring attacks', relapsing into a similar state. Initially, 'she took very little interest in her surroundings' and 'it was with difficulty that she was persuaded to eat'. Apart from an arthritic knee, the result of an accident, she felt in good health. Morton noticed that she seemed 'anaemic and weak'. On examination, she was found to have 'a large thrombosed pile and a fissure'. According to Marguerite, this had been caused by 'unnatural sexual intercourse early in June of this year'. Dr Morton thought that this 'might have been caused' by such activity.

Marguerite took the opportunity on first examination to point out the small injury to her neck, which, she said, Ali Fahmy had inflicted on her shortly before the shooting. Once the other formalities of admission had been completed, she was put to bed with a sedative, sleeping soundly until eight the following morning.

She awoke to find five other female inmates sharing the dormitory. 'I saw a nurse sitting at the end of my bed,' she recalled, 'She looked young and pretty under her white cap.' The 'nurse' was a prison officer and very well disposed towards the new arrival. 'Better this morning, Fahmy?' she asked, taking Marguerite's hand.

Marguerite's broad experience of life helped her to get on well with her fellow remand prisoners. 'The other women were mostly there for drunkenness,' she observed, 'or for having tried to commit suicide, which is not, I think, a crime in France.' In the next bed was a young girl of 18 who had killed her baby (English law on infanticide was not reformed until 1929). She knew a few words of French and Marguerite was able to communicate with her in an Anglo-French patois.

As would be the case at trial, the language barrier was an advantage that Marguerite could exploit. Although wardresses would have been present during conversations with visitors, it is unlikely that any of them spoke French or, if they did, well enough to understand what was being said.

Though Marguerite had presented as 'depressed, dazed and listless' to Dr Morton, she quickly recovered her equilibrium, keen to secure her patrimony. Her spirits were boosted by the first of a series of visits by the faithful Major Bald, beginning the process of negotiation with the Royal Household described later in this book.

The first shots of Marguerite's defence came at the inquest on Ali, held at Westminster Coroner's Court, Horseferry Road, on Wednesday 12 July. Public interest in the case was already enormous and, despite a sweltering heat that approached 90°, a crowd had started to form outside the little courthouse at 12.30, an hour and a half before the proceedings were due to begin. 'The house windows looking on to the mortuary,' reported the *Pall Mall Gazette*, 'were crowded with eager spectators.'

The Coroner bore a strange name and possessed an even stranger personality. After just eleven years', mainly prosecution, practice at the Bar, Stephen Ingleby Oddie had been appointed Westminster Coroner in 1912. He accepted the offer of this gloomy post with wild enthusiasm. 'I trod on air!', he later recalled.Some of his personal prejudices also verged on the eccentric: 'The ordinary Englishman, he believed, did not have a taste for homicide and disliiked guns always preferring a simple fist fight. He does not in a quarrel suddenly produce a pistol . . . as is the common practice of certain other nationalities . . .'

Marguerite, of course, was a woman of a certain other nationality who, on any reading, had suddenly produced a pistol during a quarrel and shot her husband dead. Wisely, she did not attend the inquest. Freke Palmer correctly advised his client that she would do herself no good by giving evidence and she remained in Holloway Prison, comfortably accommodated in the hospital wing, well away from less savoury inmates, while her solicitor did battle on her behalf.

In Marguerite's absence, the proceedings were little more than a formality, but there was the chance for her lawyer to put questions to the small band of witnesses and Freke Palmer was anxious to sow some seeds in the public mind. Reporters crammed into the tiny courtroom to hear Said Enani confronted by allegations of Ali's misconduct, with an occasional glimpse of humour:

PALMER: Did he call her in front of other
people a prostitute?
ENANI: Yes, they used to exchange names.
PALMER: They exchanged compliments?
ENANI: Yes, she called him a pig.

There was much talk of threats and punch-ups
('they used to exchange hidings,' said Enani, with
an incautious smile), before Palmer made some
veiled, but potentially explosive, suggestions of
homosexuality:

PALMER: Did she complain about you and
her husband?
ENANI: No.
PALMER: Did she complain that he would
go up to your room and spend an hour
with you before he returned to her?
ENANI: Yes . . .
PALMER: Was not one of the complaints
she made that he used to spend the day
going out with men of a very bad
character?
ENANI: Yes, but he never did.

It was a loyal response, but Marguerite's solicitor
went on to suggest that there had been something
'improper' between Said and Ali. He was beginning
to forge a dubious link between these innuendos
and Dr Gordon's evidence that Marguerite had
been suffering from 'external haemorrhoids', a fact

which, even in those prudish days, some newspapers reported in full. When his turn came to put questions, Freke Palmer homed in, eliciting from the doctor that 'Madame's complaint was extremely painful . . . [she said] her husband was the cause of it . . .'

In his summing up, the Coroner expressed disgust. 'It was,' he said, 'a sordid, unsavoury and unpleasant story of married life . . .' In the absence of the person accused, 'it would not be proper for a verdict to be returned in this court of anything less than murder'. The jury took their cue and, without retiring, declared a verdict of 'Wilful Murder' against Marie Marguerite Fahmy.

On Thursday 15 July, the temperature peaked at 92°. People were still dancing, despite the heat, according to a correspondent in the *Daily Mirror*, which also reported the sad fate of a van driver, found lying beside his horse and van in Kensington. At the West London Hospital, his body temperature was found to be 109°. The unfortunate man had been stripped, bled and put into an ice bath, where a fire hose was placed on him, but he died, still registering 102°. In similar vein, the *Sunday Times* recorded an inquest on a fish-fryer. Thomas Collard had been out of work for three years before getting the job. A week later he collapsed while working during the heatwave. On admission to St Andrew's Hospital, Bow, his temperature was 107°. Medical opinion was that the man had died of sunstroke. His employer disagreed. Death, he thought, was due to the shock of getting work. The steam and heat did not affect the boss. 'Indeed', he added, 'I have got fat on it.'

An umbrella spontaneously burst into flames in Barrowgate Road, Chiswick. Sixteen deaths were reported by the *Daily Mail* in the first week of hot weather, during which *The Times* had solemnly warned its female readers, 'wise women are buying Harris tweeds for the winter'. Two MPs defied convention and attended the House in shantung suits, but they were to have little opportunity of wearing them. *The Times* had been right. On Monday 16 July, temperatures plummeted, the heavens opened, and 1923's summer was all but over. In pouring rain, Folkestone Town Council asserted the Englishman's right to be miserable by voting 6–4 to ban Sunday dancing. 'Praise God from Whom all Blessings flow', sang the crowd of rejoicing, but bedraggled, Wesleyan and Baptist demonstrators outside the town hall.

That Monday, 'a woman of a very ordinary type' walked into 70 avenue des Champs-Élysées in Paris, the premises of Louis Vuitton et Cie. The woman was Yvonne Alibert, who calmly asked for the two gold-fitted handbags (together worth nearly £4,000) 'as they were the property of sister'. Mindful of Ali's telegram and the shooting (which had been featured in the French press), as well as possible legal complications with the Fahmy family, Vuitton refused to hand over the goods (Marguerite, it will be remembered, had tried to get hold of one of the handbags in June). It looks as if Yvonne was acting on instructions from Marguerite, who was by no means isolated in prison. She could receive visitors, including her maid, Aimée Pain, who may have contacted Yvonne on Marguerite's behalf.

Remand prisoners at this time had the liberty to correspond by letter or by telegram. Though her correspondence was subject to scrutiny and her visitors monitored, Marguerite was able to keep in touch with her friends and advisers in Egypt, as well as on both sides of the Channel. And sometimes she would contact an enemy. A large portrait photograph of Marguerite, discreetly veiled, taken at the 'World Swiss Photo-Studio Cairo', dated 1923, seems to have been sent by Marguerite to Ali's sister, Mme Said after the killing. In Marguerite's hand, a patently insincere endorsement reads '*à Madame Said en toute sympathie. Mounira*' ('to Madame Said with every sympathy. Mounira').

In the meantime, on 18 July, Marguerite had made her second appearance at Bow Street court. The air in Court Number Two was still as frowsty as ever, but slightly more bearable than it had been in the heat of the previous Tuesday. Shortly after midday, Marguerite again entered the crowded courtroom, now very much the grieving widow. Wearing no jewellery and dressed in a black crêpe-de-Chine 'coat frock', she pressed a dark fur to her face, the upper part of which was also obscured by a black waxed straw hat. More fashion-conscious reporters noted that she had cream silk stockings and high-heeled black patent-leather shoes. The *Daily Graphic* was not the only newspaper to take on board the image of 'a frail figure . . . [in] deep mourning . . .'

Marguerite's sister, Yvonne, now safely back from Paris, wept quietly, another Frenchwoman murmured '*Bonne chance*', and an interpreter was sworn in to translate Said Enani's evidence, given for a second time and, as at the coroner's court, laboriously noted down in a longhand deposition. As Said told the now familiar story of marital disharmony, 'tears rolled down [Marguerite's] cheeks and fell on to her hands clasped in her lap'. Beattie's evidence of the happenings that stormy morning caused 'Madame Fahmy's sobs to burst out anew . . . she buried her face in her arms . . .', petulantly shrugging off the hand of a wardress, who had tried to give her prisoner a consoling pat on the arm. From time to time, it was said, Marguerite would look vacantly at the witness-box as the evidence was being given, heaving a long sigh.

Much the same pattern occurred at the adjourned hearing on Saturday morning, 21 July, when Dr Gordon gave his testimony. As he came to Marguerite's allegations about her husband's sexual behaviour ('certain complaints which she attributed to her husband's practices'), this increasingly important element in Marguerite's defence was duly emphasised. She slumped forward on the wooden bench of the dock, covered her face with her fur, and sobbed convulsively. At intervals, a woman prison officer handed her a bottle of smelling salts. At the end of the hearing, Marguerite, apparently in a state of collapse, had to be helped from the dock by two wardresses.

Marguerite was committed to stand her trial at the Old Bailey, where her case would receive the formal judicial title 'R v. Marie Marguerite Fahmy'. The 'R' stood for 'Rex', for all prosecution on indictment was in the name of the King. The fate of this Frenchwoman, former mistress of the King's eldest son, would be decided by a judge and jury, the bedrock of the English legal system, which – in theory – was immune to outside influence.

CHAPTER 14

NOBLE ROT

Although they were going to have to deal with the crisis provoked by Marguerite by killing her husband, both Thomas and Lascelles were relatively young (in their mid-thirties) and would have sought advice from the most senior royal counsellors, those closest to the King. 'Just at the end of the Mall loomed the Olympian figures of Lord Stamfordham . . . and his assistant Clive Wigram.' Stamfordham and Wigram, military men, were both eminent Victorians of a very different stamp from Thomas and Lascelles. Some nine years earlier, as we shall see, Stamfordham had skilfully protected the reputation of another member of the Royal Family, in circumstances that had some similarity to the problems faced by Thomas and Lascelles.

Lord Stamfordham, as Sir Arthur Bigge, had been appointed Private Secretary to George V in 1910. Son of a Nothumberland vicar, his social background was relatively modest, but redeemed by a good showing as an officer in the Royal Artillery. Stamfordham served as Private Secretary to Queen Victoria in the last years of her reign and, by 1923, had spent many years in royal service. A small, neat man, Stamfordham was notable for his 'rasping voice, old-fashioned courtesy and an irrepressible penchant for sporting metaphors'. Reactionary in many of his attitudes, 'a very strong Tory', he nevertheless could exhibit a measure of practical good sense. After the inconclusive election of late 1923 and facing the prospect of the first-ever Labour government, Stamfordham wisely conceded, that Labour ought to have a fair chance when in office.

Wigram, 'tall, handsome and athletic', came from the family of an Indian civil servant. After Winchester came service as an officer in the Indian Army. Wigram has been described as 'sporty and down-to-earth' with the 'chauvinistic views typical of many army officers'.

Neither man could be accused of being intellectual, but in 1915 Stamfordham's cunning had prevented another royal scandal involving love letters and attempted blackmail from becoming public. His experience would prove helpful in dealing with the new challenges facing the Royal Household.

The scandal that Stamfordham had so expertly spiked related to some thirty incautious love letters written by an earlier Prince of Wales, the Prince's grandfather (Edward VII), to Daisy, later Countess of Warwick, his mistress during the late 1880s and early 1890s, celebrated as 'one of the most beautiful and interesting women of the age'.

In the first years of the twentieth century, the Royal Household seems to have been morbidly concerned with destroying private correspondence to avoid damaging revelations. Much of Queen Victoria's private diary has been consigned to the flames and, in accordance with the will of Edward VII, a 'vast number' of his unsorted papers, including many personal letters, were burned by Regy Esher, who assisted Lord Knollys (Edward's Private Secretary) in the dismal task. During 1913, an extraordinary act of vandalism took place after George V ordered 'the destruction of a mass of material relating to George IV', held in the Royal Archives.

By 1914, the extravagant Daisy Warwick was desperately short of money and was on the verge of bankruptcy. Her financial embarrassment was, of course, relative. 'When she inveigled eloquently against the evils of capitalism at drawing room meetings and Fabian conferences she was conscious of a comfortable feeling that the system, with all its inequalities and iniquities, would probably last her time.' Daisy was still able to travel, luxuriously accommodating herself as befitted the wife of an English peer, but she needed serious money to maintain her lifestyle.

While in Paris, she met Frank Harris, the seedy journalist and dubious friend of Oscar Wilde, now best known for the claims of sexual prowess set out in his autobiography *My Life and Loves*. Harris, then an undischarged bankrupt who had fled to

France to avoid his own creditors, assured Daisy that her memoirs, if sold in America, could earn an enormous sum of money. This was a typical instance of absurd exaggeration by Harris, but Daisy was impressed by his glib patter. Years before, Max Beerbohm took a shrewder view of the man, writing in the wake of the Oscar Wilde trial, 'Frank Harris is going about as a howling cad seeking whom he may blackmail.'

Word reached the Royal Household that the letters might soon be on the market. Stamfordham was shown some of the letters and considered them to be 'very bad', particularly the references to Queen Alexandra when Princess of Wales. King George V, naturally anxious to protect his mother from ridicule, commanded his Private Secretary to resolve the matter without publicity.

One of Daisy's chief creditors was Arthur du Cros, an Irish businessman and MP, founder of the Dunlop Rubber Company. A social climber, du Cros was anxious to present himself as a loyal servant of the Crown. Stamfordham wisely had no intention of negotiating directly with Daisy at this stage. On the other hand, du Cros was in regular touch with her and, also in contact with Stamfordham, acted for a time as a useful go-between, unconnected with any legal manoeuvring.

Unknown to Daisy, Harris and du Cross however, Stamfordham is said to have employed private detectives to shadow the parties.'

Buoyed up by Harris's blarney, Daisy fired off

an ultimatum to the Royal Household, threatening to sell the letters in America. In the end, the strongest weapon in the royal armoury proved to be the law of copyright. Though the letters were the property of Daisy Warwick, the copyright was vested in King George V as heir and successor of his father, who was the author. A secret interlocutory injunction was obtained by the Royal Household in July 1914, prohibiting Daisy for the time being from parting with or showing the letters, but she disobeyed and was suspected of renewing her attempts to sell them.

Stamfordham contemplated an application to commit Daisy to prison for contempt of court, but realised that this could end in disaster, with an appeal and the possibility of the whole affair becoming public. In 1915, he consulted the Prime Minister. H. H. Asquith, evidently rather amused by all the fuss, dubbed Stamfordham 'the Impeccable' and 'the Sinless One' in a private letter written to his confidante, Venetia Stanley. Nevertheless, Asquith appreciated why Stamfordham was so worried about the letters and was aware of the considerable disquiet felt in the Royal Household. Stamfordham was deeply concerned that the letters would reveal 'corruption around the court . . . precipitating a constitutional crisis'.

Fearing that Harris had taken some of the letters to America, Stamfordham at last decided to approach Daisy directly. She was questioned by Stamfordham and the then royal solicitor, Charles Russell, at her home, Easton Lodge in Warwickshire. Afterwards, showing ruthless determination on the part of the Royal Household, a watch was put on Daisy's movements and her mail was intercepted'.

In July 1915, at a further hearing on the application for an injunction, the matter was finally resolved (after private negotiations between legal representatives) by an undertaking by Daisy's solicitor that the letters should be destroyed. A large proportion of Daisy's debts was paid off by du Cros. He was knighted the following year.

Stamfordham had succeeded in preventing the name of an earlier Prince of Wales from being dragged into a major scandal arising from failure to observe the hoary adage, 'Do right to every man. Don't write to any woman.' Although the present problem facing the Royal Household bore some similarity to the Warwick case, major differences in factual background ruled out many of the options available to Stamfordham in 1914–15. The scene was set for a highly sophisticated cover-up, orchestrated by the talents of Godfrey Thomas and Tommy Lascelles, already veterans in the thankless task of clearing up after the Prince of Wales.

CHAPTER 15

CONSPIRACY

Smart plotters do not leave a paper trail and criminal agreements are not, as a rule, written down in neatly typed paragraphs to be signed, sealed and delivered. For fear of prosecution, such compacts are best not physically recorded at all. The Gunpowder Plot was exposed by an incautious letter. In the 1920s (long before shredding and deleted emails) an open fire or a stove was the conspirator's best friend.

Finding out what has been carefully concealed by clever people is challenging. A holistic approach is the best (perhaps the only) way to get an idea of what was agreed, when it was agreed, and by whom. Assessment must begin with careful consideration of direct factual evidence, drawing reasonable inferences where necessary. In unravelling conspiracies, the most valuable assistance frequently comes from circumstantial evidence. 'Circumstantial evidence is very often the best. It is evidence of surrounding circumstances which, by undesigned co-incidence, is capable of proving a proposition . . .'

In this story, all these elements taken in the round disclose a wealth of coincidence, undesigned or otherwise. This shows that the Establishment, in the form of the Royal Household, the Director of Public Prosecutions and the trial judge, agreed to do whatever was necessary to preserve the reputation of the Prince of Wales, even if this meant interfering with due process of law.

Available evidence points to a compact made between the Royal Household and Marguerite, which involved the return of the letters (possibly in exchange for money), associated with an undertaking that Marguerite's full character would never be revealed to the jury. There would be no reference to the Prince's affair with Marguerite and his name would be kept out of the trial. For these vital purposes, the Royal Household colluded with the Director of Public Prosecutions and the trial judge. Arguably, this created a conspiracy to pervert the course of justice.

Inevitably, York House in St James's Palace lay at the epicentre of the conspiracy. Although the successful suppression of scandal in the Warwick case was in the relatively recent past, present circumstances posed new dangers. Marguerite, though physically within the jurisdiction of the English courts, was a French national, resident in Egypt. Copyright in the letters belonged to the Prince of Wales, but seeking to restrain Marguerite from publishing or selling the letters by English court injunction was pointless, even dangerous. Stamfordham's tactics had succeeded in 1915, but this was during the first year of the war, when media attention was focused elsewhere. On that occasion, he had succeeded in preventing virtually all documentary evidence of the proceedings from reaching the public domain, but there was no guarantee that Thomas would be able to do the same in changed circumstances.

Eight years after the Warwick case and in peacetime, the woman in question had been charged with the capital offence of murder, with every indication of a sensational trial to come. Irrespective of any revelations about the Prince, Marguerite's predicament was going to be the focus of intense media interest. Even modern 'super injunctions', giving anonymity to applicants and ordering the suppression of evidential detail, do not always prevent the ultimate exposure of wrongdoing by celebrities. In 1923, before these legal developments, a civil court process running in tandem with preparations for Marguerite's murder trial would have been too risky and was not a credible option.

Marguerite, legally represented at Bow Street Police Court on the morning of the murder, had the benefit of independent legal advice at an early stage. She might want to make reference to the Prince during her evidence, perhaps with a view to gaining sympathy with the jury or to enhance her character in some way. Marguerite might blurt out anything. She was a loose cannon, as Thomas and Lascelles must have known.

One bonus point for the Royal Household was

that Marguerite had been remanded in custody awaiting trial (in those days, bail was not granted to defendants charged with murder). Although she could still make mischief for the Prince by communicating with associates in France and elsewhere, the Royal Household at least knew where she lived – in Holloway Prison, very much her fixed abode for the next month or so.

How, then, to communicate with Marguerite? How 'to square this case', how to 'get all these letters back', as the Prince had written so desperately in 1918? Although, in the Warwick case, Asquith agreed with 'the Impeccable' that 'it is a golden rule never to traffic or parley with blackmailers', the problem posed by Marguerite demanded a more devious approach, consistent with Godfrey Thomas's training in the Foreign Office. The Royal Household benefited from the contribution of two young courtiers, well versed in the ways of the post-war world. Thomas, steeped in Foreign Office methods, knew the value of secrecy and disinformation. Lascelles, his sharp intellect superbly focused on the job in hand, was a worthy assistant.

With secrecy as the watchword, there was a distinct downside in trying to negotiate with Freke Palmer, Marguerite's solicitor. Marguerite's instructions to Freke Palmer were, of course, privileged and confidential. In the first days after the shoooting, Thomas would have had no idea what Marguerite had said or might be saying to her solicitor, but if she had not yet talked about the letters and revealed her relationship with the Prince, there was no point in spreading knowledge of the affair wider than it had already gone.

Furthermore, attempts by a third party to persuade Freke Palmer into advising his client to stay silent on particular matters could be construed by a prickly lawyer as an attempt to interfere with the course of justice. Even if Freke Palmer had been aware of what was at stake, a canny advocate might not relish the prospect of being drawn into a matter oblique to the defence of his client, who faced the capital charge of murder, which on its particular facts was unconnected with the predicament facing the Royal Household.

From Marguerite's point of view, she would need to be careful what she communicated to her English solicitor (although recommended by the trusted Dr Gordon), at least during the first days after the shooting. Freke Palmer was something of an unknown quantity. She had not had any dealings with him before. Her trusted Egyptian lawyer, Maître Assouad, was far away in Cairo. If she wanted to bargain with the letters, to make use of that sensitive collateral to help her walk free from the Old Bailey, it might be better to negotiate with the authorities via a third party. All in all, bringing Marguerite's English solicitor into the equation was to nobody's advantage.

Given the upper-class backgrounds and attitudes of Thomas and, especially, of Lascelles (with that barely concealed hatred of his old school, Marlborough), there may have been another factor at work militating against contact with this particular solicitor in the sensitive matters of Marguerite, her evidence, and the Prince's letters.

Frederick Freke Palmer, then 62, was born in India, the son of an army officer. Although Freke Palmer was related to several 'county' families and a baronetcy lurked somewhere in his family tree, Lascelles would have marked him down at once as middle class and not entirely sound. The younger son of a gentleman might practise as a barrister, but the profession of solicitor was another matter. Royal solicitors, chosen for their utter respectability and rarefied clientele, might constitute an exception, but attorneys who practised in the rough and tumble of the lower courts were a suspect race.

Freke Palmer had a fashionable practice and was lauded as 'an expert divorce practitioner', 'a sound lawyer' and 'brilliant advocate' in the Police Courts (as today's Magistrates' Courts were then known). He was said to have been 'scrupulously fair and honest with his clients, rich or poor, wise or foolish, and often did wonders for them'. Regarded as shrewd and as a 'smart lawyer', he had made a name as solicitor-advocate in some sensational, and very sordid cases involving prostitution and 'White Slavery'. A well-read man, Freke Palmer owned a large library and his collection of Chinese porcelain would have sent Queen Mary into raptures. No matter, it seems. Freke Palmer was a 'hands-on' solicitor (and had been educated at Marlborough . . .).

No evidence has been found to show that Freke Palmer took any part in negotiations that led to the return of the letters and in securing Marguerite's guarantee of silence about her liaison with the Prince. On the basis that for various reasons (including his unsatisfactory professional and social background) Freke Palmer was not deemed a suitable repository for royal confidences, there had to be another means of finding out Marguerite's intentions. In the Warwick case, Stamfordham had used Arthur du Cros as a go-between ahead of launching legal proceedings against Daisy.

Given the facts of Freke Palmer's position and considerations of legal etiquette, there was no question of the Royal solicitor attempting to negotiate with Marguerite unilaterally, in the absence of her defence lawyer. Furthermore, one vital lesson learned from the Daisy Warwick affair was the paramount importance of strict secrecy. Stamfordham, an old military man, had shown himself adept at devious manoeuvring in securing this aim, making use of a 'neutral' go-between to sound out available options, reducing the risk not only of loose contact but of loose talk.

The choice of someone wholly unconnected with actual or potential legal process was essential. In that patriarchal age, such an intermediary would be male. The man would have to know Marguerite very well. He would have to be trusted by her. He would have to be reasonably intelligent. He would have to speak fluent French. Above all, he would have to be a trustworthy keeper of royal secrets. And, with considerations of class omnipresent, he would have to be one of the Breed.

Major Ernest Herbert Campbell Bald MC, late 15th Hussars, would be the man.

CHAPTER 16

THE GO-BETWEEN

T his galloping major had already enjoyed a colourful life. Ernest Bald was born in 1872, third son of John Bald, a whisky magnate, originally from Alloa in the central belt of Scotland. Ernest grew up in a household with a large cohort of servants, including a butler, footmen, hallboys, several resident maids, and a governess. Although the family background was in trade, young Master Bald would receive a first-class gentleman's education. At 13, after his father had taken a lease of the historic Monzie Castle in Perthshire, Ernest was sent to Eton. Here he had a distinguished sporting career, rowing in the College Eight, playing for the 1st XI at cricket and taking a leading role in the incomprehensible 'Wall Game'. A popular figure, he was elected a member of the self-elected Eton Society ('Pop') in 1890. One good friend from Eton days was George Cornwallis-West, second husband of Lady Randolph Churchill (the couple first met at Warwick Castle during a weekend party hosted by Daisy, Duchess of Warwick).

After Sandhurst, Ernest Bald was commissioned

into the 15th Hussars, a fashionable cavalry regiment, and promoted to captain in 1899 shortly before the start of the Boer War. In South Africa, he began his service with the Pietersburg Light Horse, a cavalry unit hastily created to replace the ill-starred 'Bushveldt Carbineers' (BVC). The BVC had been tainted by the 'Breaker' Morant affair and the execution of two Australian lieutenants convicted by court-martial of killing Boer prisoners and a German missionary in cold blood.

Bald later served in the Imperial Yeomanry with Bendor, Duke of Westminster, the start of a long friendship. An excellent horseman, Bald was a keen shot and 'fisher' (his talents honed on Scottish grouse moors and in highland rivers), an enthusiasm for gentlemanly sporting pursuits that he shared with Bendor.

After the Boer War, Bald – like many other officers in peacetime – found himself stranded on the Reserve List. Although comfortably off, he evidently had a restless disposition and by 1910 was managing a timber forest in Mexico, where he was visited by George Cornwallis-West. The following year, Bald travelled to the USA, planning to visit one of the hugely fashionable ranches in Wyoming (kept by the likes of 'Buffalo Bill' and the equally bibulous English remittance man, George Calverley-Rudston) to shoot elk and other unfortunate mammals. In the event, he married one Goldia Routt of Chicago in November 1911, but the marriage seems to have lasted only a few weeks, failing shortly after the SS *Cedric*, with the happy couple on board, docked in Liverpool.

Once back in Europe, unattached, and with a private income, Bald took pleasure in the casinos and *maisons de rendezvous* of France, making the acquaintance of Marguerite (then styled 'Mme Maggie Meller') at Deauville shortly before the Great War. As a result of his friendship with Bendor, he joined the Machine Gun Corps (Motor), becoming the Duke's ADC and serving in Egypt. As we have seen, on 21 March 1916, the Duke of Westminster led a squadron of Rolls-Royce Armoured Cars, his gift to the nation (Bendor insisted that his cars should be commanded only by cavalry officers). In a daring night-time raid, the squadron rescued a large number of English sailors kept prisoner in humiliating conditions by pro-Ottoman tribesmen. The Duke, nominated for a VC, had to be content with the DSO (though only one rung down on the medal ladder), while more junior officers, such as Ernest Bald, were awarded the MC. Bald subsequently merited a mention in dispatches and was also the recipient of a rather wackier honour, 'The Order of the Nile, Fourth Class'.

Towards the end of the war, Bald was attached to the RAF in an administrative post and was finally transferred to the retired list early in 1919. Under the heading 'Special Qualifications', his service record states, 'Can speak French'. After the war, Bald divided his time between rooms at the Orleans Club, near St James's Street in the West End and the family estate at East Haugh, near Pitlochry. Bald, with his outstanding service record and circle of influential friends, is a character that leaps from the pages of a John Buchan novel. Bald's South American activities give him a touch of Richard Hannay, but the closest resemblance is to Sir Archibald Roylance, the amiable Old Etonian owner of a 'gentleman's shooting lodge' in Ayrshire. Archie Roylance features in several of Buchan's 'shilling shockers', including *Mr Standfast*, *Huntingtower* and the sublime *John Macnab*.

Buchan's description of Archie Roylance's den in *Huntingtower* encapsulates the tweedy world of Major Bald, to be richly savoured when back on his native heath and well away from the grime of London. Like the fictional 'Mains of Garple', East Haugh (a neat granite house with a large turret on one side) could have sported 'a fair-sized room . . . a bright fire . . . [with] the scent of peat', its walls adorned with 'the horns and heads of big game, foxes' masks, the model of a gigantic salmon, and several bookcases . . . with books and maps . . . mixed with decanters and cigar-boxes on the long side-board'. With *The Field* and 'a pile of new novels' on display, Archie's drawing-room created 'the very shrine of comfort'.

Bald too moved in upper-class circles and his name can often be found in the Society columns of *The Times*. His sister, Mary Verena Bald, married Algernon Hay-Drummond (known as Algernon

Hay), a kinsman of the Earl of Kinnoull and Bald's close contemporary at Eton. Ernest Bald and the Algernon Hays were very close, often forming a threesome at Society weddings, as when 'Captain Ernest Bald and Mr and Mrs Algernon Hay' gave a 'silver tea kettle' to a newly affianced pair in 1909, joining aristocratic fellow-donors such as the Earls of Cawdor and Mansfield and the Hon. Mrs Keppel, then mistress of Edward VII.

Bald's friendship with the Duke of Westminster, an intimate of the Prince of Wales, is an important connection in this story. The family relationship between Algy Hay and Ernest Bald establishes another link in the chain of circumstance. Examination of Hay's background also discloses a yet further connection, this time with Godfrey Thomas.

After Eton, Hay had joined the Foreign Office and, during the Great War, worked closely with Godfrey Thomas, who was first deputy head, then head, of the 'cipher room', in charge of King's Messengers. In 1919, Thomas left the Foreign Office to become the Prince's Private Secretary. Hay succeeded him in charge of the King's Messengers, already exercising the highly confidential responsibility of ferrying the private correspondence of the Prince of Wales to destinations in the United Kingdom and in Continental Europe. Lucky recipients had included Marguerite ('Maggie Meller') and Fredie Dudley Ward.

Thomas was highly regarded during his years at

the Foreign Office. Hay too had qualities that marked him out from the common run. 'Wily old Algy! He knew how to talk . . . to anyone, from a Royal Duke to a scullery-maid. He never let anyone down or gave anything away.' Hay was in a position to give sound advice to his brother-in-law as go-between on a delicate mission.

Whether or not Bald was aware, before the hulla-baloo of the Savoy shooting, that Marguerite had come to London, he is on record as having 'frequently visited' her from the very first day of her committal to prison on 10 July until at least mid-August, a period of over five weeks. These journeys wrenched Bald from the comfort of club-land and the West End, away to the much less agreeable neighbourhood of Parkhurst Road, N. Here stood Holloway, Marguerite's gaol, a Victorian Gothic monstrosity of the dreariest kind.

In making these visits, Major Bald surely had motivations beyond those of mere past acquaint-ance, fond memories of an old flame last seen in wartime Paris and Deauville. He was an ideal candidate, from the point of view of the Royal Household, to sound out Marguerite's intentions. Properly briefed, he would be discreet and his sterling qualities would enable him to manage the mercurial personality of the Prince's former mistress.

With Bald's London club so close to York House, there was no problem in walking the few steps to York House, where he could convey Marguerite's demands to Thomas and Lascelles, returning to Holloway with whatever response the Royal Household saw fit to make.

Judging by the frequency of Bald's visits and the lengthy period over which they were made, negotiations appear to have been protracted. The dearth of French speakers among the staff at Holloway has been noted earlier. Discussions could be carried on in French without risk that a sharp-eared prison wardress would understand. Sitting either side of a cheap deal table, in a bleak whitewashed room with barred windows, Marguerite and the Major discreetly horsetraded the most intimate secrets of the Prince of Wales.

Marguerite knew that Bald was close to the Duke of Westminster and that Bendor was close to the Prince. It is impossible to rule out a demand for money. Although she was a rich woman in her own right, Marguerite had a highly acquisitive streak. Financial arrangements between the Royal Household and awkward claimants are not unknown. A substantial sum is said to have been paid a few years later to a mistress of the Duke of Kent, younger brother of the Prince, on condition that she left the country.

Marguerite, despite the considerable difficulties facing her as she prepared to go on trial for her life, is likely to have been a tough negotiator. She must have known that the Prince was desperate to get his letters back, with no idea of what Marguerite might say in court in the course of what promised to be a sensational trial. She also had the support of some powerful friends, receiving visits, flowers and scent from the Baroness Émile d'Erlanger and *la duchesse de Westminster* (although Marguerite did not specify which of Bendor's two deeply wronged wives had beaten a path to her Holloway door).

It is impossible to know the exact detail of what passed between the Royal Household, Major Bald and Marguerite, but by mid-August 1923, it appears that a settlement had been reached, in terms satisfactory to both parties, 'and his [the Prince's] name will be kept out', as Lord Curzon later reported. Marguerite's past life would not be the subject of dissection before the jury. In return, Marguerite would not breathe a word about her princely affair during the Great War.

For the Royal Household, the primary task was to recover the incriminating correspondence, which was housed far away in Egypt. Marguerite agreed that the letters would be surrendered to the British High Commission in Cairo. As we have seen, Maître Michel Assouad, Marguerite's able lawyer and confidant, most probably took charge of the letters brought over by Marguerite in November 1922. There could be no question of Assouad or some other ordinary civilian – Egyptian, French or British – travelling from Egypt to England with such correspondence. The possibilities of loss, general skullduggery, or seizure by some officious or corrupt customs official, ruled out that idea completely. On the other hand, a British official, armed with a diplomatic *laissez-passer* and free from the risk of arbitrary seizure of documentation, could safely transport the precious cargo from Egypt to an expectant York House in London.

Marguerite was allowed to send letters abroad (although, as has been shown, Special Branch intercepted all her correspondence, reading the contents before onward dispatch). She would have been able to give Maître Assouad, by letter or wire, instructions to hand over the letters in his possession. The authorities could then be sure that she was keeping her side of the bargain.

Always a cute operator, Marguerite knew that the bundle handed in to the British Residency would contain most – but not all – of the correspondence. She knew that after five years there was every chance that the Prince was not likely to remember exactly how many letters he had written. As noted earlier, Marguerite extracted some samples from the pack, left for safe keeping in Paris. Here they would remain, out of the hands of her former lover – whether as the Prince of Wales, King-Emperor, or Duke of Windsor – for nearly fifty years.

On 15 August, Bald had a meeting at Holloway with the Deputy Governor and made a curious request, immediately relayed to the Prison Commissioners and Scotland Yard. 'Application was made to me today by a Major Bold [sic] . . . that a teacher of languages might be permitted to attend here in order to teach [Marguerite] the English language.' Cronin noted that, according to the Major, 'the prisoner herself had wished that the suggestion made could be carried out' and the ostensible reason was to help Marguerite understand the trial proceedings.

The Prison Commissioners, seemingly forgetful of the lack of French speakers in the system, minuted their agreement to Cronin 'provided that you can arrange for the necessary supervision to ensure that nothing improper passes and that you satisfy yourself as to the character and bona-fides of the teacher'.

Bald returned two days later with a 'slip' (probably a letter of introduction) which gave details of the proposed tutor, a Mrs M. Barton. Cronin asked the Commissioners to make enquiries, 'nothing being known of her here', adding that 'Major Bold [sic] proposes that the lessons should be given three nights weekly from 4.30 to 5.30 p.m. This could be arranged without great difficulty.'

The date of Major Bald's last recorded visit and interview with the Prison Commissioners may help explain why Mrs Barton came into the picture. Five days before, 12 August 1923, was 'the Glorious Twelfth', the day when grouse-shooting begins. The major, a keen shot, perhaps felt that he had done his duty by Marguerite, the Prince and his good friend the Duke of Westminster during five weeks' attendance at Holloway. In the earlier part of August, Bald might have told

Godfrey Thomas or Tommy Lascelles, each equally familiar with the timetable of the London Season, of his anxiety to get back to the grousebutts. Now he could return to East Haugh, his comfortable shooting-lodge, happily rejoining fellow 'guns' on the Perthshire moors only a few days into the grouse season and happily in time for blackgame shooting, which started on 19 August.

At this point, Major Bald disappears from Marguerite's story, but his friendship with Bendor continued, as noted by Winston Churchill in a letter to his wife, Clementine, written in 1928. Churchill described a fishing party in Scotland, on the Duke of Westminster's Rosehall estate, with Bendor, Coco Chanel and one of his ADC's Ernest Ball [sic].

Major Bald died in 1938, leaving the bulk of his estate to his sister, Mrs Algernon Hay. Characteristically, he made generous provision for the staff at East Haugh, arranged a large bequest to help disabled soldiers, and left £250 to 'Musgrave Castle Smith', an old Eton friend and fellow army officer, 'in appreciation of his sterling qualities'. In the late summer of 1923, Major Ernest Bald had given ample proof of his own sterling qualities as an officer and a gentleman.

CHAPTER 17

THE REAL DEAL

The Prison Commissioners sought information from the Metropolitan Police about the proposed teacher of English. 'Mrs Barton appears to have been employed at Scotland Yard', wrote the Secretary of the Prison Commissioners, presumably on the basis of information provided by Major Bald, 'Can you say if she is a reliable person please.'

No trace of Mrs Barton was found in criminal records. An approach was then made by Scotland Yard staff to Special Branch, whose report had been shown to Superintendent Parker, in overall charge of the murder enquiry, within two days of the shooting.

Norman Kendal, a Deputy Assistant Commissioner of the Metropolitan Police, dealt with the request. Kendal, then aged 43, was already a high flyer at Scotland Yard. Educated (like Lord Stamfordham) at Rossall School, a minor public school in the north of England, and Oriel College, Oxford, he practised as a barrister before war service, in which he was severely injured. Kendal's endorsement to the police file reveals that a 'Miss Baker' had come into the frame, probably because her name had been given as a character reference. 'Miss Baker', minuted Kendal firmly, 'is highly respectable & unless you have something agst her I propose to say that we have nothing agst Mrs Barton'. On 20 August, Kendal wrote to the Prison Commissioners, informing them that 'We have no objection to Mrs Barton and know nothing of her', adding a highly significant endorsement, which forges another link in the chain of circumstance surrounding the agreement to protect the name of the Prince. 'Colonel Thompson of the N.V.A.,' wrote Kendal, 'tells me that she is an old subscriber and quite respectable.'

The NVA, the 'National Vigilance Association', was founded in 1885, at the prompting of several earnest social reformers, including the campaigning journalist W. T. Stead and the Victorian feminist Josephine Butler. Its aim was 'the enforcement and improvement of the laws for the repression of criminal vice and public morality'. Shocked by the extent of prostitution, often involving very young girls, and by the Contagious Diseases Act of 1869, which authorised the humiliating medical examination of women merely suspected of prostitution, the NVA successfully pressed for legislative change. The Criminal Law Amendment Act of that year reformed the law on female prostitution. Unfortunately, thanks to the 'Labouchère Amendment', tagged on to the original Bill, all adult male homosexual behaviour was criminalised, 'in public or in private', creating a notorious 'Blackmailers' Charter', which endured until the reform of 1967.

Like many well-intentioned attempts at changing the human condition, the NVA was not content to campaign on its original remit of helping women in the 'unfortunate class'. From the 1900s, the association began to attack what it perceived to be 'pornography', a widely defined category which included the novels of Émile Zola, duly banned by the Home Secretary in 1906.

By 1923, Miss Annie Baker (the referee noted by Norman Kendal in his Special Branch memorandum) was Secretary and Director of the NVA, with Colonel Thompson as her assistant. Col Thompson was editor of the portentous *Manual of Vigilance Law* (4th edition) and Miss Baker, already a formidable campaigner, had written a book modestly entitled *A Romance of Philanthropy: Being a Record of the Principal Incidents Connected with the Exceptionally Successful Thirty Years' Work of the National Vigilance Association*.

The NVA had forged strong links with other self-important bodies, such as 'The Association for Social and Moral Hygiene' and 'The London Council for the Promotion of Public Morality', whose efforts to suppress misbehaviour in London's parks and open spaces has already been noted. In 1923, the NVA and LCPPM jointly lobbied the Home Office for action against 'objectionable books and press reports'.

There was, however, a distinctly sinister side to this phalanx of do-gooders. W. J. H. Brodrick, a London magistrate, who was chairman of the NVA in 1923, made his trenchant views known to yet another moralising lobby, 'The Association for Moral and Social Hygiene'. Young male prostitutes were, according to Mr Brodrick, 'usually diseased . . . a pest and a nuisance . . . I should be glad to see them put in a lethal chamber . . .' Although some of the work of these organisations may have been prompted by noble aims, there is more than a whiff of self-righteousness in the activities of these 'prudes on the prowl', a mordant description of the genre given by young Winston Churchill in the 1890s.

In its campaigns in the early years of the century, the NVA had benefited from the legal advice of Archibald Bodkin, who closely identified himself with the NVA's work. Bodkin was a member of the NVA, becoming its 'standing counsel' and eventually sat on the board of management.

Bodkin, with a family background in law, was born in 1862. After putting him through Highgate School, his barrister father had insufficient funds to send Bodkin to university (which might have broadened his social outlook). Instead he went straight into the law, where his practice, apart from some liquor licensing work, consisted almost entirely of criminal briefs in which Bodkin almost invariably appeared for the prosecution. 'By upbringing he was a rigid Victorian . . . a vigorous prosecutor with a high success rate,' widely regarded as 'tough and unfeeling'.

Bodkin materially advanced his legal career in the Great War, while Treasury Counsel (senior prosecutor at the Old Bailey), for his work in spy cases, mostly involving German nationals, but occasionally French-speaking Belgian defendants. At this time, Bodkin needed reliable interpreters, most of whom (given the absence of men at the front) were women.

Appointed Director of Public Prosecutions in July 1920, Bodkin would no longer have been able to work directly with the NVA. With the knowledge we have of his methods, it is clear that Bodkin took a close interest in the Savoy shooting from the outset, with access to the growing police file, including Special Branch papers on Marguerite. Although he would not have countenanced her way of life, Bodkin would take Marguerite's side against a husband depicted by her as a monster of oriental depravity. In her prosecutor, Marguerite had found a true friend, whose influence in the trial process was enormous, extending from the earliest stages of a criminal enquiry to the trial itself, including a very close relationship with judges, far closer than would be considered desirable today. A deeply conservative figure, Bodkin would have agreed with Godfrey Thomas and Stamfordham, 'the Impeccable', that the Prince's name must not be drawn into the trial process at any cost.

Mrs Barton, that 'old subscriber' to the NVA and 'teacher of languages' links Bald to Bodkin. Bald also links Bodkin to the Royal Household. Given what we know of the world of Ernest Bald – a huntin', shootin', and fishin' cavalry officer with an eye for wicked ladies – it is virtually inconceivable that the major could have come up with this odd choice of 'teacher' all by himself.

In the absence of Major Bald and during the three weeks before the trial started on 10 September, it was in the interests of the Royal Household and the DPP that an independent channel of communication should be maintained beyond that which existed between Marguerite and her lawyers. A call from York House to the DPP's offices at Richmond Terrace, or a talk over lunch in a gentleman's club, may have secured the services of Mrs Barton, an eminently respectable rabbit plucked from Sir Archibald Bodkin's black silk hat.

Marguerite, the decidedly unreformed 'pupil', hardly fitted the expectations of the NVA. As one of the best-known and top-ranking courtesans in Paris, she lived a world away from the front-parlour moralising of Baker, Barker and Bodkin. Nevertheless, Mrs Barton was clearly a fluent French speaker and her connection with the work of the NVA must have given her a few conversational gambits. In her world far away from High Society, lairds, field sports, galloping majors and Scottish lochs, Mrs Barton seems to have served as a trusted interpreter discreetly selected by the DPP. Though she presumably reported back to Bodkin, there may not have been very much to worry about. Agreement about the letters had been reached and Marguerite, though her moral character was not of the highest, stuck to the bargain and would keep her silence about links with the Prince.

Put simply, the choice of Mrs Barton bears all Bodkin's fingerprints. Her selection ostensibly by Major Bald seems to have been a deliberate tactic to distance Bodkin, the prosecutor, from appearing to have direct contact with Marguerite.

One disparity remains unsolved. Mrs Barton had, according to information supplied by Major Bald, 'apparently been employed at Scotland Yard', but Norman Kendal, a senior officer in Special Branch, had stated firmly 'we . . . know nothing of her' in answer to the question put by the Prison Commissioners. The exchange is recorded in the general police file on Marguerite, which would have been available to relatively junior officers attached to the investigation. If Kendal was trying to put others off the scent, it may be because Mrs Barton had previously played some role in sensitive Special Branch work involving Bodkin, either as a senior prosecutor or, since 1920, as DPP.

Whatever she was doing there, it is clear that Mrs Barton did not go to Holloway Prison to be a teacher of English. In Marguerite's own words, 'I have always regretted not having learned English. Never has my regret been keener than during my sad detention and trial.' Marguerite described in some detail her period of remand in Holloway and mentioned the visits of Major Bald, but made no reference to Mrs Barton, to a teacher, or to any intensive course in the English language.

Other elements of the deal between the Royal Household and Marguerite also involved Bodkin's participation. As has been noted earlier in this chapter, Bodkin took a lively interest in the progress of the police investigation. He almost invariably considered each case personally and would visit crime scenes, with a view to telling his staff how to conduct the prosecution case. Although Bodkin had to respect the demarcation line between his department and the Metropolitan Police in the conduct of the criminal enquiry, in tandem with the sloppy detective work, Bodkin was carefully selecting prosecution witnesses for the inquest and in committal proceedings at Bow Street Police Court. His list of expert witnesses, as we shall see, omitted the name of Sir Bernard Spilsbury, the forensic pathologist whose testimony could materially have strengthened the case for the prosecution. Other important witnesses were also overlooked.

Even for his time, Bodkin was extremely prudish, disliked saucy seaside postcards and relished the prosecution of their publishers. More seriously, 'his contempt for lewd books was unbounded'. In 1922, he banned James Joyce's *Ulysses* from sale in England and, five years later, was instrumental in the prosecution of Radclyffe Hall for her celebrated novel *The Well of Loneliness*, which to modern eyes seems a very decorous, even dull, salute to lesbian love.

The office of Director of Public Prosecutions, founded in 1879, had grown in importance during the early years of the twentieth century. As an example, though the selection of trial judge ought not to be influenced by the prosecutor's wishes, a senior member of the then DPP's staff wrote a revealing letter to the then DPP, Sir Charles 'Willie' Mathews, shortly before the internationally famous trial of Dr Crippen in October 1910 for the murder of his wife, Belle Elmore. 'This is one of the criminal trials that . . . the L[ord] C[hief] J[ustice] ought always to try . . . he [the judge] told me if you thought so too he would take it . . .'

The selection of High Court judge for the September session at the Central Criminal Court was nominally a matter for the court administration, headed by the 'Clerk of Arraigns'. Rigby Swift, then aged 49, had been appointed a High Court judge three years earlier by the almost equally youthful Lord Chancellor Birkenhead, formerly Sir F. E. Smith KC. Both men had deep roots in the Liverpool area and both were enthusiastic Tories. Swift had sat as Unionist [Conservative] MP for St Helens for eight years until 1918 (present-day appointees are usually more discreet about their politics). Intellectually, however, the two men were poles apart.

F. E. Smith had enjoyed meteoric success after

taking First Class Honours in Jurisprudence at Oxford and was the youngest Lord Chancellor to be appointed in modern times. Rigby Swift, two years his junior, was never an Oxbridge man, practising in Liverpool for a decade and a half before testing the water in London. 'Wherever I am,' he once declared proudly, 'can be summed up in one word – Liverpool.'

The eighth child of a solicitor (his mother's maiden name was Daft), Swift's practice was nurtured by local legal connections and his bluff, no-nonsense manner brought him a great deal of work. Legal biographies and obituaries tend to the hagiographic, but – reading between the respectful lines – it seems that Swift's chubby features and ruddy complexion were due to a fondness for drink, a failing not exactly unknown in the legal profession. One of Swift's 'marshals', young barristers who learned on the job by accompanying a judge on Circuit, remembered how Swift would begin the judicial day with a stiff whisky or two at breakfast time.

Swift's unashamedly provincial manner was exemplified by 'a deliberate Lancashire drawl', which caused him to be known in the courts, half-humorously, as 'Rigbah'. He considered himself, with some justification, to be a 'plain man', believing in 'the wholesome deterrent of flogging'. A keen churchman, Swift was a churchwarden and possessed all the in-built puritanism of the English middle class. He preffered the bible to any other book. Swift's description of himself, as 'an early Victorian', could have been shared by Sir Archibald Bodkin.

This recently appointed, narrow-minded, socially malleable and manifestly provincial judge was an easy target for the DPP. The campaign to keep the Prince's reputation unbesmirched by scandal would have an invaluable ally. Though the task of recovering the love letters had been a tricky and long drawn-out affair, only completed in late August, persuading the judge to prohibit revelations about Marguerite's true character was not likely to have been a serious problem. In the privacy of the judge's room, Bodkin might say to Swift, 'Of course, judge, there's no question of fettering your judicial discretion or in any way suggesting that you should take a particular course of action, but there is something very important I think you ought to know . . .' A discreet reference to the involvement of royalty was probably all that was needed to persuade Swift to agree an embargo on any revelations about Marguerite's past life before she met Ali Fahmy in 1922 which, in the circumstances of the case, would be a powerful factor in securing acquittal.

The legal process had to bear the external appearance of a normal murder trial. It is impossible to know how far knowledge of the Prince's affair with Marguerite had filtered, but the paucity of references in contemporary British diaries and correspondence, coupled with the complete absence of any mention in the British press, suggests that very few knew about the liaison and that even fewer were aware of the love letters and their potential danger. These would be secrets well kept.

For the Crown, Bodkin selected an experienced team of barristers, known as 'Treasury Counsel'. Percival Clarke, son of the great Victorian advocate, Sir Edward Clarke, led for the prosecution, assisted by Eustace Fulton, also from a distinguished legal family. Clarke certainly went through the motions, but the application made under the Criminal Evidence Act to explore Marguerite's character was feeble, a half-hearted exercise, as if Clarke knew in advance that the judge would not allow any examination of Marguerite's background and meeting Ali in 1922.

The lodging of documents and the giving of unsolicited advice to the DPP from the Fahmy family and lawyers was understandable, because Bodkin was directing the prosecution of a woman charged with murdering their young relative. Much more unusual is the presence in the DPP's file of copy correspondence and statements from Marguerite's solicitor, Freke Palmer. At that time, the defence was not obliged to reveal its hand in advance. Witness statements and accompanying documentation could be kept back, to be produced during the trial, often with a useful element of surprise when it was too late for adequate response by the prosecution. In this case, however, copy letters from Freke Palmer, with statements of witnesses deposing to various matters connected with her defence, were lodged with the DPP. Although Freke Palmer may not have been privy to negotiations about the letters and Marguerite's silence, he clearly knew that something was in the wind and that it was safe to supply information to the Crown.

This was to be a Show Trial with a difference. The authorities *wanted* Marguerite to be acquitted. A murder conviction would – quite simply – have been catastrophic for the Crown.

CHAPTER 18

THE PRINCE OVER THE WATER

Like a child at play, blissfully unaware of some looming family crisis, the Prince of Wales spent the latter part of that summer largely untroubled by the danger which so deeply worried his closest advisers. In denial (not for the first or the last time) about unpleasant matters, the Prince carried on just as before. He was content to leave the hard graft of bolstering his reputation as Prince Charming in the capable hands of his two secretaries.

At the date of his appointment as Assistant Secretary, in November 1920, Tommy Lascelles was utterly smitten by the charming Prince. Before long, however, the Prince's often wayward, unpredictable and essentially selfish nature caused Lascelles to revise his view. His royal master was becoming hard work. Two years after Tommy's appointment, the Prince paid a backhanded compliment to his backroom boys, telling them how he was getting 'a pretty good insight of all the drudgery & toiling that you & Godfrey [Thomas] do for me'.

A memorandum prepared by Lascelles for Godfrey Thomas in 1922 gives a good insight into what they felt about their boss at the time of the crisis with Marguerite. The Prince failed to appreciate that his position as Prince of Wales was entirely reliant on popular support. 'When you get down to bedrock,' wrote Lascelles, 'you have to admit that, in the long run, the Prince of Wales's title, his estate, his income and his many little privileges all depend on public goodwill. You can't afford to alienate that goodwill.' In a letter to Lascelles written a few years later, Godfrey Thomas also summarised the problems posed by a hedonistic Prince of no great intelligence or perspicacity. The Prince would always believe that provided he carried out his public duties, 'his private life is entirely his own concern.'

With Stamfordham and Wigram very likely in the picture, the question arises whether the King was aware of what was happening and, in particular, of the risks connected with the Fahmy affair. Courtiers, presumably for reasons of security, at this time seemed reluctant to set down detailed accounts of problematic royal behaviour. Sir Brian Godfrey-Fausset was Equerry-in-Ordinary to the King. On 24 July 1923, two weeks after the shooting, Sir Brian joined the monarch for a morning walk in the garden of Buckingham Palace. 'He was very interesting,' noted the courtier, adding with maddening discretion, 'and spoke to me about some confidential matters . . .' The 'confidential matters' were not specified and there the matter rests. More recently, the Registrar of the Royal Archives, having trawled through all items of potential relevance, found no material relating to the Fahmy trial.

With one possible exception, the Prince's surviving letters to Fredie Dudley Ward between July and November 1923 completely ignore the matters which were so sorely troubling his secretarial staff that summer. As we shall see, there is a reference to a 'crazy physical attraction' in a letter written from Balmoral probably at the end of August that year. Nevertheless, the Prince may – for once – have taken the advice of his secretaries and agreed not to put anything in writing about Marguerite (having made such a rod for his own back with those 'bloody' wartime love letters). Perhaps, however, he was simply playing the ostrich in a potentially disastrous situation.

In the days after the Savoy shooting, the Prince carried out his usual round of public 'stunts', including military inspections, unveiling war memorials, attending charitable garden parties and country fairs. On 25 July, the Prince once more showed his immature, neurotic side, feebly trying to explain why he had stormed out, effectively in a 'hissy fit', from a party given in London by Alistair Mackintosh. 'Fredie darling,' he wrote, 'I do hope I'm asked to dinner on Friday . . . I've tried to get you on the 'phone 2 or 3 times, but was unlucky . . . I was very depressed last night at Ali's party as you probably saw when you came in with Michael [Herbert]. I just wouldn't stick it

& fled the house!!' Given that Fredie's equivocal involvement with Michael Herbert, noted already, dated back some five years and was well known to the Prince, his childish behaviour that night was ridiculous, though by no means unusual.

Back in London, the Prince resumed the round of parties, dances and nightclubs and, on 5 August, with Marguerite safely in custody, made what seems to have been his first trip to France since February 1919. Much of the intervening period had been taken up with the Empire tours and visits to the USA, but it is remarkable that he stayed away for such a long period from a country already familiar to him. As 'Earl of Chester', the Prince took train, ship, and train to Le Touquet, spending 'a few days' there, returning on 8 August.

From the days of Queen Victoria, the royal family had decamped to Scotland in August. Reluctantly visiting his parents at Balmoral from time to time, the Prince would billet himself in castles, country houses and shooting lodges, some little better than the 'wet, granite hovels' of Evelyn Waugh's *Decline & Fall*. A poor fisher and indifferent shot, the Prince would also try his hand at golf during the day, playing poker after dinner in the evening.

This year, on 15 August (shortly before Major Bald made his last recorded visit to Holloway), the Prince travelled to Scotland with Bruce Ogilvy as equerry. Just a week later, in circumstances discussed further on in this chapter, he abruptly changed his plans and returned to London. There are reasons for believing that this 500-mile journey was linked to a much longer journey from Egypt made by a British diplomat.

In Cairo, at the British High Commission, Archibald Clark Kerr (later Lord Inverchapel) was Acting Counsellor, second in command to General Allenby, the High Commissioner. Archie Kerr has been fulsomely described as an 'attractive Highlander, unconventional, very entertaining and good company'. The son of John Kerr Clark (from a long line of Lanarkshire tenant farmers), Archie was born in Australia, where his father had made a fortune from ranching sheep on an industrial scale. Archie's roots were in Scotland, where – rather like the whisky-rich John Bald – his father had provided the family with an ancestral home, the quaintly named Crossbasket Castle in Lanarkshire. After school in England in the obscurity of 'Bath College', Kerr joined the Foreign Office in 1906. Highly intelligent, with a robust sense of humour, Kerr (who inverted his last two names by deed poll in 1911) was a great networker, marked down as a high flyer from an early stage.

In 1910, Harold Nicolson, another rising Foreign Office man, met Clark, four years his senior. In his youth, he was Harold's closest friend. They always remained on close terms. Clark's sister, Muriel, was romantically involved with Nicolson's future wife, the writer Vita Sackville-West, thus creating a mixed foursome of some distinction. Kerr, who was proud of his Scottish ancestry, bought an estate of his own, Inverchapel, near Greenock, in which he installed his mother.

A dutiful son, Archie Clark kept up a very detailed correspondence with his mother for many years. Unfortunately, letters for the period July to October 1923, covering the Savoy shooting and its aftermath, appear not to have survived and his official correspondence is largely confined to political matters. In Scotland, Clark's gregarious personality won him many friends, not least among the landed gentry. On leave from various diplomatic postings, Archie Clark was a welcome guest at weekend house parties and shoots. As in the case of Major Bald, Clark had overcome his middle-class background to become an honorary member of the Breed.

Archie Kerr's Foreign Office credentials connect him to Algernon Hay and via Hay to Godfrey Thomas and the Prince, but this was by no means his only connection with royalty. He had visited Glamis in 1922, joining the roll-call of suitors for the hand of Lady Elizabeth Bowes-Lyon. The parade of the lovelorn included Lord Gorrell, Lord Gage, 'Christopher Glenconner, the Scottish chemicals heir', and James Stuart, a future Cabinet Minister. The Prince's younger brother, Prince Albert, later King George VI, finally secured the prize. Archie was left feeling 'tired and battered and dismal' on news of the royal engagement, but the episode illustrates how far he had clambered up the social ladder.

In July 1923, Allenby returned to England for three months' furlough, thus avoiding the intense heat of the Egyptian summer at a date long before the introduction of air conditioning. His younger subordinates had to cope as best they might with the fierce temperature.

Although the High Commission had been much occupied earlier in the year in attempting to resolve problems created by nationalist leaders such as Saad Zaghloul, it has been said that a comparative relaxation in Egyptian political tensions meant that both Allenby and Clark Kerr were able to take some leave. The political situation was volatile, crises could flare up at any time, and in 1923 there were no jet aircraft available to fly people back in a matter of hours.

Kerr's return to Britain was not flagged very far in advance. On 20 July (ten days after the Savoy shooting), Gerald Delaney, Reuters' correspondent in Cairo and heard a rumour that Clark Kerr was going home in August. In 1923, the journey from Egypt to England took at least five days. One route was via steamer from Alexandria (the SS *Helouan*, used by Marguerite and her sister Yvonne the previous November) to Trieste and thence by the Orient Express to Paris and London. Another was also by sea, from Alexandria to Marseilles and onward by train.

Archie Kerr was the only senior diplomat to have left the High Commission between Allenby's departure in July and the much later return home of Kerr's deputy at the Residency, Arthur Wiggin (with Owen Tweedy, Wiggin kept Kerr closely-informed of the Egyptian scene), who visited London during mid-September. Given the wealth of connections and coincidences, plus the pressing need for security at the highest level, Archie Kerr is the most likely bearer of the letters to England.

In yet another coincidence, Major Ernest Bald bowed out of the Royal Household's secret enterprise, job done, on Thursday 17 August 1923, a day or so after Archie Kerr left Egypt. Earlier that month, as already noted, Marguerite faced no problems in writing or telegraphing to Maître Assouad with instructions about the letters, her communications duly monitored by Special Branch, who could confirm that Marguerite was keeping her side of the bargain. There would have been no difficulty for Algy Hay, head of the cipher department at the Foreign Office, wiring Kerr with a discreetly worded request to bring back a particular package. Indeed, Kerr may have already known, even in the latter part of July, that something was in the wind.

With Thomas and Lascelles careful to husband the Prince's secrets in London, two clues support the view that knowledge of the affair was transmitted to Egypt that summer on a restricted basis, confined to a handful of senior officials at the High Commission.

The first marker is associated with Arthur Wiggin, who worked with Tweedy at the High Commission. In September, during his period of leave in

England, and as we shall see later, Wiggin made a point of attending Marguerite's trial at the Old Bailey. He wrote a vivid account of his experiences to Kerr, then far away in Inverchapel. This interest in the fate of Marguerite sits well with other evidence of special knowledge held by Kerr and close colleagues.

Another indication is found in the reply by Colonel Owen Tweedy, waggish liaison officer at the Residency, to an enquiry from Alexander Keown-Boyd, Director-General of the European Department of the Egyptian Ministry of the Interior. Tweedy, with Arthur Wiggin, enjoyed a very close relationship with Clark Kerr, even to the extent of sending the First Secretary a very vulgar (but extremely funny) limerick later that year as part of an official dispatch to his friend.

Early in November 1923, Keown-Boyd had referred Tweedy to a month-old Egyptian news-paper report, alleging a relationship 'of an intimate nature between "Madame Fahmy" and "one of the British princes"'. Tweedy replied that the story 'came here from England originally in August'. Keown-Boyd, despite being in charge of British intelligence operations in Egypt, had clearly not been in the loop. The British colony in Cairo was tight-knit, gossip a way of life. The fact that the story was known to a few officials in the Residency during August and was kept confidential in the meantime emphasises the aura of secrecy surrounding the return of the letters. This also supports the contention that it was Kerr, armed with *laissez-passer*, who took the letters to England in the middle of that month.

Archie Kerr, presumed bearer of this most sensitive cache of letters, returned to London from Egypt on Tuesday 21 August. The Prince had spent the previous weekend at Glamis Castle, joining the Duke and Duchess of York, various other Bowes-Lyons, and his equerry, Bruce Ogilvie. Just a year before, the Visitors' Book had included the name of Archie Kerr, who kept up a desultory correspondence with the Duchess despite the rejection of his suit. On Monday, the Prince motored over to the ancient Redcastle, near the Moray Firth, home of Colonel and Mrs Baillie of Dochfour, but in the event spent only one night there.

The Prince was driven to Nairn on Wednesday 22 August, where he unveiled a memorial to the Seaforth Highlanders and, after lunch, opened a bazaar. Evidently in relaxed mood, the Prince 'made a humorous and effective little impromptu speech, which set everybody laughing'. Photographers snapped 'Our Smiling Prince'. Later in the afternoon, apparently without any sign of distress, the Prince made a sightseeing trip around the nearby Cawdor Castle, guided by Lady Cawdor herself.

However, instead of proceeding with his usual round of Scottish summer engagements, the Prince – quite unexpectedly – boarded the overnight train from Inverness to King's Cross, travelling straight to York House. He stayed there the following night, returning to Perth by the Friday overnight train from London. The Royal Household quickly put out an official explanation for this curious return journey and, on 24 August, *The Times* obediently reported:

> The Prince of Wales arrived in London yesterday morning from Inverness to complete the arrangements for his Canadian visit and to settle details of various autumn engagements.

Eagle-eyed readers might have recalled that, only three days earlier, 'The Thunderer' had confirmed that 'plans have now been completed for the forthcoming visit of the Prince to his ranch', setting out a detailed timetable of a trip claimed (apparently without irony) to be 'a complete rest after the strenuous series of engagements which he has carried out continually for many months now . . .'

A story circulated in the Royal Household that the Prince had dashed down to London because he had 'a pain in the tummy wh[ich] convinced him he had appendicitis and must be operated on immediately!' The popular press, unaware of any health concerns, seem to have been not wholly convinced by the official announcement. The *Daily Express* suspiciously reported the 'flying visit', while the *Daily Mail* headlined, more damagingly,

'The Prince's Hustle'. Whatever may have been the reason for this mysterious visit, the Prince returned to Scotland on the Friday night.

While the Prince could be impetuous and demand changes of plan at the last minute, accounts of this episode read oddly. On the afternoon of Wednesday 22 August, he was plainly in good spirits, making an amusing speech before touring Cawdor Castle. The pain and discomfort associated with a grumbling appendix must have come upon him very suddenly and, if there is any truth in the rumour, it is remarkable in such circumstances that he would have risked a long overnight train journey, bumping along railway tracks for some ten hours.

Doctors attend princes, not vice versa. Expert medical opinion was close at hand. The Royal Household in Scotland had several distinguished physicians and surgeons, most of whom could have attended at relatively short notice without the Prince having to make an arduous train journey of over 500 miles. Aberdeen, directly connected to Inverness by rail, accommodated Sir John Marnoch, Professor of Surgery, who had successfully removed the appendix of the Prince's brother, the Duke of York, in 1914. The Prince visited his brother in the Aberdeen nursing home and would have been aware of Albert's high opinion of the surgeon. 'He is really a very nice man. One gets to know the surgeon so much better after the operation.'

Attention to chronology suggests a third ground

for those journalistic suspicions implicit in the *Daily Mail* headline, 'The Prince's Hustle'. On the footing that Archie Kerr had played postman for the Prince's letters, acting as King's Messenger from Cairo to London, the bundle of correspondence would have been in the Prince's office at York House by Wednesday 22 August. That was not the end of the matter, prompting one burning question. *Were* these the letters written by the Prince to Marguerite during the war or might they be forgeries, with the genuine letters retained for some future demand? With knowledge of Marguerite's past, anything was possible. Only the Prince himself could positively identify letters written so carelessly five or six years earlier.

The correspondence could have been brought up to the Prince in Scotland by one of the 'handpicked team', but the sudden arrival of someone like Lascelles or Legh from London might have drawn unwanted attention on the part of hosts, or servants, at Redcastle or the scene of the Prince's next house party, Drummond Castle, home of the Earl and Countess of Ancaster. In any case, we know that the Prince was keen to destroy 'those bloody letters' which had plagued him for so long. 'I just must get all these letters back somehow,' he had written in 1918. Their final destruction and long-delayed victory over that tiresome French 'pol' could be carried out more discreetly in the privacy of his own apartments than anywhere else.

Perhaps on the journey down from Scotland, the

Prince, often prey to dyspepsia, his mind awash with thoughts of Marguerite and the impending crisis, suffered awkward abdominal twinges and demanded expert medical opinion after his arrival in London. In any event, stories about appendicitis emerging from St James's Palace might serve to put people off the scent.

On the Thursday evening, before going north to Inverchapel, Archie Kerr met Harold Nicolson, his old friend. 'Dine Archie Kerr & see him off to Scotland,' wrote Nicolson in his diary. There is no record what was discussed at this intimate dinner, but there is strong evidence – as will be seen in the next chapter – that these two close friends talked about both the panic besetting York House during the past few weeks and the solution so recently achieved with Archie Kerr's help. Nicolson, who knew some of the 'handpicked team' well, had no particular love for the Prince of Wales, descriptions of whose 'red face' and 'little red hands flicking all the time about his neck-tie' had been, as we have seen, acerbically noted in his diary.

Despite the rigours of the overnight train journey and alleged groin strain, the Prince displayed the rudest of health that Saturday, playing golf at Gleneagles, morning and afternoon, before joining the Ancasters for an eventful week at Drummond Castle. Lady Ancaster was an American and something of a royal headhunter. 'Eloïse goes in for royalties now,' wrote Jean, Lady Hamilton in her diary, 'and always has one, if not two, at every small party that she has . . .' Among the outgoing house party, whose members dutifully signed the Visitors' Book, were the Duke and Duchess of York, in company with Edwina and Dickie Mountbatten (perhaps best described as 'neo-royalty').

The Ancasters' next guest shift, running from 26 August to 1 September, produced a crop of autographs from the Prince, his brother Prince George (later Duke of Kent), 'Fruity' Metcalfe, his future wife Alexandra ('Baba') Curzon, Bruce Ogilvy, J. J. Astor, Violet and Kathy Menzies (from a prominent Perthshire family), with Audrey and Dudley Coats completing the assembly.

The Prince used his stay at Drummond Castle to pursue 'little Audrey', much to the annoyance of her husband, exceedingly rich from the profits of the Coats cotton spinning empire. Undeterred by the jealousy of her spouse, the Prince continued to take pleasure in Audrey for some years. 'Personally I don't think the Prince cares two straws about her except for purely physical reasons,' wrote Joey Legh's wife in 1925.

On the last day of the house party, the Prince replied to 'a very sweet letter' from Fredie Dudley Ward, now reduced to the role of confidante (it seems, from available correspondence, that the Prince did not meet Fredie on the night of his flying visit). Though concerns about Marguerite had been somewhat allayed, the Prince desperately needed a sounding-board. 'Please come up to

London either 3rd or 4th Septr to give me that hiding,' he wrote enigmatically, mindful also of his impending journey to Canada, 'I just must see you before I sail . . . cos I've got so much to tell you.' The air at Drummond Castle had been 'electric . . . never have I had such an exciting week as this . . . & should be lucky if I escape without a hell of a row'. Perhaps mindful of past careless correspondence, the Prince added, 'no more on paper darling!!' Hoping that Fredie would see him in London 'tho' I don't deserve it at all', he was 'in a queer state of mind just now . . . very lost and all muddled up'.

The Prince spent part of the weekend with his parents at Balmoral, the kind of sojourn that usually encouraged gloomy thinking. An undated letter to Fredie may date from this time and, if so, suggests severe depression felt about the consequences of his wartime liaison with Marguerite, as well as more recent traumas. Admitting that his relationship with Fredie could now never be 'absolutely satisfactory', the Prince succumbed to despair. 'I once lost my head over a crazy physical attraction. Look at the result. Just made a fool of myself. Nothing left of it but nausea.'

The Prince managed to get away from the stifling atmosphere of Balmoral by the mid-morning train from Ballater on Sunday 2 September. His express drew into King's Cross at 6 p.m., three hours before the Dover Pullman arrived at Victoria

Station. On board was the Foreign Secretary, Lord Curzon, returning from a three-week 'cure' at a French spa, Bagnoles-de-l'Orne in Normandy.

These were leisurely times for politicians. Stanley Baldwin, the Prime Minister, began his usual vacation at Aix-les-Bains on 27 August and was not minded to return to London – whatever the reason – for at least a month. Unfortunately Signor Mussolini (the new Italian Prime Minister) unsportingly bombarded the Greek island of Corfu on 27 August in revenge for the death of an Italian general, supposedly murdered by Albanian bandits. The *Daily Mail*'s headline proclaimed 'ITALY IS RIGHT' and Lord Rothermere's press flagship once again saluted 'the great Italian leader for whom we in this country entertain so well-deserved an admiration'.

In the absence of senior government figures, the Foreign Office struggled to divine the government's intentions in the crisis. Should the dispute be referred to the League of Nations? Should the British Government argue for a bilateral resolution between Italy and Greece? In the event, Curzon reluctantly agreed to break off his holiday.

Waiting to greet the Marquess on the platform, in a small compound railed off from crowds of reporters, photographers and onlookers, stood Sir William Tyrell, Assistant Under-Secretary at the Foreign Office, accompanied by two junior colleagues, Harold Nicolson and Alan Leeper. Both Nicolson (already making his name as the author of books on Verlaine and Tennyson) and Leeper were bright stars at the Foreign Office, close advisers of Curzon during tortuous negotiations at the Lausanne conference of 1922–3. That evening, Curzon's train was an hour behind time and the three Foreign Office officials were obliged to dine in the station buffet.

The Marquess was in pain, partly from his chronic back condition, but also from phlebitis. In no mood to stay for long in his London residence, Curzon spent the night at 1 Carlton Gardens, receiving the Italian Ambassador the following morning in a brief attention to official duty. Soon the ailing Marquess was on the way to Kedleston, his much loved Palladian country seat in Derbyshire. Nicolson and Leeper accompanied him to St Pancras. The latest developments in the crisis were summarised on the short journey, but there was time to wait before the train left for Derby. 'He sat there in his compartment at St Pancras,' wrote Nicolson, 'his foot outstretched on its green baize rest reading the telegrams which had arrived overnight.'

Although the ramifications of the Corfu incident dominated conversation, the Marquess was open to diversion. His interest would have been aroused by a piece of gossip, most likely imparted by Harold Nicolson, who, as we know, dined with Archie Clark Kerr on 23 August, while Curzon was away in Normandy. Back in Kedleston and on the eve of Marguerite's trial, Curzon scribbled a note to his wife (Grace Curzon disliked Kedleston, preferring to stay in Hackwood, their country house in Hampshire). What Curzon wrote, in the early hours of 9 September 1923, amounted to a leak of information which would have severely disturbed the Royal Household had they known of it. The letter, a classic 'smoking gun', is hard evidence of the deal struck with Marguerite in Holloway, awaiting trial for the murder of her husband:

> My Darling Girl
> . . . In London the other day I heard a piece of news which may amuse you if you do not know it already. The French girl who shot her so-called Egyptian prince in London and is going to be tried for murder, is the fancy woman who was the Prince's 'keep' in Paris during the war . . . and they were terribly afraid that he might be dragged in. It is fortunate that he is off to Canada and his name is to be kept out.

The Marquess would stay on at Kedleston (always notoriously reluctant to answer the single telephone kept in his butler's pantry) until his return to London on 21 September. This remarkable letter shows that Curzon, Foreign Secretary, number two in the government, and an immensely important public figure, had been wholly unaware of these sensitive matters until a few days before the trial started, fully a month and a half after the Savoy shooting. Although, in the case of Daisy Warwick, Stamfordham had seen fit to consult the Prime Minister, H. H. Asquith, about problems posed by compromising royal letters, no such approach seems to have been made to Stanley Baldwin. The Royal Household had been content to keep the elected government of Britain in the dark about serious malfeasance on the part of the heir to the throne.

By the time the Foreign Secretary had put pen to paper, the Prince was already at sea. A night or so before his departure, as requested, Fredie Dudley Ward had visited the Prince at York House for a heart-to-heart. 'I feel so much better having got all that off the chest to the one and only soul I can or care to,' he wrote from his suite aboard the *Empress of France*, shortly before sailing from Southampton on 5 September, 'I've taken a pull already & am going to try not to take life so seriously and not to worry . . . my life is worry . . .'

CHAPTER 19

THE 'GREAT DEFENDER'

Within a short time of her arrival at Holloway, Marguerite had also been visited by Freke Palmer and Collins, his managing clerk, continuing the lengthy process of taking instructions in preparation for September's murder trial. Freke Palmer must have worked in French. His briefs to counsel was punctilously prepared and Marshall Hall's clerk considered that defence counsel had been 'magnificently instructed'.

Freke Palmer, after taking Marguerite's instructions at Holloway, and with the dry-runs of inquest and committal behind him, knew that this was to be no easy case to defend, despite what he had already gleaned about Ali's background and character.

There was no doubt, too, that Marguerite had kept a pistol for some time, well before she came to England. It might be difficult to persuade a jury that she had not known how to use a pistol bought with the express intention of protecting her jewellery. And why had she fired that first shot? Was it, as she said, to discourage Ali from assaulting her, or was it to establish that her gun was in working order before she used it to fatal effect? Moreover, there was the dangerous evidence of John Beattie, apparently supported by the post-mortem report, which suggested that Marguerite had shot her husband from behind, as he was trying to call the lapdog back into their suite.

The state of the criminal law in 1923 also seemed to put Marguerite at a disadvantage. The general rule, then as now, was that the prosecution, having brought the case against a prisoner, had to prove that case 'beyond reasonable doubt', so that at the end of a trial the jury would only convict if they were sure that the defendant was guilty. At that time, however, there was a presumption in law that all homicide was murder, 'unless the contrary appears from circumstances of alleviation, excuse or justi- fication'. In Marguerite's case, there could be no reasonable doubt that (for whatever reason) she had fired the three shots which killed her husband. That being so, the presumption applied and it was then for her to satisfy the jury that, in the circumstances (classically described in 1762 as 'accident, necessity, or infirmity'), she was not guilty of murder.

With all these considerations in mind, but happily freed from worry about financial constraints, Freke Palmer's first choice as leading counsel had been Sir Henry Curtis-Bennett KC. Marguerite's friends, however, were insistent that the defence team should be headed by an even more famous name. Accordingly, Palmer telephoned Edgar Bowker, head clerk at 3 Temple Gardens, the chambers of

Sir Edward Marshall Hall. Negotiations between solicitor and barrister's clerk for the instruction of leading counsel in a serious case resemble a complex mating dance. Fees are the major preoccupation, amid a welter of backstage bargaining in which the barrister plays no overt role. Significantly, Marshall Hall had not accepted a brief in a capital case since 1921. Lucrative civil work had taken up the intervening months and, as a result, such important murder trials such as those of Herbert Armstrong and Bywaters and Thompson took place without his forceful presence. All three defendants were hanged.

Marshall Hall had several times expressed his reluctance to be instructed in sensational murder cases, but, true to form, the great man soon relented under his clerk's pressure and a fee was agreed. The agreed 'marking' on the brief was 652 guineas, one of the highest fees he ever earned at the Bar. During the negotiations, Freke Palmer had been anxious to impress upon Bowker that the Fahmy affair was no run-of-the-mill murder case, one that might be defended by an Old Bailey hack. Indeed, no less than three counsel were eventually retained in Marguerite's defence. Marshall Hall would have the assistance of Sir Henry Curtis Bennett, with Roland Oliver (later to be an abrasive High Court judge) as junior counsel.

Marshall Hall had enjoyed a professional relationship with Freke Palmer for thirty-five years, from the day the solicitor had first seen the young, white-wigged barrister on his feet in the dingy surroundings of Marylebone Crown Court in 1888. He had then marked Hall down as a 'winner' and, despite the vicissitudes of the other man's tempestuous career, rarely had reason to change his original view.

Nearing the age of 65 in the late summer of 1923, Marshall Hall was at the height of his fame and fortune, literally a household name. He looked every inch the great advocate. A handsome, comparatively youthful-looking and well-built 6' 3", he had a commanding presence that dominated the courtroom. Yet in many ways his character, 'childlike, uncontrolled and mercurial', was a far remove from the popular conception of the lean, ascetic lawyer coldly and dispassionately expounding his case.

Never an academic lawyer, he was first and foremost an advocate. In his criminal work, he was at his finest as a defender. His attempts at prosecution were half-hearted, when not actually disastrous. Too often, when prosecuting, he would act as a 'supplementary counsel for the defence . . . and once he seems to have suppressed a most damaging piece of evidence against a prisoner . . .'

Edward Marshall Hall was born in Brighton in 1858, son of a well-known local physician. Described as 'sulky, rebellious and disobedient', he spent two years at Rugby School, where he would 'barter revolvers and guns and jewellery'. After matriculating at St John's College, Cambridge, he took a two-year sabbatical and bummed around Paris, living 'an amusing life with the students and artists of the Quartier Latin' and learning to speak excellent French.

In his unconventional early life, he developed two useful attributes. One was a skill at dealing in jewellery and precious stones, a useful supplement to his earnings at the Bar; the other was an almost encyclopaedic knowledge of firearms, which he was able to employ to great advantage in a number of criminal trials. He was a keen shot and in his early days at the Bar most of his winter weekends were spent shooting.

His reputation as the 'Great Defender' began with the unpromising Marie Hermann in 1894. This skinny, miserable-looking London prostitute of 43 had battered one of her few remaining clients over the head with an iron bar and deposited the body in a large trunk. 'Take care of that box,' she had told removal men, 'it contains treasures of mine.'

Marshall Hall persuasively argued that the fatal blows had been struck in the course of a struggle with her client, a burly, drunken man. Against the odds, he secured a verdict of manslaughter and the emotional force behind his submissions helped to secure a favourable verdict. Melodramatic as his words and actions seem today, they created a strong emotional atmosphere in court which propelled the jury far beyond a quiet assessment of the issues.

'Remember,' he implored, tears streaming down his cheeks at the end of a three-hour speech, 'that these women are what men make them; even this woman was at one time a beautiful and innocent child.' Right on cue, the prisoner began to sob in her place in the dock as Marshall Hall, with histrionic deliberation, gravely challenged the jury: 'Gentlemen, on the evidence before you, I almost dare you to find a verdict of murder.' Then, pointing to his client's pathetic form, he added the deathless plea, 'Look at her, gentlemen of the jury. Look at her. God never gave her a chance – won't you?', and sat down to tumultuous applause.

To modern eyes, this episode possesses all the risible qualities of the death of Little Nell, but a jury of the 1890s would have been used to such a florid, declamatory style in popular fiction, in the newspapers, and, above all, in the theatre. Anyone who has heard early recordings by turn-of-the-century actors such as Irving and Beerbohm Tree will immediately detect this tone. Such exuberance would become an essential part of the Marshall Hall repertoire, and went on, too long, into the years after the Great War, when juries were less ready than their Victorian counterparts to accept theatrical ham served up before them in court.

'My profession and that of an actor are somewhat akin,' said Marshall Hall, proud of his membership of the Garrick Club. 'There is no backcloth . . . there is no curtain, but out of the vivid dream of somebody else's life, I have to create an atmosphere, for that is advocacy.' He seemed to identify himself with his client, going beyond the strict role of advocate, 'speaking as if the prisoner's thoughts, actions and impulses were his own'.

He would nurse his juries, selecting 'the most intelligent or the most amenable member', addressing himself particularly to this figure until he was satisfied that that person had been won over, before moving on to the next, and so on, through the twelve. Another facet of Marshall Hall's character, however, was demonstrated by his petulant aside. The Great Defender was vain, hot-tempered and indiscreet. He had no scruples about bullying witnesses and cut more than a few ethical corners. Clashes with the judiciary had on occasion brought his practice near to ruin.

In addition to these undoubted character defects, his working method was largely intuitive: 'He never had a plan of campaign, or, if he had, he never was faithful to it. So far from preparing his speeches, he scarcely knew what the next sentence was to be himself . . .'

For forty years, Marshall Hall had battled his way through the courts and in the late summer of 1923 he was instructed to appear in possibly the most sensational trial of them all. His reaction, upon reading Freke Palmer's immaculately prepared instructions, was to agree with the solicitor that this could be an uphill struggle, yet it was a fight in which the old warrior could identify with his client's predicament. Marshall Hall had his own bitter experience of marriage. His first wife had announced during their honeymoon in Paris that she did not love him: the couple separated in 1888 after five years of constant bickering. A few months later, she died from the effects of an illegal abortion, after an affair with an army officer.

Although he lived happily with his second wife, Marshall Hall was always prone to recall the misery of earlier years. 'Marriage,' he said late in life, 'can be one of the most immoral relationships in the world.' His impulsive nature immediately sympathised with Marguerite Fahmy, seemingly vulnerable and alone in a foreign country. She needed a champion and Marshall Hall would be her man. Furthermore, they shared another painful experience. For years, Marshall Hall had been a martyr to piles.

Back at Scotland Yard, Divisional Detective Inspector Grosse was preparing his case. Information began to flow in from Egypt. An unsigned, vituperative attack on Ali and his family, written from Cairo, was sent directly to Grosse. It may have been written by a disaffected ex-employee, who appears not to have been a native English speaker and whose disparaging references to Islam suggest that he was a Coptic Christian:

Dear Sir
Aly Fahmy made the acquaintance of his wife at the Semiramis Hotel . . . where she was staying with her daughter, a very pretty girl of sixteen [sic]. Here is the motive for his death. As a rich Mussulman he would

316

try for the daughter as mistress by the side of the mother. Mahomedan morality.

His as secretary, Said Enani eff[endi], was well-known as his master's pimp and very probably worse than that, as morality does not exist in this country.

Ignoring this diatribe, Grosse had to make some effort to ascertain Marguerite's background before the trial started. The Paris Prefecture of Police was contacted late in July and responded with a short background report on Marguerite, dated 7 August, which established that she had no criminal convictions recorded against her in France, though she had earned quite a reputation since her youth. '*De naissance très modeste . . . elle se lança de bonne heure dans la haute galanterie . . .*' ('Of very humble birth . . . she soon joined the ranks of high-class fast women . . .') With gallic prudence, the statement did not identify any of Marguerite's former clients, whose publicity-shy ranks included many influential French citizens, as well as the Prince of Wales.

Grosse also received information, on 26 August, from Dr Said, Ali's brother-in-law, who had returned to Egypt in the interim, probably for Ali's funeral on 3 August 1923. The elaborate procession, which was filmed as a newsreel by pioneer Egyptian cineaste, Mahmoud Bayoumi, took place in Cairo. The silver-draped coffin on which lay a bright red fez, was carried on one of Ali's expensive limousines, accompanied by a long procession of children, carrying candles and mourning wreaths. Ali's family were now gearing themselves up for some unwelcome revelations at the trial. Ex-Chief Inspector James Stockley of Scotland Yard, who had retired in 1911 and was now operating as a 'private enquiry agent', was instructed by Dr Said to make detailed enquiries in Paris about Marguerite's character and background.

On 2 September 1923, after his return, Stockley called on Grosse, telling him of his instructions. He had been able to collect a 'considerable amount of data', contained in a six-page report marked 'CONFIDENTIAL', which he passed on to the police.

Stockley had spent four days in France 'with the assistance of an agent of mine, who for many years, in an official and unofficial capacity has been acquainted with Paris'. The wording of Stockley's report suggests that the former Chief Inspector did not speak French. 'I beg to state', he began, in wonderful police jargon, 'that . . . I proceeded to Paris . . .' There, with the help of his agent, he secured an interview with Madame Denart, Marguerite's old madame.

The intrepid ex-detective was also told by the manager at Louis Vuitton, Frank Theobald, about the Fahmys' visit to the Château de Madrid, but this reference in Stockley's written report would not have pleased the restaurant management. 'I heard that Madame Fahmy was in the habit of encouraging her husband to some place outside

Paris, called I think the Château,' wrote Stockley, 'where she used to introduce him to all sorts of not altogether desirable people and to encourage him to drink.'

'The enquiry necessitated much going backwards and forwards,' reported Stockley, who hinted that he had heard something about the royal connection, 'Of course, I heard a great many stories that might or might not be true, but the matters I shall deal with I believe to be substantially true . . .' Stockley's finding that 'amongst people in Paris there is a very strong feeling in favour of Madame Fahmy' was yet another factor that emphasised the dangerous consequences for the Royal Household of a conviction and death sentence, events that risked international repercussions.

At this time, Said Enani was found to be back in Paris, ostensibly waiting for Dr Said, who 'was expected to pass through . . . on his way to London' to attend Marguerite's trial. Said was living it up at the Hôtel Majestic, the scene of much marital strife between his late employer and the accused woman. 'He is staying alone,' revealed Stockley, 'but frequently has various ladies to his apartment. The people at the hotel are rather careful about him and ask him to pay up his account pretty frequently . . .'

The report provided confirmation that the three telegrams had been sent on 9 July, as alleged by Dr Said. In a last-minute flurry, for the trial was to begin in three days, further information was sought from the Paris police on 7 September. 'Phoning was not satisfactory. Paris could not hear', so a letter was sent by Air Mail from Croydon, as well as a telegram suitably subscribed 'HANDCUFFS . . . LONDON'.

The time for Marguerite's trial was fast approaching. On Wednesday 5 September, the archaic Grand Jury at the Old Bailey was sworn in to find, as a formality, a 'True Bill' against the prisoner, enabling the indictment to be preferred against her the following Monday. Press interest in the case began to revive and references to Marshall Hall's long and colourful career appeared in the social columns.

The coming of September was a welcome relief to journalists, the summer doldrums being blown away by several international crises. After Mussolini's Italian troops had bombarded Corfu, and the Spanish military coup, Germany too was in turmoil: claiming unpaid war reparations, France had occupied the industrial lands of the Ruhr in January. By the end of August, a catastrophic inflation, partly engineered by the German government to erode its foreign debt obligations, produced a rate of 23,000,000 marks to the pound. And from Germany there appeared in September the first photograph of the man the *Daily Graphic* referred to as the 'Bavarian Mussolini' and the *Daily Mail* called 'Herr Hittler' [sic].

CHAPTER 20

CURTAIN UP

People started queuing outside the narrow public entrance to the Central Criminal Court well before dawn on Monday 10 September 1923. 'Endeavours to be present [were] as strenuous as in the case of Crippen', thirteen years before. One woman sent her chauffeur down to Newgate at eight o'clock that morning, armed with a £10 note and instructions to reserve a place, but he had no takers.

The Old Bailey, as the Court is better known, presents a formidable appearance to its visitors, a grim and grimy structure, faced with unpolished Cornish granite and the grey Portland stone of the notorious Newgate gaol, which formerly occupied the site. Court Number One, home of so many grave criminal trials, stands on the first floor, leading off the large marble staircase and hall, the latter decorated with coloured mosaics on suitable juridical themes. By 10.30, when the court day began, every available seat was taken and many people stood at the sides and back.

In front of the judge's dais, beyond the seat of the court clerk ('Clerk of Arraigns' in Old Bailey argot), stood the imposing Treasury table, designed for the display of exhibits. Nearby sat a number of police officers, including Divisional Detective Inspector Grosse, the acting officer in the case. Behind him, in counsel's row, probably looking through the notes of his opening speech, sat the principal prosecuting counsel, known as 'Treasury Counsel'. Percival Clarke, a tall, thin, colourless man of 51, was a son of the great Victorian advocate Sir Edward Clarke, who had successfully defended Adelaide Bartlett (in a classic Victorian poisoning case) and appeared on behalf of Oscar Wilde in the first of the three trials of 1895.

Percival Clarke's 'junior' was Eustace Fulton, an experienced barrister also from a distinguished legal background. Sharing, indeed cramming, into counsel's seats were the defence team (Marshall Hall, the bulky Curtis-Bennett and their junior, Roland Oliver), accompanied by a clutch of lawyers representing the Fahmy family. Cecil Whiteley KC and J. B. Melville sat alongside Dr Abdul Fattah Ragai *bey*, an Egyptian lawyer, for Madame Said. The latter, sombrely dressed, had settled herself quietly at the back of the court. Edward Atkin, described as 'the well-known . . . authority on Egyptian and Eastern affairs', appeared with Dr Abdul Rahman el-Bialy *bey*, for another of Ali's sisters, Aziza, now Madame Roznangi.

These family lawyers had no status in the trial and were unable to take any direct part in the proceedings: they merely held a 'watching brief', no doubt with instructions to keep a careful note of the evidence, which might later prove to be relevant to the disposition of Ali's substantial estate in Egypt. Other members of the Bar, wholly unconnected with the proceedings, also squeezed into counsel's seats. Among them were two barristers in wig and gown, Ivy Williams and Helena Normanton, who caught the eye of the press. Women lawyers were a novelty in 1923.

High above the legal representatives, in the public gallery, could be seen an 'Egyptian woman' who had headed the queue of would-be spectators and 'an elegant Frenchman with the mark of Paris stamped on his clothes'. Opposite the lawyers, on the other side of the courtroom, were two empty benches awaiting their complement of twelve jurors.

Elsewhere, reporters balanced their notebooks where they could, while others, who had shamelessly used their influence with well-disposed members of the Bar, quickly secured their places. One high-minded barrister had refused to co-operate with two women friends who begged him for tickets. 'The evidence is likely to be of such a nature,' he told them severely, 'that I am not going to raise a finger to help anyone to listen to it, least of all women.'

Amid the excited buzz of conversation, ushers, policemen, journalists and spotty junior solicitors' clerks hurried about on their last-minute errands. At the rear of the court, dressed in morning coat and striped trousers, stood Edgar Bowker, who would accompany Marshall Hall throughout yet another celebrated defence, leaving his clerk's duties at Temple Gardens in other hands for the duration of the trial.

Three sharp knocks silenced the company and heralded the arrival of the judge. Everyone stood. In robes of scarlet trimmed with ermine, Mr Justice Rigby Swift entered court with the Sheriff, both carrying the traditional bouquets, a seasonal mélange of red and white roses. 'Oyez, oyez' cried an usher, making standard, antique reference to the judge's powers of 'Oyer and Terminer and General Gaol Delivery', a venerable phrase, partly of Norman-French origin, which referred to the process of hearing and determining issues at trial, with the power to commit to prison or to release defendants. The judge, round-faced and rubicund, bowed to counsel and settled himself in the enormous, throne-like chair which stood underneath the great Sword of Justice.

As the Clerk of Arraigns intoned the name 'Marie Marguerite Fahmy', another little procession made its way up the narrow staircase into the dock. Necks craned forward to get a first glimpse of the accused: Marguerite, conscious of the value of first impressions, was dressed as befitted a tragic widow. 'Madame Fahmy [was] in deep mourning, which emphasised the pallor of her complexion . . .', and she wore a black tailored coat, trimmed with fur, with a small cloche hat, whose wide brim and short veil cast a shadow over the upper part of her face. Her lips appeared pale, pressed tightly together, as she swayed momentarily when approaching the front of the dock. Holding her arm was a wardress, reported by the *Daily Express* as being 'a good looking young woman, whose neat and kindly personality suggested a ministering VAD' – a volunteer nurse from the Great War.

Even before the indictment was put to Marguerite, Marshall Hall was on his feet, eager to make his presence and personality felt from the start, knowing that the press would be hanging on his every word. The interpreter, Harry Ashton-Wolfe, was about to be sworn in, but Marshall Hall insisted that one interpreter was insufficient in the circumstances and asked for another to be brought in. The idea was that the first should interpret the evidence to Marguerite as she sat in the dock and the other would be used to translate to the court any French oral testimony and documents.

The indictment was simple enough, containing only one count, the particulars of which read 'MARIE MARGUERITE FAHMY on the 10th day of July 1923 in the County of London murdered Ali Kamel Fahmy *Bey*'. Initially, Marguerite 'did not seem at first fully to comprehend' what was being put to her, despite Ashton-Wolfe's translation, so the indictment was read a second time. '*Non coupable*' ('Not Guilty'), she responded, in a loud, clear voice.

A gaggle of people summoned for jury service then made its way into the packed courtroom, each anxious to know whether he or she would be selected to try this sensational case. The jury was made up from their number, the Clerk reading the names aloud from a little piece of card. Margaret Anne Barnwell, George Edmund Galliford, James John Butler, Frederick George Strohmenger, William Cronin, James Atkinson, Ernest William Turner, Arthur Mee, Herbert Horace Holt, Herbert Bracey Eyles, Mary Ann Austin and John Thomas Bailey took their seats in the jury-box. Marshall Hall appears not to have exercised the defence's right to challenge up to seven prospective jurors: perhaps his long experience had led him to believe in taking his jury as he found it.

The two women were described by the *Evening Standard* as 'matronly-looking, wearing good-rimmed spectacles and dressed in black': both would have had to have been over 30. The very thought of women jurors remained controversial. In May, the *Daily Express* used the headline 'CAN JURYWOMEN UNDERSTAND?' in reporting a civil case in which Mr Justice Darling, reactionary as ever, had discharged a number of women from jury service. 'It is hardly worthwhile keeping three women on the jury,' said the judge, barely concealing his contempt for the female mind, '[as] the evidence appears to be of a technical character.'

The Clerk of Arraigns read the indictment out to the jury, adding, 'To this indictment she has pleaded "Not Guilty". It is your charge to say whether she be guilty or not.' After a moment's silence, Percival Clarke rose to his feet, waiting for that flicker of the judge's eye which means that prosecuting counsel can embark on his opening statement, a précis of the Crown's case against the prisoner, indicating the principal witnesses and the likely nature of their evidence.

How much Clarke knew about the royal dimension is unclear. Written instructions from the DPP to his junior, Eustace Fulton, survive, but make no reference to the Prince and his involvement with Marguerite. However, as the Royal Household was already well aware in this case, sensitive matters are sometimes best dealt with by word of mouth. In his role as Senior Treasury Counsel, Clarke had worked closely with Bodkin in the prosecution of other grave criminal trials and would have had the DPP's confidence. From background information available to him, including the statements from people who would not be called to give evidence, Clarke would have been well-informed about Marguerite's background as a high-class Paris sex worker, contrary to her carefully constructed image as world-weary innocent. The way Clarke expressed himself in the course of the trial, particularly when applying for permission to cross-examine Marguerite about her relations with other men, supports this view. Clarke probably knew something about Marguerite's relationship with the Prince, as his conduct as prosecutor was a lacklustre affair, 'going through the motions', with vital issues left unexplored, important witnesses not called, and the defence effectively given free rein to create a monstrous scenario of depravity and cruelty on the part of someone no longer alive and able to answer back.

The apparently formidable case against Marguerite was set out by Clarke in a short speech, lasting under an hour and delivered in a dry monotone. Its character contrasted sharply with the episodes of human rage and passion, the references to high life in Egypt and France and to the violent tragedy that had occurred in London during the great thunderstorm exactly two months before.

Counsel's first words were prosaic: 'Madame Fahmy was married to her husband in December last. Her husband was in the diplomatic service and was a man of wealth and position.' Clarke went on to chronicle the brief courtship: 'In December she adopted the Mohammedan religion. Whether it was necessary or not, I do not know . . . Their natures seemed to be entirely unfitted one to the other . . . He is said to have been a quiet, retiring nervous sort of man, 22 years old, and she a woman rather fond of the gay life . . .'

Reference to events of 9 July, prior to the final scene in and around suite 41, led Clarke to his deadliest evidence, the recollections of John Beattie, the Savoy's night porter. 'Just as the porter was going away,' said Clarke, 'he heard a slight whistle behind him and, looking back, saw the deceased man stooping down, whistling and snapping his fingers at a little dog which had come out of the suite. In that position this man was last seen before he was killed.' Clarke emphasised to the jury that the post-mortem report on Ali was consistent with the Crown's contention that he had been shot from behind.

If this crucial evidence were to be accepted by the jury, it would completely demolish any suggestion of self-defence, or of a provocation so immediate as to reduce the case from one of capital murder to the lesser conviction of manslaughter, punishable not by hanging but by a term of imprisonment.

The defence did not have to indicate the precise nature of their answer to the charge before the trial began. But Clarke had the advantage of knowing, from Dr Gordon's statements in the July proceedings, what Marguerite had said immediately after the shooting. Trying to anticipate the line Marshall Hall would take, Clarke told the jury of Marguerite's assertion that Ali had advanced towards her threateningly in her bedroom (counsel seems to have delicately eschewed any reference to Marguerite's allegations of sodomy). 'She rushed for a revolver and fired it out of the bedroom window. She expected it to frighten him, but he still advanced towards her and [she] . . . pulled the trigger. She was surprised it went off, as having previously fired it from the window, she thought it would be unloaded . . .'

'This statement,' Clarke declared, slowly and with great emphasis, 'would have to be considered to see if the facts proved were consistent with the story she told.' He pointed out that Ali could not have been shot from Marguerite's bedroom: the shooting had, beyond any doubt, occurred in the corridor. Furthermore, the crushed beads, torn from Marguerite's white evening dress, had been found in Ali's room, which suggested that the final quarrel had taken place there, not in her own bedroom, as she had said.

'Coming to this country,' concluded Clarke in a chilly passage designed to eliminate the possibility of a French-style defence on the grounds of *crime passionnel*, 'persons are bound by the laws which prevail here. Every homicide is presumed to be murder unless the contrary is shown. From her own lips, it is known that she it was who caused the death of her husband. And in the absence of any circumstances to make it some other offence, you must find her guilty of murder.'

Before Clarke could call his first witness, a policeman who would produce a plan of the fourth floor at Savoy Court, Marshall Hall was on his feet again. His intention seems to have been purely tactical, with the aim of securing the jury's attention. Having earlier made a fussy application for two interpreters to be sworn, the great man now declared that he was 'willing to take the responsibility of not having the evidence interpreted to the accused'. The judge agreed, no doubt hoping to save a little public time.

After the plan had been produced and perused, it was the turn of the first important witness to testify. Said Enani came into court, 'a short dapper figure in a well-tailored blue suit', a man whose elegant manner and excellent English could not absolve him from being Egyptian and a non-Christian. To the defence, he was a very dangerous witness indeed: he had known the couple intimately and had been with them up to an hour or so before Ali's death. Unchallenged, he could damn Marguerite in the jury's mind as a hard, ambitious, pistol-packing woman with a violent temper, who had given Said's neurotic young master as good as he gave her and sometimes more into the bargain.

Marshall Hall knew all about Marguerite's allegations of impropriety between Ali and Said, as well as the other allegations about Ali's bisexuality. But luck plays its part in advocacy and, just after Said had begun to give evidence, his credibility began to be undermined by the simplest of tactical ploys.

Said Enani was, of course, a Muslim. Nowadays, a copy of the Koran would be available in court, but in 1923 the Old Bailey did not have one available. So Said was sworn on the New Testament. He had just started to describe Ali's family background, when Marshall Hall stood up and interrupted. Seizing the moment, he asked an innocent-seeming question, knowing full well what the answer was: 'My Lord, I should like to know on which book the witness has been sworn.'

A court usher confirmed that it was the New Testament, whereupon, ignoring Percival Clarke (who was, after all, just beginning to examine his own witness) and looking straight at the jury, Marshall Hall asked Said pointedly: 'Does the oath on the Bible bind you?' Said stated that it did and the judge expressed himself content, but Marshall Hall had sown a seed in the jury's mind. Perhaps this saturnine Egyptian had something to hide. It was all looking a bit fishy. Later, during cross-examination, a juryman, taking the bait, stood up and expressed concern. Was an oath taken on the New Testament really binding on a Muslim? Said replied, a shade too glibly: 'We do not swear in our country on books. We swear on the name of Almighty God only.'

Marshall Hall, exploiting the situation to the hilt, boomed out: 'I suggest your oath does not bind you and you know it does not – and there are Egyptian lawyers here whom you know who will say so.' Although he was quickly stopped by an irritated Rigby Swift, the tactic had worked and doubt clearly remained in the ranks of the jury about Said's credibility. The harsh language of Marshall Hall's intervention is a strong indication that he knew, before entering Court Number One, that he could attack Said Enani's character with impunity.

Marshall Hall had begun his cross-examination with a carefully worded reference to the relationship between master and secretary:

MARSHALL HALL: How long had you known Ali Fahmy?
SAID ENANI: About seven years.

MARSHALL HALL: Before he came into his money, you lived together?
SAID ENANI: No.

The phrase 'lived together' was a telling one, despite Said's denial. The jury could work out for themselves that, seven years ago, Ali had been only 16, and Said several years older. Marshall Hall pressed on with his covert suggestion:

MARSHALL HALL: . . . Did you say, he [Ali] was an Oriental and rather passionate?
SAID ENANI: Yes.
MARSHALL HALL: Did you tell Dr Gordon 'I've lost my job. I gave up ten years' job with the government to take this. Now I am a ruined man'?
SAID ENANI: Yes.
MARSHALL HALL: You were very much attached to Fahmy?
SAID ENANI: Yes . . .

Ali's florid appeal, begging Marguerite to join him in Cairo, was read out in full, as was the series of telegrams sent in October 1922, speaking of Ali's supposed grave illness. Using this episode, Marshall Hall launched another character attack on Said Enani, which, under normal circumstances, should have prompted a warning from the judge, rapping his pencil on the judicial dais, as was Rigby Swift's habit:

MARSHALL HALL: I am putting it to you that you and Fahmy conspired together to make false statements in order to induce this woman to go to Egypt.
SAID ENANI: No.

All this suggested a dark conspiracy between the two men to lure Marguerite to Egypt, though, as sometimes happens to the best advocates, Marshall Hall asked one question too many:

MARSHALL HALL: And the result of that is that this unfortunate lady comes out to Cairo?
SAID ENANI: She advanced her date only. She had agreed to go to Egypt [but] he wanted her before the time fixed.

A hint of Marguerite's venality and her true motive in marrying Ali emerged in one short exchange:

MARSHALL HALL: Do you know that Fahmy had implored her to marry him and that she had refused?
SAID ENANI: She said she would consult her lawyer.

Questions about Fahmy's palace disclosed a local custom, the revelation of which may have startled the more respectable business people on the jury:

MARSHALL HALL: You gave the order for the things in it?

SAID ENANI: No, everything was chosen by Fahmy.

MARSHALL HALL: Didn't you get commission on the orders?

SAID ENANI: Of course I got commission. [Laughter]

MARSHALL HALL: Ten per cent on half a million francs?

SAID ENANI: No, five per cent . . .

But the thrust of Marshall Hall's cross-examination, once the hint about Said's relationship with Ali had been driven home, was to present Marguerite as the abused wife, brought to the East on a false pretext, imprisoned and brutalised by her super-rich husband. A generalised sexual decadence, unquestionably Eastern, was canvassed:

MARSHALL HALL: You have known of Fahmy's intimacies with many women?

SAID ENANI: Yes, sir.

MARSHALL HALL: Do you know he treated them brutally, one and all?

SAID ENANI: No, sir, I cannot say brutally . . .

MARSHALL HALL: He was entitled by law to have four wives, was he not? . . .

The next part of the cross-examination was not fully reported in the newspapers. Marshall Hall, preparing the ground for Marguerite's evidence, 'put to the witness that Fahmy was a man of vicious and eccentric sexual appetite, but this the secretary loyally denied'.

The following passage, towards the end of the four-hour cross-examination, affords a good example of the way Marshall Hall could get his message across, ending with yet another sideswipe at Said, a venal, corrupt character, too close to his master for the comfort of decent English people.

MARSHALL HALL: Was not the Mme Fahmy of 1923 totally different from the Mme Laurent of 1922?

SAID ENANI: Perhaps.

MARSHALL HALL: Has every bit of life been crushed out of her these six months?

SAID ENANI: I do not know.

MARSHALL HALL: From a quite enter taining and fascinating woman, has she become miserable and wretched?

SAID ENANI: They were always quarrelling.

MARSHALL HALL: Did she say you and Fahmy were always against her and it was a case of two to one?

SAID ENANI: Yes.

MARSHALL HALL: Did you say if she

would give you £2,000, you would clear out of her way?

SAID ENANI: I said if she would discharge me I should be pleased to go away . . .

Other aspects of Ali's character were also exploited by Marshall Hall, who mercilessly used Said Enani as a sounding-board for many of Marguerite's accusations of cruelty, compiled since the beginning of the year with a view to an expensive divorce settlement.

Later in his cross-examination, Marshall Hall returned to the theme of intimacy between the two men:

MARSHALL HALL: Did you address Fahmy as 'Baba'?

SAID ENANI: Mme Fahmy used to call him 'Baba' because there is a story of Ali Baba . . . I used to refer to him, too, as 'Baba'.

At the very end of his questioning, Marshall Hall waved a copy of the cartoon from *Al Kashkoul*, in which the relationship between Ali, Said Enani and Said's own secretary had been lampooned:

MARSHALL HALL: Was not the relation ship between you and Fahmy *bey* noto rious in Egypt?

Said, of course, disagreed, and this further, blatant innuendo of homosexuality should have been the moment when the judge intervened to tell Marshall Hall that he had gone too far, risking exposure of Marguerite's own character if she were to give evidence. Percival Clarke, rising to re-examine his witness, complained, rather lamely, that the cartoon seemed to reflect on Said Enani's moral character, but Rigby Swift chose to make light of the situation, employing a poor example of judicial witticism in this capital case, an unpleasant echo of Mr Justice Darling's laboured jokes in murder trials:

JUDGE: It does not reflect on anybody's moral character, except perhaps the artist's. [Laughter]

Although the judge added, obtusely, that the only suggestion of the cartoon had been that the three men were inseparable, the jury would have taken on board the defence allegation that Said and Ali had been homosexual lovers.

The last witness of the day was potentially the most deadly. John Beattie, the night porter, a man with no axe to grind, gave his recollection of the fatal night, perfectly in accord with Percival Clarke's opening statement. Hardened observers wondered how the old pro would deal with the seemingly insurmountable fact that Ali had been whistling for an errant lapdog literally seconds before his wife had shot him dead.

The skilled advocate known when <u>not to ask questions</u>. Marshall Hall, barely cross-examined this most dangerous of witnesses, confining himself with the gentle suggestion, itself no more than a polite ridicule, that the man could not possibly have heard someone whistling above the roar of the storm.

Taking a great risk, Marshall Hall did what only the most seasoned criminal advocates dare to do in the face of such damning material. He ignored it.

The second day of Madame Fahmy's trial dawned wet, cold and windy. Only a few of the crowd, several hundred strong, were destined to find seats in the public gallery, spearheaded by an 'elderly, grey-haired woman [who] was the first to dash in . . .'

On Monday, the jury had been rewarded with a drive, ordered on their behalf by the judge after the court had risen at 4.15 p.m. Unfortunately, while they were being ferried along Archway Road, the charabanc broke down and they were obliged to spend an hour or two locked up in a hotel billiard-room until a replacement arrived. By court order, the jury was under the care of 'the Sheriffs, Bailiffs Monk & Lake & Mrs Bellini' and that evening spent their first night confined to the Manchester Hotel, Aldgate, their enforced home for the duration of the trial.

Once they had assembled in their jury-box, a few minutes before the court was due to sit, they

339

were treated to the well-rehearsed ritual which now invariably heralded the arrival of the Great Defender. An impression of majesty, with a touch of the valetudinarian (among other ailments, Marshall Hall's haemorrhoids frequently played up), seems to have created a striking and unforgettable effect.

'He would be preceded by a panoply of medical apparatus. First, his clerk [Bowker] would arrange his air-cushion; then there would be a row of bottles to set up on the desk containing smelling-salts and other medicines; there would also be some exquisite little eighteenth-century box, containing some invaluable pill; his noting pencils, green, red and blue, would be arranged in a row and, last, but not least, his [throat] spray would be ready to hand, which, according to his opponents, he would be certain to use in order to divert the attention of the jury when the case was going against him. Finally, when all was prepared, and the judge was waiting, the great man himself would come in . . .'

In addition, a footstool would be placed in position, for him to rest his legs, which were severely affected by varicose veins and the phlebitis which made standing for long periods extremely painful. He would manoeuvre the footstool or inflate a pneumatic cushion (very necessary for the great man's comfort) at tactically appropriate moments, just as he would do with the spray, 'hissing and gargling . . . to the distraction of both counsel who was speaking and the jury who were listening . . .'

Marguerite made an affecting entrance. She was seen to walk 'with short steps across the dock, which she entered supported by a wardress and fell listlessly into the chair . . .', frequently making use of smelling salts during the day's proceedings.

The first witness to be called was Arthur Marini, night manager at the Savoy, for whom the shooting of Ali Fahmy had become something of a personal nightmare. His account of the scene in and around the corridor outside the Fahmys' suite went smoothly enough, until he testified that he had understood Marguerite to remark that the couple had been quarrelling about a divorce.

Percival Clarke had not mentioned such an argument in his opening speech and Marshall Hall pounced, scenting danger. If the shooting had been the result of the couple quarrelling about a divorce, it would undermine Marguerite's defence that she shot Ali in self-defence to avoid serious sexual assault and also fearing for her life.

MARSHALL HALL: I should like the
    French of that, because it is quite new.
JUDGE: It is new to me and probably
    the prisoner and perhaps you would like
    it interpreted.
MARSHALL HALL: I would.

Although Marguerite could not understand English and her counsel had waived the need to translate everything to her, she knew that a problem had arisen. 'Madame Fahmy raised her head and listened with an alert air.' Marshall Hall left his place, as if to emphasise the significance of the occasion, went to the dock, and spoke to his client in French. The *Daily Telegraph* reported that, 'She replied in a few words and then relapsed into her former nonchalant demeanour.'

The little episode indicates how easily a court and jury can be misled. Marshall Hall went on to ask Marini why he had not said anything about the divorce at the committal proceedings in July, in an attempt to weaken the force of what could be seen as a dishonest embellishment to her orginal story. Marini replied that he had simply responded to questions put to him in court at the time. 'I had to answer "Yes" or "No",' he said plaintively.

In fact, his original statement to the police (not ordinarily available to the defence, a declaration made less than four hours after the tragedy), quoted Marguerite as saying, 'We were quarrelling over my divorce that was to take place shortly in Paris.' Percival Clarke does not seem to have made any application to the judge, as he could have done in the circumstances, to get her original statement before the jury. Either the son had not inherited the forensic talents of his father or, more likely in the circumstances, he was sleepwalking through the prosecution.

Marshall Hall's fluent French was already standing his client in good stead. After Clement

342

Bich, the hotel's assistant manager, had rendered one of Marguerite's despairing statements, '*J'avais perdu ma tête*', as 'I have lost my head', Hall suggested that she could have said '*J'avais perdu la tête*', meaning, 'I was frightened out of my wits'. The witness agreed that this was a possible alternative interpretation.

With the arrival of Police Sergeant George Hall in the witness-box, attention shifted to the fatal weapon, a menacingly black, .32 semi-automatic Browning pistol, about 6 inches by 4 inches and weighing some 20½ ounces.

George Hall does not seem to have had the sharpest mind. Producing the pistol as an exhibit, Sergeant Hall referred to it quite wrongly as a 'revolver'. He was sternly corrected by Marshall Hall, who knew his weaponry backwards, but the clumsy officer soon afterwards compounded his error in his answer to a pertinent question from the foreman of the jury. The juryman had pointed out that 'certain automatic weapons continued to fire as long as the trigger was depressed' and, therefore, unless the user was remarkably nimble in handling the gun, it would be practically impossible to fire a single shot. According to Sergeant Hall, the pistol would fire as long as the trigger was pulled: the gun definitely did not need pressure on its trigger for each shot. His assertion was completely wrong.

The next witness, Robert Churchill, would try to put matters right. A burly man, Churchill was the country's leading firearms expert and had given evidence in a host of criminal trials. He had examined the pistol, manufactured in Herstal, near Liège, by the famous Fabrique Nationale d'Armes de Guerre, and numbered 127303. Its .32 calibre was shared by all the cartridges, cartridge cases and bullets recovered from the scene of the shooting. These latter items were suitable for use in the pistol and were each marked 'SFM', standing for the Société Française des Munitions, in Paris. Churchill told the court that the full capacity of the pistol was eight rounds (seven in the magazine and one in the barrel). He had test-fired the pistol himself and found that it was in perfect working order and not liable to accidental discharge.

Percival Clarke, picking up the foreman's point, asked, 'Is it a weapon that continues to fire when the trigger is pressed or does the trigger require pressure for each shot?' Churchill contradicted Sergeant Hall, giving a reply that seemed ominous for the defence: 'The trigger has to be pulled for each shot. It is automatic loading, but not automatic firing.'

The pistol was loaded by inserting a clip of cartridges in the hand-held butt, a process that did not require much force. With the clip in place, the gun could be primed by pulling back the sliding breach cover (which lay over the barrel) about three-quarters of an inch and then releasing it. This was a much more forceful exercise than loading, and required some strength and experience of the weapon.

Another dangerous aspect for the defence lay in the degree of effort required to fire the gun. 'The pull of the trigger,' said Churchill, 'is eight and a quarter pounds. It is not a light pull.' Furthermore, the pistol had a threefold safety provision: the magazine had to be in place; the normal safety catch needed to be pressed (usually by the thumb); and the butt safety grip – on the rear of the butt – had to be squeezed by the palm of the firer's hand as the trigger was pulled. Churchill again affirmed, at the end of Clarke's examination-in-chief, that this was not the sort of weapon to go off accidentally.

Marshall Hall had worried long and hard about this firearms evidence. Churchill was the most important prosecution witness after Said Enani and the tactics that had been successfully employed the previous afternoon to smear Ali's former confidential private secretary were not available to challenge the evidence of a world-renowned gunsmith. Marshall Hall was only too aware that the mere process of getting the pistol into operation suggested that Marguerite knew full well how to use it.

Before the trial started, Marshall Hall had called in to Whistler's, another Strand gun shop, where he enlisted the help of a Mr Stopp, whom he had known for half a century. Together, they minutely examined a similar .32 Browning, which was brought along to court. Years earlier, in a murder trial at Stafford Assizes, Marshall Hall's courtroom demonstration of a revolver had helped secure his client's acquittal. He would keep the idea up his sleeve for possible use on Madame Fahmy's behalf later in the trial.

For the moment, though, the need was to perform a damage-limitation exercise on Robert Churchill. A slice of ham was served up. 'I want you to give me your careful attention,' said Marshall Hall to Churchill, using his most magisterial manner as he rose to cross-examine. He turned solemnly, looking straight at the judge. 'A great deal depends on this witness's evidence and I shall be some time with him.' Rigby Swift, quite used to this sort of technique, blandly assured counsel that there was no time limit, as long as the questions were relevant.

To assist the dramatic effect, the pistol loaned by Messrs Whistler was produced from a box and a second, dismantled one was set out on the exhibit table. Holding the first gun in his hand, Marshall Hall put numerous technical questions to the gun expert. These seem to have been largely irrelevant, designed simply to impress the jury with Marshall Hall's expertise, so that his ultimate submissions, arguments that might not strictly accord with the facts of the .32 pistol's mode of operation, would thereby gain credence.

When the judge asked Marshall Hall if he wanted his pistol made an exhibit, there was a short diversion. Counsel had replied, lightly, that he was afraid it might get lost. Rigby Swift made another little joke, accompanied by a plaint not entirely favourable to the defence:

RIGBY SWIFT: You are much safer without it. [Laughter] If there were fewer of these things in the hands of the public, we should not be here so often and I look forward to the day when it will be a criminal offence to have a revolver [sic] . . . A revolver can be of no legitimate use in this country.

The crux of Marshall Hall's questioning was the fact that, once the pistol had been primed by pulling back the breach cover and releasing it, and the weapon fired, another bullet would automatically enter the chamber. Churchill agreed that if someone, thinking to clear the barrel of a loaded pistol, discharged a single shot, it would immediately be replaced by another bullet.

The suggestion was then made by Marshall Hall that, when the pistol was tightly gripped, 'a very small pressure' on the trigger would discharge several shots. This proposition does not accord with the working of this type of pistol and was in manifest contradiction to Churchill's earlier evidence about the substantial eight and a quarter pound pull on the trigger required for each shot. For some reason, Churchill did not robustly disagree with what was being put to him, as surely he should have done. Contemporary reports state simply that 'Mr Churchill hesitated and the pistol was passed round the jury', who tested the mechanism, using a dummy cartridge. Perhaps Marshall Hall's battery of footstool, air cushion and throat spray was being put to use yet again.

Sensing his advantage, Marshall Hall quickly brought the expert back to the loading mechanism, which he had been exploring just a moment before:

MARSHALL HALL: An inexperienced person might easily reload the weapon thinking that, in fact, he was emptying it?
CHURCHILL: Yes.

Marguerite, of course, was that 'inexperienced person'. During Churchill's evidence, she lost her earlier impassivity and showed rather more interest in the proceedings than might have been expected from an *ingénue*. 'Mme Fahmy made notes with a blue pencil on a sheet of paper . . . while her glance travelled continuously from counsel to witness and back again. While her leading counsel was handling the pistol, Mme Fahmy showed great interest . . .'

Towards the end of the gunsmith's evidence, the judge showed that he was still concerned about the evidential conflict with Sergeant Hall. Churchill was able to settle that point, at least, by an analogy that veterans of the Great War, possibly some of the jurymen themselves, would have appreciated. 'A lot of people think these pistols are like Lewis guns. They are not. Each bullet requires separate pressure . . .' His last words also struck a jarring note for the defence: 'It's impossible to load this pistol with the safety catch on.'

If Marshall Hall had won his game with Said Enani hands down, his spar with Churchill was less successful, although some students of the Fahmy case have maintained that this was a great triumph of cross-examination. Marguerite was still vulnerable. She had killed her husband with a large, deadline handgun, indubitably her own property, a lethal pistol far removed from the small revolvers, .22 or less, which were at that time thought of as suitable for ladies to carry in their handbags for self-protection. What was more, to fire the Browning required a considerable degree of skill and application. It was not a weapon designed for pinpoint accuracy, but three of its bullets had struck her husband and one had ploughed its way neatly through his left temple.

The advent of Dr Gordon, whose fleshy face had been snapped outside the Old Bailey that day, beneath a light grey trilby, gave a much-needed tonic to flagging defence morale. In some ways, the doctor was a curious witness for the Crown. He had been the accused's medical adviser, was on friendly terms with her, and had visited his patient in Holloway several times while she was on remand. Nevertheless, the prosecution is under a duty to call witnesses 'capable of belief' and, given the hidden background to the case, Percival Clarke showed no reluctance in calling him to give evidence.

Dr Gordon described how Marguerite had consulted him during the first week of July and made the first clear reference in the trial to those tiresome, painful haemorrhoids, doubtless aggravated by the hot and sticky weather of the brief heatwave. On the fatal morning, he had found Marguerite 'very dazed and frightened' after the shooting, but she had remembered to hand him the letter in which she had set out her reasons for cancelling the booking at the London nursing home and returning to Paris.

Of the greatest importance was what Marguerite had told her doctor in the dawn light of 10 July, while they had sat huddled in the inspector's room at Bow Street with the great storm still rumbling overhead. At the trial, Dr Gordon expanded somewhat on his written statement, composed that same day. In particular, his account of Marguerite's words now included an allegation that 'Fahmy had brutally handled and pestered her' in the suite, before advancing threateningly in her bedroom.

The judge wanted to know whether Madame Fahmy had explained what she meant by her husband having 'brutally handled her'. 'She told me that Fahmy had taken her by the arms in the bedroom,' said the doctor, adding, 'She showed me a scratch on the back of her neck about one and a half inches long, probably caused by a fingernail. She said it was caused by her husband.'

The doctor was not asked, it appears, whether this injury might just as likely have been self-inflicted, and Marshall Hall, seizing the opportunity, persuaded Gordon to agree that the mark was consistent with 'a hand clutching her throat'.

So far, Dr Gordon seems to have been pussy-footing around the allegations of sodomy. Cross-examination on the point was brief but effective. Bowdlerised reports appeared in the press, the *Daily Telegraph* reporting that 'Madame Fahmy had complained that her husband was very passionate and that his conduct had made her ill. Accused's condition was consistent with the conduct on the part of her husband which she alleged . . .', behaviour described by the *Daily Sketch* as 'violent ill-treatment'.

Another fragment of evidence useful to the defence was Gordon's 'clear understanding', from Marguerite's words, of her belief that the pistol had become unloaded by the single shot she had earlier fired through a window of the hotel suite.

Prosecution evidence also included the post-mortem and the testimony of three witnesses from the Savoy staff. Some hours after the shooting, a chambermaid, Ellen Dryland, had spotted the cartridge case in Marguerite's bedroom. A few days earlier, she had found the Browning pistol under the bolster while she was making the bed. With considerable aplomb, she had put the gun in a drawer of the bedside table. Next morning, she was surprised to find it tucked into the fabric and the back of an armchair. Sharp-eyed valet Albert Dowding had found one of the bullets in the corridor a week after Ali's death. Jane Seaman, housekeeper at the Savoy, told how she had handed the bullet found by the valet to Clement Bich, the assistant manager.

The Crown's case ended with the police evidence, mostly of a formal character, with no significant disputes. DDI Grosse told of seeing Fahmy's body in the mortuary at Charing Cross Hospital (an account which reduced to tears Mme Said, unhappy recipient of Marguerite's callously endorsed portrait photograph of herself). He also described examining the scene of the fatality, none too carefully as it seems, before his first encounter with Madame Fahmy at Bow Street.

French-speaking Detective Sergeant Allen gave Marguerite's answer to the charge, though the newspaper copy garbled 'He has told me many times "kill me" . . .' into 'He has told me many times that he would kill me . . .', just as some reports of Fahmy's impassioned letter to Marguerite in September 1922 turned '*Torche de ma vie*' ('Torch of my life') into the more apt 'Torture of my life'.

CHAPTER 21

CENTRE STAGE

Marguerite was going to have to go into the witness-box and tell her side of the story. That much was clear. There was no doubt that she had fired the shots that killed her husband and only she could give real force to the gamut of allegations that had been made about Ali in cross-examination, and which would be amplified in her counsel's opening speech to the jury. Marshall Hall's invariable practice was to explain carefully to a defendant the pros and cons of giving evidence and secure written authority for the decision.

He began his opening speech for the defence on a low key, pointing out the three possible verdicts of murder, manslaughter or outright acquittal. The kernel of Marguerite's defence would be 'justifiable killing because she was in fear of her life'.

Marshall Hall neatly tackled Percival Clarke's description of Ali as a 'quiet, retiring nervous sort of young man', quoting the physical description set out in the post-mortem report: 'a man of five feet nine or five feet ten, muscular and strong'. This he contrasted with Marguerite's vulnerability. 'Her position is an extraordinarily difficult one,' he argued, 'as she is a stranger in a strange land. She speaks no English and understands practically none and every word that she will give in evidence will have to be . . . translated. The effect . . . will no doubt be seriously lessened before it comes to your ears.' In fact, Marguerite would be greatly assisted by the need for an interpreter. This slows down the pace of questioning (always fairly slow because of the need to make notes of evidence), allowing extra time to deal with awkward questions.

Sensibly, he did not try to whitewash Marguerite's character completely. 'The accused is perhaps a woman of not very strict morality,' he conceded. '. . . She is an extraordinarily attractive woman and when they first met, she was as infatuated with [Fahmy] as he was with her.' He moved quickly to the association between Ali and Said Enani. Said, he alleged, 'had been very ungracious to her . . . she was very jealous of his influence over her husband'. Said was a bad lot. 'I am not going to say much about the so-called secretary and great personal friend, Said Enani. You will form your own opinion as to the sort of influence he had over Fahmy.' Together, this odd couple had enticed Marguerite to Egypt by trickery.

Marshall Hall's foray into homophobia was accompanied by a measure of racism. Marguerite, the older woman, had been attracted to the younger Ali, who had used his 'Eastern cunning' to make himself agreeable to her. 'You have to consider,' he added, 'the relationship between East and West and the extraordinary pride an Eastern man takes in the possession of a Western woman . . .' Marguerite had been left in Egypt 'absolutely at the mercy of his entourage of black servants'.

Briefly digressing from his theme and plainly to introduce an element of mystery, Marshall Hall made reference to the sealed document Marguerite had written in January 1922, alleging that Ali had sworn on the Koran to kill her. The paper had been opened by her lawyer, Maître Assouad, in the presence of two barristers. 'Whether or not the contents . . . are evidence depends very much on the line Madame Fahmy takes in the witness-box. I cannot say what the contents are because I am not entitled to at this stage . . .'

Reference to the Muslim marriage brought 'dramatic gestures and heightened inflection [as] counsel continued to outline the story', using his trump card, the allegations of sodomy:

> After the marriage ceremony was over, all sort of restraint on Fahmy's part ceased. He took her away up country. He developed from an attentive, plausible and kind lover into a ferocious brute. That is her own language and I adopt it. She discovered for the first time that he not only had the vilest of vile tempers, but was vile himself, with a filthy perverted taste. From that day onwards down to the very night, within a few moments of the time when a bullet sent that man to

eternity, he was pestering her [for unnatural sexual intercourse] . . . She will tell you that . . . he kept a black valet to watch over this white woman's suite of rooms, conditions that really make me shudder . . . that state of obedience which a black man wants from a woman who is his chattel.

A long catalogue of Marguerite's grievances followed, including an allegation that Fahmy had once refused to let his wife travel in his car, sending her in a tram instead, accompanied by a black servant: 'She could not go anywhere without these black things watching her.' Then, 'to a hushed court', Marshall Hall read out the anonymous letter that Marguerite had received at the Savoy on 3 July, two days after their arrival, with its references to the 'craftiness' of Easterners, poison and possible accidents. Neither the judge nor prosecuting counsel made any attempt to stop Marshall Hall reading out this very dubious document, which, apart from any other defect, was of unknown origin and of little relevance to the direct issue that the jury was trying. But an air of unreality, a touch of hysteria, was beginning to pervade Court Number One.

'Fahmy's threats were not empty threats,' continued Marshall Hall, warming to his subject. 'Orientals have the power of carrying out their threats. Madame Fahmy was guarded by an irresponsible black Sudanese' – in reality, Ali's diminutive valet – 'who was absolutely the creature of his master. Fahmy had said, "You shall not escape me. In twenty-four hours you will be dead." That threat was made on the night before the tragedy . . .' Marguerite, 'a poor, wretched woman suffering the tortures of the damned', had fired the pistol in desperation as Ali 'crouched for the last time, crouched like an animal, crouched like an Oriental . . .'

He came to his peroration, the usual strong meat of the Marshall Hall style. 'I submit that this woman, driven to exasperation by the brutality and beastliness of this man, whose will she had dared to oppose, thought that he was carrying out the threat he had always made and that, when he seized her by the neck, he was about to kill her.'

That reference to seizure by the neck dovetailed neatly into the evidence of the day's last witness. Although, by the rules, Marguerite should have been the first to be called, Marshall Hall, not for the only time, broke precedent and produced the Medical Officer from Holloway, Dr J. H. Morton. During his speech, Marshall Hall had referred dramatically to 'a new and wonderful piece of evidence' that had emerged 'thanks to His Lordship's intervention'. It was a clever way of exploiting Rigby Swift's concern about Dr Gordon's testimony, which had mentioned a scratch mark at the back of Marguerite's neck.

The judge had asked for a report from the prison and Dr Morton confirmed that Marguerite had been admitted with three abrasions in the same place. It added little to what Dr Gordon had already described. Marshall Hall then asked an outrageously leading question of his own witness:

> Were those marks consistent with having been caused by a man's hand?

The answer was affirmative, but as in the case of Dr Gordon's evidence, no one seems to have canvassed the possibility of self-infliction. By now it was late in the afternoon and the judge was growing a little worried about the direction the case was taking. It was important to ensure that Marshall Hall should not be seen to be making the running. When the court adjourned for the day, he warned the jury not to come to a definite conclusion before they had heard all the evidence.

Marshall Hall's opening address resembled the heavy shelling that precedes a battle assault. He was softening up his target, using his dramatic style to the full, appealing to a jury that was likely to have been inimical to homosexuality and suspicious of foreigners, especially 'black' ones. Frequent references to the perceived decadence of the East, to the guile of the 'Oriental', would have struck a chord in an English jury.

In childhood, some of the jury's complement of twelve would have had the *Thousand and One Nights* as nursery reading, with exotic tales of the court of Haroun al-Raschid, magic carpets, and the journeying of Sinbad the Sailor. In the expurgated version available to Victorian youngsters, readers would have missed the earthy humour and scatological wit of the complete series, but there would have been much to excite the imagination, even if the stories were a poor guide to contemporary realities in the Near and Middle East.

There was a distinct possibility, too, that one or more of the jurymen had done war service in the eastern Mediterranean. Before the fiasco of the Gallipoli landings in 1915, many British troops had been stationed in Egypt and, further east, the Arabian subcontinent, Mesopotamia and Palestine had all been theatres of war against the Turks. Troopships bound for India would have had to pass through the Suez Canal, putting into Port Said or Ismailia.

Anyone who had spent time in Egypt while serving in the armed forces or who had travelled there as an English civilian would have been exposed to the prevailing prejudice against things Eastern in general and against nearly all things Egyptian in particular. Egyptians were regarded, by and large, as a shifty bunch. The *Daily Mail* lambasted them as 'the most volatile and feather-headed race in the world', a statement that reflected the view that Egyptians were not only incapable of running their own affairs, but were thoroughly ungrateful to Britain into the bargain. Nevertheless, the British in Egypt continued to believe in their mission. That they had never begun to understand, let alone accept, the ways of the native population is evident from contemporary press coverage.

It would be surprising if this pervasive contempt for the Egyptian people had not found its way into the minds of those who comprised the jury in the Fahmy case. Their outlook would have been, in all probability, a hopeless mishmash when it came to anything Middle Eastern.

The recent triumphs of Lawrence of Arabia had given substantial, supposedly unwanted publicity to the strange little man who had fought for his beloved Arabs in the Great War. The slick salesmanship of Lowell Thomas, an American journalist, had much to do with the creation of the Lawrence legend in the years after 1918. The image of Lawrence in his spectacular white, flowing Arab costume was striking enough, but this breathlessly romantic impression of 'the East' was by no means the first manifestation of the English public's interest in such things. At least since the turn of the century, there had been a glut of novels written about dusky sheiks, women innocent or 'fast', desert sands, cool oases and searing passion. Stuffy, puritanical England went wild about the desert myth.

One of the most successful exponents of this genre was Robert Hichens, who had originally made a name for himself in the mid-1890s with *The Green Carnation*, an exploitative novel inspired by the world of Oscar Wilde, written just before his fall. Hichens had travelled extensively in the Arabic-speaking world and was a prolific author. *The Garden of Allah*, set in Morocco, ran to forty-three editions between 1904 and 1929 and was made into a film in 1917. Probably his best-known work was *Bella Donna*, published in 1909.

The setting of the novel is Egypt and there are parallels with the Fahmy case. The sinister Mahmoud Baroudi, 'of mixed Greek and Egyptian blood', embodies a dangerous combination of Western manners and Eastern deceit. '[Baroudi] was remarkably well-dressed in clothes . . . which he wore with a carelessness almost English, but also with an easy grace that was utterly foreign . . . Probably he was governed by the Oriental's conception of women as an inferior sex . . .' Hichen's description of Baroudi had been read by a wide public for nearly fifteen years by the time H. V. Morton made his slighting references to Ali Fahmy in 1923 as an Egyptian, 'too well dressed to look right' and whose 'dangerous magnetism' attracted white women.

Ruby Chepstow, 'a woman with a past' and married to the virtuous Nigel Armine, slips aboard Baroudi's *dahabeeyah* on the Nile, falling helplessly in love with the brutal Easterner, attended by 'a huge Nubian'. '[Baroudi] acknowledged calmly that he had treated her as a chattel. She loved that . . . She felt cruelty in him and it attracted her.' In this regard, *Bella Donna* exemplifies the myth of the potent sheik, an unbridled sexual animal with rape perpetually in mind.

Baroudi's target was the white woman. Marshall Hall's condemnation of Ali Fahmy could have sprung directly from the pages of *Bella Donna*. Baroudi, '. . . like a good many of his smart, semi-cultured, self-possessed and physically attractive young contemporaries had gloried in his triumph among the Occidental women . . . [striking] a blow at the Western man'. He was 'one of those Egyptians who go mad over the women of Europe . . . their delicate colouring and shining hair'.

Baroudi's evil influence prompts Ruby to poison Nigel, but the plot is discovered in time to save his life and, ruined, Ruby wanders off alone into the desert night. *Bella Donna*, forgotten today, was a popular success for some twenty years after its publication. In September 1923, just as Marguerite's trial was starting, news came that Pola Negri, the smouldering Hollywood film star, would be appearing in a film of the novel.

Elinor Glyn (then mistress of Marquess Curzon) had employed a desert theme in *His House* (1909) and during the next decade Katherine Rhodes wrote stories of 'the fire and passion of the relentless desert'. Another blockbuster from the Mystic East first appeared in 1921, perhaps the greatest (or most notorious) of them all. Promoted by an elaborate hype, *The Sheik*, by E. M. Hull, had gone through a hundred editions in English by mid-1923 ('E. M.' stood for Edith Maud, the wife of a Derbyshire pig farmer). An accompanying dance tune, *The Sheik of Araby*, had sold 250,000 copies as sheet music in England alone, where gramophone recordings of it were made by four different bands between March and August 1922.

The film based on the book was a sensation, at

any rate in the Western world. Starring Rudolph Valentino, *The Sheik*, as the *Evening News* reported in July 1923, 'has been shown in 1260 cinemas in Great Britain', where the Paramount Film Corporation estimated that five million people had paid to see it.

In the novel *The Sheik*, tomboyish Diana Mayo unwisely contemplates 'an expedition into the desert with no chaperone . . . only native camel drivers and servants'. There she is captured by Sheik Ahmed Ben Hassan, 'the handsomest and cruellest face she had ever seen . . .' and taken to his tent. Breathlessly, she asks, 'Why have you brought me here?' Prompted by the classic reply, 'Are you not woman enough to know?', Diana succumbs to 'the flaming light of desire burning in his eyes . . . the fierce embrace . . . [of] the man's pulsating body . . . the touch of his scorching lips'. He was an 'Oriental beast . . . in his Oriental disregard of the woman subjugated', presenting 'a hideous exhibition of brute strength and merciless cruelty . . .' This purple prose might have come from Marshall Hall's opening address to the jury in the Fahmy case.

Having thus far lived their ordinary lives amid this welter of misinformation about Egypt and the Arab world, Marguerite Fahmy's jury were unlikely to have taken a detached, dispassionate view of her relationship with the dead man. For good measure, the Tut-Ankh-Amun discoveries high-lighted Eastern exoticism, a distant remove from

363

the humdrum world of suburban London in which most of the jury lived.

The first would-be spectator to arrive, at 2 a.m. on Wednesday morning, was young Mr James Stewart of Lancing, who told the *Pall Mall Gazette*'s reporter that he had been a ship's steward in charge of the Fahmys' suite, when they had travelled aboard the SS *Nile*, possibly before Christmas 1922. Mr Stewart was determined to see the show. At 2.30 he had refused £5 from a 'well-dressed man' for his place and later a woman unsuccessfully offered him '£3 and 50 cigarettes'. The police soon started to break up the queues that were forming in Newgate despite a very chilly wait, but not before another young man received the day's best offer, 'to keep him for a week at one of the best hotels in London', made in vain by a prosperous-looking gentleman.

The *Daily Telegraph* reported that Marguerite seemed 'brighter and more alert' when she entered the dock, which she did for once without the assistance of a prison officer. The start of her evidence was delayed by legal wrangling, during which the jury were sent out of court. Percival Clarke, very properly, had told Marshall Hall that he intended to cross-examine Marguerite 'as to whether or not she had lived an immoral life', to show that she was 'a woman of the world, well able to look after herself'. The judge would now have to make a ruling about the issue of Marguerite's past character.

Marshall Hall made a show of resisting a damaging

attack. 'The only effect,' he told the judge, '. . . would be to prejudice the jury unfavourably against this woman. I have not opened the case that she is a woman of moral character . . .' Clarke, mindful of the dirt about Marguerite set out in ex-Chief Inspector Stockley's confidential report, said that he wanted to dispel the idea that this was 'a poor child practically domineered over by this man'. He was entitled, he felt, to ask how she treated other men and in any case defence counsel had opened that she was an immoral woman.

Since 1898, when, for the first time, a prisoner had been allowed to give evidence on his or her own behalf (as opposed to merely making an unsworn statement from the dock, which had little evidential value), an accused had been shielded from questions about character and background. That protection could be lost, at the judge's discretion, depending on how the defendant's character was being presented at the trial and also if imputations of bad character had been levelled by the defence against prosecution witnesses.

The judge, aware of the danger that the Prince's name would emerge, declared emphatically that the jury should not be told much about Marguerite's eventful past, ruling that prosecuting counsel would have to confine himself to questions about Marguerite's relations with Ali Fahmy, which was to say, since mid-1922. 'Sir Edward has said that she was a loose woman,' he observed, 'but he said it in such a way that he gave the impression . . .

that she was an innocent and most respectable lady. It is a difficult thing to do, but Sir Edward, with all that skill we have admired for so long, has done it . . .' The judge, ignoring the savage attack on Said Enani's character, passed over the accusation of homosexuality. 'Although I thought there was going to be an attack . . .,' said the judge, flying in the face of plain fact, 'there really was no attack made on his character.' Relying on inside information, just before the trial started, Lord Curzon had been absolutely right to predict that the Prince's name would be kept out of evidence at the trial.

The jury filed back in, to be told that they were now to be deprived of newspapers for the duration of the trial, since they would report the substance of the legal argument. 'I am sorry to deprive you of them,' said the judge, sympathetically. 'It must be very boring to be shut up all the evening without a newspaper, but I am bound to do it.'

Marguerite was then called to give evidence in her own defence. She was seen to falter as she approached the witness-box and required the help of a wardress to complete the short journey. Rigby Swift intimated that Marguerite could give her evidence from a chair and as she took her seat, it was possible for most of those in court to see her clearly for the first time. The *Evening Standard* thought that Marguerite 'was not so much beautiful as interesting looking. Small, mobile features; a rather petulant mouth, large expressive eyes – such was the picture framed by a black mushroom hat and flowing black veil.' The *Daily Sketch* saw her as 'dark haired and lustrous eyed', an altogether more flattering description than that afforded readers of the *Daily Mail*, which ungallantly claimed that Marguerite was not 'the handsome woman of the photographs', but rather 'of a pronounced Latin type'.

When Marguerite stood up to take the oath, Marshall Hall, recalling his recent, very effective destabilisation of Said Enani, prudently suggested that, as Marguerite was now a Muslim, she should be sworn on the Koran. As before, the judge said the witness could be sworn in any way that was binding in conscience and Marguerite took her oath on the Bible. Unlike in the case of the unfortunate Said, nobody seems to have thought the worse of her for doing so. But then Marguerite was European.

Harry Ashton-Wolfe, the official court interpreter, a stocky man with close-cropped hair and a luxuriant black moustache, stepped forward to translate the oath into French. In barely a whisper, Madame Fahmy declared, '*Je jure*' ('I swear'). Marguerite was again demurely dressed in black: it struck Ashton-Wolfe, he later wrote, as a peculiar thing that a woman should be mourning for a man she had herself killed.

Marguerite's evidence began with some very brief personal details. She told the court that she had divorced Charles Laurent after his desertion, but the jury were never to be aware of Marguerite's blunt words to old Madame Denart in 1918, that she would 'kick him out' after six months of marriage. She claimed that she had lost an annual allowance of 36,000 francs (£450) from Laurent when she married Ali. Marshall Hall then read out the civil contract of marriage to Fahmy, including the provision that he should pay her a dowry of £2,000. Ali had only paid her £450, she said, conveniently forgetting the jewellery and other costly gifts made to her both before and after the wedding, estimated to be worth 200,000 francs (£2,500).

The pace began to hot up when Marguerite started to describe her life as a Muslim bride. 'Her low, musical voice carried well as she answered in rapid French the questions put to her. Now and then there was just the ghost of a shrug of the shoulders. Occasionally, the black-gloved hands toyed with a grey silk handkerchief . . . sometimes pressed to eyes or mouth.'

After her sister Yvonne had returned to Paris (possibly because she and Ali had been getting on rather too well), Marguerite was left alone with Fahmy *bey*. 'There were twelve black men as servants in the house,' she said, 'but no other white women apart from my maid and I.' After a quarrel, Ali had sworn on the Koran to kill her, an allegation that enabled Marshall Hall to make a second dramatic reference to the document Marguerite had composed on 22 January 1923.

Although the trial process had been subject to

outside interference to protect the reputation of the Prince of Wales, the appearance of due process had to be maintained and such blatant over-egging by Marshall Hall was too much for the judge. Rigby Swift tetchily intervened to express disapproval of mysterious documents that did not properly form part of the evidence. 'This court,' he said portentously, 'is not a receptacle for waste paper . . .' Marshall Hall responded by claiming that he had simply wanted to show that 'on a particular day this woman wrote a particular document and I wanted her to identify it'. 'Quite irrelevant,' declared the judge. 'You might as well say that on Christmas Day 1920 she sent a Christmas card to her lawyer.' On that abrasive note, the matter ended, at least for the moment.

Marshall Hall wisely shifted attention to the scenes on the Nile en route for Luxor. 'The first day,' said Marguerite, '[Ali] tried to frighten me and fired a revolver several times above my head. He had three revolvers.' She had often tried to leave him, but each time she did so, he would cry and beg her to stay, promising to reform. Once he had got her aboard the *dahabeeyah*, however, Ali's attitude had changed. He had frequently struck her, saying 'You can never leave me any more', eventually locking her into her cabin, evidence that Marguerite gave 'in a choking voice'.

Marguerite's letter to Maître Assouad was read out, providing an opportunity for more racial mileage. 'I was terrified,' Marguerite claimed, 'I was alone on board and surrounded by black men.' She described her 'horror' of the 'black valet', who was 'always following her', even to the extent of coming into her room while she was dressing. Her complaints to Ali had met with a dismissive response, distinctly resembling dialogue from *The Sheik*: 'He has the right. He does not count. He is nothing.'

She claimed that she had been forced to take the tram to visit a Cairo cinema, because Ali had denied her the use of a car. In the presence of 'Said Enani and four black men', Fahmy had delivered an unprovoked blow to her chin on her return to the mansion with Mukhta *bey*. 'I fell against the door, suffering excruciating pain . . . next day I was treated for a dislocated jaw.'

All this neatly led to revelations of the sexual decadence of non-white society. 'Madam Fahmy proceeded in a faltering and hesitating voice to describe her relations with her husband . . .' The press drew a veil over these intimate details, though it was noted by the *Evening Standard* that 'only three women got up and left [the public gallery] when Madame Fahmy was being asked questions of such a nature that she finally buried her face in her hands'. After she had endured this sexual abuse, said Marguerite, Fahmy had again threatened to kill her with a pistol in Cairo, crying, 'I am all powerful; I shall be acquitted.'

In Paris, Ali had refused to pay her Chanel dress bill of 18,000 francs (£225). 'He told me to get a lover to pay for them,' she sobbed, 'he said he would call me the worst name in the French language – and it hurt.' After a visit to the Folies Bergère (where unknown to the jury, Marguerite had once solicited for custom), her decadent husband had proposed to visit a 'notorious place'. Taking a higher moral stance than circumstances justified, 'she refused as it was not a fit place for her and her sister'.

Marguerite recounted further argy-bargy, including an absurdly melodramatic incident during which, she alleged, Ali had seized her by the throat and threatened to horsewhip her. Yvonne Alibert had come to her elder sister's rescue, brandishing a pistol in her hand.

At this point, the fatal Browning was passed to Marguerite by the interpreter, Harry Ashton-Wolfe, who 'fully expected that she would shrink and hesitate . . . As unconcernedly as if it had been a toy, she took the deadly, blue [sic] weapon in her hand . . .' The *Daily Telegraph*, however, reported a 'strained face' as she briefly let it slip on to the ledge of the witness-box: '. . . in the tense silence it seemed that some great weight had crashed on the wood'.

Marshall Hall, the great opportunist, took his cue. 'Come, Madame Fahmy,' he said softly, 'take hold of the pistol. It is harmless now.' Marguerite 'attempted to pull open the [sliding cover of the] magazine, but without success and, rising to her feet, said she was unable to open it'. This was a delicate moment for Marguerite. She

371

had admittedly been in possession of a lethal firearm, apparently for some time (though Marshall Hall was keeping this aspect deliberately vague). Did she know how to use it? There had to be an explanation of why, in the early hours of 10 July 1923, Marguerite's pistol was loaded and capable of being fired. Marguerite's story was that Ali had himself cleaned and loaded his wife's gun in Paris, saying that she ought to have something with which to protect her jewellery. 'It's all ready to fire,' he had told her, before leaving for his short visit to Stuttgart in mid-June. Marguerite maintained that she had never known how the pistol worked: 'I know nothing of the mechanism.'

MARSHALL HALL: Had you ever fired
a pistol in your life before 9 July?
MARGUERITE: No.

Probably mindful of the inherent improbability of this evidence (bearing in mind that Marguerite had owned a pistol for years and that two rounds were unaccounted for), Marshall Hall quickly changed tack to resume allegations about Ali's sexual habits: 'Several times . . . she put her hand to her forehead and once she almost broke down and applied her handkerchief to her eyes . . .' She could not escape Fahmy, she said, even in Paris. Marguerite spoke emotionally of the man 'Costa', otherwise *Le Costaud* or 'Hercules', who 'owed his life and his liberty' to Ali and 'would carry out any orders given him', including, it was said, Fahmy's threat to disfigure Marguerite with 'sand in a bottle and acid from accumulators'. 'Costa' was an Algerian who had been expelled from Egypt and a 'horrible man'. At this point, 'Madame Fahmy rested her head on the front of the witness-box and sobbed loudly. Counsel paused for some moments until she had composed herself . . .'

Yet another strange document was read out to the court by Marshall Hall. Written in Marguerite's hand, over Ali's signature, this was a product of bitter marital feuding and purported to be an agreement between the couple providing that Marguerite could live as she pleased, even commit adultery, without fear of divorce, but that, if she did so, Ali would feel himself free to call her a 'filthy name', which the newspaper reports did not reveal. When Marshall Hall read certain 'improper phrases . . . Madame Fahmy covered her face with her black gloved hands' in a show of modesty, presumably the object of this forensic exercise.

Marguerite had consulted the private detective in Paris because of Ali's behaviour, though not, it seems, the police, even though one day, as she was being driven with Said Enani and 'Hercules' to Neuilly, a western suburb of Paris, Fahmy had said that he was looking for a house in which to imprison her. She had agreed to come to London only because her daughter, Raymonde, was at school there. Marguerite had not seen her for nine months. Tears welled up.

MARSHALL HALL: Did you think you would be safe in London?
MARGUERITE: I passed from despair to hope and from hope to despair.

Rigby Swift asked if she would like to pause, but Marguerite dried her eyes and went on to describe the incidents at the Riviera Club and the Molesey Casino. Appearing to speak of the Sunday night before the shooting, she told how 'Fahmy came to her room . . .' (the *Daily Telegraph*'s cryptic report breaks off here), where, it seems, he sodomised her yet again. 'I told him that I preferred to die rather than go on living in the way I was doing. He said, "You have a revolver", and pointed to the open window [of the suite], saying, "It's quite easy. There are four floors."' Marguerite could either take her own life or jump to her death.

It was now one o'clock and, as Marguerite left the witness-box at the start of the lunchtime adjournment, reported the *Daily Telegraph*, 'she almost swooned and a second wardress ran to her assistance and, with the marks of tears on her face, the prisoner was half carried into the dock'. There would be a good deal more swooning before Marguerite had finished her lengthy testimony.

CHAPTER 22

A FRAIL HAND

glance at the public gallery, where all the
seats were filled, would have revealed a
substantial majority of women, among
whom were 'girls who did not appear to have been
more than 18 . . . Some seemed to have come
with their mothers . . .', each eager to hear these
unsavoury tales of Franco-Egyptian married life.
After lunch, the first three rows, it seems, were
filled with 'shop assistants released from their
counters for the weekly half-holiday . . .'

Arthur Wiggin, 2nd Secretary at the British High
Commission in Cairo and now on leave from
Egypt, somehow managed to secure a seat in the
crowded court. Part of a small coterie at the
Commission with knowledge of the Prince's
wartime affair, Wiggin wrote to Archie Clark Kerr,
secure in his Scottish fastness, giving his impressions of the trial:

My Dear Archie . . .
I spent three hours at the Old Bailey
during Marshall Hall's defence of Madame
Fahmy. It was the most hair- and

gorge-raising experience of my life. Nothing of what really took place has appeared in the press. It simply couldn't! Rows of fashionably-dressed young women sat with flushed cheeks and glittering eyes as Hall detailed monstrosity after monstrosity. Her acquittal was certain after the first speech.
. . . Yours ever, Arthur

The delicate problem of Marguerite's haemorrhoids began the afternoon's evidence. Ali had told her to 'go to the devil' and 'take a lover' when she had asked him for money to pay for the operation in London. That was why, she said, she had decided to return to Paris, but Ali had furiously told her, 'You will not escape me. I swear to you that in twenty-four hours you will be dead.'

These uncorroborated assertions paved the way for the pivotal evidence – the shooting itself. 'I took the pistol from the drawer,' Marguerite told a hushed, expectant court. 'I knew that it was loaded. He had told me so and I had not touched it since the day he went away [to Stuttgart]. I tried to look into it to see if there was a bullet . . . I tried to do as I had seen him do to get the cartridge out of it . . . I had not the strength to pull sufficiently to make the cartridge fall out.'

MARSHALL HALL: Why did you want to get the cartridge out of the barrel?
MARGUERITE: Because he said he was

going to kill me and I thought I would frighten him with it . . . I was shaking it in front of the window when the shot went off.

MARSHALL HALL: What did you think was the condition of the pistol after it had been fired?

MARGUERITE: The cartridge having been fired, I thought the pistol was not dangerous.

Marguerite was now claiming that the pistol had been fired out of the window, not during the thunderstorm, immediately before killing her husband (as she had told Dr Gordon at Bow Street police station), but earlier the previous evening, before the party had left to see *The Merry Widow* at Daly's Theatre.

She had been alarmed by Fahmy's threats, made at about 7.30 p.m., after he had seen her luggage packed up and ready for her return to Paris. He had taken his photograph from her dressing-table, torn it up and flung the pieces at her. 'Pale and aggressive', he handed back a tie-pin she had given him before their marriage. 'As you are going away,' he had said, contemptuously, 'do not forget your presents to me,' adding, 'You will see; you will see.'

At the theatre, Ali had said, 'Even if you manage to escape from London and get to Paris, Costa will be waiting for you,' and at supper had again threatened to disfigure her. In a disturbed state of mind, and frightened of the storm, Marguerite had not gone to bed, but had just written 'a letter or two' (including the one discharging Dr Gordon) when there was a loud knock at her bedroom door. 'Sobbing and occasionally throwing back her head and shutting her eyes, [Madame Fahmy] described the tragedy.'

Fahmy had banged on the door, shouting, 'You are not alone, then. Open. Open.' She let him in and saw that he was wearing a *djellaba* and dressing-gown, his night clothes. Ali asked her what she was doing. 'I said I had sent a cheque to the doctor and asked him, "Are you going to give me any money to leave tomorrow?" He said, "Come into my room and see if I have any money there for you."'

In terms that resembled the more purple moments of Robert Hichens and E. M. Hull, Marguerite described the drama that took place in her Egyptian husband's bedroom. He had produced some pound notes and about 2,000 francs, which he held sneeringly before her. *The Times* reported that when Marguerite asked him for the French money to cover her travelling expenses, Fahmy said, 'I will give it to you if you earn it', and started to tear off her dress. The unreported suggestion was that, unless Marguerite submitted yet again to his unorthodox sexual demands, despite her painfully inflamed condition, she had no hope of escaping to Paris.

'He struggled with me. I ran to the telephone, but he tore it out of my hand and twisted my arm. I hit him and ran towards the door. He struck me and spat in my face. I rushed to the corridor, where there were several people . . .'

It had, of course, been Ali who had first emerged from the suite, closely followed by his wife, and both had accosted the long-suffering night porter, showering him with mutual recriminations. Beattie's evidence suggested that it had been Ali who was more frightened of Marguerite's temper, rather than the other way round, but that was not what Marguerite was saying from the witness-box.

She had been ordered back to her room. There she saw the pistol on top of a suitcase, where she had left it some hours before. Ali banged on the door again: 'I was very frightened and felt weak,' she recalled. She was now sobbing convulsively, tears running down her cheeks, as she told how Ali had come towards her, saying, 'I will revenge myself.' Marguerite picked up the pistol. Ali shouted, 'I'll say that you threatened me,' and by some unexplained means Marguerite managed to slip out from her room, through the lobby of the suite, and into the hotel corridor.

'He seized me suddenly and brutally by my throat. His thumb was on my windpipe and his fingers were pressing in my neck. I pushed him away and he crouched to spring at me, saying "I will kill you."'

At this point, 'her voice broke into a moan, and

between her sobs she lifted her left hand and tapped excitedly on her black hat, as if this movement helped her to get through this ordeal. She stretched a frail hand across the witness-box and, closing her eyes, sobbed out, "I now lifted my arm in front of me and without looking, pulled the trigger. The next moment, I saw him on the ground before me . . . I do not know how many times the pistol went off."'

Marguerite's examination-in-chief ended on an impressive note:

> MARSHALL HALL: When you threw your arm out when the pistol was fired, what were you afraid of?
> MARGUERITE: That he was going to jump on me. It was terrible. I had escaped once. He said, 'I will kill you. I will kill you.' It was so terrible.

Marguerite had already spent some four hours in the witness-box before Percival Clarke rose to cross-examine. Experienced counsel can often sense the unspoken mood of a court and it is likely that Clarke was aware of a distinct change in the atmosphere since his opening speech on Monday morning. The case was beginning to develop a momentum of its own; a mist of unreality was gradually befogging the courtroom.

There were a number of improbabilities and inconsistencies in Marguerite's story. She had, for example, just given a very wobbly account of escaping into the hotel corridor from a murder-bent Ali. Could he really have been about to jump on her in so public a place? Clarke had the material for some very awkward questions, but this was to be a lacklustre cross-examination. Indeed his first question could only have served to strengthen the defence case:

CLARKE: Were you afraid he was going to kill you on that night?
MARGUERITE: Yes, I was very afraid.

Yet a little later it seemed that Clarke was beginning to make progress:

CLARKE: How long have you possessed a pistol?
MARGUERITE: I had a pistol during the War in 1914. A second one was given me two years ago . . .
CLARKE: What did you have a pistol for if you did not know how it worked?
MARGUERITE: It is the usual thing in France to have a pistol.

Clarke then made a major tactical blunder and, seeming to go behind the judge's firm ruling about Marguerite's character, clumsily started to ask personal questions about her family background. Marguerite proudly told the court that Raymonde, her only and much loved daughter, had been legitimised by her marriage to Charles Laurent. Her defiant answers to this insensitive probing probably enlisted the jury's sympathy, as did this foolish, unanswered question:

> CLARKE: Was your father a cab driver in Paris?

Rigby Swift was very angry. 'Does it matter whether he was a cab driver or a millionaire? I do not want a long inquiry into the lady's ancestry . . .' but Clarke, treading a delicate path, seemed not to take the hint. After Marguerite had told him, a little riskily, that she had a number of friends in Paris of 'wealth and position', he asked:

> CLARKE: Can I correctly describe you as a woman of the world?
> INTERPRETER: The meaning is not the same in French.
> CLARKE: A woman with experience of the world?
> MARGUERITE: I have had experience of life.

This world-weary answer did much for Marguerite and probably impressed the jury, who might have been surprised to know just how extensive Marguerite's experience of life had been. Clarke's cross-examination was foundering, but before the court rose for the day, he managed to score a rare success:

> CLARKE: Would it be right to say that this black valet my friend has spoken of is a boy of eighteen?
> MARGUERITE: Yes, he was fairly young.
> CLARKE: Is he only five feet high?
> MARGUERITE: Yes, he is very small.

And she agreed that it was customary for wives of Egyptians to be attended by servants. The long day was near its end. Clarke tried a last attempt to impress the jury, asking sternly:

> CLARKE: Madame, were you not very ambitious to become his wife?
> MARGUERITE: Ambitious, no. [Here she wiped her cheek] I loved him so very much and wished to be with him.
> CLARKE: . . . What did you do while he was being so cruel? Sit down quietly?
> MARGUERITE: Only once I boxed his ears when he had beaten me very much . . . He beat me so much when I did so that I never dared do it again. I never boxed his ears in public.

Clarke's last question of the day seemed callously worded and Marguerite's answer, in contrast, was consistent with the poignant response of an abused widow. In keeping with her role, she again appeared to faint before leaving the witness-box and had to be almost carried down the stairs to the cells by a wardress and a male prison officer.

Barely three hours after Court Number One had adjourned for the day at 4.30 p.m. on Wednesday 12 September, people again began to congregate around the public entrance to the Old Bailey. By 11 p.m. there were about fifty, and an hour later that number had doubled. By 2 a.m. several hundred people had gathered in Newgate Street, defying the persistent attempts of police to move them on. In one of the side streets, pretty girls, smartly dressed, were seen sitting on rubber cushions, 'bivouacking' on sandwiches and oranges. One man, asked by the *Pall Mall Gazette* why he had come, responded, 'Well mister, it's life, ain't it?' The trial of Madame Fahmy was now the acknowledged sensation of the year.

When the case resumed on Thursday morning, Marshall Hall used another diversionary tactic, aiming a blow at Clarke's faltering cross-examination. Madame Fahmy, he told the judge, found it very difficult to understand Ashton-Wolfe's French, as he spoke in a low voice. Counsel asked if Maître Odette Simon, a 24-year-old French barrister, might be allowed to sit near the witness-box and 'hear if the questions were translated properly'.

The judge agreed, but before Percival Clarke had posed more than a question or two to

Marguerite, Marshall Hall was again on his feet, this time objecting to Ashton-Wolfe's translation. 'I very much deprecate these difficulties about the interpreter,' said Rigby Swift testily. 'He seems to me to have been performing his difficult duties very well . . .'

Ashton-Wolfe was discharged with thanks and Mlle Simon took the interpreter's oath. She was staying with relatives in England after the French courts had adjourned for their vacation at the end of July and had been eager to see an English trial. Odette, one of 80 women barristers in France, had practised law for some four years. Wearing, 'a navy blue costume with a white collar and a large-brimmed dark hat, trimmed with bluish-green brocade', she gave her translation from the well of the court, standing between the judge and the witness-box.

There had been a strategic dimension to Marshall Hall's request. The previous day, Helena Normanton, Mlle Simon's English barrister colleague, had sent counsel a note in which she wrote that Mlle Simon was anxious to 'offer you her aid as witness or otherwise, if you care to avail yourself of it . . .' After the court rose, Marshall Hall invited Mlle Simon to tea in the Bar Mess, soon realising the advantage that would accrue to the defence by presenting 'the romantic situation . . . of one gifted young Frenchwoman helping another in her hour of extreme peril in a foreign country . . .' Helena Normanton, the first woman to practise at the English Bar, had been a suffragette, a pacifist during the Great War, and was active in feminist causes. Normanton was not easily ignored ('she was enormous', recalled one contemporary) and, despite obvious differences in their political standpoints, Marshall Hall was only too glad to have had her help in setting up this clever tactical exercise.

Marguerite was reported to be 'more composed than she had been the previous day' and was able to step into the witness-box unaided. At first, during Clarke's resumed cross-examination, she sat very still in her black marocain dress and hat, which, the *Evening Standard* reported, accentuated 'the olive tints of throat and face', delivering answers almost too calmly, as Clarke investigated how far her complaints about Ali derived from the divorce dossier. Rightly, prosecuting counsel was concerned to know why Marguerite had stayed with so brutal a husband, regularly appearing with him in public places.

CLARKE: While you were in Paris before he went to Germany, were you leading a very gay life – I do not mean immorally gay – but going to theatres, dining etc.?

MARGUERITE: Yes, we were going out every evening.

CLARKE: When your husband went to Stuttgart on 17 or 18 June, why did you not leave him while he was away?

MARGUERITE: [Giving a slight shrug] Where could I have gone to? If I had gone to my flat, Said Enani would have come to fetch me back the next day.

CLARKE: But you had lived in Paris all your life and had many friends there of influence and wealth?

MARGUERITE: I did not want my friends to know all about my sorrow, because I thought they would laugh at me. Except for two or three intimate women friends, I have always tried to save appearances.

Marguerite's stated reasons for not leaving Fahmy were manifestly weak and Clarke pressed home his advantage by putting questions about the document, containing 'improper phrases' and supposedly giving Marguerite the right to commit adultery. Fahmy, she said, had dictated it, 'because he was always so brutal when he wanted a thing to be done . . .'

CLARKE: Did you write that letter in order to assist in your divorce?

MARGUERITE: I never produced it. It was so degrading.

Amid this demonstration of modesty, her voice began to quaver. Gesticulating wildly, she related an unconvincing story that Ali had insisted that she wrote the letter, as he was unable to form the French characters.

CLARKE: If this were a genuine document, why did he not write it himself?

MARGUERITE: It was 2 o'clock in the morning and I did not wish to prolong the scene which preceded the writing . . . He said 'write' and I wrote.

It seems to have been at this stage in cross-examination when Clarke's feeble prosecution was at last appearing to make some progress, that Marshall Hall's mischievous spirit again asserted itself. Robert Churchill, the firearms expert, was still in court, sitting at the exhibits table. While Clarke was putting questions to Marguerite, Marshall Hall left his seat, a conspicuous progress in which he was obliged to disturb several other barristers, and went over to where Churchill was sitting.

Marshall Hall quietly asked Churchill to dismantle the pistol, also whispering some questions about partridge shooting which had started on 1 September that year. In what seems to have been a carefully calculated exercise the jury was distracted from concentrating on a particularly weak part of Marguerite's testimony.

Marshall Hall would not have felt the need for distraction when Clarke came to question Marguerite about the sexual side of her marriage. Madame Fahmy coped very well with what was probably a fairly discreetly worded inquiry into the allegations she had made about her husband's amorous inclinations. Tears could be seen in her eyes as she declared that her relations with Ali had 'never been quite normal'.

> CLARKE: I take it that from the time of his first objectionable suggestion you hated your husband bitterly?
>
> MARGUERITE: I loved my husband and, when he had been so bad, I despaired and I told him I hated him. I did not hate him, but only what he wanted me to do.

Clarke's cross-examination was beginning to nose-dive. The trend was accelerated by some very awkward questioning about knowledge of the pistol's mechanism. It is a golden rule of cross-examination that counsel should not, if at all possible, reduce a witness to tears. To be fair, Marguerite had tended to the lachrymose from the moment she had stepped into the witness-box, but Clarke went over the previous day's old ground in far too much detail, even to the extent of putting the pistol back in her unwilling hands.

Calmness gave way once more to emotion. 'She wept while speaking, supporting her head with one hand and with the other made gestures deprecatory, emphatic, disdainful . . .', reported the *Evening Standard*, and, when Clarke put to her that she must have known that there were other cartridges in the gun, she cried out, 'I don't know

389

anything of its mechanics. I . . .' before breaking off in distress. She burst into loud sobbing and fell back into her chair.

The effect of Clarke's heavy-handed questioning was to rob many of the prosecution's stronger points of their force. If she had, as she said, fired the first shot out of the window early in the morning, how was it that no one, apart from her maid, had heard it? The thunderstorm was not then raging. 'Did you not fire that first shot to see that the pistol was in working order,' Clarke had asked, but she maintained that she had only been trying to get the bullet out of the gun, using the pistol only to frighten Ali.

The white Chanel evening dress was passed to her, and tears again welled up in her eyes as she pointed to the back of the garment, where Ali had torn off some of the small beads in the course of the struggle. She affected to shudder as the dress was handed back to a court usher, but had sufficient composure to parry Clarke's next question:

CLARKE: Did you know that your husband was completely unarmed when you pointed the revolver [sic] at him?
MARGUERITE: I did not know; he often had a pistol in the jacket of his dressing-gown. The thunderstorm was so awful and I was in such a terrible state of nerves I do not know what I thought of it at the time.

Soon afterwards, Clarke came to the end of his cross-examination in a distinctly downbeat way:

CLARKE: Were you not fully aware that when your husband attacked you, you could immediately have rung the bell and got assistance?

MARGUERITE: I could not speak English. What could I say?

CLARKE: Could you not have got your maid to stay with you that night?

MARGUERITE: She had gone to bed and was on the eighth floor. I had no telephone to her.

Marshall Hall's short re-examination was largely taken up with Rigby Swift's 'waste paper', the declaration that Marguerite had written in January 1923, and that she had left, sealed, with her lawyer, Maître Assouad, 'only to be opened in case of her death'. It had, in truth, virtually no evidential value, merely reiterating what Marguerite had been saying in evidence, but, predictably, Marshall Hall was able to maximise its dramatic effect. Without objection from judge of prosecuting counsel, the whole of the document was put before the jury, a useful reminder of Marguerite's wholly uncorroborated claim that Ali had sworn on the Koran to kill her.

Yvonne Alibert gave evidence that broadly supported her sister's case – no surprises here – as

391

did Aimée Pain, the maid, with whom Marguerite had spoken at such length in Bow Street police station just hours after the shooting. Aimée confirmed her mistress's story of the pistol going off between 8.30 and 9 p.m. on the night of 9 July (an incorrect time, by any reading, as Marguerite was then uncomfortably seated in Daly's Theatre), but had somehow forgotten to mention this to the police, because she was 'so upset'.

Eugéne Barbay, Marguerite's faithful chauffeur, came close to over-egging the pudding on his mistress's behalf:

> CLARKE: What do you mean when you say she was always crying?
> BARBAY: She had her handkerchief to her eyes.
> CLARKE: Even at the dressmaker's or dinner or the theatre?
> BARBAY: She always had red eyes. She was always trying to stop.
> CLARKE: Oh, she did try to stop sometimes?
> BARBAY: Yes, but for never more than half an hour at a time.

With descriptions of Marguerite's bruised face in Paris, given by Hélène Baudry, the concert singer well known in France (if not in England) and *protégée* of the Prince's friend, François de Breteuil, the defence evidence closed. It remained for

Marguerite's advocate to make the speech of his lifetime.

Marshall Hall, rising painfully from his seat, began his closing address just before 3.30 in the afternoon, not the best time to start a keynote speech. The jury had already been subjected to nearly four hours of evidence that day and concentration inevitably tends to slip after lunch.

As was his custom, he began quietly. There were only two issues in the case: 'Either this was a deliberate, premeditated and cowardly murder, or it was a shot fired by this woman from a pistol which she believed to be unloaded at a moment when she thought her life to be in danger.' Mindful of the ruins of Clarke's cross-examination, counsel dared to assume that the jury were already well disposed towards his client: 'You must not allow your sympathy for this poor woman to interfere with returning a proper verdict,' he adjured. 'Do not descend to little, minor or petty details, but take a broad view of the facts . . .' That 'broad view' would become, as the speech progressed, a projection of Ali Fahmy as a monster of Eastern depravity and decadence, whose sexual tastes were indicative of an amoral sadism towards his helpless European wife.

'She made one great mistake, the greatest mistake any woman can make: a woman of the West married to an Oriental,' said the Great Defender, turning the jury's attention to the slight figure in the dock, so quietly dressed in black, her chin resting on her hands, calm now after the tears and emotion of her evidence.

'I daresay the Egyptian civilisation is and may be one of the oldest and most wonderful civilisations in the world. I don't say that among the Egyptians there are not many magnificent and splendid men' – here came the sting – 'but if you strip off the external civilisation of the Oriental, you get the real Oriental underneath and it is common knowledge that the Oriental's treatment of women does not fit in with the idea the Western woman has of the proper way she should be treated by her husband . . .'

And that husband was not the 'nervous, retiring young man' of Percival Clarke's instructions (Marshall Hall had given his jejune opponent a clever backhanded compliment to 'the way he had performed a difficult and thankless task'). Not at all: the 'mysterious document' that Marguerite had composed herself in January 1923 showed how afraid she was that some of Fahmy's 'black hirelings' would do her to death.

'In 1923, in the midst of civilised London, it seems odd that such a threat should have had any effect on the woman. But think of Egypt,' he contrasted. 'It is the curse of this case that there is something we can't get at, that is, the Eastern feeling.' The dead man's personal private secretary had possessed that 'Eastern feeling' in abundance. 'One almost smiles when my friend asks "Why did you not get Said Enani to protect you?",' said

Marshall Hall, appearing to take the jury into his confidence. 'You have seen Said Enani and have heard something about him. Is he the kind of man you would have as the sole buffer between yourselves and a man like Fahmy? . . . Do you believe anything said by Said Enani that was hostile to this unfortunate woman?' Defence counsel was now in full xenophobic flight, with no sign of a rebuke from the judge. 'I suggest that it is part of the Eastern duplicity that is well known.'

Spicing his argument with gratuitous references to colour, he continued, 'Do not forget Costa [sic], that great black Hercules, who came day after day for orders, and who was ready to do anything. Don't you think she had ground for fear of this great black guard who owed his life to Fahmy?'

It had all been an Easterner's plot to lure Marguerite into a kind of white slavery. 'Picture this woman,' he invited the jury, 'inveigled into Egypt by false pretences, by a letter which for adulatory expression could hardly be equalled and which makes one feel sick . . . At first, all is honey and roses. He shows her his beautiful palace, his costly motor-cars, his wonderful motor-boat, his retinue of servants, his lavish luxuries, and cries "Ah, I am Fahmy *Bey*; I am a Prince." This European woman became more fascinated and attracted to this Oriental extravagance . . .'

As the end of the court day approached, Marshall Hall, knowing that he would be unable to finish his speech in one piece, developed his 'Eastern 'feeling' theme, giving the jury something to mull over that evening in the close confines of the Manchester Hotel.

'The curse of this case . . . is the Eastern feeling of possession of the woman, the Turk in his harem, this man who was entitled to have four wives if he liked – for chattels, which to we Western people, with our ideas of women, is almost unintelligible, something we cannot quite deal with.'

Overnight, a massive police operation outside the Old Bailey prevented any queues forming, but, as ever, the courtroom was crowded almost beyond capacity when the trial resumed. Even some barristers were content to stand during the proceedings. Public interest in the trial was now intense; it attracted press attention throughout the world and was one of the first major criminal trials to have been the subject of news reports on the radio. British listeners had to wait until 7 p.m. each day for their information, a restriction imposed on the BBC to protect the interests of newspaper proprietors.

Most people thought that Friday 14 September would bring the jury's verdict on Marguerite's innocence or guilt of murder and there was a perceptible tension in Court Number One when Marshall Hall resumed his final address to the jury that morning. He soon came to a consideration of Fahmy's character, a central feature of his speech. Ali might have been only 22 or 23 but he had 'learned a lot and had many mistresses'.

Referring to the time Marguerite had come home with Mukhta *bey*, after the visit to a Cairo cinema, Sir Edward's voice rang with indignation as he told of the blow in the face given to Madame by Fahmy before an Egyptian friend to whom he laughed and joked after having shown his 'mastership of this Western woman'.

This brutal behaviour extended into the bedroom. Fahmy was 'a great, hulking muscular fellow' who was able to force his will upon his wife. Before launching into his attack on Ali's depravity, Marshall Hall eyed the public gallery. 'If women choose to come here to hear this case, they must take the consequences. It is a matter of public duty that I must perform.' In the event, none of the women spectators left court while defence counsel wrestled with the vexed question of sodomy.

'The whole sex question is one of mystery,' announced Marshall Hall, in a curiously worded passage. '. . . Nature gave us the power to get morphia from the seed of the poppy, gave us alcohol, and cocaine from the seed of the coca plant in Peru. Probably there are no better things than these in their proper places. Probably thousands in the War had cause to bless them. Just as they are the greatest boon to men and women, so probably these three things taken together are three of the greatest curses that are in the world at the present moment. It is not their legitimate use; it is the abuses of morphia, alcohol and sex that give all the dreadful trouble in the world.'

Fahmy, declared counsel, had 'developed abnormal tendencies and he never treated Madame normally'.

There had been no direct evidence before the court to prove that Ali had taken drugs, but these references to morphia and cocaine were most probably designed to create the image of Ali as a drug-crazed sex fiend. The more sensational newspapers regularly printed stories about the 'drug menace', a threat commonly imputed to the activities of 'black' people.

The thrust of Marshall Hall's untidy, emotionally charged argument was that Ali Fahmy, an 'Oriental', effectively a black man in the eyes of the all-white jury, had disqualified himself from their consideration, mainly by reason of his race and his sexuality. Employing a popular canard, Marshall Hall implied that, because Ali had been bisexual, he would invariably practise sodomy as his preferred mode of intercourse with women.

Viewed dispassionately, Marguerite's defence was less than coherent. Did she shoot Ali in the hotel corridor because she thought he was going to kill her or because she feared that he would force himself sexually upon her again? How did this fit in with the virtually unchallenged evidence of John Beattie? The Great Defender would simply pass that by.

Rational argument went out of the window. Marshall Hall would choose to rely on rough patriotism and homely sentiment. '. . . Maybe she thought she would be safer in London than in

Paris. There are people who even in 1923 . . . have a high opinion of English safety and English law. She may have thought that it would be a little more dangerous for these black emissaries to work their fell purpose at the bidding of their master.' Tugging hard at the jury's heartstrings, he added, 'I wonder how many mothers have braved a great many dangers to see the child they loved. Because her child was illegitimate, maybe Madame Fahmy loved it all the more.'

Visibly sweating now and in great pain, Marshall Hall turned up the dramatic pressure as he came to the night of the shooting and the great thunderstorm. 'You know the effect of such a storm when your nerves are normal. Imagine its effect on a woman of nervous temperament who had been living such a life as she had lived for the past six months – terrified, outraged, abused, beaten, degraded – a human wreck . . . Imagine the incessant flashes of lightning, almost hissing, as you remember, it seemed so close . . . She saw her husband outlined by a vivid flash in the doorway and there to her hand on the valise she saw the pistol – harmless, she thought . . .'

Then came one of the great moments of Old Bailey mythology. 'They struggle in the corridor. She kicks him and he takes her by the throat. Do you doubt it? The marks are spoken of in the prison doctor's report.' From his seat in counsel's benches, Marshall Hall physically imitated how, according to the defence, Ali had 'crouched like an animal, crouched like an Oriental and then it was that the pistol went off'.

He had picked up the gun, the very gun Marguerite had used to kill her husband, and pointed it at the jury as he made submissions about its mechanism, with a view to establishing, contrary to the facts, that very little pressure on the trigger would discharge several shots. Marshall-Hall repeatedly manipulated the pistol, keeping the jury's attention, with the aim of emphasising his argument. To represent the fatal shots, he gave three loud raps on the wooden shelving in front of him and, 'amid a tense silence, the pistol rattled to the floor as it had fallen from the hands of Mme. Fahmy'. Causing some people in court to shout out in surprise. (In fact, the gun had slipped out of his hand.)

There followed another moment of silence, maximising the dramatic effect, before Marshall Hall reminded the jury that Marguerite had said (her words), '*Mon chéri, ce n'est rien, responds-moi*' ('Sweetheart, it is nothing, speak to me'), as Ali lay dying. 'What a place,' he said, 'for a deliberate planned murder – the corridor where the lift was going up and down and people were moving about. Would she choose the Savoy Hotel for such an act? Would she have left at the hotel the address of the nursing home to which she was going? Would she have wired to Paris, saying she was going there the next day? . . .'

Then he did something very naughty indeed.

Percival Clarke's conduct of the prosecution's case had been a drab and uninspiring affair, in marked contrast to the triumphant abilities of his father, Sir Edward Clarke, in 1923 still alive, though retired. Marshall Hall, with some cruelty, played on this unhappy comparison. 'To use the words of my learned friend's great father many years ago at the Old Bailey in the [Adelaide] Bartlett case, "I do not ask you for a verdict. I demand a verdict at your hands."'

This would have been a good moment on which to have finished, but there was still the last advantage to be wrung from the 'Eastern feeling'. As with the fictional Mahmoud Baroudi, so it had been with Ali Fahmy. 'Eastern men, as I have said, are courteous, civilised and elegant, but underneath lies the Eastern temperament and the Eastern idea of how a woman should be treated. In some cases, a Western wife is a triumph for an Eastern man to possess; Eastern men are proud of such a possession, but they are not prepared to sacrifice their right of domination.'

Then came the peroration, delivered as shafts of September sunlight intermittently penetrated through the glass roof of the court:

'You will remember, all of you, that great work of fiction, written by Robert Hichens, *Bella Donna*. Some of you may have seen the masterly performance given of it at one of our theatres. If you have, you will remember the final scene, where this woman goes out of the gates of the

401

garden into the dark night of the desert. Members of the jury, I want you to open the gates where the Western woman can go out, not into the dark night of the desert, but back to her friends, who love her in spite of her weaknesses; back to her friends, who will be glad to receive her; back to her child, who will be waiting for her with open arms. You will open the gate and let this Western woman go back into the light of God's great Western sun.'

At the final words of his speech, delivered almost in a whisper, Marshall Hall looked up and pointed at the glass ceiling of the courtroom, 'where the bright English September sun was streaming in and suffusing the packed court with its warmth and brightness', after which, manifestly exhausted, he sank back into his place.

CHAPTER 23

VERDICT

Marshall Hall's was an almost impossible act to follow, but, for once, prosecuting counsel's arid delivery made some impact, as Percival Clarke struggled to bring the debate back into the realms of reason. 'You have had the advantage,' he told the jury in a quiet monotone, 'of listening to two dramatic speeches from one of the most powerful advocates at the Bar. I shall try and take you from the theatrical atmosphere which has prevailed in this court for three or four days . . .' Clarke's final speech, for all its dryness, began promisingly. In the theatre, for example, the 'Blood and Thunder' school was no longer as fashionable as it had been before the war, and, it might be supposed, some jury members now possessed a relatively sophisticated approach to life's problems.

The last words of that mighty defence effort had been paraphrased from the pulp fiction of *Bella Donna*. Introducing themes from that Edwardian sensation was risky, as Clarke was quick to point out, and a less impulsive advocate than Marshall Hall would have reflected at length before making use of such material. Clarke referred to *Bella Donna* as a play (Mrs Patrick Campbell had felt herself miscast as Ruby Chepstow in a 1911 West End production), 'a strangely unfortunate play, I think, to recall to your mind. You will remember that the woman who went out into the desert, out into the dark, was the woman who had planned, and very nearly succeeded in murdering her husband. In that respect, it may be that the smile between the play and this case is somewhat alike [sic].'

Additionally, there were unspoken dangers in the indiscriminate use of *Bella Donna* by the defence. Around midnight on 3 October 1922, Percy Thompson, a 32-year-old shipping clerk, had been stabbed to death in an Ilford street while walking home with his wife from the local railway station. His assailant, twelve years younger, was Frederick Bywaters, who had been the lover of Thompson's wife, Edith, for over a year before the murder. Edith had destroyed the letters he had written to her; Bywaters, for reasons of his own, had kept her correspondence.

Edith Thompson and Frederick Bywaters were tried for murder at the Old Bailey in December 1922. Much of the prosecution's case against Edith derived from those love-letters. There was no direct evidence that she had known beforehand of Bywater's plan to murder her husband, but there were references to powdered glass, to poisons, and to *Bella Donna*, a particularly unfortunate choice of reading material. Prosecuting counsel (the

Solicitor-General, Sir Thomas Inskip KC) made much of the *Bella Donna* theme. Edith Thompson was convicted of murder and hanged. Hichens's potboiler helped seal her fate, even though she had herself described the character of Ruby Chepstow as 'abnormal – a monster utterly selfish and self-living'.

Marguerite Fahmy, an experienced woman and a decade older than her husband, was a far more suitable candidate for the role of *Bella Donna* than Edith Thompson, who had been no more than a bored, day-dreaming Ilford housewife. Mrs Thompson had gone to the gallows accompanied by remarkably little public sympathy. Would Marguerite's jury, more astute perhaps than their Victorian counterparts, take a cooler, more sceptical view of the evidence than that suggested by the emotional flummery of Marshall Hall?

It was easy, said Percival Clarke, 'to speak ill of those who are dead'. Marshall Hall had tried to introduce prejudice against Fahmy, so that the jury would think that he, a brute, had deserved to die. 'I have no brief for the dead man,' Clarke told his listeners, reminding them of Marguerite's early lapse from the path of virtue, her illegitimate child, but carefully avoiding any detail about later relationships: 'From the age of sixteen upwards, this woman had had experience of men and the world.' Just like *Bella Donna*.

So far, so good. But Clarke ought not to have reminded the jury of his hideously inept question about the occupation of Marguerite's father, lamely attempting to justify the unjustifiable by explaining that it was asked 'merely to show the ambition of the woman'.

No doubt he pointed out the discrepancies in Marguerite's story: the pistol, first said to have been fired shortly before Fahmy had attacked her, later said to have gone off before the visit to the theatre; the scene of the struggle – was it in her bedroom, as she had originally said, or his, where the small pearls torn from her dress had been found? And those improbabilities: would such a woman, a pistol owner for some nine years, not know how to use it? And there was her shaky account, of how the action had been transferred from the suite into the hotel corridor.

Clarke had begun his speech just after midday and it was now after 3 p.m. Marguerite had listened to both speeches without the services of an interpreter and was having to use her imagination to divine what these strangely dressed English lawyers had been talking about for so long. As Clarke's wearisome arguments ploddingly unfolded, dreariness unbroken by the sort of dramatic gestures that were Marshall Hall's stock-in-trade, Marguerite appeared to think that all was lost. 'She sat with her head hanging limply forward and her black gloved right hand supporting her forehead. Now and again . . . her eyes were closed and . . . tears were trickling down her cheeks.' In the closing moments of Clarke's address, she also seemed unable to keep still. 'Her head moved from side to side and she twisted and untwisted her handkerchief round her fingers.'

The jury could be forgiven, with the day's speechmaking now well into its fourth hour, for not absorbing the Crown's better points. There was, for example, the fact of Marguerite and Said Enani dancing together to the music of the Savoy Havana Band in the hotel ballroom that fateful night. Marguerite had said that she had danced just a couple of steps in an atmosphere of crisis. 'I care not how many steps it was,' said Clarke, 'whether one step or two steps, or whether it was to the door or round the room. Was this desperate woman in a painful condition dragged off to dance . . . Whatever evidence is there at all except that she went of her own free will?'

At last, he encapsulated the Crown's case. Fahmy, as the evidence of John Beattie and the post-mortem had proved, was shot from behind while bending down, playing with a dog. 'What really happened,' he suggested, 'was that the accused, angry, cross, quarrelling, went back, lost her temper and her head, seized the pistol which she knew was in working order and fired it at her husband.' All very well, but the prosecution had never fully explored the true reasons for so violent an outburst of temper on Marguerite's part. The jury would have to do what they could with the material before them.

That material now came to be reviewed by Mr Justice Rigby Swift in his summing-up, which, as a punctilious reporter noted, began at 3.27 that Friday afternoon. The judge at first appeared to be hostile to the accused, an impression reinforced by his particularly grave tone of voice. 'Unless you find something to your satisfaction, something which has been brought home to your minds, that the killing of Ali Fahmy by this woman was not murder, you are bound to return a verdict of wilful murder. This is not a case of giving the accused the benefit of the doubt . . .' In other words, the old presumption that all homicide was murder, unless the contrary could be proven, might yet serve to hang Marguerite Fahmy.

The judge's compliment to Marshall Hall ('a brilliantly eloquent speech made by one of the foremost advocates at the Bar') was followed by a disparagement, as is often the case with plaudits from the Bench: 'You have heard a great deal about the bad character of the dead man, but . . . the prisoner is not to be acquitted because you believe that [he] was a bad, and, indeed, a detestable character. It is no . . . excuse for homicide that the person killed was . . . a weak, depraved or despicable person . . .'

Swift's initial apparent antipathy to Marguerite can be seen as a tactical exercise. Judges minded to 'row out' a defendant (that is, to persuade a jury to acquit) often begin summing up in this way, which can strengthen the effect of later observations favourable to the accused.

And yet that character assassination of Ali Fahmy had left its mark, a seed planted by the defence in the fertile soil of contemporary English prejudice. 'I have had many years' experience, but I am shocked and sickened at some of the things which it has been our duty to listen to in the course of this case.' In a clear reference to the eager curiosity of the trial shown by a large number of women, the judge continued: 'These things are horrible; they are disgusting. How anyone could listen to these things who is not bound to listen to them passes comprehension.'

Turning to the evidence, the judge resumed a stance seemingly antipathetic to the defence. If Beattie's testimony was right, then the killing was unjustified, unexplained and amounted to murder. The jury had to examine Marguerite's story: if they decided that it was untrue, there was no answer to the charge. Was there, asked the judge, corroboration of her version of events? According to Rigby Swift, there was, and the tide of the summing-up began to flow strongly in Marguerite's favour. What she had told Dr Gordon early on the morning of 10 July at Bow Street police station was 'substantially the same story' as her evidence in court and was 'not a tale that has been concocted by the legal advisers'.

Furthermore, said the judge, 'the letter written to Dr Gordon about her leaving for Paris was strong corroboration of her story' and the finding of the bullet in the accused's room, and of the beads in

Fahmy's room, was a 'really remarkable corroboration' of her story. With respect to the judge, it is
difficult to see how any of these elements could
corroborate Marguerite's account of the central
issue in the case: how she had come to fire three
shots at her unarmed husband in a hotel corridor.

Late in the afternoon, Rigby Swift asked the jury
if they would like a short break for tea or to adjourn
till the next day. A majority was in favour of going
on, but, noticing the lack of unanimity, the judge
decided to resume the case on Saturday morning.
Mlle Simon whispered to Marguerite that the case
would not, after all, finish that day. Marguerite,
who had sobbed spasmodically throughout the
judge's address, prompted by his frequent references to 'murder', covered her face in her hands
at the news of the postponement, stood up, swayed,
then collapsed into the arms of her two wardresses,
who needed the assistance of a male colleague to
carry the defendant bodily downstairs from the
dock.

Almost as soon as the court had risen that Friday
afternoon, women and men started to loiter around
the public entrance to the Old Bailey. As
Marguerite's prison taxi pulled away from the rear
of the building, someone in the crowd shouted
out to her, 'Good Luck, Fahmy!' That cloudy, cold
and windy night, the City of London police were
in energetic mood and kept the crowd on the
move, but as fast as they cleared people away from
the door, another group took their place.

Marguerite spent a restless night in the hospital wing at Holloway, despite the usual sedative. Just before she left for court, a well-wisher gave her a sprig of white heather. By 8 a.m., an enormous crowd had gathered outside the grim courthouse and, half an hour before the trial resumed, Court Number One was jammed to the walls. In a helter-skelter rush to get the best places in the public gallery, several women tried to climb over the rows of seats, tearing their stockings as they attempted to get the best vantage point.

Rigby Swift posed three possible verdicts. Guilty of murder; Guilty of manslaughter; and Not Guilty altogether. Accepting Marshall Hall's argument, the judge effectively dismissed the issue of manslaughter. The element that would reduce murder to manslaughter was provocation, 'some physical act . . . so annoying or aggravating as was likely to destroy the self-control of an ordinary reasonable person'. The judge observed that there did not seem to have been anything in the nature of provocation at the moment of the shooting. Marguerite had alleged that Fahmy had spat at her, but that was barely sufficient by itself and had occurred too long before the shooting.

If, however, the jury accepted that Fahmy had seized Marguerite by the throat, this could lay the foundation for a defence of justifiable homicide and a verdict of Not Guilty. The jury should pay close attention to evidence of the Fahmys' marital life. 'You are not to say,' warned Rigby Swift, 'here is an Oriental man, married to a Frenchwoman and therefore things were likely to be so and so . . .' The judge's seemingly moderate approach to the consideration of that stormiest of marriages soon vanished. Swift had been deeply swayed by Marshall Hall's speech and now began to dwell on the theme of 'abnormality', adopting, in less inflammatory language, the agenda of race and sexuality set down by the Great Defender.

'If the evidence shows you that these two people were not ordinary normal people, as you and I understand people, and . . . that their relationship was not the ordinary, normal relationship of husband and wife, you might more readily believe [the defendant's] story of what happened . . .' Said Enani's important evidence was dismissively treated, with a veiled reminder of Marshall Hall's accusation of homosexuality. 'He was, and is, in a difficult position and it is for you to decide whether all that has been said about him is justified . . . You must remember he was the dead man's friend. They were inseparable.' On the other hand, the so-called 'secret document' of 22 January 1923, once referred to by Swift as so much 'waste paper', was now to be regarded as throwing 'a good deal of light upon the relationship of these parties . . .' and as confirming Marguerite's contention that Ali had often threatened to kill her.

The judge had been particularly shocked by another peculiar document in Marguerite's hand, the one in which Ali was meant to have condoned her adultery. 'It is a disgraceful and disgusting document,' sermonised the judge, taking the paper at its face value, 'which shows to us that the relationship between these two people was not the ordinary relationship of man and wife to which we are accustomed in this country.' That relationship was 'something abnormal, something extraordinary', as were the events which took place at the Savoy Hotel on the night of the tragedy. Marguerite's evidence about Ali's alleged sexual tastes was 'shocking, sickening and disgusting . . . If her husband tried to do what she says, in spite of her protests, it was a cruel, it was an abominable act . . .'

The contrast between West and East, so much a feature of Marshall Hall's two speeches, was endorsed by the judge. 'We in this country put our women on a pedestal: in Egypt they have not the same views . . . When you hear of this woman being followed by a black servant, you . . . must not allow your indignation to run away with your judgement.'

When the judge came to review the evidence of the witnesses in the trial, one eye-witness, who would have seen almost everything of relevance to the killing of Fahmy *bey*, was not mentioned. This witness had never been called to give evidence in any of the legal proceedings, though he had been in and around the Fahmys' suite throughout the material time. He was the Nubian valet, the diminutive, 18-year-old youth who, according to his late master, did not matter and was nothing. The police did not bother to take a statement from him. Even his name is unknown.

Rigby Swift's summing-up, now heavily slanted in favour of the accused, ended with a simple question: 'Has Madame Fahmy made out to your satisfaction that she used that weapon to protect her own life?' After three bailiffs had been sworn to keep them in 'some private and convenient place', the jury filed out of court at 12.24 p.m. Marshall Hall spoke a few sentences of comfort in French to Marguerite, and Maître Assouad shook her by the hand in encouragement, before, smiling wanly and looking very pale, she returned to the cells to await the verdict. Court Number One emptied and people tried to snatch a brief lunch.

Almost exactly an hour later, an usher returned to court, indicating that a verdict had been reached. Marshall Hall and his corpulent sidekick, Curtis-Bennett, hurried back into court, closely followed by the Clerk of Arraigns. Three sharp knocks again rang out to mark Rigby Swift's return to his place on the Bench.

Marguerite, 'very composed', dressed still in deep mourning, with a black, low-brimmed hat and veil, moved slowly into the dock, where she sat awaiting her fate, her head resting on her hands. Asked to stand, she stared straight ahead at the judge, not venturing to look at the jury as they returned. Some women sitting behind the dock stood up, 'trembling visibly', noted the *Evening Standard*, as the Clerk inquired: 'Members of the jury, are you agreed upon your verdict?' 'We are', said the foreman. 'Do you find Marguerite Fahmy guilty or not guilty of the murder of Ali Kamel Fahmy *bey*?'

Marguerite clasped her hands together, putting them to her chin as if in prayer. The official court interpreter, Ashton-Wolfe, was surely not the only spectator to have waited, with thumping heart, during the momentary but profound silence.

'Not guilty,' replied the foreman. A woman shrieked and the court erupted into cheering, stamping feet and tumultuous applause. Marguerite, giving what the *Daily Mail* described as 'a little gurgling cry', collapsed into her seat and wept, black-gloved fingers pressed against her face. Her two wardresses fought back the tears; both women on the jury were visibly moved and one, Mrs Austin, broke down completely, covering her face with her handkerchief as she sobbed aloud.

'Clear the court,' shouted Rigby Swift above the pandemonium. It took nearly five minutes before order could be restored and the jury asked if they found Marguerite guilty or not guilty of manslaughter. The foreman's reply was the same as it had been to the previous question and Rigby Swift, beckoning to Ashton-Wolfe, said brusquely, 'Tell her that the jury have found her not guilty and that she is discharged. Let her go.' Marguerite was helped downstairs, to be seen by the prison doctor, while the young and vivacious Mlle Simon was thanked by the judge for her assistance and the jury were discharged from further service, if they so wished, for ten years.

Marshall Hall, as an old campaigner, would have known the likely verdict from tell-tale signs as the jury returned. Generally speaking, if juries are going to convict, they appear solemn and do not look towards the dock. The evident expressions of relief on the faces of some of the male jurors, even, here and there, a slight smile, showed that this was to be yet another notch on Marshall Hall's forensic gun.

His triumph, however, was tarnished by physical distress and pain. Feeling too ill to see Marguerite, he was helped to the robing-room by Bowker, his clerk, and said that he felt 'all in'. He had committed more than his usual share of nervous energy to the Fahmy case and, drenched in perspiration, was given a good towelling down and change of clothes by his clerk, before slipping out of a side door to avoid the waiting crowds.

People who had been cleared from the court milled around in the Main Hall on the first floor of the Old Bailey, waiting vainly for Madame Fahmy to appear. But she remained below and the crowd mistook Yvonne Alibert for her sister as she emerged, weeping tears of joy, after a brief embrace with Marguerite in the room underneath the dock. A foolish woman, smartly dressed, who pushed her way over to Yvonne, kissed her on the cheek and breezily exclaimed, 'Bravo, I'm so glad you're free as I've often been to Paris', was rightly awarded first prize in the *Daily Sketch*'s 'Imbecility Stakes'.

Helped by Maître Assouad, Yvonne made her way with difficulty down the broad marble staircase, smiling through her tears and exclaiming, according to the English press, *'Mon dieu! Mon dieu! C'est magnifique, c'est terrible.'* Outside, a solicitor's young clerk had broken the news to the waiting throng, shouting 'She's acquitted!' As Yvonne reached the steps leading into the street from the Old Bailey's main entrance, the crowd rushed forward, shouting 'Bravo the Madame', and Yvonne, now relishing the impersonation, responded with her arms outspread in triumphant gesture. Hats were thrown into the air and weeping women clutched at her body, in the mistaken belief that this was indeed the sensational Madame Fahmy.

Yvonne managed to scramble into a waiting car, where she joined some of Marguerite's Parisian friends. After police had cleared a path, Yvonne leant out of the car window, blowing kisses to the crowd and shouting *'les anglais sont très bien'*, as people climbed on to the cars and taxis trapped in the crush, waving handkerchiefs, walking-sticks and umbrellas.

Marguerite, now a free woman, remained in the Old Bailey for three-quarters of an hour, as anxious as her defender had been to avoid the ordeal of recognition. Police obligingly lined up outside the barristers' entrance in Newgate Street, successfully diverting the crowd. Marguerite gave a last hug to one of her wardresses before finally quitting the scene of her trial. Almost unnoticed, she left by the Lord Mayor's entrance at the rear of the building, her small, limp form lying motionless against the back seat of a cab.

Travelling with the weary Marguerite in the back of the taxi was Maître Odette Simon, who had rapidly advanced from being volunteer interpreter to the status of friend and confidante. A suite had been reserved for Madame Fahmy, not at the Savoy, with its tragic associations, but at the more discreet Princes' Hotel, which then stood at 190–96 Piccadilly. Some six years earlier, the Prince of Wales – agog to hear the latest salacious stories about Paris 'tarts' – had joined intimate friends there to celebrate the Duke of Westminster's birthday.

Waiting for Marguerite's arrival were her Egyptian lawyer, Maître Assouad, her sister Yvonne, Dr Gordon and numerous French well-wishers. Steps were taken at once to secure the maximum commercial advantage from Marguerite's notoriety. The press thronged the hotel lobby, desperate for the chance to interview Madame. Representatives came from all over the world: one large syndicate of American newspapers sent an open cheque. Despite the fact that the *Weekly Dispatch* and the *Evening*

418

News claimed to have had an exclusive right of interview, accounts of Marguerite's first words in freedom appeared in several other papers, though the *Sunday Pictorial*, obliged to disappoint its readers, made out that Madame Fahmy had been 'forbidden to pose or interview by her medical advisers'.

Dr Gordon was on hand to supervise his patient's welfare and almost her first action on reaching the hotel, after wiring the good news to Raymonde, safely in Paris, was to telephone Dr Morton, the prison doctor, with whom she seems to have struck up a close friendship. While the newshounds crowded around her (no doubt after suitable financial arrangements had been made with Maître Assouad on his client's behalf), she sat quietly in her Egyptian-style armchair, occasionally sipping a small glass of Benedictine and smoking cigarettes, which, from time to time, she generously pressed upon the reporters. Still dressed in black, she wore a single string of pearls and bracelets on each wrist. It was noticed that Marguerite, hatless for the first time since her trial began, was wearing her hair 'caught up with side curls', not bobbed as she had been in July. She looked wan and drawn.

'*Je n'ai aucun plan pour l'avenir*' ('I have no plan for the future'), she began, tactfully adding, '. . . *je dois render homage à la justice anglaise*' ('I must pay my respects to English justice'). She still felt dazed and '*abroutie* [stupefied]' from the effects of the sedative injection she had received in prison.

419

'*Laissez-moi ajouter que j'ai souffert atrocement durant les débats de ne rien pouvoir comprendre de ce qui se disait autour de moi, alors que ma vie était un jeu . . .*' ('Let me add that I suffered terribly during the trial from not being able to understand what was said about me, when my life was just a [courtroom] game . . .')

'Maggie Meller' could now afford to relax a little. Unable to follow much of the evidence, her thoughts had wandered, she recalled, causing her to muse on the jury, 'what we French call "bourgeois" – people who had left quiet lives in quiet homes, their simple pleasures and their businesses, to sit in judgement . . . What did they think of Marguerite Fahmy, I wonder, and the life so different from their own? Were they shocked at . . . the simple, brutal truth?' She also remembered how Percival Clarke had fidgeted with his gown, how his wig had gone awry, and how he had punctuated those bloodless questions with a nervous cough.

From time to time, she had understood a word or a phrase. The judge's use of the word 'murder' had scared her terribly, but she was downright annoyed when she heard prosecuting counsel scornfully describe her as 'that woman of 32'. '*Voyons, messieurs*', said Marguerite tartly, 'a woman of 32 is not old!' She was also unhappy at the contrast drawn between her age and that of her young husband. 'Surely his youth did not excuse his violence, his wickedness and, shall I say, his terrible abnormalities?'

It was those very 'abnormalities' and the controversial issue of interracial marriage that was the subject of much of the home-grown press comment on the Fahmy case in the next few days, now that the papers were free from reporting constraints operative during the trial. The *Evening Standard* censured 'the readiness with which the French inter-marry with coloured people . . . with whom we hardly mix at all' and, in the same edition, 'A Barrister' warned that '. . . white women take serious risks in marrying outside their own race and religion . . .', mooting the possibility of forbidding 'mixed marriages' altogether. 'Where a white woman weds a coloured man,' adjured the sleazy *Reynold's News*, '. . . she does so at her peril.'

The *Sunday Pictorial* warned parents of young English girls about the dangers lurking in Continental resorts such as Deauville, where 'a considerable proportion of the holidaymakers live East of Suez . . . the men are often handsome, frequently rich and entertaining . . .' (It was obviously safer to stay in Bognor.) 'A woman who marries a man not of her own race is taking a step that leads . . . to disaster . . . As a slave she has been taken and as a slave she will be held.' The *Daily Mirror*, too, emphasised 'the undesirability of marriages which unite Oriental husbands to European wives' and, without naming E. M. Hull and her school, roundly condemned 'women novelists, apparently under the spell of the East, [who] have encouraged the belief that there is

421

something especially romantic in such unions. They are not romantic. They are ridiculous and unseemly.'

Concern was expressed about the interest taken in the case by women, who had loitered about or queued for hours for the chance of a seat in the public gallery. To the *Manchester Guardian*, the 'blend of squalor and cheap glamour of great wealth provides exactly the mixture which stimulates a Central Criminal Court crowd. The sightseers seem to be equally divided between the seedy hangers-on who specialise in murder trials and fashionable women in furs . . .' The *Law Journal*, noting that many of these richer women had secured their seats with the help of connections in the City of London, wondered if the Corporation 'might consider whether the most important criminal court in the country ought to be reduced to the level of a playhouse . . .'

The allegations made in respect of Ali Fahmy's sexual behaviour could only be hinted at, but, even with the prudery of the time, hints could be broad ones. The *Illustrated Sunday Herald* informed its readership that Fahmy was 'master from boyhood of satiating his eastern voluptuousness . . .', while *Reynold's News* produced a 'SECRET HISTORY OF THE TRIAL – WHERE THE NEWSPAPER REPORTS STOPPED SHORT', written by 'One Who Was There'. The text did not live up to its titillating title. 'Nobody who was not present [sic] at the trial can have any idea of the horror . . . too dreadful even to be hinted at . . . the abnormal and extraordinary relationship between man and wife . . .' This sort of behaviour was foreign to our shores, as the *Daily Chronicle* soothingly confirmed: '[Fahmy's] particular vices are commoner in the East than here.'

In *John Bull* the usual mixture of racism and sexual prurience was laid on with a trowel. 'From the desire for many wives and for women of a certain class, he [Ali] now developed a . . . sexual perversion which should have unfitted him for human friendship.' Homosexuality was not directly mentioned, but Ali was supposed to have become 'completely unsexed . . . all became as nothing to him beside the one mad desire to live unnaturally'.

Perhaps the most telling commentary, certainly the most self-righteous, came from a *Sunday Express* editorial headed 'THE CHRISTIAN ETHOS': 'It must not be imagined that this just verdict opens the door to the perilous anarchy of sentimental pity and maudlin compassion in cases of murder by a wife of her husband . . . on the contrary, it closes the door upon it. If Ali Fahmy had been a normal husband, the jury would not have acquitted his wife.' The verdict Not Guilty was 'a vindication of womanhood against the vices that destroyed Rome . . . the horrors which brought down fire from heaven upon the cities of the plain . . .' Forty years later, the writer Macdonald Hastings put the argument more crudely: 'The reason why Madame Fahmy shot her . . . husband . . . was because he was a sodomite.'

The *Sunday Express* was convinced that 'the status of women in our Western civilisation is immeasurably higher than it is in the Orient'. One contemporary snippet of news was overlooked by the sanctimonious commentators. Rose Little was a young woman who had been married in February 1923. Three days later, her husband had knocked her down. Thereafter he did so every Sunday, without fail. These were 'little tiffs', the man told Sittingbourne magistrates, who ordered him to pay his wife maintenance at the rate of just £1 per week.

A feeling that there was more than a whiff of humbug in English reactions to moral issues raised in the Fahmy trial was fanned into a blaze in Egypt, already in political ferment after the return from exile on 17 September 1923 of the veteran nationalist leader Zaghloul. The British had packed him off to the Seychelles two years earlier and his homecoming was, inevitably, a triumph, coming a month before the first elections of the semi-independent Egyptian state.

Nationalist sentiments were especially prickly at this time: the Foreign Office gravely minuted that the Fahmy trial was being used to stir up anti-British feeling in, of all places, Switzerland. Reports of Marshall Hall's comments and the judge's summing-up, which appeared to endorse what the defence counsel had said, were received with indignation in Cairo and Alexandria.

The Bâtonnier of the Egyptian Bar sent a long cable of complaint to the British Attorney-General, Sir Douglas Hogg. Marshall Hall's response was a sorry apologia: 'Any attack I made was . . . on the man Ali Fahmy and not on the Egyptians as a nation . . . The only thing I remember saying that might be misunderstood was that it was a mistake for the Western woman to marry this Eastern man . . . If, by any chance, in the heat of advocacy, I was betrayed into saying anything that might be construed as an attack on the Egyptians as a nation, I shall be the first to disclaim any such intention . . .'

Almost alone among the English press, the *Daily Chronicle* saw merit in the Egyptian protest. 'The impression might be gained,' it wrote, 'that English opinion, in condemning the depravities of Ali Fahmy, was led to regard these as characteristics of Egyptian society . . .' Sir Henry McMahon, British High Commissioner in Egypt between 1914 and 1916, shared this balanced, unsensational view of the East: 'It is a mistake to imagine . . . that women in Moslem countries are regarded as intellectually negligible. In numerous cases, they have claimed and obtained high positions . . .'

In Egypt, the *Mokattam* spoke for other Arabic newspapers (patronisingly referred to as the 'native press' in the *Egyptian Gazette*): 'The error which was committed by Sir Marshall Hall [sic] and

425

Mr Justice Swift . . . is not, however, the first mistake committed by Westerners . . . as the majority of people in England are ignorant of family life in Egypt . . .' Recalling the Russell divorce case of earlier that year, a juicy saga of aristocratic bedroom fun, the *Mokattam* forcefully pointed out how easy it would be to judge 'the highly civilised English community, relying on the reports of crimes and the cases of divorce which appear daily in the London press'.

Ali Fahmy's reputation was a casualty amid all these outpourings of justified wrath. In the light of the unpalatable allegations made at the trial, the Egyptian government felt bound to issue a statement, which claimed that although Ali had enjoyed the reputation of being a 'notable and personal friend of King Fuad . . .', this was incorrect. His only meeting with the monarch had been at the foundation-stone ceremony at the Maghagha hospital. Ali was described, ungenerously and inaccurately, as having been 'of modest extraction and practically uneducated, except for the veneer acquired in the demi-mondaine [sic] . . . a libertine of the cosmopolitan type'. A more measured epitaph came from the newspaper *Al Lataig Al Musarawa*: 'Those who surrounded him . . . called him the Prince of Youth. The public, high and low, was a spectator of his prodigality and they regretted deeply that his great wealth brought such little profit to his . . . countrymen.'

Marguerite, heavily veiled, caught the boat-train

426

at Victoria on 23 September. Wearing a black crêpe gorgette, black cloak and hat, and clasping a bunch of white roses, she travelled back to Paris with her sister Yvonne. *Le Figaro* commented wistfully, '*Elle a quitté Londres et ses brouillards où elle a tant souffert*' ('She has left London and its fogs, where she has suffered so much'). In the meantime, she had received shoals of congratulatory telegrams, several offers of marriage (one from an earl, another 'in perfect French', from a professional man in northern England) and a theatrical agent had tempted her, but without success, to appear on the Paris stage.

Before she left, she afforded the *People* a second interview in which, unbelievably, she expressed herself 'too distracted to think of any fortune which her Oriental husband might have left her'. Reflecting on her awkward religious position, 'her wonderful eyes grew dim with tears . . . "I am afraid of what our Church will say",' she murmured.

The French press, preoccupied that summer with recurrent domestic political crises and with France's ill-advised occupation of the Ruhr, had largely ignored Marguerite's fate until the start of her trial. At first, some of the references to her were disparaging, as when *Le Temps* spoke of '*Madame Marguerite Fahmy Bey, mieux connue à Paris sous le nom de Maggie Meller . . .*' ('. . . better known in Paris as . . .'), but the mutual distrust between England and France soon surfaced.

The *Manchester Guardian*'s Paris correspondent

reported that 'the execution of Mrs Thompson gave a shock to French public opinion'. Indeed, no woman had been guillotined in France since 1887, whereas in Britain a dozen women had been hanged in the same period. English juries were described as '*si rigoureux* [so harsh]' by *L'Intransigeant*; while *L'Illustration* commented, '*En matière d'homicide, on sait que les jurys anglais se montrent toujours impitoyables*' ('With regard to murder, one knows that English juries always show themselves to be merciless').

The schoolboy prurience of the English press was absent in France and the racial element less evident. Ali had been '*un despote maladif* [a morbid tyrant]', but the emphasis was on the shattered dreams of this elegant Parisian woman. 'LE MIRAGE DE MAGGIE MELLER' was front-page news in *Le Gaulois*: '*Pauvre petite princesse des mauvaises mille et fois nuits! Tout ce malheur est né d'un mirage* . . .' ('Poor little princess of the unlucky Thousand and One Nights! All her ill-fortune was caused by an illusion . . .') Marguerite had been '*L'esclave de son mari, le jouet de ses caprices*' ('The slave of her husband: the plaything of his whims').

From being regarded as an unlucky *demi-mondaine*, Madame Fahmy was fast becoming a latter-day St Joan, a symbol of French womanhood, on trial for her life before a tribunal of the flint-hearted and sexually repressed English. Percival Clarke's faltering cross-examination was transformed by *Le Temps* into an interrogation '*fourmillant de pièges extrêmement difficiles à éventrer'* ('swarming with traps extremely difficult to break out of'). The presence of Mlle Simon, *'une jeune et jolie Parisienne'* had, in France at least, just the effect that her defender had hoped, *'prêtant son concours à une compatriot malheureuse assise sur le banc des accusés'* ('giving her help to an unfortunate compatriot seated in the dock'). Though Marshall Hall had delivered *'une brillante plaiderie'* ('a sparkling address'), prosecuting counsel had responded with *'une réplique froide et monotone'* ('a cold and monotonous reply').

The perils of dictation over the telephone were exemplified in the reporting of the judge's name; several newspapers referred to him as 'Ribby Swist', whose summing-up was regarded by *Le Figaro* as *'extrêmement severe pour l'accusée'* ('extremely hard on the accused'). The verdict was a surprise to many. *L'Intransigeant* reported a conversation between two astonished travellers in a Paris commuter train, shortly after the news of Madame Fahmy's acquittal had reached the Paris newsstands at 4 p.m. on 15 September. One said *'C'est extraordinaire . . . Jamais je n'avais cru les Anglais capable de cela'* ('It's extraordinary . . . I never thought the English capable of it'), while the other replied, *'Avec leur rigorisme – C'est inoui!'* ('With their severity, it's unheard of!').

Le Canard Enchaîné took a sideways look at the trial and at Marguerite herself, about whom the satirical weekly nursed no illusions. A spoof interview with Marguerite began, in deadpan style, '*C'est avec une joie patriotique que la France entire l'acquittement de Mme Fahmy . . .*' ('The whole of France has greeted the acquittal of Mme Fahmy with patriotic joy . . .') – an absurd exaggeration followed by a dig at Madame herself. '*Mme Fahmy, qui quelques confrères appellant Mme Maggie Meller – car elle n'a jamais épousé M. André Meller . . . était Mme Grandjean avant de devenir Mme Fahmy*' ('Mme Fahmy, who some friends call Mme Maggie Meller, because she wasn't married to Mr André Meller . . . was Mme Grandjean before becoming Mme Fahmy'). The reference to 'Grandjean' may have been to her former lover, Jean d'Astoreca.

'Maggie Meller' had come to symbolise, wrote *Le Canard*, the virtues of the French race: *gaieté, esprit de détente (si l'on peut dire), en opposition avec le sérieux hypocrite des* Anglais [gaiety, spirit of relaxation (so to speak), as opposed to the solemn hypocrisy of the English]'. '*Détente*' was a play on words: it also means 'trigger'. Marguerite, '*notre illustre compatriote*', confided her plans for the future. She was thinking of going back to the Folies Bergère. With waspish humour, *Le Canard* gives her supposed reply: '*Mais, cette fois, sur la scène et non plus au promenoir*' ('But this time on the stage and not walking about again'), a jibe at the days before the Great War when she had plied her trade as a good-time girl at the Folies.

The parallel with Jeanne-Marguerite Steinheil, a woman of loose morals also widely thought to have escaped justice after murdering her husband, was not overlooked. By this time, Mme Steinheil had become Lady Abinger and was living in England. Marguerite, supposed by *Le Canard* to have met her there, calls her *'une copine* [a close mate]'.

The article ended on a savagely accurate note. 'Will you be inheriting your husband's fortune?', she is asked. The reply is perfect. *'Grands yeux étonnés, délicieusement ingénus, "Certainement, puis qu'il est mort?"'* ('With great astonished eyes, deliciously innocent, "Of course. He's dead, isn't he?"')

After leaving the Old Bailey and the scene of one of the greatest triumphs of his long career, Marshall Hall had gone straight down to his country cottage at Brook in Surrey to rest. The telegraph boy brought the old campaigner a pleasant surprise that Saturday evening, a cable from Madame Fahmy, who had resumed her maiden name for the occasion: *'De tout mon Coeur je vous suis profondément reconnaissante – Marguerite Alibert.'* ('With all my heart, I am deeply grateful to you.')

The next day was Marshall Hall's sixty-fifth birthday, which he marked by replying gallantly and at some length to Marguerite's wire. Paying tribute to her testimony, *'bravement donnée* [bravely given]', he apologised for not having personally congratulated her after the verdict, excusing himself on the ground of her manifest exhaustion. *'J'espère que l'avenir vous donnera beaucoup de*

*moments heureux pour remplacer les misères passes.
C'est encore une fois que "la vérité est triomphante"
. . .'* ('I hope that the future will give you many
happy times to replace the sad occasions. "Truth
is triumphant" once again . . .')

Marguerite's telegram was soon followed by a
letter, elegantly expressed and written from Princes'
Hotel:

> *Septembre 15me 1923*
> *CHER MAÎTRE – J'arrive et dans cette
> ambiance de Bonheur un regret m'attriste, celui
> de n'avóir pu vous prendrer la main et de vous
> dire merci. Mon emotion était si grande que
> vous me pardonnerez d'avoir fermé les yeux et
> de m'être laisser emmener. – Votre profondément
> reconnaissante M. FAHMY.*

> [DEAR MASTER – I arrive and in this
> happy atmosphere one regret saddens me,
> that of not being able to take your hand
> and thank you. My emotion was so great
> that you will forgive me for having closed
> my eyes and for allowing myself to take my
> leave – your profoundly grateful M. FAHMY]

Before she left, Marguerite had visited Marshall
Hall in his chambers at 3 Temple Gardens. Bowker,
his clerk, showed Marguerite into his comfortable
room, overlooking the River Thames, with original
Victorian caricatures decorating the walls, within

which the Great Defender sat at his Chippendale desk, with red morocco inset. From time to time, Bowker heard 'laughter in the room, her rather shrill voice mingling with Marshall Hall's . . . measured tones'. Marguerite visited Marshall Hall in London on later occasions, fuelling speculation of an affair, though she was careful to record in her memoirs that she had been formally presented to his wife.

In 1924, Marshall Hall was instructed as prosecuting counsel in the murder trial of Jean-Pierre Vaquier, a Frenchman accused (and ultimately convicted) of poisoning a pub landlord in Surrey. In whimsical mood, Marguerite wrote '*Je savais par les journaux que vous étiez contre l'accusé et de de ce fait je me plaignais – mais oui!!!*' ('I've learnt from the papers that you've been acting against the defendant and don't think much of this – yes indeed!!!').

The year before, just after the end of the trial, Marshall Hall had an ulterior motive beyond personally receiving the thanks of his attractive client. He dearly wanted to add her .32 Browning semi-automatic to his already extensive collection of firearms. Normally, acquitted people are given back any of their possessions that have been used as exhibits at their trial, but the pistol had been imported illegally. Marshall Hall's first step was to get Marguerite's disclaimer and he wrote out a note, in English, addressed to 'The Chief of Police, Scotland Yard', asking that the Browning automatic pistol, 'Exhibit No.2 in the trial of Rex v. Fahmy', might be handed to him. Marguerite obligingly appended her signature to the document.

Shortly before she returned to France, Marguerite wrote yet another billet-doux to her saviour, saying how pleased she was that at last the English newspapers were telling the truth about her. Maître Assouad had penned a neat demolition job on Ali Fahmy for the *World's Pictorial News* of 23 September and the first instalment of her own hastily cobbled together memoirs was published the following day in the *Illustrated Sunday Herald*, also appearing in the *New York World* and *Le Petit Parisien*.

Marshall Hall, determined to get hold of the pistol, began a campaign. Although there was at first some official reluctance, the matter was resolved in an extraordinary way. Sir Wyndham Childs, who may have revealed confidential Special Branch information about the Prince and Marguerite to his old friend, duly minuted: 'I think we should refuse to hand it over on Madame Fahmy's request. It would be another matter entirely if we handed it over to Sir E. Marshall Hall as a small memento of a case in which he made such a thrilling speech.' Two letters were sent from Scotland Yard to Marshall Hall on 11 October 1923. The first was an officially worded refusal of his request, on the grounds that Madame Fahmy had been in unlawful possession of the pistol and the Commissioner therefore could not recognise her authority to hand it over. The other, also signed by Wyndham Childs, was a personal note which made a confidential invitation: '. . . if you would like to send somebody round to see me in about a month's time, [the Commissioner of Police] will be happy to send you the souvenir . . . which you desire. My only regret is that the lady did not get a "right and left" . . .'

Marshall Hall's delighted reply confirmed an 'old pals' act' of sizeable proportions. Long-ago shooting expeditions to the moors of Forfar were recalled: 'I often think of our happy times at Hunt Hill and our journey down together on that awful night . . .' and 'Fido' Childs's phrase, 'right and left' (presumably a suggestion that Ali Fahmy's genitalia should have been blasted away), was enthusiastically echoed: 'PS I think I know where the left barrel ought to have proved effective and I agree.'

'Fido's' private opinion of Marguerite was not much more generous than his attitude to her husband had been. The first instalment of Marguerite's memoirs had provided a colourfully embroidered account of her arrest and detention at Bow Street police station. 'Naturally, one does not believe all the statements made by this hysterical woman,' he minuted crustily, 'but I would like to know what "E" Division have to say . . . about it.'

Officialdom was anxious to tidy away the troublesome Fahmy case as soon as possible after the verdict and Madame's very welcome return to the land

435

of her birth, but the vexed issue of how both Ali and Marguerite had been able to get into the country, each carrying guns and ammunition, continued to worry the Home Office until well into December. One harassed official fruitlessly canvassed a faint possibility: '. . . I suppose these two had not applied for an import licence?', but there was no doubt that the guns had been illegally imported. 'Customs must not search persons without reasonable cause for contraband . . .', responded the red-faced Customs and Excise. 'Obviously it would not be right . . . to subject every person landing to a personal search . . .'

The Savoy's management must also have harboured the wish that a very tiresome episode in its history would soon be over and forgotten. Towards the end of September, a development in the hotel's entertainment policy provided a welcome distraction from the sordid revelations of the Fahmy trial. Wilfred de Mornys, musical director at the Savoy, announced the introduction of a second resident band, the Orpheans, which would join the already highly successful Savoy Havana Band. The *Evening Standard* saluted the Orpheans' début under the title 'LONDON'S BRIGHTER EVENINGS'. 'Last night, I heard the Savoy Orpheans play in the splendidly re-decorated Savoy Hotel ballroom . . .', wrote a correspondent. 'They play beautifully with a swing and rhythm that set the feet stepping and tapping almost unconsciously . . .' In his diary, Arnold Bennett wrote of the 'wonder-band', who 'played bad music well'. His novel, *Imperial Palace*, was based on the Savoy, Bennett's favourite hotel, not least because François Latry, the hotel's *maître cuisinier*, had created the famous *omelette Arnold Bennett* in his honour.

The hotel's publicity machine was in top gear, emphasising that the band contained a number of top American musicians and had a '£900 piano with its double keyboard [which] is making some interesting experiments with the fox-trot rhythm . . .' The *Radio Times* promised listeners that the Savoy Orpheans would be a feature of the winter's entertainment. 'They will play at the Savoy Hotel, whence the music will be transmitted to a land wire to 2LO, and so, through the ether to your receiving sets.'

In England, amid such gentle diversions, memories of the antics of that unwelcome pair of foreigners, Ali and Marguerite Fahmy, began to fade from the public mind, wholly unaware of the lady's chequered history as mistress of the Prince of Wales.

CHAPTER 24

SHOW TRIAL WITH A DIFFERENCE

M adame Fahmy had been triumphantly acquitted in a wave of popular sympathy, but in reality this had been a Show Trial. In the 1930s and 1940s, the notorious trials of supposed traitors or enemies of the people in Hitler's Germany or Stalin's Russia were fake processes, condemnation assured. In the England of 1923, the prosecuting authority (with the Royal Household hovering in the background) desperately wanted an acquittal.

The dire consequences of a conviction for murder were only too obvious. Sentence of death was mandatory. The Home Secretary would then have to decide whether to advise the King to commute the sentence to one of life imprisonment. The agreement reached between Marguerite and the Royal Household in August, with the aim of ensuring her silence about the liaison, could be in jeopardy. Anything could happen in the weeks during which Marguerite's life lay in the balance. Although strenuous efforts were made in the interwar years by the Home Office to prevent condemned prisoners publishing statements in the newspapers, explanations, justifications and pleas for mercy would often leech out. Even if Marguerite were to be reprieved, she was not the type to take incarceration meekly. Her lobby of powerful friends would ensure that Marguerite maintained her media access. The Prince could still be 'dragged in' to the noisome world of *l'affaire Fahmy*.

Although in retrospect it is not surprising that Marguerite walked free from the Old Bailey, her defending advocate had taken a gloomy view of her chances of acquittal when he was initially instructed by Freke Palmer, in the first days after the shooting. Although he must have received an indication before the start of the trial that Marguerite was safe from cross-examination about past character, Marshall Hall knew that his client's past life could very possibly put a noose about her neck. Evidence about her real character was kept to a minimum, a state of affairs ensured by the judge's ruling. By imputing to her husband sexual behaviour of the very basest sort (thus shifting the moral spotlight away from the wife), Marshall Hall went a long way towards securing a favourable verdict. The sexual dimension, coupled with a crude racism, served Marguerite well, although it would be churlish to underestimate the considerable histrionic talents she demonstrated in her own defence.

When he made his eyecatching entrance into Court Number One, Old Bailey, on the morning of 10 September 1923, Marshall Hall knew that he could cross-examine Said Enani robustly, with

439

no risk of putting Marguerite's character in issue. He may have had a hint from Bodkin. Marguerite's family always thought that Marshall Hall knew, before the trial, about her affair with the Prince and the importance of the love letters. Family tradition held that, on the last day of the trial, when things seemed to be going badly for Marguerite, Marshall Hall somehow brought the letters to the attention of the judge, who intervened at this very late stage to ensure acquittal. The nature of the trial process rules out this possibility, but there is no doubt that the letters were in play from the time of the shooting in mid-July.

Marshall Hall may have visited Marguerite in Holloway, though there is no evidence that he did so. At this time, it was unusual for counsel, particularly Leading Counsel, to hold pre-trial conferences with clients in capital cases. Sir Patrick Hastings, a younger contemporary of Marshall Hall, made it a rule never to see an accused person in prison, the risk was that one defendant might say something to counsel directly which (perhaps confincing him counsel's written instructions) could hamper the conduct of the defence.

If Marguerite had been 'squared' by the Royal Household (with the assistance of the DPP) in mid-August, as seems to be the case, the terms of the agreement regarding the issue of past character must have come to the attention of the defence team. Confidential information about the hidden background to the case may also have leaked out from Marshall Hall's old friend, Sir Wyndham ('Fido') Childs, head of Special Branch.

'Fido' Childs, as has been shown, was aware of the Royal Household's interest in Marguerite at an early date and, despite his very senior position in the Metropolitan Police, seems to have been a bit of a gossip. A year or two later, General Sir William Horwood, Commissioner of Police for the Metropolis, would issue a sharp rebuke to his garrulous deputy. In a tartly worded minute, the Commissioner relayed concerns that had been expressed by the Prime Minister, Stanley Baldwin. Childs had been 'making a great deal too much' about security matters 'while attending dinners and weekend house parties'. Horwood summoned 'Fido' to his office at Scotland Yard, telling him that 'he <u>must absolutely close down discussing "shop" when outside the office</u>'.

Although Marshall Hall knew that he was on safe ground with regard to Marguerite's character, the most famous biography of Marshall Hall, published only six years after the trial and written by the Hon. Edward Marjoribanks MP (elder half-brother of Quintin Hogg, later Lord Hailsham), contains this odd passage:

> The cross-examination of the secretary [Said Enani] had been a very delicate matter; if Marshall, always excitable and indiscreet, had in any way attacked the man's character, this would have entitled

441

the prosecution to attack that of Madame Fahmy and it would have been a fatal mistake to attack that of his secretary . . . it was of vital importance that she should not be distressed by the introduction of other matters . . . Mr Roland Oliver [junior counsel for the defence] sat like a watch-dog . . . to restrain his leader . . . Marshall Hall obtained all that was necessary . . . without once attacking the witness himself.

The suggestion that Marshall Hall had not attacked the character of Said Enani is nonsense, underlined by the author's absurd reference to Marguerite as a 'fragile creature who had been in the power of this decadent Oriental millionaire'. Marjoribanks devoted eighteen pages of text to a detailed summary of the trial, written very much in Marguerite's favour. 'Enquiries of the most expensive kind . . . in Paris', he wrote, had produced 'two youths who had been associated with [Ali] Fahmy', duly sitting in court, 'in case there should be any doubt as to the "prince's" true character'. Marjoribanks, however, gave no hint that the Prince of Wales had ever played any part in the past life of 'Madame Fahmy'.

Marjoribanks – educated at Eton and Oxford – was the son of Lord Tweedmouth, a courtier and 'Lord in Waiting' to George V. Given his link to the Royal Household and other contacts shared with the Prince, it is hard to believe that Majoribanks knew nothing about the Prince's liaison with Marguerite by the time the biography was published in 1929, even if news of the love letters had been kept under wraps by the Prince's secretaries. Marjoribanks also knew gossipy 'Chips' Channon, confidant of Grace Curzon, whose husband, Marquess Curzon, had blurted out royal secrets in a letter to her written in September 1923.

Robert Bruce-Lockhart, the adventurer and journalist, considered Marjoribanks to be unbalanced. 'When he became excited,' Bruce-Lockhart noted, 'there was something abnormal about his mentality.' In 1932, supposedly after a second jilting by a girlfriend, Marjoribanks committed suicide by shooting himself in the heart with a shotgun. His uneven, unreliable account of the Fahmy trial, strongly pro-Marguerite and contained in a bestselling book of the day, has the air of an exercise in disinformation.

With regard to the selection of witnesses for the prosecution, Archibald Bodkin had responsibility for deciding who would give evidence for the Crown at the inquest and in committal proceedings at Bow Street Police Court. His list of expert witnesses, however, omitted the name of someone whose testimony could have materially strengthened the case for the prosecution. The omission is remarkable.

Sir Bernard Spilsbury, the one and only 'Honorary Pathologist' to the Home Office, was the most famous pathologist of his day. Making his name in the Crippen case, he had appeared for the prosecution in a series of high-profile murder trials (Seddon, 'Brides-in-the-Bath', 'Button and Badge', Bywaters and Thompson) and had been knighted in January 1923 after his evidential triumph in the Armstrong poisoning trial the previous October. The sensational background to Marguerite's case rendered this a true *cause célèbre*.

Spilsbury was a prosecutor's dream. He cut a commanding figure in court, dealt in certainties, could put spin on the facts, and played games with the truth, sometimes even embellishing evidence in support of his propositions. Spilsbury had given evidence in several high-profile firearms cases, including Jeannie Baxter (1913), Norman Rutherford (1919) and Dunn and O'Sullivan (1922), the IRA murderers of Sir Henry Wilson. In all the circumstances, the absence of Spilsbury – who was in England and available to be instructed by the Home Office – is a glaring omission on Bodkin's part, underlining the lack of drive to secure a conviction.

Although Robert Churchill, the firearms expert, would be called to give evidence as a witness for the Crown, the effect of his testimony was blunted by the absence of forensic evidence from Spilsbury, his frequent collaborator in controversial firearms cases.

The post-mortem on Ali Fahmy's body should have provided the prosecution with its deadliest ammunition. It was conducted by a House Physician

444

at Charing Cross Hospital, on the day after the shooting, who clearly lacked significant experience of forensic pathology. Examination of Ali's body (his *djellaba* was quaintly described as looking 'rather like a tennis shirt') revealed seven different wounds collectively representing the tracks of the three bullets fired from Marguerite's gun.

The forensic evidence manifestly supports Beattie's account of seeing Ali, seconds before he was shot, bending down and whistling to Marguerite's errant lapdog. The first bullet in the back brought him down, a second passed through the side of the neck, and the *coup de grâce*, delivered neatly through the left temple, was fired by Marguerite from a closer range, as suggested by the slight blackening around the entrance wound.

Surviving accounts of the trial suggest that, somehow or other, the effect of the post-mortem findings got 'lost in the wash', as lawyers say when important facts become overwhelmed in a mass of other evidence. In fact, Marguerite had shot Ali Fahmy straight through the head at point blank range. Spilsbury, at the top of his form as the country's most famous forensic pathologist, could have exploited these known facts to deadly effect, but in this case the magic words 'SPILSBURY CALLED IN' would not be appearing on newspaper hoardings.

As July progressed, Bodkin began to receive advice (not always welcome) from the Fahmy family. Shocked and outraged by the shooting of their much-loved only brother and fearful of Marguerite's designs on his fortune, Ali's sisters joined forces to seek legal advice. They wanted to see Marguerite convicted of murdering their brother. Expensive Egyptian lawyers were recruited to the cause and, as has been seen, an English private detective, ex-Chief Inspector Stockley, was sent to Paris with a view to digging some dirt about Marguerite's past life. Marguerite's life as a high-class prostitute, her acquisitive streak, her cynical approach to marriage, her violent temper, even her lesbian interests, were duly recorded for the information of police and the DPP. The wording suggests that Stockley spoke no French and was wholly reliant on an interpreter for his information, most of which seems to have come from Mme Denart, the 'old woman' who had managed Marguerite at the start of her career.

Dr Abdul Ragai *bey*, an Egyptian barrister, prepared a lengthy memorandum on the case, written in reasonably clear English, highlighting the differences between English law and *sharia* practice. The family also instructed an English solicitor, W. Stewart Craigien of Gray's Inn Square, in a further attempt to persuade the DPP to call 'some witnesses proving murder premeditation'.

On 22 August, Dr Said, his wife, and Dr Ragai arrived in London, installing themselves in the Hotel Metropole, then one of London's smartest hotels, situated in Northumberland Avenue, easy walking distance from the DPP's office. Ragai immediately wrote to Bodkin, asking to know what was happening with regard to prospective witnesses from Egypt, 'waiting for an answer and apologising for my bad English'. A DPP official minuted sniffily, 'This letter was found this morning "on my doormat". I do not think in view of my letter to Mr Craigien that we need deal with it.'

Craigien had been told that, 'in view of the nature of the statements', Bodkin was 'not of the opinion that the presence of such witnesses in England need be procured'. A week later, after Ragai's report had been submitted to an unenthusiastic DPP, Craigien wrote that his clients had 'expressed surprise that you have not thought it necessary to interview them', adding the forceful rider that 'they might be able to give you information regarding the dead man . . .'

The Ragai memorandum cited aspects of *sharia* law which would have been unacceptable in 1920s England. There was provision for 'moderate disciplinary punishment for each disobedience [by a wife]', quoted from a legal textbook *Mohammedan Personal Law* by Kadri Pacha, as well as 'the right to forbid [the wife] to leave the house without permission'.

Ragai was on stronger ground in his submission regarding evidence of premeditation and motive. He pointed out that Marguerite could have deposited her jewels for safety with the hotel (the Savoy was quite used to that sort of thing) and did not need to carry a gun to protect them. Furthermore, if she was unhappy with Ali, she could simply have stayed in Paris. As to allegations about Ali's sexual demands, Ragai argued plausibly that Marguerite had 'seen many men before the deceased . . . some of whom might have had this perversion'.

Three witness statements were submitted to the DPP by Ragai, but their evidence would never be heard by the jury. The wording of the statements suggests that each witness was broadly credible and that they had not been schooled by the Fahmy camp. The head of the perfumery department at Cicurel's (the most expensive store in Cairo) deposed to Marguerite's extravagance and her 'quite polite' husband's weary acceptance. A Cairo modiste remembered that Marguerite was 'continually talking about Ali', who, she claimed, 'wished to indulge in unnatural vice but that he could die before she would allow him', a declaration that does not sit well with other evidence about brothel practices in Paris. Marguerite also said that she had a 'programme' of her own against Ali, which she would carry out in Europe and 'then everyone would know of it'.

The most important witness to be ignored by the DPP was Mahmoud Abul Fath. Born in 1885, Mahmoud was far from being *fellaheen*, enjoying a middle-class, academic background. He became Ali's secretary for a time (later to be succeeded by Said Enani) and in 1922 joined the staff of the prominent Cairo newspaper *Al-Ahram*, of which he later became editor. Mahmoud had links with the nationalist Wafd Party and his media career led to interviews with leading Egyptian statesmen and international figures. As has been noted in Chapter Six, Mahmoud was with Ali during the visit to Paris in the summer of 1922. During the Tut-Ankh-Amun season, Mahmoud joined Ali and Marguerite on board the *dahabeeyah* for the mysterious visit made by Howard Carter and General Sir John Maxwell.

Mahmoud would have given evidence that he had once been 'on very intimate terms' with Marguerite, a connection that may have begun during her 1921 visit to Egypt. Marguerite told Mahmoud, who spoke fluent French, a great deal about her private and personal affairs. With a striking familiarity to what she had said to Mme Denart before marrying Charles Laurent, Marguerite admitted to Mahmoud that she was only marrying Ali for his money. Her conversion to Islam was purely to exploit rights that accrued to her under *sharia* law.

Marguerite knew that if Ali died childless, she would get only a quarter of his fortune, but if she had a baby, the child would get half or all, depending on its gender, and she spoke of trying to get pregnant. She expressed hatred for Ali and again boasted that she had a programme in mind. 'You will hear of it. Everyone will,' she said. After the fulfilment of her 'programme', she would sell all Ali's property in Egypt, returning to Europe to live alone on the proceeds. 'She gave me plainly to understand,' Mahmoud told G. L. Moriarty, an

English barrister based in Cairo, 'that some time in the future she intended to kill him.'

Mahmoud's account of Marguerite's own words, showing her growing hostility to Ali, her greed, threats and obsession with money, reads coherently and is consistent with other accounts of these disagreeable aspects of her character. The DPP was obliged to put forward witnesses whose testimony was relevant, admissible, and capable of belief by a jury. Bodkin, almost certainly for reasons connected with pressure from the Royal Household, manifestly failed that responsibility.

Thanks to the judge's ruling, which wholly ignored the suggestions of venal conduct and of homosexuality that Marshall Hall had put to Said Enani, Marguerite's own background escaped searching inquiry. Percival Clarke's ill-judged question about the cab driver father had backfired on the prosecution and the jury were left with the impression that Marguerite was a divorcee who had enjoyed a number of affairs and whose love child had been legitimised by marriage to Charles Laurent. The jury were not to know the truth: that Marguerite had fifteen years' experience of working as a high-class courtesan.

A further matter that seems not to have been canvassed was whether Marguerite had known the content of the three telegrams, each worded 'NOTHING TO BE DELIVERED TO MY WIFE ON MY ACCOUNT DURING MY ABSENCE. FAHMY', sent off during the interval of *The Merry*

Widow. Marguerite had made an unsuccessful attempt to collect one of the expensive Vuitton handbags while Ali was away in Stuttgart in June. Her reaction to the discovery that Ali was pre-empting any attempt to clear those plush Paris stores of all the expensive goods held on his account was likely to have been a violent one. Clarke appears not to have made any use of these telegrams in his cross-examination of Marguerite, leaving the jury unaware of their existence.

Marguerite also escaped searching inquiry about her financial circumstances. In evidence, she claimed that she was effectively penniless in London, wholly dependent on her husband. There is no doubt that Marguerite was already an extremely wealthy woman when she married Ali. The evidence suggests that she could easily have afforded to pay for both the operation and the journey back to Paris, where, the previous month, she had bought another horse for her already considerable stable.

A more delicate topic, and one handled inadequately by the prosecution, was the vexed question of Madame's piles. Just how long had she been suffering from this painful complaint? Because questions about Marguerite's background were off limits, the fact that some prostitutes have practised anal intercourse from time immemorial, as the surest way of avoiding conception, was never canvassed before the jury.

Another important element that never came to the jury's attention was Ali Fahmy's mysterious journey from the Savoy to the Piccadilly area, made at the height of the tremendous thunderstorm. Such late-night excursions had been a feature of Ali's life both in Cairo and in Paris. Despite this and despite compelling newspaper reportage, the DPP ignored the episode, endorsing his file, 'What happened between 1.45 and 2.30 is not known.' That sweltering Monday in London must have been a time of intense emotional pressure, accompanied by a desire for relief, away from his increasingly bad-tempered wife. The relationship with Marguerite was at an all-time low: he had long doubted her fidelity, and with reason. He was now openly talking about divorce. She was accusing him of cruelty both physical and sexual; and, come hell or high water, she was going back to Paris the next day, leaving him to spend his Season in London alone and shamed.

There may have been a sexual motive for leaving the hotel, or Ali may simply have wanted to get away from his fractious wife for a while. He was away for perhaps an hour, ample time for a physical liaison or a visit to a club, and Ali was quite rich enough to have paid his cab driver to wait until he decided to return to the Savoy (Marguerite's chauffeur, very much *parti pris* in her favour, is unlikely to have been roused on this occasion). Ali's exact destination remains a mystery. It could have been any one of a number of late-night clubs in the West End, many operating illegally.

Mrs Kate Meyrick, 'Queen of the Night Clubs',

had fallen foul of the licensing law on numerous occasions, operating drinking clubs in Gerard Street (the infamous '43') and, later, in Newman Street, near Oxford Circus. Kate remembered seeing Ali, with his 'graceful, dignified carriage, good looks and the vague air of mystery that seemed to brood over him'. On her account, Ali took French leave from Marguerite during their short London stay, entering the club around midnight with 'some beautiful and exquisitely gowned woman', always with a 'wiry Egyptian' (perhaps Said Enani) in attendance. Ali confided that he was jealous of Marguerite. 'She fascinates me, but . . . I feel that she possesses a stronger personality . . . I'm almost frightened of her beauty and her brilliant intellect . . . When I'm with her I have a feeling of intellectual inferiority.' On the night of the shooting, a dark-eyed girl, 'conspicuously restless', waited for Ali, but he did not visit the club that night.

Ali could have taken his pleasure elsewhere or spent time in one of the other seedy West End clubs. Whatever happened could very possibly have acted as a spur to the bitter row that raged in the suite immediately before Ali was killed. Clarke did not ask Marguerite about her reaction to Ali's absence and for her part she was hardly likely to have wanted to introduce this sort of evidence into the case. Police took no steps to follow up the story. So the jury, unless they could remember July's newspaper reports, knew nothing about that rain-sodden journey. Said Enani made no mention of the trip. Perhaps the loyal secretary, not for the first time, was covering up for his master's indiscretion, out of regard for his surviving family.

What did happen on that stormy night in the summer of 1923? Marguerite's story of the crouching Oriental, ready to leap on her in a hotel corridor where, even at that late hour, people were passing and re-passing, is intrinsically ridiculous, as is her melodramatic account of Fahmy demanding his favourite sexual activity, accompanied by the waving of banknotes before his wife's helpless eyes. Much of the rest of Marguerite's narrative was culled from self-serving material compiled with an eye to an expensive divorce settlement and to lay a foundation for her defence if, in the end, she decided to give effect to her 'programme' and kill her husband.

By the summer of 1923, evidence shows that Marguerite had already made up her mind to rid herself of this tiresome, jealous, unfaithful and sometimes abusive husband. Ali had made up to her younger sister and was now planning to divorce Marguerite and marry another woman. England would have been the venue of choice. Egypt, Ali's home turf, was impossible. Paris knew too much about the lifestyle of the 'little French lady'. In England, Marguerite had valuable aristocratic connections and, well aware of the social calendar, very likely knew that the Prince of Wales would be in London for the Season. The veiled hint of blackmail, which had so worried the Prince in

1918, could easily be revived. Those foolish wartime letters deposited with Maître Assouad in Cairo would be Marguerite's trump cards. And, with great prudence, she seems to have ensured that one or two examples were in the safekeeping of a Paris friend.

Matters came to a head in the early hours of 10 July 1923. From what we know about Marguerite's tough, combative character, her avarice, her failure to manage Ali, his growing exasperation with her (as exemplified in his attempt to prevent Marguerite getting possession of the Paris jewellery), it was now or never. This was no *crime passionnel*. The risks to Marguerite were enormous, but so was the prize of fabulous wealth. With her domestic affairs in crisis (and, it must be allowed, suffering the torments of haemorrhoids, aggravated by the hot, sticky night), she finally decided to kill Ali Fahmy. With respect to the great Agatha Christie and her school of detective fiction, murder – even premeditated murder – is not always a neat and tidy affair. The rawness of human emotion, of hatred, anger and greed, may play a part in the killing process. With risk already calculated, the final decision to kill may be only a matter of moments.

When Ali left the apartment to call in his wife's lapdog, Marguerite simply went back to her room, picked up her pistol, already loaded as was her custom. Having fired once out of the window to check that it was working, she ran back into the corridor and shot her husband dead. The idea that

Marguerite, a pistol-packer for nine years, did not know how the firearm worked is laughable.

The flawed decision to protect Marguerite's character from exposure indicates beyond doubt that the judge, a recent appointment and relatively inexperienced, had been suborned by the DPP (a strong and highly reactionary character) on the Prince's behalf. In this most sensitive of trials, the prosecution gave Marguerite an easy run, ignoring vital cross-examination material. The defence, extraordinarily, supplied important evidence for the Crown. Potentially damaging witnesses were simply not called. The judge prevented the exposure of Marguerite's background in circumstances where her character should have been brought out. If the jury had known about her true background, her defence would have lacked credibility. She risked being convicted of murder, with its mandatory death sentence.

The family of Ali Fahmy benefited from the legal assistance of Cecil Whiteley, an experienced KC, who held a 'watching brief' on their behalf. Whiteley would have told his clients that the judge's ruling about character was wrong in principle. The family were aware that the judge's decision had been motivated by the need to protect the reputation of the Prince of Wales, for Marguerite was not quite the 'petite French lady' she pretended to be . . .

All in all, the Royal Household and the DPP had done a very neat job.

CHAPTER 25

'*MON BÉBÉ!*'

Within two weeks of the verdict, the story about Marguerite and her Prince found its way into one of the most scandalous gossip sheets in France. The *Cri de Paris* alleged that Marguerite, as 'Maggie Meller', had 'old and deeply rooted relations with one of the British princes'. Although the piece did not directly name the Prince of Wales, readers were given a broad hint the identity of her lover. 'These relations,' it was said, 'were the main factor contributing to her acquittal.'

The story was quickly taken up in Egypt, where opinion was still smarting from Marshall Hall's xenophobic closing speech. On 4 October, *El Sabat* (The Sabbath) added an even more sensational rider: 'The relations between Maggie Meller and the English prince appear to have been of a more intimate nature than could be imagined. It is said that the daughter of Maggie Meller is not a stranger to the Prince and that she lives in England and is being brought up at his expense.' The newspaper mooted that 'British Justice' would find itself in a critical position, with a public 'who take the utmost care to see that British Jurisdiction [sic] is always out of the reach of outside influence, whatever its origins may be'.

The article was based on 'a telegram received by the "[*Al*] *Ahram*" from London'. Owen Tweedy, at the British High Commission, noted drily, 'Prince Mohammed Ali [pretender to the Egyptian throne] will tell all his friends this story which will certainly be believed.' Though allegations about Raymonde and her schooling are without foundation, there is substance in comments about 'outside influence' affecting the due process of Marguerite's trial. Whatever the source of *Al Ahram*'s information, however, there would be no debate in England about the role of the Prince in the verdict. No hint of the affair would appear in the British press.

A word in the right ear, nothing on paper, could be sufficient to prevent publication of any gossip thought undesirable. Documentary evidence of a request to spike a particular story at this time is rare, though examples exist which show that people close to the royal family felt free to approach editors in sensitive cases. Marshall Hall, too, enjoyed a cosy relationship with Rex Blumenfeld, editor of the *Sunday Express*, asking him to keep his reporters from speculating about the size of his fee, following an unsuccessful defence in a murder trial. In Marguerite's case, however, it should be remembered how effectively the Royal Household, represented by Godfrey Thomas and Alan Lascelles, managed to confine knowledge of the affair to a very small circle of people. Even Curzon, the Foreign Secretary, knew nothing until a few days before the start of the trial. Strange as it may seem, the story may simply not have been picked up by British newshounds.

Despite the discreet reportage of evidence in the Fahmy trial carried in the more respectable French press and Marguerite's coy published account of her life in *Le Petit Parisien*, the *International Sunday Herald* and the *New York Times*, titillating news of the allegations made against Ali in court had seeped out into the wider world.

Marguerite's whiter-than-white memoir provoked grim laughter in Paris. On 25 October 1923, a fairly well-researched article appeared in *Le Dechaîné*, a satirical weekly. The revelations, titled *Quelques Dètails Nouveaux Sur La Vie De Maggie Meller* (A few new details about the life of Maggie Meller), was accompanied by two photographs, one showing her standing, with Raymonde, alongside her expensive chauffeur-driven limousine; the other, in her '*costume de travail* [working clothes]', showed Marguerite lying invitingly on a sofa and dressed in little more than a slip. *Le Dechaîné* promised its readers that Marguerite would be shown '*comme une prostituée haut de gamme* [as a top-ranking prostitute]'. Marguerite would later claim that the photograph was doctored.

Although in her memoirs Maggie had castigated Ali Fahmy for usurping the title of 'Prince', she had taken the horsewhip to a maid, 'Mademoiselle

Lucienne Dusunneaux', who on her first day at work had unwittingly addressed Marguerite simply as 'Madame', rather than 'Madame la Princesse'. Lucienne, subsequently sacked, turned whistle-blower and described a prolonged ordeal at Marguerite's hands. Lucienne admitted, however, that she had put up with the abuse because she was well paid. Marguerite, she claimed, had some-times dressed in her maid's clothes, to be beaten and abused by male customers, before walloping the clients herself. *'C'était des scènes inimaginables'* ('There were unimaginable scenes'), added a shocked Mlle Dusunneaux, not embarrassed in the least to tell *Le Dechainé*'s readers how Marguerite had once asked her what she felt while being walloped. 'It's easy,' said the maid. 'You take my place and I'll take yours' – a pert reply that provoked yet another beating with Marguerite's *cravache* (horsewhip).

The maid's story may not have lost in the telling, though a measure of sadomasochism was clearly part of Marguerite's *menu du jour*. The article was on firmer ground in alleging that Marguerite had murdered Ali for gain. The allegations in *Le Dechainé* contain inaccuracies, but the story contains credible elements and stands up reasonably well. The article claimed that Marguerite had decided to kill Ali after discovering his relationship with another woman, named as 'Jacqueline Wolt'. Marguerite had discov-ered that Ali intended to divorce her, which meant that she would lose out financially.

At the *maison de rendezvous*, the journal alleged, she had conspired with Sonia de Thèval and Ginette Folway to do away with Ali. In fact, Marguerite could take care of herself and needed no help from the Paris *madame* and her cotery at 20 rue Bizet to perfect her 'programme' against Ali. Rather more accurately, however, Ginette – described picturesquely as *'marchande d'amour'* ('seller of love') – was revealed to have been the lover of a French MP, M. Mandel, as well as M. Pereire, member of the enormously rich banking dynasty and director of the *Banque Transatlantique*.

Le Dechainé noted that the publicity surrounding the case had done Marguerite no harm. She had received many proposals of marriage, but instead had chosen to go back to General Mehmet Sharif *pasha*, her protector in wartime Egypt. She was spending time with him at 20 avenue de Messine in the 16th and the couple had been seen recently at the opening of Les Acacias, a new nightclub, *'ou se pressaient toutes les notabilités du monde, du demi-monde, de la politique et du Boulevard'* ('where they were surrounded by celebrities of every backround, people from the world of politics and from Society').

Although by 1923 Marguerite had ceased to make herself available in *maisons de rendezvous*, the paper nevertheless peddled some prurient allegations about lesbian activity involving Marguerite, Sonia and Ginette. After this, *Le Dechainé* got into its stride with a clear reference to royal involvement in the affair: '*Le Prince de Galles, de son côté, ne pouvait refuser d'influencer les Juges en reconnaissance des heures qu'il avait passé dans les bras de la meutrière.*' ('The Prince of Wales, for his part, could not refuse to influence the court, in view of the hours he had spent in the arms of the murderess.')

In loose translation, the article suggested that Marguerite knew before the trial started that she was on to a winner. The tone is scurrilous, relying in part on the allegations of a maid who had been dismissed by Marguerite, but the kernel of the story is consistent with a belief, well beyond the offices of *Le Dechainé*, that the British Royal Household had interfered in the trial, perverting the course of justice to protect the Prince and, by doing so, had saved Marguerite's neck from the gallows.

Worse came the next day. *Cupidon*, a French erotic fortnightly edited by Lionel d'Autrec (pseudonym of the anarchist Maurice Vandamme), discussed *Le Mémoire de Maggie Meller*, publishing its review under a weighty heading, *de sodomia feominarum* – a Latin phrase resembling some obscure Papal Bull from the depths of the Middle Ages.

Though Marguerite had undoubtedly been acquitted after showing the hotel doctor *son derrière outragé* (her outraged behind), she should not take Parisians for fools. Over the years, she had entertained Egyptians and Japanese men at *maisons de*

462

rendezvous, clients who had very special sexual predilections. There was a pointed reference to *marcher dans la voie tracée par les princes* [walking in the way traced by princes]. Thought this probably alluded to Ali as 'Prince' Fahmy, the use of the plural when coupled with the explicit reference to the Prince of Wales in the recent issue of *Le Dechainé*, may have been a deliberate attempt to implicate him.

Meanwhile, the Prince was safely out of the way in Canada. Once upon a time he would write as many as three letters a day to Fredie, but now things had cooled there would be gaps of ten days or more in his correspondence. On 27 September, he wrote from 'E P Ranch, Perisko, Alberta', where he was immured in the wholly masculine company of 'G' Trotter, Godfrey Thomas, 'Fruity' Metcalfe, the ranch manager, and an official from the Duchy of Cornwall. Wistfully calling up old memories, the Prince wrote, 'Darling, I dreamt about you last night . . . a queer dream & rather confused (but a bit naughty – in fact very!!).'

The Prince returned to England on 21 October. In petulant mood, he wrote angrily to Fredie from Plas Newydd, as the guest of Lord Anglesey, complaining that he would have to represent the King at the funeral of Andrew Bonar Law, the former Prime Minister. '. . . Bonner [sic] Law's funeral on Monday . . . means that I can't hunt with the Quorn.' At the service, this grown man of 29 behaved like a spoilt boy, paying no attention to the ceremony, fidgetting and making his acute boredom only too obvious to the distinguished congregation .

Through her lawyer, Maître Assouad, Marguerite had told journalists in London that she would never return to Egypt. However, on 20 October 1923 Marguerite boarded the SS *Esperia* at Naples, bound for Alexandria, where she arrived two days later. Once his client was safely in Cairo, the Maître announced to an astonished world that Marguerite was pregnant by her late husband, the happy event to occur the following April. This declaration did not sit comfortably with Marguerite's claim that Ali practised anal intercourse and, as will be seen, attempts to record the 'birth' of a phantom baby led to farcical court proceedings in Paris, involving Marguerite and a certain Cassab *bey*.

This was not the only piece of extraordinary news that month. Marguerite's 16-year-old daughter, Raymonde Laurent, wrote a well-publicised letter to a friend in Cairo, informing one and all of her intention to embrace Islam. She had privately sworn to become a Muslim if her mother were acquitted of the murder charge and regarded the verdict as no less than 'a miracle of the Moslem faith'.

The reason for these bizarre developments is not hard to divine. There had been much gossip in the newspapers about the diminution of Ali's fortune by reason of his gross extravagance, but once the dust had settled it had become apparent that he had left an estate valued at some £2.5 million and no will. Marguerite's chances of inheriting all or part of this vast sum were considerably hindered by the fact that it was she who had killed him. A Muslim court would demand more than a 'Not Guilty' verdict: she would have to satisfy them of her complete innocence in the matter. Failing that, the estate would be divided, half between Ali's three surviving sisters and the other half to his closest male relative, a paternal uncle, who worked in Ali's office at Cairo and used to complain that he was badly paid.

Much to Marguerite's chagrin, the administrator appointed to superintend Ali's estate was his brother-in-law, Dr Assim Said, who was not well disposed towards her. Marguerite's lawyer began an action in the Egyptian probate court, the *Meglis Hesbi*, to have Dr Said replaced as administrator by someone less hostile to her interest. The case drifted on into the New Year, was twice adjourned in January and again the following month, when Marguerite, now back in Paris, was invited to appear before them. Events in Paris involving the bogus baby were to overshadow the decision of the Egyptian court.

In the meantime, another startling development was reported by a French newspaper, which claimed during November that Marguerite was to be married to Said Enani. Said issued an angry denial to the London correspondent of *Al-Ahram*, saying that he was minded to consult his lawyers about the rumour. He did not have very much time in which to do so: early in January 1924, he died of pneumonia, a complication of *encaphalitis lethargica* ['sleepy sickness'] in Paris.

Back in York House, the partying continued. In mid-December, the Prince had enjoyed a 'queer evening' with Jean Norton (Beaverbrook's mistress) and two other lady friends, spending time at the Embassy Club with 'Duddie' (Fredie's estranged husband) and 'Ali' (Mackintosh). 'A- has gone to Paris for a few days. I guess something big is going to happen . . .'

Early in the New Year, the Prince made his first visit to Paris since February 1919. Accompanied by Godfrey Thomas and the ubiquitous 'Fruity', he installed himself at the Meurice yet again as the 'Earl of Chester'. The visit was supposed to be unofficial, but his arrival at the Gare du Nord made front-page news, accompanied by photographs of *le Prince Charmant*, elegantly attired, already regarded as the apogee of style.

From his first night, 9 January 1924, as if making up for lost time, the Prince showed himself determined to make the most of what Paris could offer. That Monday, he took a party to Ciro's at 6 rue Daunou, near the Opera, where the company dined and danced into the small hours. Although the Prince was officially attended by his Private Secretary, the official press release did not name 'Fruity'. The party was guarded by the Prince's

Special Branch detective, Sergeant Albert Canning, 37, 'the giant of Scotland Yard', a police officer whose ability and discretion had greatly impressed the Prince.

Though the visit was supposed to be *incognito*, the French press scented glamour in the Prince's return to Paris. He was *adorablement jeune* (adorably young) and *exactement comme son grand-père* (exactly like his grandfather), Edward VII, who had been enormously popular in France.

The hedonistic Prince could not completely escape public duties. On Tuesday 10 January, he inspected the damage caused by a recent flood of the River Seine and duly called on President Millerand at the Élysée Palace. That night, 'very much incognito', he attended *un théâtre des boulevards*. Next day, after lunching with his old friend Jacques de Breteuil, he dined at the British Embassy, guest of Lord Crewe. 'We tried to make [the evening] an amusing one for him,' wrote Crewe to Lord Stamfordham, 'and . . . finished up with a dance at which all the available good looks were collected.' Crewe felt 'very glad indeed that the Prince has broken the ice of coming here after the war . . . whenever he comes over again in a quiet way, he will not find himself bothered by too much public attention & will be able to interest & amuse himself in his own way'.

On the last day of his short visit, the Prince rode with 'Fruity' in the Bois de Boulogne, before going on a stag hunt in the forest of Villers-Cotterêts to the north of Paris, a messy affair that sometimes ended with hounds devouring the exhausted prey. 'I believe the Prince enjoyed his hunt very much, though it was as unlike Melton [Mowbray] as possible,' wrote Lord Crewe. Not a wit exhausted, the Prince was reported to have visited, for a second night, that *théâtre des boulevards*', most probably the Folies Bergère. In a letter to his wife, Alexandra 'Baba' Curzon (daughter of the Marquess), 'Fruity' described how, during their stay, he and the Prince 'went staghunting [and] to the Folies Bergère', as well as dining at the British Embassy.

With their track record in the pursuit of pleasure, it is scarcely conceivable that the Prince and 'Fruity', two veteran roustabouts, would have gone out for an evening without female company. 'Fruity', for his part, had no qualms about using ladies of the town to service his bachelor needs. Later that year after visiting a New York prostitute he accidentally left behind several letters written to him by the Prince of Wales. In Paris, a remarkable, wholly extraordinary, reunion of the Prince and Marguerite, the two wartime lovers, may have taken place, perhaps during that first month of 1924.

The managing director of the Ritz Hotel was Claude Auzello (originally from Nice), who, in 1922, had married the former Blanche Rubinstein of New York. Blanche had travelled across the Atlantic with the silent film star Pearl White, and

Pearl had featured in several film shorts, shown under such gripping titles as *The Exploits of Elaine* and *The Perils of Pauline* (most famously seen tied to a railroad track as an engine thunders towards her).

The Ritz had long been Marguerite's favourite hotel in Paris and it is not surprising that a friendship developed between Marguerite and Blanche, two young women who had already seen a great deal of the world. Blanche's account of her friendship with Marguerite, posthumously ghosted by her nephew, Samuel Marx (Hollywood script writer and producer of *Lassie Come Home*), is an affectionate memoir, sloppily written with events and dates all mixed up, but the amount of credible background detail in the text suggests that Blanche knew Marguerite quite well.

Blanche claimed that Marguerite asked her to make up a party with the Prince. That evening, the story went, 'The Prince's personal equerry was along to make the foursome complete.' In an attempt to avoid gossip, Blanche was be a front, a 'mustache' [nowadays a 'beard'].'

The quartet was said to have ventured out into 'Paris night life a few more times', but Marx tantalisingly provides no dates for these occasions. Blanche did not arrive in France until around 1922 and the Prince did not visit Paris between February 1919 and January 1924, so Blanche's first encounter could not have taken place before 1924.

Blanche's recollections of partying with the

Prince in Paris may be merely a recycled episode from Marguerite's past. From one viewpoint, it seems unlikely that the Prince would have taken the enormous risk of going back to Marguerite, in view of the strenuous efforts made by the 'handpicked team' at York House to recover his letters and keep his name out of a sensational and sordid trial.

On the other hand, although Marguerite had used the letters for purposes of blackmail, she had not attempted to sell them in the years between 1918 and 1923, given their enormous value, particularly in the American market. Furthermore, the correspondence had been returned, presumably destroyed by the Prince. Marguerite had kept her side of the bargain by not revealing, during the course of the trial and the subsequent media-fest, all that she knew about the Prince and his ways. There had been no 'kiss and tell'. The Prince, for his part, would remember the intensely physical relationship, the 'crazy physical attraction', enjoyed with *'mon bébé'*, still an attractive woman who could provide him with sexual adventures well beyond what was available from the well-bred ladies in England.

Today, people prominent in the media – 'celebs', politicians, American Bible-belt preachers, even members of the British royal family – seem strangely impelled to indulge in bizarre sexual adventures, risking exposure and ridicule, high-octane activity possibly fuelled by the very fact of celebrity itself.

In late January 1924, after the Prince's Paris visit, Marguerite took Raymonde – now a very sophisticated and self-possessed 17-year-old – to watch the 1924 Winter Olympics, staying at the Palace Hotel, Chamonix. A French reporter noticed Marguerite's *silhouette* (the outline of her figure), accompanied by her daughter, a vision *brève et blonde* (slight and fair), which evoked looks of sympathy from other hotel guests. Marguerite may not have relished the reference. She would become increasingly jealous of her daughter's looks, rivalry that would eventually produce a complete rupture of the relationship.

Three months later, the Prince made his next visit to Paris in very different circumstances. An enthusiastic, but not the best 'seat', the Prince was prone to falling off his horse while hunting or riding in point-to-points. On 8 February 1924, the Prince was exercising one of his hunters at Billington Manor, near Leighton Buzzard, prior to going out with the Whaddon Chase. He was thrown, pitched on to his right shoulder, and broke his collarbone. The local GP, one Dr Square, appropriately dressed 'in hunting kit', attended the stricken Prince.

Notwithstanding this injury, the reckless Prince was back in the saddle just over a month later, riding in the Army point-to-point at Arborfield Cross, near Wokingham, on 15 March. This time, his horse 'pecked' (stumbled) and fell, throwing the Prince, who suffered concussion and bruising to his face. Obviously dazed, the Prince was carted off on a stretcher, to the delight of the *paparazzi*.

Out of action for some weeks, the Prince decided to visit Biarritz, accompanied by the pleasure-loving 'G' Trotter, where he stayed at the Hotel Helianthe, meeting his old friend the Duke of Westminster. On Monday 14 April, the Prince and Trotter (but not, it seems, 'Fruity') arrived in Paris, where his usual apartment at the Hotel Meurice had been reserved. The trauma of his riding accident overcome, the Prince was seen to be looking 'quite well and apparently quite recovered from his fall'.

Meanwhile, Marguerite's campaign to win her share of Ali's fortune proceeded apace. In April, however, her plans came to a temporary halt, in circumstances that bear distinct resemblance to a Feydeau farce. Hiding behind a tapestry in the entrance hall of a clinic at 82 rue Dareau (only some 300 yards from Marguerite's birthplace), on the evening of 9 April 1923, was Commissioner Michet of the Paris police, normally stationed across the Seine in La Muette, a district of the 16th *arrondissement*.

Marguerite had called him in to hear a short conversation between herself and a marvellously shady character, Yusuf Cassab *bey*, a Syrian money-lender and carpet merchant, normally resident in Cairo. Stepping from his place of concealment, the Commissioner arrested Cassab on charges of attempted fraud and hauled him off to prison. Cassab had, in effect, been 'shopped' by Marguerite.

Cassab, who in the past had sold carpets to Ali Fahmy, told his story to the *juge d'instruction* (investigating magistrate) three days later. The whole matter revolved round finding an *'enfant du miracle'* ('miraculous child') for Marguerite, who was not pregnant, and never had been. Under Muslim law, a posthumous son could inherit a proportion of his father's estate, variously stated as a quarter or a half. A generous two-year period, it seems, was allowed for any such claim to be made. If evidence could be produced to show that Marguerite had borne a son, she would become, indirectly, a substantial beneficiary. The problem, of course, was that she was not pregnant. So the child would have to be a fiction, recorded in the documents as having died shortly after its birth.

Enter Cassab *bey*. On 15 October 1923, Cassab met Maître Assouad, surely not by chance, in the Café de la Paix in Paris. Cassab agreed that Marguerite's chances of getting her hands on the money were slim. The wily merchant told Assouad that he had an idea that would annoy the Fahmy family, and had a meeting with Marguerite to discuss his plan. Shortly afterwards, she left Paris for Cairo, where the pregnancy was announced, much to the discomfiture of Ali's family, who immediately stated that they would contest her claim.

Cassab, too, returned to Egypt, where he approached a friend with medical connections in

Paris, one Dr Kamel. On 11 January 1924, Cassab telegraphed to Marguerite: '*Je m'embarque. Je serai le mercredi 27 à Paris. J'ai des sérieuses propositions à vous presenter.*' ('I'm on my way. I shall be in Paris on Wednesday the 27th. I have some important proposals to put to you.') On arriving in Paris, he went to see her. Marguerite had moved from her apartment in the avenue Henri-Martin, possibly to escape the attentions of the press, and was now living at an equally plush address in the rue Georges-Ville. According to Cassab, Marguerite told him that she had cleared his plan with her lawyers, but that she had not so far been able to find a doctor willing to certify the birth of the phantom child.

Cassab introduced Marguerite some weeks later to Dr Kamel at Claridge's Hotel. Kamel had found someone willing to provide a false certificate for 200,000 francs (£2,500), half payable on signing the contract, and the balance paid when the birth certificate was handed over. Before this meeting, however, Cassab had received a disturbing letter from his son in Cairo, telling of a visit of a member of the Fahmy family, who were already deeply suspicious about Marguerite's 'pregnancy' and the 'shameful things' going on in Paris.

The family had evidence that damned Marguerite on three counts: first, a certificate that showed that she had undergone an ovariotomy; second, a declaration from Holloway that she was not pregnant during her imprisonment there; and, third, testimony about her private life in Paris. If, said the family representative, Marguerite was willing to withdraw her declaration of pregnancy, the family would pay her £15,000 in settlement of her claim against the estate.

When Cassab showed Marguerite his son's letter, her temper got the better of her, not for the first time. She had never had an ovariotomy, she declared angrily, merely an operation to remove her appendix (presumably the operation she had in 1918, just before the break-up with the Prince of Wales). Headstrong as ever, Marguerite brushed aside the settlement offer and told Cassab that she was going into the clinic the following Friday, probably 4 April. In court, Cassab tried to make out that he had no idea where the clinic was and had paid a M. Finance, a *marchand de cotton hydrophile* (cotton-wool salesman) some 250 francs for the information. The clinic at 82 rue Dareau was run by Madame Champeau, a professional midwife, married to a doctor.

At 11.05 a.m. on 9 April, the curtain rose on the last act of this long-running comedy. A domestic servant, employed at the clinic, called at the Registry of Births at the town hall of the 14th *arrondissement*, to announce that a boy had been born at the clinic on the 7th. Probably to the knowledge of Madame Champeau, the doctor officially appointed to verify births had already left with the day's list and the pink form that was an essential document of record. In his absence, the registrar's clerk made an informal note of the claim.

Forty minutes later, a Mme Renée Masdurand, midwife at the Champeau clinic, hurried into the town hall, claiming that, as a matter of great urgency, the birth of the child should be formally recorded, because it had taken place on the 9th, not the 7th. 'We don't have the official doctor available', she was told. 'Give me the pink form,' insisted the midwife, 'Madame Champeau . . . is going to see the doctor. She'll show him the child and return the form.'

The clerk reluctantly handed one of the precious forms to Mme Masdurand, telling her to return it before the office closed that afternoon. 'I'll bring it back at 5 o'clock,' promised the midwife, but it was not returned and, in the event, was never signed by the doctor. The reported birth was a hoax. Plainly, an attempt had been made to hood-wink the Registry, a plot that came to nothing, as *Le Canard Enchaîné* suggested, because Marguerite, who had suddenly realised that she was in danger of being found out, and thus risked prosecution, decided to shop Cassab that very evening.

The hearing of Marguerite's allegation of attempted fraud against Cassab ran to some five days. He claimed that he had been entrapped by Marguerite, who had originated the plot and was in it up to her ears. Marguerite, on the other hand, said that Cassab was himself part of a campaign by the Fahmy family to persecute her:

476

this does not explain how her lawyer came to announce a bogus pregnancy the previous October, and Marguerite, of all people, had most to gain from the subterfuge. Putting on a brave face, she attended the hearing swathed in mink and generously exonerated Mme Champeau, wife and mother, from complicity in the affair. 'That woman has five children,' said Marguerite, 'and is most certainly a victim of the machinations of Cassab *bey* . . .'

When Madame Champeau came to give evidence, she told of being pestered, almost threatened, by Cassab to take part in the deception, but she had refused any involvement. She admitted sending her staff to the town hall, but it was merely to report the births of two other children, a month earlier, on 5 and 10 March. She had never asked 30,000 francs (£575) for the false certificate, as Cassab had claimed.

It was all quite absurd. The Paris press gleefully recounted the attempts of the principal conspirators, Cassab, Marguerite and the '*doctoresse*', Mme Champeau, to extricate themselves from the mess. '*L'AFFAIRE CASSAB BEY OU LES MÉLI-MÉLOS DE LA RUE DAREAU*' ('THE CASSAB BEY AFFAIR OR THE MIX-UPS IN THE RUE DAREAU') headlined *Le Figaro*, while *Le Canard Enchaîné*, under the heading '*NOUVELLE INNOCENCE DE MADAME FAHMY*' ('NEW INNOCENCE OF MADAME FAHMY'), mercilessly sent up Marguerite for a second time.

She had been photographed sporting a mink coat and superb pearl necklace. '*Toute de monde souvient de Mme Fahmy bey qui, pour avoir simplement tué son mari, eut, à Londres, à subir toutes sorters des désagréments.*' ('Everybody remembers Madame Fahmy *bey*, who, for simply having killed her husband, had to undergo all sorts of unpleasant things in London.')

Le Canard wittily suggested that Marguerite had realised that the scheme was '*une infahmie*', before turning in the unfortunate Cassab to the police. '*Elle veut bien tuer ses maris tant qu'on voudra, mais dire un mensonge, ça jamais!*' ('She's willing to kill as many husbands as you like, but tell a fib – never!')

M. Barnaud, the investigating magistrate, decided that there was insufficient evidence against Cassab, who was released at the end of April and immediately returned to Cairo, undertaking not to communicate with Marguerite again.

Marguerite had been shown up as a less than honest participant in a ludicrous plot and, by declaring a pregnancy, albeit a false one, she had also undermined the allegations about Ali's sexual preferences made so robustly by her defence at the trial. Marguerite, once the envy of the *demi-monde*, was now the butt of jokes.

Two weeks earlier, the Prince had spent the first evening of his April visit to Paris at the gala opening night of the new Embassy Club, or Le Jardin de ma Soeur, at 17 rue Caumartin, not far from the Opera. Among the *glitterati* were the Maharajah of Kapurthala (Marguerite's old friend from Deauville and Tut-Ankh-Amun days), Lady Cunard, Prince Thurn und Taxis, 'the Prince of Persia', Ahmad Shah, with an enormous contingent of Americans

The company was entertained by the swarthily handsome Maurice Mouvet and his American partner, Leonora Hughes, an internationally famous dancing duo, who had also performed at the sister Embassy Club in London, where Leonora's sexually charged 'shimmy shake' was a great attraction. Marguerite, though she loved dancing, 'did not care for such eccentric dances such as the Shimmy'. She preferred to dance in the English fashion (whatever that may have meant), which she found 'very correct'.

Though the Prince's Paris stay in April 1924 began respectably enough, bad habits quickly reasserted themselves. Later that night and on two further nights of this Holy Week, the future Supreme Governor of the Church of England went late night clubbing to Jed Kiley's raffish Montmartre establishment. There appears to be no record of other social activities during Tuesday and Wednesday, except for lunch with Lord Crewe at the British Embassy. Maundy Thursday found him an invitee at a private dinner given by the Marquis and Marquise de Polignac (an American, the former Nina Crosby) in the intimacy of Henri's

Restaurant in the place Gaillon. Coco Chanel was to be among the guests. The Marquis was managing director of the Pommery champagne company.

An episode related by Coco Chanel serves as a good example of how the Prince could get what he wanted, even if it meant compromising a close friendship. Coco had recently become the mistress of the Prince's close friend, the Duke of Westminster, who had arrived in Paris only the day before and was staying at Malmaison. Bendor was attracted to Coco because, like Marguerite she was attractive, 'sexy, witty and brainy with an acid tongue'.

Coco later claimed that the Prince had suggested meeting for a pre-prandial drink in her apartment, where they had an early evening fling, a story that – given the royal form in that department – seems entirely plausible. Later Coco and the Prince, accompanied by 'G' Trotter, went to 'a night club' but, perverse as ever, Coco declared that she would rather have gone home to bed. In truth, she was looking forward to seeing Bendor again for the first time since Christmas. The little Prince of Wales could not compete with the mighty Duke.

The next day, Good Friday, brought an emotional, as well as a physical, hangover from that three-day binge. Coco may not have been the only physical entanglement to upset the neurotic Prince. Marguerite was in town, in the process of extricating herself from involvement in the fake baby plot. If (despite all that had happened) the Prince had decided to risk another liaison with Marguerite, a discreet physical encounter – in the privacy of her apartment – is just possible.

That night in his suite at the Meurice, the Prince penned his London confidante a rambling screed of maudlin introspection headed 'Good Friday'. Solipsistic outpourings by the Prince were common during their long correspondence, but this example seems particularly dark. 'I'm off to Le Touquet tonight,' he wrote, later using the third person singular to emphasise his feelings of emotional torment. 'He's got pretty rotten on this trip . . . God, what a bloody life this is & it's a great pity I was not <u>killed</u> in the Army p[oin]t to p[oin]t . . . Your very sad little David.'

CHAPTER 26

ENDPAPERS

During the 1920s, Inspector Alfred Burt was entrusted with 'personal and intimate enquiries . . . outside the province of official duties', sometimes involving 'pretty women', which suggests that he may have had a role in compiling the (now missing) Special Branch file on Marguerite, opened after her first attempt at blackmail late in 1918.

Special Branch duties included observations and reports about the activities of women deemed to pose threats to the Prince. A Miss Mary Agnes Stanford was one such stalker, already the subject of police attention when, in May 1927, she was seen lurking near the Royal Palace in Seville during a visit by the Prince to King Alfonso. Mlle Marie Catherine Jeanne Geoffroy of Paris, another obsessive fan, who had written the Prince 'an incoherent letter', was observed loitering near the Hotel Meurice.

The Prince's private life, away from these harpies, was neatly encapsulated by 'Cholly Knickerbokker', byline of Maury Henry Biddle Paul, short, chubby and very camp gossip columnist of the American

Hearst press. 'All of Edward Windsor's romances,' mused Cholly, '– has any of us fingers and toes to count them?' In due course, keeping company with Marguerite, Wallis Simpson would be afforded the accolade of a Special Branch report, alleging that she was having an affair with the deliciously named Guy Trundle, a West End car salesman with upper-class contacts. The report must surely have been compiled without the knowledge of the Prince, already deeply besotted with his new mistress. The Trundle-Simpson affair has been doubted, but Superintendent Canning, the compiler, was a very experienced officer (posted to Special Branch in 1909), with many years' service in the field of royal protection.

In the later 1920s, the Prince made nine visits to Paris, some official, others 'strictly private'. After 1929, Paris visits became much less frequent. In 1930, the Prince moved from York House to Fort Belvedere, near Windsor Great Park. Fredie Dudley Ward helped the process of refurbishing of a gothic folly designed by Sir Jeffrey Wyatville for the profligate King George IV and the Prince spent a good deal of his leisure time at the fort, during the period of his infatuation with Thelma, Lady Furness.

The royal visits, some official, some 'strictly private' to Paris in the later 1920s, included a bizarre trip to Paris in mid-February 1929. By this time, leading members of the 'handpicked team' were almost at their wits' end dealing with the capricious Prince, who had behaved particularly badly during an East African tour the previous year, complaining bitterly that he had been forced to break off an enjoyable visit (including sensual delights offered by Kenya's 'Happy Valley' community) simply because of his father's grave illness in November 1928.

Although the Prince had visited Paris previously in winter, weather conditions were exceptionally bad; there was a bitterly cold spell, the worst for nearly half a century. The thermometer recorded $-8°$ in central Paris on the evening of 14 February the day of his visit. The Prince was taking a calculated, even callous, risk in leaving the country so precipitately. The King was in poor health, still recuperating at Bognor from the severe respiratory illness contracted the previous November and a sudden relapse was always a possibility. 'The King is desperately ill,' wrote Lady Lee in January 1929, 'and we are all very despondent about his prospect of recovery.'

The Prince gave Special Branch minimal warning of his trip, made at only one day's notice, with Inspector Palmer in tow. Whatever prompted this mysterious wintertime journey, which had to be made by ship in stormy cross-Channel conditions, the Prince 'requested . . . that the . . . arrangements be kept strictly private and wishes his movements to be kept from the press'. The journey was made after his feelings for Audrey Coats (whom he had first pursued at Eloïse Ancaster's

Drummond Castle houseparty in August 1923) had cooled and some months before he met Thelma, Lady Furness, at an agricultural fair in Leicester.

It has been claimed that the Prince continued to see Marguerite from time to time in Paris until he took up with Wallis Simpson, but such an extended time span seems unlikely. There is a remote possibility that the Prince met Marguerite clandestinely during his visit to a very chilly Paris in February 1929, but no material has been found to suggest any intimate contact after that date.

By early 1929, Lascelles had decided to leave the Prince's service. Not long before, exasperated by the behaviour of the Prince of Wales and Prince George, he had written to his wife, 'I am certainly getting too old for the society of the Windsors; they bore me stiff, I'm afraid . . .' A little later, he reflected wistfully on the Prince's reluctance to face up to his Imperial destiny. 'I always feel now as if I were working, not for the next King of England, but for the latest American millionaire.'

Lascelles, was not alone in his despair. Godfrey Thomas shared some of his reservations the Prince, but it was out of the question that both men should resign at the same time. The pair had grappled with so many hair-raising moments caused by the selfishness and arrogance of the Prince over the past decade of royal service. They had coped manfully with the most severe difficulties, including the consequences of the Prince's affair with

485

Marguerite, the return of the love letters, and the risky procedure of keeping the Prince's name out of a most scandalous trial.

The true reasons for the problems repeatedly faced by both men over the decade could not easily be communicated to anyone beyond the confines of York House.

The York house staff grumbled about the Prince's behaviour, but, as has already been noted, there seems to have been reluctance to commit intimate details of the Prince's shortcomings to paper. Nevertheless, just a month before the mysterious last-minute trip to Paris, Admiral Halsey (the 'old salt') reported that the Prince 'had begun to visit Night Clubs again prompting unpleasant comments in some quarters.

The Prince's behaviour was now hopelessly erratic. At Le Touquet in August 1929, as recounted by Lady Rosslyn, 'the Prince of Wales turned up at the Casino . . . quite drunk and quite incapable of standing.' Freda, it seems, was with him at the time. The Prince was then 35, approaching middle age, and a dispassionate appraisal of his life shows little to commend. He had developed a vain, shallow, sometimes treacherous character, almost maniacally self-indulgent, yet constantly looking for someone who would tell him what to do, someone who would say things that few others would dare to say, someone who might even treat him with scorn.

There were some good qualities. The Prince

liked adventure, he loved to travel, and he was, above all else, a modern man in his public life. He intensely disliked the heavy hand of protocol, relishing a more relaxed approach, in manner as well as in dress. His power to charm and to put nervous people at their ease was a very attractive attribute. Furthermore, despite frequent periods of gloom and introspection, the Prince could show a sense of humour. His description of an Italian princess having 'a face like a bottom' can still raise a smile. More seriously, both during and after the Great War, the Prince showed a warm regard for the servicemen who faced hardships in the trenches, in the air and at sea, privations that he would never be called upon to endure. There were glimmerings, too, of a social conscience when confronted with the problems of unemployment and social deprivation that beset Britain during the interwar years.

Over the years since the end of the Great War, the ceaseless efforts of Thomas and Lascelles, with the help of Special Branch and even the DPP, had succeeded in papering over cracks that regularly threatened to cause irreparable damage to the Prince's reputation. Strangely, bearing in mind the seriousness of the challenge that Marguerite posed to the Royal Household and the notoriety of her trial, there are surprisingly few references to be found in contemporary letters, diaries and other documentation.

In good measure, this is due to a deliberate

process of destruction. The Prince tore out and destroyed sections of his personal wartime diary referring to his affair with Marguerite. His compromising love letters no doubt suffered the same fate, after they were surrendered as part of the compact between Marguerite and the Royal Household. The Special Branch file, probably prepared in response to the 'regular stinker', Marguerite's bombshell of November 1918, cannot now be traced in the Metropolitan Police archive. (As has been shown earlier in this book, these papers, which existed in 1923, seem also to have contained 'horrible accusations' against the Prince.)

The language used by both Thomas and Lascelles in private correspondence, quoted earlier in this chapter, may give an explanation. The overarching requirement was to preserve secrecy, almost at any cost. In the case of Marguerite, the two secretaries succeeded brilliantly in heading off a major scandal, the narrative of which has remained carefully interred for the better part of a century. In this task, they were aided by several factors. Putting aside the question of whether the Prince took up briefly with Marguerite after the trial, the heart of the affair had taken place in France during the Great War. Only a few people closest to the Prince knew about the relationship during this very disturbed period. The Prince's mistress was French, unknown to English Society, many of whose members would simply have regarded her a 'French tart' of little or no consequence, an attitude exemplified by the dismissive language of Curzon's 1923 letter to his wife (using pejorative expressions such as 'fancy woman' and 'keep'). Thomas, an old Foreign Office hand, also knew the importance of not writing down sensitive material or, if a note had to be made for any purpose, ensuring that it was quickly destroyed. Communicating information on a 'need to know' basis is not a new method.

Finally, although the episode was probably the most serious problem encountered by Thomas and Lascelles during their tenure of office, it was one of many crises to beset the Prince's secretaries during the 1920s. After Marguerite had been 'squared', the letters returned and destroyed, and silence maintained at the trial in accordance with the unwritten compact, her sting had been drawn. The secretaries were thus free to move on and await the next scrape their young master would fall into.

After the farcical end to the phantom baby case in April 1924 and with the Prince off to Le Touquet, Marguerite decided to leave town for a while. Early July found her enjoying the summer season in Carlsbad (Karlovy Vary), Czechoslovakia. Described as 'The Queen of Bohemian Watering Places' in the *New York Herald*, the resort was overflowing with rich foreigners, Marguerite's favourite quarry. President Masaryk was there, along with an assortment of the Austrian aristocracy and the American super-rich, a Rothschild or two, Viscount Cowdray, and the renowned violinist Fritz Kreisler.

Throughout the 1920s and beyond, Marguerite relentlessly pursued her aim of acquiring as much of Ali's fortune as possible, claiming that she had never been paid her *dot* (marriage portion) and that some exceedingly valuable jewellery belonged to her. In France, taking action against the Fahmy family, she had succeeded in obtaining jewellery held by a sequestrator after the French court had taken into account the fact of her acquittal on the murder charge in England. This appears to have been the Louis Vuitton jewelled handbag, worth 450,000 francs, which was handed over because it bore her initials. There was also the little matter of a 'gold-studded diamond mounted dressing-case, equipped with gold-stoppered bottles and golden-backed brushes', valued at £4,000 sterling. Some disputed items were retained by Van Cleef & Arpels, pending the outcome of judicial proceedings.

Returning to Egypt to prosecute other parts of her case, however, could be risky. She was determined to obtain a settlement of not less than 64,000,000 francs. She would donate half to Moslem causes (or so she said) and could live decently on the balance.'

In 1928, she again set foot in Egypt and installed herself in the Hotel Continental in Cairo. Suing the Fahmy estate, she claimed £82,000 in arrears of income, demanding an annual payment of

£6,000, but her attempt to get a share of Ali's estate was doomed from the start. Memories of her trial in England and Marshall Hall's xenophobic tactics were still fresh. 'It will be remembered,' wrote Sir Percy Loraine, the British High Commissioner, 'that this sensational case caused a great deal of ill-feeling in Egypt.'

The Fahmy family counterclaimed. At the hearing, the court showed hostility from the outset and her very identity was called into question before there was any argument on the merits of her case. Put simply, *sharia* law did not recognise the right of a woman to inherit if she was responsible for the death of her husband, except (possibly) if he had a gun in his hand at the time of the shooting. In April 1929, the *sharia* court heard the arguments of both parties, examined the shorthand record (now lost) of the trial and refused to accept evidence of Marguerite's acquittal at the Old Bailey, deciding that this was a case of premeditated murder. The case was decided in favour of the Fahmy family.

Undaunted, Marguerite approached the British authorities in Egypt, demanding intervention on her behalf. Although the bulky Foreign Office file on this application does not make mention of her relationship with the Prince of Wales, the seriousness with which her claim was viewed suggests an unspoken tension. The matter was considered at the highest level and the facts put before Arthur Henderson, Foreign Secretary in

Ramsay MacDonald's Labour government. If Marguerite had simply been a French national complaining to the British authorities about a local court decision in Egypt, her situation would surely not have merited such serious attention to her plight.

A British official considered her case to be 'excessively delicate'. Arthur Booth, the Judicial Adviser, minuted his view that 'it cannot be said that the Sharia Court is bound by the decision in London. Nor do I think that the judgment is so bad that it can be said to be a mockery of justice', as Marguerite's English lawyer had argued. Booth, in a poignantly worded postcript, indicated how difficult it was for an outsider dealing with questions of Egyptian law and practice. 'In my hurry to get some sort of note to you . . .,' he wrote, 'I have not been able to find out exactly what Sharia Law requires in order to admit a husband-killer to a share in the estate – probably a difficult thing to get really clear as most questions of Sharia Law are.'

Back in England, the Foreign Secretary considered the papers. 'We cannot intervene,' minuted a senior civil servant, 'Madame Fahmy was, I think, a Frenchwoman before her marriage & I shd have thought that if there was to be intervention in her behalf the French Minister might have had the privilege of opening the ball.'

Marguerite lodged an appeal against the *sharia* court decision, but her claim was dismissed in

April 1930. Seven years later, she visited Egypt for yet another court hearing, but it seems that this attempt also failed. Despite these setbacks, Marguerite remained a rich woman, well able to exploit a complement of wealthy male admirers.

As 'Maggie Meller', she proved excellent copy for media worldwide throughout the later 1920s, her various courtroom battles reported salaciously in the American press. Endlessly recycled headlines, including such gems as *Mystery of Princess Fahmy's Bogus Baby*, *Notorious Maggie Mellor*, and *Couldn't Kill Her Husband and Grab His Millions*.

After 1930, Marguerite's name appeared less frequently in the newspapers, although the *villégiature* columns of *Le Figaro* give a fair idea of her pre-war travels within France. These notices, inserted by the rich and famous (or those who hoped to be so regarded) recorded their presence at fashionable seaside resorts, capital cities and spas, always her favourite working territories. Between 1930 and 1937, Marguerite was to be seen in Vienna, Budapest, Cannes, Venice, Bad Homburg, Capbreton (near Biarritz) and St Malo. Gratifyingly for Marguerite, who loved a title, entries might randomly juxtapose her name with members of the aristocracy, as in July 1931 when she found herself alongside 'Mme la Baronne Rudolphe d'Érlanger' when staying at Néris-les-Bains, a spa in the Auvergne. More revealingly was a record, dated 2 September 1932, of visitors to Vittel, the Vosges spa famous for its mineral water, where

Marguerite's name followed that of 'Maître Assouad', her Egyptian lawyer, who may have been enjoying more than a merely professional relationship with his former client.

Vladimir Barjansky painted Marguerite's portrait. Like many other Russian *emigrés*, Barjansky fled to France after the 1917 revolution, settling in Paris. He was socially well-connected, and his homosexuality also appealed to Marguente, who enjoyed the company of gay men, perhaps a welcome diversion from the demands of her heterosexual companions.

Marguerite's final memoir was written by Michel Georges-Michel, who had met her first at Deauville just before the Great War. After the trial, their paths had crossed in Venice and at a ball in Cannes, where Marguerite – elegantly masked – appeared from nowhere, put two fingers to Georges-Michel's temple, declaring only too evocatively, '*Pan! Pan!* [Bang! Bang!]'. A local wit composed a couplet in honour of Marguerite's notoriety humorously suggesting that 'cruel men' should put their hands up promptly if Maggie Mellor came along.

The memoir, portentously titled *La Vie Brillante et Tragique de la Princess Fahmy Bey, parisienne*, was written very much under her direction and published in France on 30 April 1934. By this time, Marguerite's affair with the Prince was long past and she may have felt released from earlier undertakings of confidentiality. Although she described meeting the Prince during the Great

War, the account is discreetly written, though leaving the reader little doubt that the relationship was physical. By use of the expression *on se tutoie*, a French readership would be aware that Marguerite and the Prince had been on intimate terms. Marguerite also revealed that the Prince had written love letters, though no hint was given about their ultimate fate. Marguerite also claimed in her memoir that she was regularly shadowed by *spadassins* (hitmen), supposedly agents of the Fahmy family, although this is probably an invention. Nothing untoward ever happened to her.

Georges-Michel's book appeared as a cheaply bound paperback, part of a crime collection that included accounts of the Dreyfus affair, a life of Laçenaire (the legendary thief graphically depicted in the 1945 film *Les Enfants du Paradis*) and the fate of the Borgias. This second memoir seems to have made little impact in France, and none at all in England. Marguerite, now well over 40, was beginning to slip from public gaze.

Raymonde, who had married Raymond Fischof La Foux in December 1929, bore a close resemblance to her mother, although her eyes were blue rather than grey-green. As Marguerite aged, she became more jealous of her daughter's looks and an unbridgeable gulf developed between the two women. Raymond La Foux took an active part in the Resistance during the Second World War and later became an economic adviser to François Mitterrand, the future President of France.

The Duke of Windsor married Wallis Simpson on 3 June 1937, after the Abdication. After their honeymoon in Austria, the pair returned to Paris, taking a suite at the Hotel Meurice, but for social entertainment 'they preferred the Ritz with its gay and crowded bar'. The next year, Marguerite moved to an apartment conveniently sited above the premises of Van Cleef & Arpels, at 22 place Vendôme (built as a nobleman's residence, the 'Hôtel de Segur') and opposite the Ritz, where she, Wallis and David would from time to time find themselves sharing the same space in its bars and restaurants. In France, during those long years of exile the Duke had to endure regular reminders of his fateful wartime affair with 'Maggie Meller'.

In September 1939, Marguerite gained a new neighbour. At the outbreak of war, Noël Coward had been appointed as head of the 'Enemy Propaganda Office' (the vaguest of job descriptions) in Paris. Coward was relieved to discover that the Ritz remained open, although the rue Cambon side (where Coco Chanel lived) lay in darkness. In the hotel restaurant, Coward and his English colleagues 'ate caviar and *filet Mignon* and drank pink champagne' as though war had never been declared. With the help of Madame Guinle, an old friend, Coward found a six-room flat in the Place Vendôme. Fortunately, it was 'opposite the Ritz, which had an excellent air raid shelter. Coward took the flat, moving in with his factotum,

Cole Lesley. They inherited a maid, Yvonne Garnier, a talkative Lyonnaise.

Coward's neighbour on the other side was Marguerite. When Cole, Lesley, Coward's factotum asked Yvonne why their neighbour had killed her husband, the maid replied firmly, *'Parce qu'il a toujours fait l'amour par la derrière'* ('Because he always made love by the back passage'). Tactfully, neither Coward nor Lesley ever mentioned the shooting directly to Marguerite. On Sunday mornings, she would be heard playing, on the piano, the wistful (and doubly appropriate) song *Someday My Prince Will Come*.

After the collapse of France in June 1940, Coward's flat was requisitioned for the use of the Gestapo, but Marguerite managed to stay on for the duration of the war, occasionally hosting card parties for friends in her apartment.

The Ritz became an outpost of the Nazi administration, led by General Karl Heinrich von Stülpnagel, and only a few carefully selected non-German civilians were allowed to enter the building. Coco Chanel, an approved resident, took a suite of rooms, where she entertained her current beau, Baron von Dincklage. Marguerite seems to have been allowed access to the Ritz, keeping her eyes and ears open, memories that served her well after the war when many were anxious to forget relationships forged with the occupying power.

After the war, Marguerite settled down to a quiet routine, *habituée* of the Ritz and a familiar figure, usually accompanied by a favourite lapdog. The Windsors, who first took a suite at the hotel in the spring of 1946, stayed for some three years before taking a rented house at 85 rue de la Faisanderie, later moving to the mansion on the Bois de Boulogne which would be their last Paris home. They also leased, then bought, a mill on the Chevreuse, not far from the Château de Breteuil, where the young Prince of Wales had spent part of his first visit to France. 'The Duke kept his ranch in Canada until 1962 and they spent a considerable amount of every year in America, but France had become their home.'

If the Duke recognised his first mistress in the *chic* venues of Paris, life with the redoubtable Wallis precluded any further attentions on his part. Nevertheless, fate had further surprises in store for the fading Prince Charming. In 1947, Cynthia Gladwyn (wife of a future British Ambassador to France) wrote a barbed description of the ex-King. 'Old, wrinkled and worried with hair that had appeared to have been dyed.' As has been well documented, the Windsors gravitated towards rich expatriate Americans (and vice versa) in Paris. As long ago as the Great War, the Prince had eagerly adopted Americanisms (for example, by writing 'ass' for 'arse') and during their affair in 1917, as we have seen, Marguerite had noticed him cutting up his food in the American manner, eating with a single hand.

By the 1940s, the Duke was speaking with an

American accent habitually using Americanisms. One well-connected transatlantic friend was Anthony J. Drexel Biddle II, husband of Margaret Thompson, a leading figure in the post war American community in Paris. Tony Drexel Biddle, a Philadelphia socialite, became US Ambassador to Poland in 1937. After the war, Tony Drexel Biddle was employed in a succession of diplomatic and government posts, including the implementation of the Marshall Plan, helping to aid the reconstruction of war-blighted European countries.

Though the Drexel Biddles divorced, both remained friends of the Duke and Duchess. In September 1951, as Hugo Vickers has noted, 'he [the Duke] and the Duchess dined with Margaret Drexel Biddle'. By this time, Raymonde Laurent (using her maiden name after her own divorce in 1949) was living at Neauphlé-le-Château in a large house where she was looked after by staff including her mother's former chauffeur and maid. Tony Drexel Biddle was a neighbour, and Raymonde's son, Raoul Laurent, then a small boy, remembers meeting the Windsors with Drexel Biddle at Neauphlé-le-Château. Raymonde, as has been noted already, bore a striking resemblance to her mother. Raoul Laurent is sure that, apart from Drexel Biddle, all present knew about the relationship between mother and daughter (not to mention mother and Duke), but not a word was said . . .

At the age of 70, Marguerite retired from her life's work, declaring that, from then on, 'I shall sleep alone in a single bed.' She died, aged 80, on 2 January 1971. After her death, Jean Patay, her last lover and director of the Crédit Commercial de France, a major French bank, destroyed the few surviving letters written by the Prince. Patay also got rid of photographs and (perhaps saddest of all) Marguerite's studbook, in which – much as Cora Pearl had done during the Second Empire – she had kept a unique record of her clients and their sexual preferences.

At the time of her death, Marguerite was still receiving handsome annuities from five or six former lovers. By way of a final twist to her relationship with the Prince, Marguerite had died in the American Hospital, situated in the fashionable suburb of Neuilly, an institution where both the Duke and Duchess of Windsor would receive treatment in their few remaining years together.

The *deuil* [obituary] announcement posted in *Le Figaro* accorded Marguerite the evocative title, '*la Princesse Fahmy-Bey*', but her tactical conversion to Islam had been shortlived. Fully reconciled to Mother Church, Marguerite – 'a Parisian to my fingertips' – was buried by Christian rite, alongside other members of the Alibert family, in the Paris cemetery of Saint-Ouen.

The story of Edward and Mrs Simpson is a well-ploughed furrow, extensively harvested and mercifully outside the scope of this book. Although Wallis cannot be considered to have been a courtesan, she and Marguerite nevertheless had a good deal in common, perhaps even as 'sisters under the skin'. Edward's neurotic, self-pitying, neo-masochistic character proved to be the perfect foil for the ambitions of both women.

Both were refreshingly un-English (unlike safe, complaisant Fredie Dudley Ward) and not in the least 'correct', and at times noisy and ill-behaved. Both were deeply self-centred. Both were social climbers. Both could be amusing, charming, witty, graceful. Both loved luxury, jewellery, clothes, the high life. Both were strong and manipulative personalities, liable to be loved or loathed. Both were determined women not afraid to take on and dominate male admirers.

In the ultimate analysis, Wallis and Marguerite were damaged characters, both scarred by unhappy experiences early in life. Wallis married an ex-King, a man she did not love, may even have despised. Cherished royal titles eluded her. Marguerite's vanity resulted in bitter estrangement from her family. And, despite having committed the perfect murder, Marguerite failed to secure the fabulous wealth and full social acceptance that she craved.

> Not all that tempts your wand'ring eyes
> And heedless hearts, is lawful prize;
> Nor all that glisters, gold.